The Experts Praise *The Marketer's Guide to Public Relations in the 21st Century*

There's no one who knows more about marketing public relations than Tom Harris, and his new edition of *The Marketer's Guide to Public Relations* is proof positive. Tom knows both sides of the equation, what it takes to successfully market a new product and what motivates the customer to buy. Marketers and publicists alike will be well served dipping into his deep knowledge base.

Harold Burson
Chairman Founder, Burson-Marsteller

Marketing public relations has come a long way in the last decade, and this book gives ample evidence why the business function is going to expand even more in the years to come. This is really a wonderful read! It is engagingly written, with tons of real-world examples. Most of all, it is both comprehensive and comprehensible; a valuable addition to anyone's library, from university student to chief marketing officer. Kudos to Tom Harris and Pat Whalen.

Joe Cappo
Author, *The Future of Advertising: New Media, New Clients,*
New Consumers in the Post-Television Age

If any marketers still have questions about the effectiveness of marketing public relations, they'll be answered with great affirmation by this new volume by Tom Harris and Patricia Whalen. It demonstrates that public relations provides greater visibility and return on invested capital compared to traditional advertising. This work is a classic in asserting once and for all that public relations is a most important element in any brand campaign.

Daniel J Edelman
Founder and Chairman, Edelman

Tom Harris talked and wrote about MPR—BEFORE it was fashionable. His new book on this exciting subject covers all the techniques that provide winning strategies for the 21st century—and will be required reading for all of us in this industry.

Al Golin
Chairman, GolinHarris

Over the years, Tom Harris has gone on from a distinguished career as a public relations executive to become one of our profession's most perceptive and insightful observers. Now he has joined forces with Patricia Whalen on a book that offers a wealth of practical wisdom for anyone who wants to realize the full potential of marketing public relations.

John D. Graham
Chairman and CEO, Fleishman-Hillard

The man who literally wrote the book on marketing public relations has done it again. Identifying the new tools at our disposal, the long-time practitioner shows us again why public relations is such an important part of corporate strategy, and how public relations continues to provide marketing support from strategy to implementation in today's companies. This is a must-read for anyone who wants to make public relations work harder and smarter in their business.

Rick Kean, Managing Partner, Business Marketing Institute
Former Executive Director, Business Marketing Association

Tom Harris is one of the most knowledgeable and respected people in the public relations business and Pat Whalen understands what works and what doesn't. People who want to learn about PR or who think they already know how it's done should read this book. It's a solid and well-written guide to successful PR marketing.

Joe Marconi
Author, *Public Relations: The Complete Guide* and
Creating the Marketing Experience

If advertising was the career choice of the 20th century, public relations is the career choice of the 21st century. Read Harris and Whalen's great guide to one of the future's best occupations.

Al Ries
Author, *The Origin of Brands*

The Marketer's Guide to
Public Relations
in the
21st Century

Thomas L. Harris

Patricia T. Whalen

Medill Integrated Marketing Communications Graduate Program
Northwestern University

Foreword by Philip Kotler

RĀC☀M
COMMUNICATIONS

THOMSON

Australia · Brazil · Canada · Mexico · Singapore · Spain · United Kingdom · United States

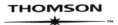

The Marketer's Guide to Public Relations in the 21st Century
Thomas L. Harris and Patricia A. Whalen

Library of Congress Cataloging in Publication Number is available. See page 288 for details.

For more information about our products, contact us at:

Thomson Learning Academic Resource Center
1-800-423-0563

Thomson Higher Education
5191 Natorp Boulevard
Mason, Ohio 45040
USA

Contents

Foreword

Beginning in the 1950s, marketers invested most of their marketing resources on TV advertising . . . and it worked! Fortunes were made by companies whose ad agencies delivered creative and memorable commercials. But this bonanza period is rapidly drawing to a close. The truth is that TV commercials, by and large, don't work anymore.

Let's look at two recent studies:

—Adworks found that TV advertising returned only 32 cents for every dollar spent.

—Deutsche Bank found only 18 percent of TV advertising generated a positive return on investment (ROI) in the short term, and less than half (45%) paid off long term.

Why is this? Here are a few of the reasons:

- Advertising saturation and clutter is leading to lessened attention. Only 36 percent of TV viewers say they watch with full attention. Of those who don't, 79 percent flip channels during commercials. Fifty-three percent turn the sound down.
- People have a time shortage and are busy with computers, video games, exercise, listening to music, talking on their cell phones, and watching movies on their DVD players.
- Seventy percent say they would buy products that would help them resist advertising. Today, there are 3 million TiVos in use that help block out TV commercials.
- The economic recession has made companies more cost-sensitive to advertising expenditures, especially when they cannot measure the ROI.
- The explosion of TV channels has seriously reduced audience reach and audience economics. In the meantime, TV advertising costs continue to rise.

The result of this decline in the effectiveness of TV advertising has led companies to search for other media that might be more effective. Here are some headlines:

"P&G Marketing Chief Critiques the Advertising Industry, Wants New Ways to Measure Ad Results and a Broad Shift to Permission Marketing"

"Network TV Does Worst Job of Proving Advertising ROI"

"GM Vice Chairman Questions Effectiveness of TV Ads"

"Automakers Threaten to Pull More Ad Spend from Networks, Plan Shift to Cable, On-Line, Outdoor, Internet, Direct Mail, Public Relations"

As mass advertising loses its cost-effectiveness, message senders are driven to other media. They discover or rediscover the power of news, events, community programs, atmospheres, and other powerful communication modalities. They are turning increasingly to marketing public relations (MPR). Al and Laura Ries recently indicted the advertising world with their publication of *The Fall of Advertising and the Rise of PR.* MPR can reach target audiences, and reach them with more credibility.

The person who deserves credit for conceptualizing MPR is Tom Harris, who wrote the first book on the subject in 1991. In this new book, Tom and his colleague, Patricia Whalen, not only show why MPR helps companies gain competitive advantage in an over-communicated society, but also how it is done by its most sophisticated practitioners. The reason for this second edition is to introduce new theory and describe new practices that have taken place since the first *Marketer's Guide to Public Relations* was published. It predicts an ever-increasing role for public relations in marketing in the twenty-first century.

Their book is a "must" book in the library of every marketer who recognizes the need to take a broader look at the changing media and markets and wants to get messages through in an otherwise attention-deficit society.

PHILIP KOTLER
S. C. Johnson & Son Distinguished Professor
of International Marketing
J. L. Kellogg Graduate School of Management,
Northwestern University

Preface

When *The Marketer's Guide to Public Relations* was published in 1991, Philip Kotler called it "not only the first book on marketing public relations, but the 'classic'." I was especially grateful to receive this endorsement from the world's pre-eminent authority on the strategic practice of marketing, and I am very pleased that Professor Kotler has once again agreed to write a foreword to this new book.

When a number of publishers expressed their interest in a new edition of *The Marketer's Guide*, I thought that revising my first book on the subject would be a relatively simple matter. How wrong I was! When I got into this book, I began to fully realize how very much the world of marketing has changed over the past decade. While the present book follows the same basic format as its predecessor, a good 80 percent of it is entirely new. It looks at the events that have impacted the practice of marketing public relations in recent years and that will further transform the practice in the immediate future. That is why it has been titled *The Marketer's Guide to Public Relations in the 21st Century*.

In the first book, I coined the appellation "MPR" to describe that area of public relations which specifically supports an organization's marketing goals. I drew a distinction between MPR and corporate public relations (which I dubbed "CPR"), the goal of which is to win the support of all of any organization's stakeholders, importantly including its employees and shareholders. Clearly, the two are inter-related because the success of an organization, be it a corporation or non-profit organization, is first and foremost dependent on the successful marketing of its goods or services. Likewise, the business scandals of recent years have made it clear that consumers want to patronize companies they perceive as worthy of their trust.

The marketing landscape has changed so dramatically over the past decade that a fresh perspective is required. The "leave-it-all-to-network-television" mindset that was dominant when the first book was written has faded. Network advertising is now much more expensive and much less efficient in reaching target audiences. Marketers in the twenty-first century are faced with a plethora of broadcast and print choices and a broad array of new media, importantly including Internet advertising. The nature of this threat to what was the conventional marketing wisdom as we entered the 90s is discussed throughout this book.

While marketing public relations had made significant strides when the first book was written, it is now accepted as an essential component of any effective integrated marketing program. The whole concept of integrated marketing communications throws all preconceived notions of what works to the winds. From the get-go, all of the prospective components of an IMC (integrated management of all communications) program are created equal. MPR has long been a key factor in marketing categories like cars and packaged goods. It has become a critical element of high-tech and healthcare product marketing in reaching not only consumers but also industry analysts and other thought leaders who influence the marketplace.

From the outset, I realized that I needed a writing partner who was an expert in certain critical areas of MPR. Professor Patricia Whalen has taught public relations and other marketing courses to graduate students in the Integrated Marketing Communications department of the Medill School of Journalism of Northwestern University for more than seven years. She succeeded me in teaching the first university course in marketing public relations. Pat combines academic discipline and real world experience. She has spent nearly twenty years in senior corporate marketing and communications positions with Fortune 500 companies. Her contributions to the book include her strategic planning process and her analysis of the latest methodologies for gaining insights about key targets and the measurement of MPR outcomes that is demanded in this age of accountability. Pat also addresses the important areas of internal marketing and business-to-business MPR, and covers the uses of the Internet in public relations, which did not exist when the first *Marketer's Guide to Public Relations* was published.

This book combines how-to-do-it advice with scores of how-they-did-it case histories. They were selected to illustrate how vital public relations has become in the marketing of some of the most successful brands in the world.

The authors hope that the cases will also stimulate creative thinking, which is still the key to breakthrough marketing. The creative spark may originate with advertising, promotion, or public relations, but it works best when it ignites all facets of the marketing program.

Thomas L. Harris
Highland Park, Illinois
January 2006

PART I

Understanding Marketing Public Relations

The MPR Explosion

The year 2000 not only marked the start of the new millennium; it was also the beginning of the second century of public relations. Public relations historian Scott Cutlip fixes 1900 as the point when the practice of public relations, as we know it, began in America. It was then that The Publicity Bureau, the first publicity agency in the country, was founded in Boston. From its modest origins, the practice of public relations has evolved into a vital business management discipline of the twenty-first century. It has simultaneously assumed an essential role in the marketing of goods and services, institutions and individuals, governments and nongovernmental organizations.

Philip Kotler, S.C. Johnson Distinguished Professor of International Marketing at Northwestern University's Kellogg Graduate School of Management and author of the world's most widely used marketing textbook, says that today public relations and direct marketing are achieving the most attention from marketers and the most growth. He attributes the growth of marketing public relations to its great versatility, its aptitude for drama, and its ability to break through the information clutter to capture attention and interest. He says that marketing public relations in the future can only go one way: up. He also states that MPR is moving into an explosive growth stage because companies realize that mass advertising is no longer the answer.[1]

Veronis Suhler Stevenson, a leading investment bank dedicated to the media, communications, and information industries, predicts that public relations will grow at a faster rate than any other communications practice aside from event planning. The bank's 2004 Communications Industry Forecast predicts that spending on public relations will rise more than 8 percent by 2008. This follows an 11 percent gain from 1998 to 2004. Most of this gain will come from marketing public relations.[2]

The use of public relations has driven spectacularly successful marketing programs for the world's best-known products. You will read about many of them in this book. Here, for starters, are a few:

- The public relations program for Toyota's hybrid Prius directed to Hollywood celebrities and environmental groups dominated the media and was so effective that the traditional launch with heavy advertising was made unnecessary. Consumer demand for the car was so great that buyers waited months for delivery.
- Seconds after the newly dismissed contestant of NBC's "The Apprentice" heard Donald Trump's fateful words "You're fired," thousands of consumers visited the *crest.com* Web site with ideas on how they would launch Crest Refreshing Vanilla Mint toothpaste. The product placement on the show drew more than 4.7 million hits on the product web site, the highest level of on-line interest in a single product in Procter & Gamble history.
- An exclusive *Newsweek* cover on Sony's Playstation2 a year before it was introduced in the United States predicted that it would become "the most successful consumer product ever launched." While that claim may have been exaggerated, PS2 sold out its initial shipment of one million sets. Because of the publicity and the buzz it generated, it became the dominant factor in the highly competitive market for video games.

- Microsoft's Windows 95, essentially an upgrade of an existing operating system, became the top-selling software program ever as a result of a two-year public relations campaign that gained 99 percent awareness before the advertising ran and the product hit the stores. The blockbuster launch also stimulated record sales for PC's loaded with the system.
- Viagra became the best-selling pharmaceutical in the world as a result of a massive media relations-driven campaign two years before it was advertised. The PR campaign was so successful that it generated 2 billion media impressions and caused doctors to write a million prescriptions in its first month on the market.

Marketing public relations works. That is why so many companies are making major commitments to MPR. They range from companies that can no longer afford the high cost of advertising to mass marketers who recognize the value that public relations uniquely brings to the marketing mix.

Herbert M. Baum, CEO of The Dial Corporation, says:

Long-term brand equity, brand-building type of advertising and marketing are absolutely necessary for sustaining the effectiveness of our brands. At the same time, sales promotion, getting the immediate sale, the short-term buck is necessary to stay in the game. The hidden weapon is PR. PR is probably more effective in changing consumer attitudes about products today than advertising. It is easier for consumers to believe a message if it's coming from an independent third party than if you are shouting it in an ad.[3]

Sir Martin Sorrell, CEO of WPP, one of the world's largest communications conglomerates that houses such advertising giants as J. Walter Thompson, Ogilvy & Mather, and Young & Rubicam, as well as leading PR firms, such as Burson-Marsteller and Hill & Knowlton, says:

All the research I've seen says that editorial publicity is better than paid-for publicity. Editorial publicity is more effective. If you can convince the editor, or someone who's writing an article, that your company knows what it's doing, that will be more effective than 'I bought an ad in your learned journal to say that my company knows what it's doing.' "[4]

Marketers Affirm PR's Effectiveness

Where public relations was once primarily associated with corporate communications, it is now widely used by marketing managers and recognized as a key component of integrated marketing campaigns.

Nine out of ten brand managers now use public relations to support their brands, according to a study conducted by McBain Associates, a New York-based market research firm for M Booth & Associates, a national public relations firm that specializes in marketing public relations. Participants in the 1999 study included brand managers from food and beverage, cosmetics, health and beauty, travel and tourism, financial services, and business-to-business services. It found that public relations is highly valued by brand managers for brand building, brand credibility, and brand vitality.

The brand managers surveyed believe that public relations works better than advertising, sales promotion, and new media:

- when editorial context is important,
- when credibility is required,
- when traditional media are impractical,
- when third party endorsement is needed, and
- when brand managers need to deliver more impact for the marketing dollars spent.

Further, the survey found that public relations works as well as advertising when audiences need to be reached in unique and special ways and when brand reputation needs to be maintained. The brand managers rated public relations and advertising as performing equally well in maintaining brand reputation. [5]

Lou Capozzi, CEO of Manning, Selvage & Lee (MS&L), a leading international public relations firm, says "the relevance, involvement, and importance of PR in the marketing mix have reached a level that the industry could only have hoped for a few years ago." MS&L sponsored a survey of chief marketing officers, vice presidents of marketing, and brand managers conducted by Impulse Research Corporation for the trade magazine *PR Week* in 2004. The *PR Week*/MS&L Marketing Management Survey found that public relations was regarded as more effective than advertising or direct marketing in a number of critical areas of marketing planning. These areas include building a brand's reputation, strategy development, generating word-of-mouth, pre-market conditioning, building a corporate reputation, cultivating industry thought leaders, and overcoming a crisis. PR was seen as only slightly less effective as advertising in launching a new product, building awareness, and in developing messages.

The survey also found that marketing managers were spending far more time identifying advertising alternatives. The alternatives they were exploring most were building buzz or word-of-mouth, targeting influentials, grassroots marketing, and media relations. All of these options have a strong foundation in marketing public relations. [6]

Marketing Public Relations: What Is It?

The designation *marketing public relations* (MPR) arose in the 1980s because of the need to distinguish the specialized application of public relations techniques that support marketing from the general practice of public relations.

Marketing public relations has grown rapidly and pragmatically to meet the opportunities of a changing marketplace. In the process, it has borrowed and amalgamated thinking from traditional public relations, marketing, advertising, and research.

Jim Dowling, who formerly headed the giant public relations firm Burson-Marsteller, said, "Public relations is . . . almost impossible to define because it has no context of its own. It is only definable in its relevance to other things. Public relations embraces a wide variety of disciplines and activities that are applied individually or in combination with a goal or objectives established by someone else. Someone like the chief executive officer, the chief financial officer, or the chief marketing executive."[7]

He has a point. Marketing public relations can be defined more precisely than the larger concept of public relations because of its relevance to marketing, specifically to helping an organization meet its marketing objectives.

Exhibit 1.1. The Many Uses of MPR

Product Promotion
- Introduce new products
- Revitalize, relaunch, or reposition mature products
- Communicate new benefits of old products
- Involve people with products
- Engage customers with products on-line
- Build or maintain interest in a product category

Building Markets
- Reach demographically defined markets
- Cultivate new markets
- Reach secondary markets
- Reinforce weak markets
- Reach lifestyle-defined markets
- Identify companies and products with special-interest markets

Advertising Support
- Extend the reach of advertising
- Counteract consumer resistance to advertising
- Break through commercial clutter
- Make news before advertising breaks
- Make advertising newsworthy
- Complement advertising by reinforcing messages and legitimizing claims
- Supplement advertising by communicating additional product benefits
- Attract visitors to commercial web sites
- Gain awareness in media where product is not advertised

Marketing Support
- Test marketing concepts
- Reinforce sales promotion campaigns
- Tailor marketing programs to local audiences
- Raise brand awareness through title sponsorships
- Create new media and new ways to reach consumers

Corporate Reputation
- Build consumer confidence and trust in the company behind the product
- Win consumer support by identifying companies and brands with causes they care about
- Position companies as leaders and experts
- Interpret the impact of emerging issues on the marketplace
- Open communication channels between marketers and consumer activists
- Communicate marketing decisions in the public interest
- Influence opinion leaders
- Defend products at risk

Sales Support
- Gain distribution
- Build store traffic
- Generate sales inquiries
- Motivate the sales force
- Win retailer support

Marketing Public Relations Defined

We define marketing public relations as "the use of public relations strategies and tactics to achieve marketing objectives. The purpose of MPR is to gain awareness, stimulate sales, facilitate communication, and build relationships between consumers, companies, and brands."

Another definition was suggested by Rene Henry in his book *Marketing Public Relations: The Hows That Make It Work!*:

> Marketing public relations is a comprehensive, all-encompassing public awareness and information program or campaign directed to mass or specialized audiences to influence sales or use of a company's products or services.[8]

The definition of marketing public relations in *Webster's New World Dictionary of Media and Communications* is "the use of special events, publicity and other public relations techniques to promote products and services." (The author, Richard Weiner, adds parenthetically, "a term popularized by Thomas L. Harris.")[9]

MPR and Marketing: Moving Together

The explosive growth of marketing public relations has been fueled by the simultaneous recognition of its intrinsic value by marketers and the ability of public relations professionals to devise programs that precisely support marketing strategies.

The late Patrick Jackson, a highly respected public relations counsel, described the relationship between marketing and public relations this way:

> Whatever an organization offers to whichever publics, the hard fact is that success lies in its sales—getting someone to sign on the dotted line, actually or figuratively. No matter what type of organization we're talking about, without successfully selling something, it fails. Therefore, both public relations and marketing ultimately exist to serve sales—the purveying of goods, services, or ideas.[10]

Philip Kotler sees a number of current developments that presage a closer working relationship between marketing and public relations in the future:

> Marketing practitioners are very likely to increase their appreciation of PR's potential contributions to marketing the product because they are facing a real decline in the productivity of their other promotional tools. Advertising costs continue to rise while the advertising audience reached continues to decline. Furthermore, increasing advertising clutter reduces the impact of each ad. Sales promotion expenditures continue to climb and now exceed advertising expenditures two to one. Marketers spend money on sales promotion, not out of choice, but out of necessity; middlemen and consumers demand lower prices and deals. Sales force costs continue to rise. No wonder marketers are searching for more cost-effective promotional tools. . . . Here is where public relations techniques hold great promise. The creative use of news events, publications, social investments, community relations, and so on offers companies a way to distinguish themselves and their products from their competitors.[11]

Marketing Public Relations Comes of Age

Where public relations was once primarily associated with corporate communications, it is now widely used by marketing managers and recognized as a key component of integrated marketing campaigns. Marketing Public Relations has finally come of age:

1. Marketing public relations is the largest and fastest growing segment of a fast-growing industry. The public relations budget of the average company now exceeds $3 million, according to the Thomas L. Harris/Impulse Research Public Relations Client Survey, divided approximately between work done in-house and by public relations firms. In 2004, clients spent one-third of their total budget for "product media relations." The preponderance of money spent by client companies with their public relations firms is devoted to programs that help them sell their goods and services. Marketing public relations now leads all public relations disciplines with its rapidly increasing importance.[12]

2. Giant international communications conglomerates are placing more importance on "below-the-line" activities, such as public relations, rather than traditional advertising. Sir Martin Sorrell, CEO of WPP, reported that these activities represented more than one-third of his firm's $6 billion in revenue in 2004. He predicts they will reach one-half within the decade.[13]

3. Companies have recognized the growing importance of marketing public relations with increasingly bigger budgets. Multimillion dollar worldwide MPR programs are being mounted with increasing regularity.

4. Public relations is playing a more central role in the development of marketing strategies. PR people are becoming integrated into brand management teams. They have become key players in product marketing teams at companies such as General Mills and are involved in marketing planning from the outset rather than being called in after the marketing strategies are set.

5. Public relations has developed sophisticated tools to measure its effectiveness. Companies are creating systems that measure not only quantity of audiences reached but also quality in communicating message points and resulting impact. Matt Gonring, vice president of marketing and communications at Rockwell Automation, says companies have become more creative in drawing the direct relationship between target audiences and the behavior of those audiences by using metrics, such as sophisticated content analysis tools. This is bringing a level of precision and focus to PR efforts that was previously unavailable.[14]

6. Companies have recognized that achievement of marketing goals is impacted not only by consumers, but also by other key audiences who have a stake in the success of the brand. Jack Bergen, senior vice president of corporate affairs and marketing at Siemens, says, "PR is the one place where you can consider multiple stakeholders. PR people understand the richness of audiences that have an interest in a company; advertisers just focus on customers. Strategy is the development of options to accomplish an objective. PR people can develop these, as they have a multiplicity of audiences and channels to reach them."

7. Public relations is increasingly covered by the marketing and business media.

As advertising, which has been covered extensively by major market newspapers and in the business press, has evolved into integrated marketing, important components of marketing campaigns, including public relations, are becoming a greater part of the story.[15]

8. The academic community is showing greater interest in public relations. Universities are responding to the growing demand for public relations practitioners trained in business and for business leaders trained in public relations. The Medill Integrated Marketing Communications program at Northwestern University offers a specialization in public relations as part of its master's degree program.

MPR: A Discipline Distinct from Corporate Public Relations

There is no standard public relations or marketing public relations organization chart. Every company structures its public relations functions to suit its own needs, but in most corporations there are significant differences between marketing-supported public relations and those other public relations activities that define the corporation's relationships with its non-consumer publics. The mission of MPR is clearly to support marketing objectives. However, a close working relationship must be maintained between corporate communications and marketing public relations, not only because of the similarity of skills and experience, but also because of the need to integrate marketing objectives with corporate objectives. Relationships with government on all levels, for example, significantly affect the environment in which the company markets its products, as do the company's public positions on a variety of existing and emerging issues that affect the public as consumer.

Corporate response to crisis situations inevitably affects consumer perceptions and consumer behavior. The now-famous Tylenol poisoning case was for Johnson & Johnson both a corporate crisis and a marketing crisis that might well have destroyed a major product line had not responsive, responsible corporate action been taken and effectively communicated to all of the company's publics, especially the consumer and the trade.

However, despite the increasing acceptance of the value of MPR in most corporations, there is considerable confusion and resistance surrounding the nature of the relationship of PR within the marketing function. There is some organizational resistance, driven by different forces and coming from different departments, to MPR. Thus, to better understand the organizational resistance to the merging of marketing and public relations activities, it may be helpful to further explore the agendas of the CPR and MPR functions.

Corporate Communication Objectives

The corporate public relations program is responsible for maintaining the long-term health of the organization by building a strong corporate reputation. This function focuses on various stakeholders beyond the customer, such as employees, communities, government regulators, and shareholders. Some of the functions it oversees are community relations, charitable contributions, employee communications, and investor relations.

This function is critical in all corporations, but it is particularly important for those firms, such as McDonald's, Coca-Cola, and Starbucks, where the corporate brand and the product brand are one and the same. People do business with organizations they trust, and if a company develops a poor reputation as an employer or is seen to have corrupt investment practices, it will not be long before its product sales begin to decline.[16]

Marketing Public Relations Objectives

The MPR function is focused more narrowly on just the product brand and its customers. Its primary purpose is to achieve third-party endorsement from key customer influencers, such as the news media. This third-party endorsement is the real key to MPR's success, and has been noticed by the great marketing minds of our time. The advertising genius David Ogilvy cited research that showed that six times as many people would read an article about a product than an ad for the same product. Al Ries has said, "PR has credibility. Advertising does not."[17]

MPR also works to create word-of-mouth "buzz" about the brand by generating news about the product and its features, holding special events to demonstrate the product, creating educational materials to facilitate usage of the product, and generating goodwill for the brand by associating it with good causes. This function can be very effective in building relationships between customers and the product brand.

As Arthur Page, one of the earliest public relations practitioners, said, "PR is what everybody in the business, from the top and bottom, says and does when in contact with the public"[18] and, most especially, when in contact with the news media. It has been called, "the cheapest form of branding known to mankind," because media coverage is free in most developed countries. But ensuring that media coverage is positive and supportive of the organization and its products is not an easy task and requires strong management skills as well as an ability to maintain credibility on critical issues both inside and outside of the organization. The marketing challenge is even greater, because, in the marketplace of the twenty-first century, the driving force is not companies with products to sell, but customers controlling what, where, and how they want to buy.

A Matter of Survival

An underlying assumption of this book is that, unless an organization successfully markets its goods and services, it cannot survive and that, therefore, its relationships with its various publics are inevitably intertwined with marketing. Many of these publics influence, to a greater or lesser extent, the success of an organization's marketing efforts, but success in the marketplace depends on building healthy relationships with non-customer as well as customer publics.

A company's community relations affect the marketplace because people want to do business with companies they know and trust. As the business scandals of the 90s showed, corporate reputation has an enormous impact on the marketplace, so do questions of product safety and efficacy, which are a key concern to both the consumer and the government. Marketers were once concerned only with delivering the right product to the right people at the right time and in the right place through the right advertising and promotion. Now they must spend a great deal of time and energy anticipating or personally interacting with state attorneys general, consumer advocates, environmentalists, political activists, legislators, and governmental agencies, whose influence on the marketing of their products can be critical.

All of these relationships with all of these publics inextricably bind public relations to marketing. These activities also closely link corporate public relations with marketing public relations, but in most organizations, they are distinct functions.

2 Marketplace Forces Driving MPR

In order to survive in an increasingly competitive worldwide marketplace, companies need to do a far more effective and cost-efficient marketing job than ever before. It is this need to get more bang for their bucks that has driven the growth of marketing public relations and the move to integrated marketing. The leave-it-all to advertising mindset is giving way to more targeted, more diverse ways to sell goods and services, maintain customer confidence, and build brand equity. This requires that custom mix of media advertising, Internet advertising, sales promotion, event sponsorships, direct and database marketing, point-of-sale merchandising, sales training, and marketing public relations, a custom mix now popularly known as integrated marketing communications.

Public relations plays the critical role in the integrated marketing process because building relationships is what PR is all about. Public relations is vitally needed to make integrated marketing work precisely because study after study tells us that consumers are finding advertising messages less credible.

Television advertising, long regarded as the be-all of marketing, has come under attack because it is expensive and not as cost-effective as it once was. Whereas saturation advertising on the "Big Three" television networks (NBC, CBS, and ABC) was once the key to reaching the mass market, network TV is going the way of general interest magazines. *Look, Collier's* and *The Saturday Evening Post* no longer exist because of the demassification of the market. They have been replaced by a multitude of special interest magazines. Likewise, consumers now have a choice of dozens, if not hundreds, of cable TV networks. The high cost of reaching a mass market has driven many advertisers from network advertising altogether. Most advertisers are now targeting their dollars to discrete markets and using a variety of ways beyond traditional advertising to reach their customers.

Marketers today have a formidable task not experienced by their counterparts in the glory days of marketing. The surefire marketing methods of the post-World War II period began to break down in the 1980s. The world changed so rapidly and fundamentally that marketers were forced to retrench and reevaluate. The tried is simply no longer true.

The marketing job is much tougher now than ever before; executives responsible for developing marketing plans must find ways to break through a climate of consumer resistance, indifference, and clutter. They must deliver a more imaginative message with greater credibility and impact.

New marketplace challenges can no longer be addressed with the same old rules. The new environment offers opportunities for public relations to play an ever-larger role in determining how the business community deals with its publics, markets its products, and interacts with a more global culture.

Public relations and marketing are being driven into a closer relationship by the same change factors that have revolutionized the very nature of business in the United States and the world.

The Mass Market Splinters

The mass market, as it was once known, is becoming a distant memory. Many new buzzwords have surfaced as firms grapple with the new diversity: "demassified market," "splintered market," "fragmented market," "niche marketing," and "micromarketing" (the splintering of consumer markets into segments defined by geographics, demographics, and psychographics).

The population has changed, necessitating a change in marketing. With the demographic shifts have come attitudinal shifts. More sophisticated shoppers with a desire for quality and diversity have emerged. Consumers are more value oriented and less brand-loyal, perhaps because there are so many choices open to them. The sophistication level of consumers has grown to a point where they no longer receive, much less believe, everything that is in the ad message.

In a 2004 special report called "The Vanishing Mass Market," *Business Week* reported that:

> For marketers, the evolution from mass to micromarketing is a fundamental change driven as much by necessity as opportunity. America today is a far more diverse and commercially self-indulgent society than it was in the heyday of the mass market. The country has atomized into countless market segments defined not only by demography, but also by increasingly nuanced and insistent product preferences.[1]

In tandem with these developments, the almost-universal audience assembled long ago by network television and augmented by other mass media is fragmenting at an accelerating rate. The mass media's decline is an old story in many respects; prime-time network ratings have been sliding since the 1970s. What's new is that the proliferation of digital and wireless communication channels is spreading the mass audience of yore ever thinner across hundreds of narrowcast cable TV and radio channels, thousands of specialized magazines, and millions of computer terminals, video-game consoles, personal digital assistants, and cell-phone screens. Because public relations is affordable, it can reach both specialized and mass audiences.

An array of new media channels has given public relations greater opportunity to reach target markets faster and with more impact than could have been imagined 20 years ago. We have evolved from land-based telephones to wireless cell phones, from nightly network news to 24/7 cable news, from snail mail to fax mail to e-mail, from encyclopedias to search engines, from yesterday's news to Google. Just Ask Jeeves.

The Decline of Network Advertising

Shrinking viewership means shrinking audiences for advertising. The Big Three of network television, the old reliable of advertising, can no longer be regarded as the only way, the best way, or, in some cases, even the right way to reach consumers. The television universe has expanded rapidly. The Fox network made it the Big Four. Independent television stations that offer popular reruns and other syndicated programming have won another chunk of the prime-time audience.

Clearly the greatest threat to the networks is cable TV. The average US household in 2004 received 100 TV channels compared to 27 in 1994, according to Nielsen Media Research. While the audiences attracted by even the largest cable stations are far smaller than those of the networks, collectively cable now has a larger audience than network.

The proliferation of channels not only offers consumers a wide spectrum of choices, but also gives advertisers a wide array of alternative opportunities to reach specific market segments more efficiently. Cable channels devoted to news, sports, arts and entertainment, movies, history, science, nature, music, comedy, food, travel, and golf enable advertisers to reach targeted audiences with added precision. While reducing costs and avoiding the waste of mass television, the sheer variety of choices puts even greater demands on marketers.

The now-universal remote control device has altered viewer behavior and has led to "zapping" commercials and "zipping" from channel to channel to sample the spectrum of available programming and/or to avoid commercials, a practice that has become known as "grazing." Personal video recorders (PVRs), which were introduced in 2000, enable viewers to skip commercials altogether and may present the greatest threat to television as an effective advertising medium.

Rising Television Advertising Costs

The new uncertainty of network television is rising simultaneously with the cost of television time. Keith Reinhard, chairman of DDB Needham and one of the advertising industry's most innovative thinkers, believes that advertisers must become more responsive to consumers' patterns of receiving information. "The consumer is not a TV viewer or a radio listener or a magazine reader. She has her own network."[2]

The high cost of television time has eliminated it altogether as an option for many advertisers. By necessity, many of these companies have chosen to reach both mass and specialized television audiences through the use of public relations. A skillfully executed PR placement can communicate more product information than an abbreviated 15-second commercial. Not only can the message be lengthier, but because it is broadcast in the context of programming, it also has a credibility that the advertising message may lack.

In their effort to reach target customers more efficiently and effectively, micromarketers are increasingly using new and specialized media, reaching consumers where they shop, working closely with retailers to develop special promotions, and using event sponsorship and other public relations techniques to reach specialized, local, or ethnic markets. The link between advertising and sales, once accepted as gospel, is now being questioned by researchers.

Consumers maintain a healthy skepticism about advertising. Industry studies have found that the majority of consumers believe that ads encourage unnecessary purchases, that advertising increases prices, and that ads encourage people to use products that are bad for them.

The Need for Integration: Consistency in Message and Purpose

Markets have become increasingly competitive, and that competition now comes not just from down the street or from around the corner, but from all over the world. We now live in a truly global marketplace. Greater efficiency and greater effectiveness are mandatory Getting more band for a back is just good; today it is mandatory. More is just better; it's necessary to survival. Few, if any marketers, can totally rely on advertising;

rather, the more successful companies are using integrated marketing communications that draw on the entire range of communications vehicles to tailor programs that speak and sell more effectively and efficiently to their customers. Public relations is vitally needed to make integrated marketing work precisely because study after study tells us that consumers are finding advertising messages less credible.

The current Medill/Northwestern University definition of IMC covers the primary concerns here:

> . . . IMC is the integrated management of all communications to build positive and lasting relationships with customers and other vital stakeholders. It is a customer-centric, data-driven approach to marketing and branding that stresses communicating to the individual by understanding needs, motivations, attitudes and behaviors.[3]

Certainly, a very important principle of IMC is that marketers be consistent in their brand messages and images across all promotional strategies. That is, not only should the firm be collectively employing advertising, direct marketing, public relations, sales promotion, and exhibition strategies as appropriate to reach key targets, but these strategies should be coordinated with one another so that there is a similar look, feel, and message across all of them.

The underlying assumption behind IMC is that the customer aggregates all product exposures into one brand image, regardless of how the company is organized or intends for the marketing strategies or messages to be perceived. Without strong coordination, that aggregated image will likely be a distorted jumble of unrelated slogans and product features.[4]

A 2004 special report on the future of advertising in *The Economist* stated:

> The advertising industry is passing through one of the most disorienting periods in history. This is due to a combination of long-term changes, such as the growing diversity of media, and the arrival of new technologies, notably the Internet. Consumers have become better informed than ever before, with the result that some of the traditional methods of advertising and marketing simply no longer work.
>
> People are tiring of ads in all their forms. A recent study by marketing-services company Yankelovich Partners says that consumer resistance to the growing intrusiveness of marketing and advertising has been pushed to an all-time high. Its study found 65 percent of people now feel "constantly bombarded" by ad messages and 59 percent feel that ads have very little relevance to them. Almost 70 percent said they would be interested in products or services that would help them avoid marketing pitches.[5]

The report states that "there are plenty of alternatives to straightforward advertising, which include a myriad of marketing and communications services, some of which could be called 'below-the-line' advertising. They range from public relations to direct mail, consumer promotions, in-store displays, business-to-business promotions, telemarketing, exhibitions, sponsoring events, product placements, and more."

In his book, *The End of Advertising As We Know It*, Sergio Zyman, former chief marketing officer of Coca-Cola, warned businessmen: "Advertising, as you know it, is dead.

It doesn't work, it's a colossal waste of money, and if you don't wise up, it could end up destroying your company and your brand." 6

The man who once spent hundreds of millions of dollars on TV advertising says the near ubiquitous 30-second television commercial has become more about entertainment than selling stuff. To Zyman, advertising is a lot more than TV commercials. It encompasses how you package your product, the spokespeople you use or don't use to endorse it, the way you treat your employees, and the way they, in turn, treat your customers, the events you sponsor, and the articles that get written about you.

"The very definition of an ad has morphed dramatically in the last decade," states *The Wall Street Journal.* "Marketers including big-spending companies such as Procter & Gamble, American Express Co. and Coca-Cola Co. are pressuring their ad agencies to look beyond 30-second TV ads as consumers become less and less beholden to the electronic hearth." The article reports that college advertising courses now go far beyond copywriting, layout and TV production. At Miami Ad School, students take courses covering guerrilla marketing, which may include street theater and improvisations; viral marketing, in which a promotion spreads via word-of-mouth or forwarded e-mails; and other unusual ad venues such as video games.[7]

Paying to Avoid Ads

A study published in 2004 by Veronis Suhler Stevenson, a New York investment bank specializing in advertising, reported that the amount of their media-consuming time that Americans devoted to media that is mostly financed by advertising, such as broadcast TV, consumer magazines, and daily newspapers, shrank between 1998 and 2003 by 56 percent. Based on current trends, by 2008, consumers will spend an average of 46 percent of their time with media that they pay for, including Pay-TV, DVDs, the Internet, and videogames. Since their production costs are paid for through sales and subscriptions, they will likely contain little or no advertising.

The Economist concludes, "This increases the pressure on media firms to become less dependent on ad revenues. For advertisers it means new ways have to be found to reach consumers, such as buying sponsored links to Internet searches carried out on sites such as Google or Yahoo! or boosting marketing services such as public relations, in-store promotions, direct mail and sponsorship. Spending on such services in America last year (2003) reached $141 billion."[8]

As if advertisers weren't having enough difficulty reaching consumers, the personal video recorder (PVR) is emerging as advertising's public enemy number one. The PVR allows you to record your favorite program on a hard drive and watch it commercial-free when you choose. The *Wall Street Journal* reported that by 2007, PVRs would be in 30 million homes, cutting traditional ad viewing by 19 percent and zapping $7 billion from TV ad budgets. *Wall Street Journal Online* reporter Emily Nelson points out:

> Thirtysomethings are the first generation of TV viewers raised on videos and cable and they are used to seeing what they want, when they want. The ability to record or watch shows at their leisure is particularly appealing to younger viewers, who aren't used to adjusting their time around a network's schedule, Prime time starts at 8 p.m. (7 p.m. in the Midwest.) and with ever longer workdays and commutes, fewer people are at home to watch TV that early."

Marketers say they're tired of paying ever-higher amounts for broadcast ads when shows keep drawing smaller audiences. It isn't even clear how many people pay attention to commercials on live broadcast.[9]

Viewers watch 20 to 30 percent more television after getting a PVR but use it to bypass about 70 percent of the ads, according to the 2003 *Business Week* special report on "The Vanishing Mass Market." They skip more than 90 percent of the ads for such product categories as fast food, credit cards and home products, all mainstays of network television advertising. [10]

Ad Agencies Become Communications Conglomerates

The advertising agency business has changed so dramatically in recent years that it bears little resemblance to the business as it was practiced in the 1950s, when it was largely an entrepreneurial business run by creative giants like Leo Burnett, Bill Bernbach, David Ogilvy, and talented lesser lights who ran hundreds of successful smaller shops. The business has evolved into an oligopoly of four publicly held global communications companies, Omnicom, IPG, WPP, and Publicis, which now account for the lion's share of the marketing communications business in this country and the world. All of them now offer their clients a menu of marketing services beyond advertising, including market research, sales promotion, direct marketing, event management, graphic design, media buying, and public relations.

While the dollars spent on public relations will likely continue to be dwarfed by advertising expenditures, PR's potential has not been lost on advertising agencies, large and small. While small ad agencies attempt to offer their clients a full menu of services including public relations, the giant global communications companies have transformed the public relations agency business by acquiring almost all of the largest PR firms.

The reasons for these acquisitions were:

1. The perceived need for a full array of services matching competitive agencies.
2. The desire to provide one-stop shopping to clients, capturing business that was going elsewhere.
3. A recognition of both the growth rate and profit potential of public relations.
4. The desire to take the opportunity that public relations offers to get closer to client top management.

Some of the advertising-agencies-turned-communications-conglomerates are reporting that "nontraditional" subsidiaries, that is, public relations, sales promotion, and direct marketing, now contribute from one-third to one-half of their total revenues and an even greater percentage of profit. That is why the mega agencies aggressively promote the total communications, or one-stop-shopping, concept to their clients. The conglomerates are making every effort to cross-sell all of their services, traditional and nontraditional, by convincing clients that a communications supermarket provides added value through better integration.

A Global Business

Public relations as a business is largely an American invention and the largest international PR firms are all US-headquartered. All of the largest firms began in this country, with the exception of the Shandwick side of the Weber Shandwick, which in the 1990s began its quest to acquire PR firms in the US, Europe, Asia, and elsewhere in the world from headquarters in the UK.

But public relations, like advertising, has become a global business. The parent organizations of some of the largest PR firms are no longer American. The Publicis Groupe, based in Paris, completed its $3 billion acquisition of Bcom3 Group in 2003, then adding the Manning, Selvage & Lee public relations firm. This narrowed the advertising world to four giant companies, two based in New York, one in London and one in Paris. These four firms (IPG, Omnicom, WPP, and Publicis) now account for more than half the industry's revenue.

These worldwide advertising conglomerates now own a dozen of the 15 largest public firms in the world. Burson-Marsteller, Hill & Knowlton, Cohn & Wolfe, Ogilvy Public Relations, and GCI Group are now owned by WPP Group; Fleishman-Hillard, Ketchum, and Porter/Novelli by Omnicom; Weber Shandwick and Golin Harris by IPG, and Manning, Selvage & Lee by Publicis Groupe.

Onetime antagonist PR firms now peacefully co-exist under the same corporate umbrella. With communications capitals moving to London and Paris, the US retains only two of the four giant firms, IPG and the Omnicom Group.

Does this global consolidation mean that the giants will take over the PR world? We think not. A wise American politician once said all politics is local. The same could be said for public relations. Despite globalization and regional alliances, every country retains its unique culture and every organization has a unique relationship with its stakeholders. The principal practices of media relations, investor relations, employee relations, government relations and marketing public relations vary widely from nation to nation. Clearly, local expertise is required to know how best to relate to the audiences that are critical to any enterprise. The US-based firms have made inroads by employing local experts abroad and by acquiring PR firms that know the territory. But there is still an appetite on the part of many companies to hire firms owned and run by nationals with whom they are more comfortable, provided they can demonstrate their ability to do the job as well as, or better than, the multinational PR firms. In Europe, there is still a preference for using domestic firms. The largest PR firms in France, Germany, Italy, Spain, Holland, and Sweden are local, but the situation is changing as large multinational companies seek coordinated global programming.

It should be noted that the largest remaining independent PR firm, Edelman Public Relations, justifiably amends the name "Worldwide." It has an extensive network of overseas offices in Europe, the Asia-Pacific, and South America. Daniel J. Edelman, chairman of the international public relations firm that bears his name, told the International Public Affairs Symposium at the United Nations in 2004 that "there will be potholes in the road but the way is clear. We'll be globalized more and more as the 21st century unfolds."[11]

Edelman said that he expects the most dramatic growth will be for agencies operating in Asia, particularly in China, Korea, and India. He also predicted that the PR business would expand in Brazil and grow in Russia with greater privatization.

In his book *How to Manage Your Global Reputation: A Guide to the Dynamics of International Public Relations*, Michael Morley, deputy chairman of Edelman Public Relations, believes that the key to successful practice of international public relations is to "think global, act local" rather than "think local, act global." He suggests that:

By thinking local, you can reach a level of understanding of the mind-set of each group of people with whom you must communicate that will make your dialogue much more successful. If you are able to think local, you will stand a much better chance of being able to put your case in terms that are comprehensible by and convincing to your local audience. Thinking local means much, much more than translating, customizing, and even localizing news releases and other communications.

It means understanding local history, customs, rituals, taboos, and prejudices. It means knowing what does and does not make news. It means respecting that a local community's perception, motivation, or priority represents a different outlook.[12]

Sir Martin Sorrell sees limits to globalization. He told *The Wall Street Journal*, "We're losing country focus which is why we're creating country managers. Our clients are doing the same thing. If you don't have someone leading the business locally, you don't get government contracts, education contracts, and political contracts." He added, "One size doesn't fit all. Consumers are more interesting for their differences rather than their similarities."[13]

The 2003 Trust Barometer Survey of 850 US and European opinion leaders conducted by Edelman Public Relations Worldwide reveals that people have a natural affinity toward companies they perceive to be part of the local community and culture. The study concludes that, in order for a global brand to succeed in a foreign market, it must build strong relationships with as many local constituencies as possible and adopt a communications policy and style that fits the market. The bottom line according to Bob Kornecki, then Global Practice Director of Edelman, is that "it's increasingly difficult to be warmly accepted in the global community unless you are an active, integral part of it, so companies must work hard to gain acceptance, one market at a time."[14]

McDonald's Corporation has 29,000 restaurants in countries around the world. Jack Daly, the company's senior vice president of corporate relations, says that his "big job is striking an effective balance between the global nature of our communications and the local nature. That, to me, is where the art and science of communication comes in. We try to employ local people to do the job so we have a greater sensitivity to issues in each of the markets."

McDonald's created Global Communications Council as part of its efforts to strike a balance between global and local needs. Daly says, "Our job is to try to identify best practices that exist all over the place and to share them. In every country, our teams can be little incubators of innovation." McDonald's intranet plays a big part in bringing this about.[15]

Blurring of Advertising and Entertainment

The networks are trying to figure out new ways to please advertisers such as incorporating their products in shows. They are striking deals to have their advertisers' products written into the script of a sitcom or drama.

Marketers will continue to look for new ways to get their messages across. That is both an opportunity for and a barrier to marketing public relations. Media placements on the editorial side, which have become known as "earned media," are more credible than paid product placement. The consumer may accept news of a newsworthy brand or a product that appears in a film or TV drama or sitcom because it naturally fits, but may reject an abundance of blatant product placements on TV shows. Product placements could become even more suspect than paid ads.

Brody Keast, vice president and manager of TiVo Inc. the leading PVR company, told *Marketing News* columnist Michael Krauss that his company, which zaps commercials, makes extensive use of public relations in its own marketing efforts. TiVo can't afford too many of those 30-second TV spots it hopes to make obsolete. Instead, the company uses a mix of celebrity product placements, word-of-mouth communications and public relations. To create buzz and gain trial, TiVo gave its product to entertainment industry and sports celebrities. Keast told Krauss, "For us, public relations has become the new advertising. We've done everything from product reviews to lifestyle stories to a massive amount of product placement with people who are influential in pop culture. TiVo has been written into the scripts of top sitcoms like "Friends" and "Will & Grace" and the monologues of late night hosts David Letterman and Jay Leno—between commercials, that is—TiVo placements that TiVo users would have a hard time zapping."[16]

Fear of TiVo has led some big time advertisers to find ways to keep their product on camera beyond traditional ad breaks. The networks have been pleased to oblige. "The Best Damn Sports Show Period" on Fox Sports Net was paid by LaBatts beer to load the bar with its products and signage and allow its bear mascot walk-on privileges. Viewers of Fox's smash hit "American Idol" watched contestants sipping Coca-Cola and Ford cars are driven exclusively in Fox television network's highly rated dramatic series "24." Stuart Elliott, ad columnist for *The New York Times,* called them "placements so pervasive that viewers must shut their eyes or change the channel to avoid them."[17] The so-called reality shows, most notably "Survivor," led the way to blurring the line between advertising and programming. Now companies can buy a whole show, an arrangement known as "branded entertainment." Sears tools have a major presence on ABC television's "Extreme Makeover: Home Edition" and Home Depot stores, salespeople and products are written into the script of "Trading Spaces" on The Learning Channel.

The Future of Advertising

Joe Cappo, who has seen the advertising business from the unique perspective of newspaper-marketing-columnist-turned-publisher of *Advertising Age*, says that ad agencies must redefine and reinvent themselves in order to survive in the future. In his book *The Future of Advertising.* Cappo predicts that the giant advertising-centered holding companies may not stay intact as presently constituted because they are made up of dozens of different companies of different sizes, different cultures, and different personalities and because "not all marriages are made in heaven, no matter how happy the couple looked on their wedding day." He thinks that some of the former owners of these units, especially those in non-advertising businesses, may want to buy themselves back and their corporate parents may find it advantageous to sell them. He notes that powerful clients will increasingly dictate the structure and ownership of their agencies:[18]

> No one denies the necessity of integrated marketing these days but the big question remains: Who will be the "general contractor" that puts all the pieces together. It could be the large holding companies but there are a couple of

problems. They are still dominated by their big ad agency holdings. And clients know that it's to their agency's advantage to assign non-advertising work to other units of their company—which may or may not be the best choice.

The ad industry is also haunted by an underlying fear that their strategic role will be usurped by management consulting firms. The consultants are close to and highly regarded by top client management, and since they aren't in the marketing services business, they aren't driven by the need to cross-sell. Cappo says the battle for communication attention can no longer depend on mass marketing and television advertising. This will inevitably require more emphasis on "below-the-line" activities, including direct marketing, event marketing, sales promotion, and public relations.

In an interview with *The Wall Street Journal*, Sir Martin Sorrell, Chairman of WPP Group said, "If you want to upset me, call us an advertising agency. The strategic objective is for two-thirds percent of our revenue to come from nontraditional advertising in five to 10 years. Because of fragmentation, TiVo and Sky Plus, clients and ourselves have to look at everything. Instead of focusing on network television, we have to look at public relations and radio and outdoor and mobile messaging and satellite."[19]

The Fall of Advertising and the Rise of PR

A book published in 2002 called *The Fall of Advertising and the Rise of PR* by marketing guru Al Ries and his daughter Laura brought joy to the hearts of PR people and shook up the ad world. In their book, the Rieses contend that marketing has entered the era of public relations. They predict that, in the future, PR will set the strategic direction for the brand and that advertising will have to follow its lead. They believe that publicity provides the credentials that create credibility in the advertising. Until a new brand has some third-party-supplied credentials, they say the consumer will ignore the advertising. They contend that "advertising doesn't build brands, publicity does" and that advertising can only maintain brands that have been created by publicity.[20]

The truth, according to the Rieses, is that "advertising cannot start a fire. It can only fan a fire after it has been started." Why? Because in order "to get something going from nothing you need the validity that only third-party endorsements can bring." Therefore, they contend, the first stage of any new campaign ought to be public relations. The Rieses' all-purpose formula is: Use PR to Build Brands and Advertising to Maintain Them. They provide numerous good examples of campaigns where the formula works. They report, "Wherever we look we see a dramatic shift from advertising-oriented marketing to public-relations oriented marketing."

The Rieses are advocating what marketing PR leaders have been preaching for years, but since the Rieses have no apparent commercial ax to grind, their words have caused many marketers to take a fresh look at public relations. Their credentials are impeccable. The Rieses normally recommend that any new marketing program start with publicity (which they equate to public relations) and only shift to advertising after the PR objectives have been achieved.

They believe that advertising should follow PR in both timing and theme and that advertising should be started only after a PR program has run its course. They conclude "For most companies today, PR is far too important to take a back seat to advertising. In many ways PR is in the driver's seat and should lead and direct a marketing program."

Exhibit 2.1. IMC Best Practices

1. Consistency in message and purpose across multiple communications tools
2. A strategic approach with clear and measurable business objectives
3. A feedback mechanism to encourage receipt of information from customers, employees, suppliers, etc.
4. The use of data to target and attract specific audiences to promotions
5. A focus on retrieving data and using it for follow-up with key targets
6. An evaluation of the financial effectiveness of the communications efforts through an ROI analysis
7. A mechanism to learn from past experiences and a commitment to improving future performance

Their book is replete with good examples of PR driving successful marketing programs. While we couldn't agree more that publicity can be invaluable in introducing new products and building new brands, we believe that there is a danger is applying this formula across-the-board to all products.

No less an authority than Harold Burson, founder chairman of Burson-Marsteller, one of the world's largest PR firms, questions whether or not PR can deliver in moving consumer staples off the shelf. "We can do well in the introduction of novelty or otherwise newsworthy items, but sustained marketing programs require continuity and repetition, which we cannot guarantee over a time span."[21] In the context of an integrated marketing communications campaign, public relations can enhance the effectiveness of advertising. Burson-Marsteller did some research years ago that showed that public relations efforts increased the credibility of advertising and even the readership.

Publicity can do wonders for a product that is truly newsworthy. If the product has real built-in news value, PR should take the lead in gaining public awareness. But some products simply can't count on a big PR blastoff to put them on the map. Publicity can work wonders for products that have a good story to tell. And while PR may have a role to play in all product introductions, sometimes the big news peg simply isn't there. Regardless of how awful a great deal of today's advertising is and how difficult it is to reach consumers with media so fragmented, we cannot see a time when mass marketers will introduce a new breakfast cereal, soda pop, burger, or beer without traditional advertising. Studies conducted by Information Resources, Inc., have consistently shown that advertising plays an important role in new product launches and is a key factor that differentiates successful products from the unsuccessful. In 2003, a consumer survey conducted by InsightExpress for Schneider & Associates, a Boston-based public relations firm, found that the most successful product launches of the year use a combination of marketing communications approaches including advertising, media relations, consumer education, special events, sampling, partnerships, endorsements and coupons to create consumer awareness of the product and its benefits.[22]

Successful integrated marketing arranges the components so they work together to move a customer toward a sale. Almost all use public relations to reach the consumer and the trade in advance of advertising. *PR Week's* Marketing Management Survey 2005 of chief marketing officers, vice presidents of marketing and brand managers found than PR was as effective or more effective than advertising in pre-marketing conditioning, generating word-of-mouth and message development.[23]

Media Relations Makes the Difference

Today's technology has given public relations the power to reach customers directly through a variety of non-media tactics ranging from e-mail and voice mail to on-line chat rooms, interactive interviews, news conferences, forums and surveys.

But never underestimate the power of media relations as a public relations tactic. While consumer confidence in television news, newspaper and magazine articles may have declined, consumers still believe that the editorial side of the media is far more trustworthy than the advertising it runs. That's why publicity is such an effective tool in integrated marketing campaigns.

The 2003 Trust Barometer Survey conducted by Edelman Public Relations Worldwide of US and European opinion leaders found that individuals are eight times more likely to believe information that they get from articles or news coverage than information in advertising. Articles in newspapers, newsweeklies, business magazines, and on radio and TV all carry an implied level of credibility with readers and viewers.

Sergio Zyman, former chief marketing officer of the Coca-Cola Company, says, "One of the biggest distinctions of all between advertising, publicity and public relations is the way consumers react to them. People are generally pretty cynical and they often attribute the worst to everyone. They know that companies pay for advertising and they know that companies sponsor events for no other reason than to get their name in the paper. That, of course, makes people a little suspicious of both. But then if a piece of information is put out by a supposedly neutral third party, people are a lot more likely to believe it: what the media says about you often has a much more significant impact on your business than almost anything else."[24]

A case in point: In 2000, American Family Life Assurance Co. a.k.a. Aflac was a relatively unknown purveyor of workplace insurance. Within four years, consumer awareness of Aflac increased from 12 percent to 90 percent, and sales increased 20 percent. That was when the company launched its enormously successful Aflac duck. *The Wall Street Journal* reported that Aflac's success was "done on the cheap" and that the company spent "Only $45 million on commercial time annually, a relatively paltry sum in the ad business." The *Journal* credited "a well-orchestrated behind-the-scenes guerilla public relations campaign" for making the difference.[25]

Two years after the ads began to appear on television, Aflac marketers noticed that actor Ben Affleck, then at the peak of his stardom, was joking about the similarity between his name and the character. When the Aflac team heard he was slated to go on NBC's "The Tonight Show with Jay Leno," they wrote a letter to Mr. Leno stating, "Ben likes being compared to his nemesis, the Aflac duck." And indeed, Mr. Affleck himself brought it up on the show.

During an appearance on ABC's "Live with Regis and Kelly," host Regis Philbin surprised Ben Affleck by pulling out the toy and making it quack. This was followed by what Aflac called "Quack attacks." Aflac toy ducks began appearing everywhere. A dozen company and ad agency executives bearing ducks in hand and sewed to their hats were seen on the outdoor set on NBC's "Today" show.

Dan Amos, Aflac's chief executive, told the *Journal,* "We can buy expensive time on the Super Bowl but when you can show up in places for nothing it's twice as rewarding and twice as profitable for the corporation."

Al Ries told *The Journal* that "without the guerrilla PR campaign, the advertising campaign wouldn't have been as effective."

The paper concluded, "The behind-the-scenes maneuvering reflects an axiom of twenty-first century advertising. In this cluttered marketing environment, simply buying TV time isn't enough." [26]

Classic MPR

Long before the Aflac duck, there were many cases of the power of PR being used to help make household names of a brand. Scott Cutlip, public relations historian and the late Dean Emeritus of the University of Georgia College of Journalism and Mass Communication, related the experience of the National Biscuit Company in his history of public relations, *The Unseen Power.*

In 1899, the National Biscuit Company decided to take the cracker out of the barrel in country and small town stores and put it in "a sanitary package." Nabisco retained the nation's oldest advertising agency, N.W. Ayer & Co., to advertise its Uneeda Biscuit in the sanitary package. In its revolutionary ad campaign, Ayer quickly discovered that it was selling more than packaged crackers, it was selling change. The Ayer campaign, on behalf of what became Nabisco, was the first to feature a staple food, ready for consumption, and sold in individual packages. It involved creation of an air-tight package, a distinctive brand name, and a trademark. In bringing this revolutionary change to a frontier America, Ayer quickly realized it would take a coordinated plan for reaching the general public through newspapers, magazines, streetcar advertisements, posters, and painted signs. It sold sanitation, then it sold crackers. This was the beginning of Ayer's pioneering in the use of publicity to support its advertisers' marketing campaigns. By 1908, the promotional publicity work had become so heavy that it was taken out of the copy department and set up as a separate department. Gradually, this work in the Ayer agency grew, and in 1920, a Publicity Bureau was set up, the first in a major advertising agency. Thus was set the stage for the emergence of the publicity agency that evolved into public relations counseling over the next half-century.[1]

This chapter will address an arbitrary list of other astonishingly successful marketing programs driven largely by public relations.

Ivory Soap Sculpture

In 1919, Edward Bernays set up his publicity office in New York City. When he died in 1995 at age 100, obituaries that appeared in *The New York Times* and scores of other newspapers referred to him as "the father of public relations." While some may dispute the legitimacy of the title, Bernays was certainly one of the first and most successful practitioners of public relations. He was responsible for some remarkably successful programs in the sphere that we now call marketing public relations.

One of Bernays's most successful campaign dates back to the mid-1920s and ran for four decades. This was the celebrated contest created by Bernays on behalf of Ivory Soap, which was then the primary product of his client, Procter & Gamble. He said that kids of the day didn't much like taking baths and getting soap in their eyes. So he devised the Ivory Soap Sculpture Contest—a contest that brought dirty kids and clean soap together. He succeeded in getting schools across the country to turn kids into soap sculptors.

Bernays wrote:

Procter & Gamble, leading American manufacturer of soap and vegetable fats, retained us for counsel on public relations early in this period (the 1920s), and we worked together on diversified projects in close consultation with management. . . . I did some research and found that many sculptors used soap instead of wax. I contacted public schools and asked them to participate in a soap sculpture contest. Within a year, we had 22 million school children doing soap sculpture and loving it; it gratified their creative instincts.[2]

Works often broke in mid-sculpture, requiring the use of several bars of Ivory in coming up with a suitable contest entry. That may have been the idea. Bernays's brochure with soap sculpture tips, which millions of children received in their schools, advised them to "use discarded models for face, hands and bath," adding, "You will love the feeling of cleanliness that comes from an Ivory soap bath once a day."

The contests continued for 35 years until 1961. Kid sculptors used up a million cakes of Ivory Soap a year, making Ivory the all-American soap.

Bernays, never modest about his accomplishments, wrote: "Soap sculpture became a national outlet for children's creative instincts and helped develop a generation that enjoyed cleanliness."

More of Bernays's Greatest Hits

Long before the public was concerned with things like carbs, cholesterol, fats, and nitrates, Ed Bernays made bacon and eggs America's favorite breakfast. By promoting the health benefits of eating a large breakfast, his efforts greatly increased bacon consumption and his meat-packer client's sales. Bernays similarily helped United Fruit Company boost banana sales by publicizing a study that showed that eating fruit helps fight cystic fibrosis.

Before the surgeon general's warning that cigarette smoking is hazardous to health, Bernays made it socially acceptable for women to smoke in public by arranging for debutantes to smoke in New York's Easter Parade. (Decades later, when the health issue arose, he helped get cigarette advertising off television.)

Before the invention of paperback books and their mass distribution at newsstands and supermarkets, on behalf of his client, America's Booksellers, Bernays convinced the country's builders to build bookshelves in new homes so that they could be filled with hardcover books.

The Father of Event Marketing

Bernays could arguably also be called "the father of event marketing." He pulled off the publicity coup of the century for his client, General Electric, in celebration of the fiftieth anniversary of the electric light bulb. He called it the "Golden Jubilee of Light" and described it as the greatest tribute ever paid to any living man. The man, of course, was Thomas Edison, and, for this event, Bernays had Edison's boyhood home moved from Menlo Park, New Jersey, to Henry Ford's Dearborn Village in Michigan and recreated a great moment in history. When an NBC radio announcer gave the signal, people all over the world switched on their electric lights, adding their personal tributes to those of President Herbert Hoover, Henry Ford, Orville Wright, Madame Curie, J. P. Morgan, and John D. Rockefeller, all of whom were assembled for this auspicious occasion.

"Bread, de Luxe"

Although he would have eschewed the description of public relations counselor for press agent, Benjamin Sonnenberg represented some of the most important personalities and business people of the mid-twentieth century. His corporate clients included Philip Morris, Texaco, and Lever Brothers.

How he helped a friend and neighbor named Margaret Rudkin is described in his biography, *Always Live Better Than Your Clients*. It relates how Mrs. Rudkin began selling her homemade bread during the depths of the Great Depression, baking the loaves in an old relic of a stove. When she and her husband needed a new one, they called Sonnenberg for help. He obliged, and, in return for the stove and his help in publicizing the bread, the Rudkins insisted that Sonnenberg have a one-third interest in their company.

Among Sonnenberg's accomplishments was the placement of an article called "Bread, de Luxe" in *Reader's Digest* in 1939. It told how Mrs. Rudkin used only the finest ingredients in her old-fashioned, home-baked bread and kneaded the dough by hand, and how she had built a quarter-of-a-million-dollar business on word-of-mouth advertising.

At the time the article appeared, production was 25,000 loaves of bread a week; three months later, it had doubled. The increased volume caused the company to turn other buildings on the farm over to bread-baking and to double the number of employees.

Mrs. Rudkin said:

> The mail, which resulted from the story, seemed to me to be absolutely staggering. By the time a month had gone by, I had received 3,000 letters and had to employ two secretaries, because each letter had to be answered individually due to the fact that most of them enclosed money or checks ordering bread to be sent to all sorts of addresses, not only in the United States, but actually in Turkey, South Africa, Canada, England, etc.[3]

The name of her company was Pepperidge Farm, and when it was sold to Campbell Soup Company in 1961 for $28 million, Sonnenberg got one-third of it in cash and stock.

The Making of the Mustang

In the late 1960s, Lee Iacocca appeared on the covers of the two leading newsweekly magazines in the same week. The cover stories in *Time* and *Newsweek* were, of course, no coincidence. They launched a carefully orchestrated national media relations campaign to introduce the Ford Mustang before the car was advertised or seen in the showroom. In his best-selling book *Iacocca*, Lee describes the key role public relations played in launching the Mustang, and, not too incidentally, Mr. Iacocca himself, as an American celebrity.

He relates how the introduction of the Mustang was conceived of three years before the car was designed. The target date was the opening of the New York World's Fair in April 1964:

> It was the ideal place to launch our car. Although new models are traditionally introduced in the fall, we had in mind a product so exciting and so different that we would dare to bring it out in the middle of the season. Only the World's Fair had enough scale and drama for the car of our dreams.[4]

Six million visitors gawked as the procession of brightly painted, sporty cars from Ford passed by. The Mustang became the talk of the Fair.

Ford had produced a minimum number of 8,000 Mustangs, so that every Ford dealer would have at least one in his showroom when the car was officially launched. Then the media relations campaign began:

> We promoted the Mustang to the hilt. We invited the editors of college newspapers to Dearborn, and we gave them a Mustang to drive for a few weeks. Four days before the car was officially launched, a hundred members of the press participated in a giant, seventy-car Mustang rally from New York to Dearborn, and the cars demonstrated their reliability by breezing through the seven-hundred-mile trips without any problems. The press recorded its enthusiasm . . . prominently in hundreds of magazines and newspapers.
>
> On April 17, Ford dealerships everywhere were mobbed with customers. In Chicago, one dealer had to lock his showroom doors because the crowd outside was so large. A dealer in Pittsburgh reported that the crush of customers was so thick that he couldn't get his Mustang off the wash rack. In Detroit, another dealer said that so many people who had come to see the Mustang had arrived in sports cars that his parking lot looked like a foreign car rally.
>
> The Mustang was destined to be an incredible hit. During the first weekend it was on sale, an unprecedented four million people visited Ford dealerships. . . . [T]he Mustang was featured simultaneously on the covers of both *Time* and *Newsweek* . . . an astounding publicity coup for a new commercial product. . . . I'm convinced that *Time* and *Newsweek* alone led to the sale of an extra 100,000 cars. . . .
>
> I had a target in mind for the first year. During its first year, the Falcon had sold a record 417,174 cars, and that was the figure I wanted to beat. We had a slogan: "417 by 4/17"–the Mustang's birthday. Late in the evening of April 16, 1965, a young Californian bought a sporty red Mustang convertible. He had just purchased the 418,812th Mustang, and we finished our first year with a new record.[5]

Twenty-five years later, Lee Iacocca had long since departed from Ford, but Mustangs were still making news. On the 25th anniversary of the Mustang, Ford's New York district sales office threw an anniversary party at the Flushing Meadows site of the 1964 World's Fair. About 250 owners of vintage Mustang parked their cars around the still-standing Unisphere. The event also drew members of regional chapters of the more than 2,000 Mustang clubs in the US. Also, a thundering herd of nearly 40 European-owned Ford Mustangs participated in an American Pony Drive. The cars, driven by Mustangers from three European countries, covered more than 7,000 miles in their two-month long odyssey, passing through 17 states with stops in 25 cities.

Eventually the car caravan headed for Dearborn, Michigan, for a visit to Ford World Headquarters and a tour of the Dearborn Assembly Plant, the only Ford plant that had built Mustangs over the entire 25-year history of the car.

Knowing a good thing, Ford staged another celebration of the Mustang on its 30th anniversary. This occasion was used to turn the spotlight on the new 1994 state-of-the-art Mustang.

What a Doll/Oh, You Beautiful Doll

That was the title of a six-page cover story in *Newsweek* on the hottest toy of the 1980s. The article was the culmination of a six-month MPR effort of what became known as the Cabbage Patch Kids "phenomenon," a campaign that made it mandatory for every kid in America to own, rather to "adopt," at least one of these cuddly, homely dolls.

The convergence of modern technology and toy-making had made it possible for every child to become a parent to a doll that was uniquely his or her own. Described by *Newsweek* as "the first toy of the industrial age," each one-of-a-kind Cabbage Patch Kid came off a computer-controlled assembly line with a different combination of hair, skin color, clothing, type of mouth, dimples, freckles, and gender. Each was packaged in a see-through package so every kid could pick a doll of his or her choice.

The kicker was that each doll came with a name and adoption papers. Richard Weiner and his public relations company depended heavily on research and the advice of child psychologists and educators, who advised that the dolls' appearance brought out the nurturing instinct in kids. The Director of the Psychology of Parenthood Program at New York University worked with the PR firm to develop a "Cabbage Patch Kids Parenting Guide," which accompanied each doll. This piece won the hearts of kids and the minds of parents and influentials and gave legitimacy to the value of the adoption idea.

The incredible success of this MPR program is a testimonial to the value of research and forward planning. Toy buyers were introduced to the Cabbage Patch Kids at the New York Toy Fair. Coleco's showroom was converted into a replica of Babyland General Hospital, generating an avalanche of trade publicity that helped stimulate the interest of the consumer media. The consumer media relations effort was launched at a New York press conference in June, even though the dolls would not be available in stores until the Christmas shopping season. Two hundred reporters attended, including magazine writers, who needed the long lead time to feature the dolls in their "what's hot for Christmas gifts" stories.

The New York press event at the Manhattan Laboratory Museum was duplicated in Atlanta and Boston. Pupils from local schools were invited along with toy buyers and their children. Each event featured a "mass adoption" by the children present.

In the fall, Cabbage Patch spokespersons hit the road for a 15-city media tour, extolling the dolls' virtues and showing them off on TV interview shows. Interviews and photo ops were arranged with local newspapers, and talk radio listeners were invited to call in with their questions and comments.

A doll sent to Jane Pauley, then the co-host of the NBC network's top-rated *Today* show, who was at home expecting a baby, resulted in a five-minute segment on the show and started the national publicity ball rolling. The other networks followed with their own stories. In the end, "the Cabbage Patch Kids were on literally every TV station and in every major newspaper and general interest magazine in America, and not just once," according to Dick Weiner. "Everybody in the United States, whether or not they were parents, knew about the Cabbage Patch Kids."

The mad rush for dolls at stores throughout the country could have resulted in a negative backlash had Coleco not pulled its advertising and had the story not been tempered by the PR decision to give away dolls to hospitals and other charities serving kids. A wire picture of First Lady Nancy Reagan presenting Cabbage Patch Kids to two

Korean children who were heart patients at a Long Island, New York, hospital was seen throughout the world.

Every kid had to have one. Some $600 million worth of dolls were sold during the first year. The success of Cabbage Patch Kids became an MPR classic because it was primarily public relations-driven. Conventional toy marketing wisdom of the time decreed that no toy could succeed without a plethora of kid TV advertising, but the PR for the Cabbage Patch Kids was so successful that it wasn't necessary to advertise until year two.

In 1989, Hasbro acquired the Cabbage Patch Kids line from Coleco. Steady marketing proved that the line had staying power and turned a trendy toy into a consistent, steady seller for years.

The Pillsbury Bake-Off

Since the first "Grand Recipe Hunt and Baking Contest" was held at New York's Waldorf-Astoria Hotel in 1949, with TV host Art Linkletter as master of ceremonies and former First Lady Eleanor Roosevelt as guest of honor, the nationwide event has become an American institution and has made Pillsbury synonymous with baking.

Thousands of men, women, and children have participated in what became known as the Pillsbury Bake-Off, which became the premier contest to select the nation's best nonprofessional cooks. Many of the winning recipes have become classics.

The event has been highly publicized through the years. At the first event, a *Life* magazine photographer captured a picture of a finalist dropping her cake upside down. Decades later, on February 29, 1988, a *Newsweek* headline proclaimed "They're Cooking for Cash: A Major Culinary Contest Shows How America Eats," and the story described how very few food ideas hit American homes with the speed and thoroughness of Bake-Off recipes, which begin to appear in daily newspapers as soon as the winners are announced.

Newsweek reported that Pillsbury could tell that people start making the recipes right away because of immediate sales of products used by the winners. One year, a Chicago supermarket chain sold a half-year's supply of Pillsbury's lemon frosting mix used in the winning recipe in just two weeks.

Pillsbury has changed the Bake-Off rules and categories over the years, to reflect both trends in American cooking habits and the development of new products. In 1949, all recipes submitted had to contain Pillsbury flour. Later, categories covering nutritious and ethnic recipes were added. In 1988, the name of the event became the Bake-Off Cooking and Baking Contest, to acknowledge the addition of recipes using Green Giant canned and frozen vegetables.

Finalists are selected from tens of thousands of entries received between June and October. After several rounds of screening, more than 1,500 selected recipes are prepared for taste panels of Pillsbury home economists. The 100 finalists are called in December and told that they have been selected for the February trip to the contest site and the opportunity to compete for cash prizes and national recognition, that is, publicity for their outstanding cooking skills.

On February 20, 1990, Linda Rashman of Petaluma, California, the grand prize winner of that year's Pillsbury Bake-Off, was pictured in *The New York Times* with her blueberry poppy seed brunch cake. The accompanying story was headlined "At the

Super Bowl of Bake-Offs, a Dream Can Be Worth $40,000." The article commented that, while the company will not divulge the cost of the Bake-Off, "it appears to be worth every penny." Gary Klingl, president of the Pillsbury's Green Giant division, explained why. He told *The Times*, "an analysis of newspapers and magazines showed that the publicity pays for the contest."

In 1996, the Pillsbury Bake-Off got the biggest makeover in its history. The updated Bake-Off included brands like Old El Paso and Progresso for the first time. By that time, tens of thousands of consumers were entering the contest, and the ante for the prize-winning recipe was raised from $50,000 to $1 million. That assured the company of maximum consumer participation and media coverage. The Bake-Off was promoted at retail outlets, where store demonstrators distributed contest entry forms. Special point-of-sale material was created for stores in African-American and Latino neighborhoods. The announcement of the winner was a major publicity coup, since the million dollar winner was, for the first time, a man. His victory was noted by all of the network nightly newscasts, and the winner himself was interviewed on the networks' popular morning and late night shows.

MPR Makes a Market

In 1963, the 3M Company formulated a marketing strategy that would put one of the company's overhead projectors in every classroom in America. 3M announced its Assistance Grant to Education program, which would award $3,000 worth of its visual communications equipment to each of 500 schools, selected on the basis of written proposals detailing their plans for use of the equipment.

The response was astonishing: 150,000 schools, more than one out of every ten eligible schools in the United States, submitted proposals! 3M gave away $1.5 million worth of equipment, which the company later admitted exceeded the total sales of visual products for the previous year.

The grants program was an investment that paid stunning dividends. Supported by a skillful grassroots public relations strategy, the program reached hundreds of thousands of teachers, principals, and school board members and caused them to think about how they would use 3M overhead projectors in their classrooms. Five hundred schools received them free, but thousands of other schools now recognized their value as a teaching tool, and the orders rolled in.

When the company shifted its marketing focus to the business market, an equally innovative—and equally successful—marketing public relations program was created on the concept of how to run more effective business meetings. The program was introduced at a New York press event, featuring Rudy Vallee and other members of the cast of the then-current hit musical, "How to Succeed in Business Without Really Trying." 3M became positioned as the business-meeting expert and the 3M overhead projector as the indispensable tool for running effective meetings. These programs not only sold overhead projectors, but 3M transparency markers and huge quantities of transparencies needed for every presentation.

4 The Trust Factor

Today's marketing managers may be required to deal with any number of consumer concerns about their company's reputation, fiscal integrity, social responsibility, and the efficacy of their products. The odds are increasing that young marketing executives will be faced with a threatening crisis situation sometime in their career.

How to deal with these problems is something they don't teach marketing students at business schools. That is why public relations is increasingly being called upon by corporations to identify emerging problems and corporate vulnerabilities in order to prepare plans for crises that could occur and to train executives on how to respond when and if the need arises. A single incident, the Tylenol murders, raised the crisis consciousness of corporate America. Since that time, the need for crisis planning has become a universally accepted management responsibility and function and one of the fastest-growing areas of corporate public relations practice.

A survey of a cross-section of US consumers, conducted by NFO WorldGroup for Golin/Harris in 2003, found not only that a crisis of trust in business had reached epidemic proportions but also that trust has a direct positive effect on brand preference and loyalty. Nearly 40 percent of the respondents said they would definitely or probably start doing business with a company or increase their business specifically because they consider the company trustworthy. Conversely, the loss of trust has an even greater negative impact on the brand. Fifty-three percent said they would definitely or probably stop doing business with a company, reduce their volume of business, or switch to a competitor because of doubts about trustworthiness.[1]

A strong corporate brand not only can help a company compete effectively in the marketplace for goods and services, but also is positive for equity, capital, ideas, and employees, according to Harlan Teller. Teller, who managed the worldwide corporate practice for Hill & Knowlton, a leading global PR firm, says that consumers, investors, and employees all want to feel good about the company behind the brand. His view is supported by a 1997 Lou Harris poll that demonstrates that when you link a product brand to a well-known and trusted corporate brand in the mind of a consumer, there is an increase in intent to purchase.[2] Ellen Ryan Mardiks, worldwide director of brand strategies for Golin/Harris International, believes that the time is fast approaching when brand strategy will equal corporate strategy.[3]

Corporate Brand or Reputation

There currently is a debate within the public relations industry on whether the goal of corporate public relations should be to manage the corporate brand or to manage the company's reputation. Paul Holmes, editor of *The Holmes Report*, believes that brand and reputation are not the same. He says, "Brand is all the things a company wants you to think and feel when you hear its name, the sum total of its communications, while reputation is all the things you really do think and feel, the result of communications plus behavior. Brand is something you build; reputation is something you earn. Brand is a promise; reputation is the result of keeping that promise."[4]

Others believe that the distinction is a matter of semantics. Bob Druckenmiller, former president of Porter-Novelli, a leading international PR firm, believes that corporations have brands and that these brands have real and perceived value at the functional level, at the personal or emotional level, and at the core of a company's character. He says that marketing-based perspective is critical to successfully building long-term value in any corporate brand by enabling it to better understand and meet the needs of its audiences.

Yankelovich+Partners, a leader in market research, recently designed a new methodology for Hill & Knowlton, called Corporate Equity Performance System (CEPS), that measures the value of corporate reputation. It provides corporations with a benchmark of how they are perceived by such key audiences as employees and recruits, customers and prospects, financial analysts and portfolio managers, opinion leaders, business peers, suppliers and the trade, regulators and other government audiences, activists and advocacy groups, academics, the news media, and the general public. The CEPS process begins with a senior management audit that provides an "inside-out" look at the company and is followed by an "outside-in" survey of key stakeholder groups. An analysis of this input defines the attributes that drive the company's behavior. Further analysis combines attribute and behavioral analysis with evaluation of the company versus its competitors.

The system is designed to identify key attributes that have the greatest potential for motivating key audiences to support the company in several key ways: to buy its products or its stock, to recommend it as a trade partner or place to work, to believe in it at a time of crisis, or to support it in the public policy arena.

Trust or Consequences

In his book, *Trust or Consequences: Build Trust Today or Lose Your Market Tomorrow*, Al Golin, chairman of Golin/Harris, expands on a concept he created early in his career, called the "trust bank." He believes that community involvement results in "deposits" of trust from its customers, that the accumulation of these deposits builds consumer confidence and that trust is especially important when the company has to make a "withdrawal" from the trust bank—when the company faces a crisis or other negative news. He contends that by saying and doing the right thing over time a company can earn your trust. He and Ray Kroc, the founder of McDonald's Corporation, shared a common vision from the beginning of their long relationship. McDonald's was virtually unknown and couldn't afford advertising back then, but Kroc insisted that his franchisees sponsor programs in their communities.

Golin believes that it is much easier to achieve the long-term objective of trust building year after year than to begin rebuilding relationships that have been damaged. His prescription for fixing-it-before-it-breaks is particularly relevant these days when so many corporations and financial institutions are under fire from their investors, customers, and employees, and under siege from states' attorneys general, federal regulators, jurists and jurors, and investigative reporters.

He says that you may be able to build a solid brand without integrating trust into the message, but it's tough to build a great one without it. Trust gives brands like McDonald's, Johnson & Johnson, Volvo, Gerber, and General Electric an edge. In commercialized markets, it says to customers, "Here's a reason beyond price why you should buy our products. Trust gives people a good feeling about what they're buying."[5]

How McDonald's Builds Trust

From the beginning, founder Ray Kroc believed that McDonald's should be committed to giving something back to the society from which the company derives its profits and putting something back into the local communities where it does business. He knew instinctively that good citizenship is good public relations, and that good public relations is good for business.

A half-century later, this dedication to giving something back remains first in the statement of McDonald's Core Values:

> We give back to the communities in which we do business. We are a local business. We must be leaders in social responsibility. Our customers view us by the positive influence we have on the neighborhood, its people, and the environment.[6]

To McDonald's, marketing public relations and community relations are inseparable, if not synonymous. From day one, McDonald's discovered that community involvement was a far more efficient and affordable form of promotion than advertising. In *McDonald's: Behind the Arches,* John F. Love points out that "community relations work has become one of the most powerful [image-producing] weapons in McDonald's impressive marketing arsenal."[7]

Al Golin, who has been public relations counsel to McDonald's for more than 50 years, says that McDonald's no longer needs to participate in community involvement to generate awareness. Today, the purposes of McDonald's commitment to community relations are to reinforce its leadership position in the fast-service field and to generate the trust of its customers.

He explains:

> The essence of McDonald's is the individual, locally operated restaurant. Each restaurant's management and employees have an important stake in the community or neighborhood where they are located. They owe their success and their jobs to the patronage of their neighbors. Therefore, it makes sense that McDonald's has an unusually strong commitment to being a leader in community citizenship in each restaurant's trading area. There is a tradition of personal local involvement in community service that extends throughout the McDonald's organization. Whatever the project, it must always deliver a tangible benefit to the community. That must come before any publicity can be generated.
>
> Community relations is both an opportunity and an obligation. The opportunity is to establish a partnership and build trust among those who use the company's products and services. The obligation is to be a responsible corporate citizen, with the understanding that there, in fact, exists a moral obligation for a business to give something back to the society from which it derives a profit.[8]

McDonald's communications efforts have the common purpose of increasing its food sales, but they also have a common goal: to preserve, protect, and enhance McDonald's image and reputation in the marketplace. The company's 1999 annual report states:

> The McDonald's brand lives and grows where it counts the most—in the hearts of customers worldwide. We, in turn, hold our customers close to our heart,

striving to do the right thing and giving back to the communities where we do business. At McDonald's, social responsibility is part of heritage and we are committed to building on it worldwide. Being an active, responsible leader in our communities instills pride among McDonald's people—the people who are ultimately responsible for providing customers with a positive McDonald's experience.[9]

Corporate Brand and Product Brand:
One and the Same at McDonald's

McDonald's has long been recognized as a leader in social responsibility. Its community involvement programs span the country and the globe. The company releases an annual "Social Responsibility Report" that tracks the company's performance and progress in four areas: community, environment, people, and economic impact.

Community performance highlights listed in the 2003 report lead off with the company's support of Ronald McDonald House Charities (RMHC), one of the world's premier philanthropic organizations. By 2003, RMHC and its local network of chapters had made grants in excess of $380 million to children's organizations around the world. McDonald's supports the management and general expenses of the charity's global office and defrays some of the costs associated with fund-raising activities and program services. The organization provides care to children and their families by awarding grants to organizations through chapters in countries throughout the world and supporting more than 180 Ronald McDonald Houses in 50 countries, where families of seriously ill children can stay while their children undergo medical attention at a nearby hospital. Other highlights include:

- The Ronald McDonald Care Mobile program, which brings cost-effective, high-quality medical and dental care directly to children in underserved communities.
- Olympic Youth Camp brought together 400 young men and women from nearly 200 countries to participate in a variety of arts, sports, and cross-cultural activities in the 2000 Olympics in Australia.
- In partnership with the Field Museum in Chicago, McDonald's helped bring "Sue," the world's largest Tyrannosaurus Rex fossil, to US cities through two traveling replicas and viewable fossil preparation labs in Chicago and Orlando.
- With the Walt Disney Company, McDonald's recognized the outstanding contributions of 2,000 exceptional young people to their local communities in 90 countries.

Marketing public relations programs at McDonald's involve the company in local communities wherever it does business, thereby generating consumer trust and patronage. Exhibit 4.1 shows how McDonald's community involvement programs serve the company's marketing objectives.

Assessing the Corporate Brand

One of the most important roles of public relations is defending products at risk and giving consumers permission to buy. Effective crisis communications restore confidence in the brand and the corporate brand behind it. A 1999 nationwide on-line survey of 10,830 Americans conducted by the market research firm Harris Interactive and

Exhibit 4.1. Marketing Objectives of Community Involvement Programs at McDonald's

Marketing objective:	To be the world's best quick service restaurant experience.
Marketing strategy:	To reinforce leadership by generating consumer trust.
Public relations strategy:	Community involvement programs
Public relations programs:	Ronald McDonald House Charities, Ronald McDonald House, Ronald McDonald Care Mobile, Olympic Youth Camp, T-Rex Education

The Reputation Institute found that the company most admired by Americans is Johnson & Johnson, a 112-year-old company best known for its baby powder and shampoo. Johnson & Johnson is a company that lives by its credo, written in 1943, that puts customers first, even ahead of shareholders. The credo begins: "We believe our first responsibility is to the doctors, nurses and patients, to mothers and fathers, and all others who use our products and services."

The Corporate Brand behind the Brand

It is no coincidence that Johnson & Johnson is still widely remembered for putting that credo into action in handling the Tylenol crises in the 1980s. Johnson & Johnson's handling of the Tylenol crisis has become a classic public relations case history. Although it has been widely told, we would be remiss not to include it here because it is the penultimate example of the successful interaction of responsible management action, media relations, and marketing communications.

The facts are well known. In September 1982, an unknown murderer contaminated Extra-Strength Tylenol capsules with cyanide. Seven people died in the Chicago area. This was followed by a rash of reports of other illnesses and deaths implicating Tylenol. From the onset of the tragedy, the company cooperated fully with the media, answering literally thousands of calls openly with all information that was available. An entire lot of 93,000 bottles was immediately recalled, warnings were wired to doctors, hospitals, and distributors, and all Tylenol advertising was suspended.

Although the company was convinced that it was blameless, it recalled all Tylenol capsules nationally within the week and, through advertising and statements to the media, offered to exchange Tylenol capsules for tablets. The public relations effort restored confidence and trust in the Tylenol brand. Johnson & Johnson's chairman, James E. Burke, appeared on the syndicated "Donahue" TV talk show, answering questions from the studio and viewing audience for an hour.

The company then agreed to allow "60 Minutes" to film its executive strategy sessions. Veteran correspondent Mike Wallace, known for his tough interviews, said of the company's actions:

Only a few weeks ago, many business experts were asserting that Tylenol was dead. Today, they are beginning to hedge their bets—change their minds—for they have seen the men who run Johnson & Johnson use the facts, the media, and huge amounts of money, as in the recall ($100 million), in a way that confounded the crepehangers. Instead of stonewalling, Johnson & Johnson has been forthcoming and apparently has managed to avert disaster.

Within two months, the product was reintroduced in triple-sealed, tamper-resistant packaging. At the recommendation of its public relations firm, Burson-Marsteller, the news was communicated by means of a 30-city "Tylenol comeback" video news conference, which reached representatives of over 600 news organizations by satellite. At the time of the murders, Tylenol was the leader of the OTC analgesic market, with a 35-percent share. By the end of 1982, its share had declined to 18 percent. As a result of its actions and openness with the press and the public, the brand had recaptured 80 percent of its market share within a year of the tragedy.[10]

Then, incredibly, in February 1986, tragedy struck a second time when it was reported that a woman died in Yonkers, New York, after taking a capsule of Extra-Strength Tylenol. After additional poisoned Tylenol capsules were found, the company again suspended sale of its capsules, this time permanently. The company again went to the consumer, this time to offer to replace Tylenol capsules with Tylenol caplets, a solid form of the product, or a cash refund.

By communicating openly and frequently with consumers through the news media and advertising, Tylenol survived its second life-and-death crisis with its credibility and integrity intact. And, remarkably, it allayed consumers' fears while simultaneously protecting its brand share. More than 95 percent of Tylenol users exchanged their capsules for caplets rather than cash. James H. Dowling, former president of Burson-Marsteller, who sat in on the Johnson & Johnson strategy sessions, said, "The great lesson here is that you can overcome bad news. You can win. You can come back."[11]

The Tylenol case has become the public relations textbook example of the right thing to do when the consumer—and the brand—are at risk. Tylenol survived two crises that might well have destroyed the brand. The company communicated openly, honestly, and frequently to all of its major stakeholders—consumers, trade customers, doctors, hospitals, and employees, directly and through the media. By leveraging the equity and reputation of its parent company, Johnson & Johnson, with all of its internal and external audiences, Tylenol was able to regain trust in its brand and retain its leadership in a highly competitive product category. Only months after the crisis, a poll showed that 79 percent of those surveyed would buy Tylenol again in the new tamper-resistant packaging and 90 percent of those people said they didn't blame the company for what happened.

Johnson & Johnson's "Trustmark"

James Burke, Johnson & Johnson's CEO at the time of the Tylenol crisis, defined a brand as "the capitalized value of the trust between a company and its customer." In explaining the high esteem in which the company is held today, Ralph S. Larsen, Johnson & Johnson's present CEO, told Al Golin that, when he was first appointed CEO, he met with his key people and told them that, when they represent Johnson & Johnson, they are representing more than a trademark. "You have a 'trustmark,'" he said. "If anybody screws it up, you'll have me to answer to!" He wanted to be sure that everyone understood that they were responsible for maintaining a name that signified more than quality products. "We're known as a caring, healing, and curing company, which has been our legacy from the beginning." [12]

The "trustmark" concept is defined by Kevin Roberts, chief executive worldwide of Saatchi & Saatchi PLC, as "a distinctive name or symbol that emotionally binds a company with the desires and aspirations of its customers." He says that "we live in an economy where people are bombarded with messages day in, day out, and brands don't cut it. First we had products—which were the equivalent of management. Next, we added trademarks and developed brands—which were the equivalent of leadership. Now we've got to move beyond brands to 'trustmarks.' A trademark plays defense. It's the way that you protect what you've already built up. It's your copyright, your patents, your table stakes. But a 'trustmark' plays offense. It's the emotional connection that lets you go out and conquer the world!"

The Ten Commandments of Organizational Trust

In his book, *Trust or Consequences*, Al Golin lays down what he calls the ten commandments of organizational trust that can help companies mend fences, strengthen relationships, and build trusted brands.

1. Focus on building trust first and restoring it second. Although companies can rebuild relationships that have been damaged by everything from product safety problems to financial scandals, it's much easier to achieve the long-term objective of building trust incrementally year after year.
2. Hold leadership accountable for trust-building efforts. The CEO, the board of directors, and a chief trust officer (CTO) will all work together to make a trust strategy happen. If the CEO demonstrates that this is a top priority for him, others in the company automatically make it a top priority.
3. Make trust bank deposits even if you're the most ethical company in the world. Whether you're 100 percent pure or just 90 percent, trust bank deposits will serve you well when an unexpected crisis or problem hits.
4. Do the right thing because it's the right thing to do. Customers want to do business with good people. When leadership is sincere about using resources to benefit employees, customers, and the community, it attracts the right sort of people.
5. Practice humility even when you have plenty to brag about. The majority of CEOs of major corporations possess a certain amount of humility. They give credit to others when it's due and acknowledge the luck involved in their own success. In this way, they guard against attitudes and behaviors that lead to distrust.
6. Base your actions on principles as much as on results. Highly trusted companies have established values-based cultures to guide their decision-making. It's not unusual for them to ask themselves: is this action consistent with what we believe as a company?
7. Avoid shortcuts. Trust is lost when people think they can get away with cutting corners or treating others disrespectfully.
8. Be patient. Creating trust isn't a quick fix. Trust emerges from a series of

actions over time: it's the cumulative power of these actions that helps change stakeholders' minds about a company or strengthens their faith in and respect for a company.

9. Take action as an individual (not just an organization). Anyone in an organization can suggest a charitable effort that the company can sponsor or form a volunteer group for a worthwhile cause. People can make a conscious effort to treat direct reports with more respect and be more honest with customers.

10. Be willing to give rather than receive when appropriate. Everything doesn't have to be measured by return on investment. From an organizational standpoint, integrity is doing the right thing even when it doesn't make perfect financial sense.[13]

How MPR Adds Value: Push, Pull, Pass

5

Marketing public relations works because of its unique ability to lend credibility to the product message. That ability is why it is more cost-effective than advertising, a subject we'll discussion greater depth in Chapter 15. Theodore Levitt, professor emeritus of the Harvard Graduate School of Business and former editor of *The Harvard Business Review,* has long recognized public relations as "the credible source." In his influential book, *The Marketing Mode,* a distinction between the public relations message and the advertising message point out that when the message is delivered by an objective third party, such as a journalist or broadcaster, the message is delivered more persuasively.[1] Levitt's recognition gave added clout to a claim long made by public relations practitioners.

Cost-Effectiveness of MPR

MPR gives companies a big bang for their marketing bucks. Most public relations budgets still remain a fraction of advertising budgets. To a marketing decision maker, MPR is a bargain because the effectiveness of an entire public relations program can be measured against the cost of one or two fleeting 30-second spots on prime-time television.

MPR's cost-effectiveness is usually measured in terms of total exposures generated and cost per impression. Frequently, the cost per thousand of MPR exposures is less than a dollar. Marketers can buy a full year's MPR program for the cost of a single, 15-second, prime-time TV spot. Increasingly, these measures are being refined to consider cost-per-target market impression, which eliminates waste exposure to nonprospective consumers and applies especially to exposures in media that appeal to a mass audience. On the other hand, with narrowcasting or special interest publications, there is very little waste exposure in the first place. In either case, the marketer can determine how cost-effective MPR is in reaching a particular target audience without a great degree of difficulty.

A widely utilized method of measuring MPR's cost-efficiency is by equating exposures to their "advertising equivalents." Many public relations people question whether an article can really be considered the equivalent of a print ad, or a TV interview the equivalent of a commercial. They believe that the implied editorial endorsement makes an article more valuable than an advertisement taking up the same amount of space in a publication or the same amount of time on a television program. They point out the difficulty of comparing a 30-minute interview with a 30-second spot on the same show. Yet, measuring MPR exposures by calculating what it would cost to buy the space or time persists, and likely will continue, because marketing clients are familiar with advertising rates, and the use of equivalencies gives them a convenient way to quantify exposures.

In Chapter 14 we address this issue further and provide some better methods for measuring MPR campaigns than ad equivalencies.

Cohesive Communication Strategies

Public relations works best when it is integral to the marketing strategy and plays a specific role in the marketing plan. Whether it is used to stretch the marketing dollar, to make advertising campaigns or sales programs work harder, or to provide a silver bullet that generates real excitement in the marketplace, MPR brings a number of unique benefits to the marketing plan.

One benefit is the opportunity to gain positive product exposure in the ever-widening selection of media. While it is becoming nearly impossible to cover the bases with the most generous of advertising budgets, there have never been more publications or television programs available as publicity outlets. An advertising plan typically concentrates on reaching the largest target audience at the lowest cost per thousand. MPR may be assigned the role of reaching primary and/or secondary markets through supplementary media. Women between the ages of 25 and 49 may buy 60 percent of products in a category, so ad dollars are allocated to reach this market at a high rate of frequency. Since MPR is not buying time and space, reaching this target market—plus the other 40 percent—through media they read, see, or hear is inexpensive. A cohesive marketing plan integrates media planning and assigns a specific role to MPR.

In *Persuasion in Marketing*, Horace Schwerin and Henry Newell observe:

> Enlisting publicity in the service of a specific product, as opposed to broader long-term company goals, has historically had observable short-term marketing benefits. . . . The most dramatic example was the exploitation of fluoridation of Crest toothpaste, beginning with securing the seal of approval of the American Dental Association and the wide dissemination of the favorable story, both in the press and in paid advertising.[2]

Other instances abound. A 1974 article about the health benefits of fiber in *The Reader's Digest* is just one example. All cereals featuring bran benefited from this publicity, even those that had not advertised for some time. Retail store audit data showed a sudden increase of 73 percent in sales after years of virtually static trends.

Successes like these, Schwerin and Newell conclude, "sometimes depend on being alert to newsworthy trends and exploiting them; in other times, on making the news yourself."

A Tripartite Approach to Marketing Public Relations

Product publicity is a strategic tool of MPR, which, in turn, is an integral element in the marketing communications plan. We suggest a new approach to MPR that encompasses both traditional marketing strategy and the "megamarketing" dimension, that is, the need to communicate with parties who are not part of the traditional marketing chain.

Push-Pull

The first two dimensions of this approach are the "push" and "pull" strategies. Philip Kotler states:

> A "push" strategy calls for using the sales force and trade promotion to push the product through the channels. The producer aggressively promotes the product

to wholesalers; the wholesalers aggressively promote the product to retailers; and the retailers aggressively promote the product to consumers.

A "pull" strategy calls for spending a lot of money on advertising and consumer promotion to build up consumer demand. If the strategy is effective, consumers will ask their retailers for the product, the retailers will ask their wholesalers for the product, and the wholesalers will ask the producers for the product.[3]

Larger MPR budgets are usually allocated to "pull" strategy programs; that is, those aimed directly at the end user, but both "push" and "pull" strategies can be, and often are, employed simultaneously.

For example, "pull" programs (such as those described throughout this book) may be designed to reach consumers through mass and/or specialized media, media tours, event sponsorships, special-audience programs, and the like. At the same time, aggressive MPR programs directed to the sales organization and the trade may be implemented to help "push" the product through channels.

"Pull" MPR results can be effectively "merchandised" to motivate the sales force. For example, a particularly effective national television news feature about the product can be shown at a national sales meeting, or good local TV interviews can be presented at regional sales meetings. With the growing importance of regional marketing, it is important to demonstrate to salespeople how MPR is specifically helping them in their territories.

"Push" tools used by MPR are:

- Trade show communications, including special publications and sponsored meetings, breakfasts, or receptions where the new product is introduced to the trade.
- Trade newsletters spotlighting new products and promotional support.
- Publicity reprints for use by salespeople on sales calls or mailed directly to buyers. (The theory is that if the media consider this news, so will the consumer.)
- Trade publication articles aimed at merchandise managers and buyers, covering product news items.
- Stories about advertising and promotional support programs, including MPR, company expert interviews and byline stories, or retailer-success programs with the product line.

Two of America's great marketing successes were accelerated through the use of "push" MPR techniques.

Al Golin recalled, "Our first job for McDonald's wasn't to sell hamburgers; it was to sell franchises." Publicity was used to draw attention to McDonald's as an attractive opportunity for investors who wanted to run their own businesses.[4]

For Sara Lee, an early feature story in *The Wall Street Journal,* "Sara Lee Builds Baking Bonanza on Heaping Slices of Quality," brought immediate demand for the company's cakes from supermarkets all over the country, leading to national distribution.

Pass: The Third Dimension

Philip Kotler introduced the concept of megamarketing in *The Harvard Business Review*. His article dealt specifically with the need for companies that want to operate in certain markets to "master the art of supplying benefits to parties other than target consumers who can singly or collectively block profitable entry into a market." Those who can block entry into a market may include legislators, government agencies, political parties, labor unions, churches, and public interest groups representing an ever-growing agenda of causes, interests, and concerns. Just as the media act as gatekeepers, determining which news will or will not enter, these parties act as gatekeepers to the marketplace.

Kotler believed that a new strategy, that of "megamarketing," is called for in order for companies to break into blocked markets. His article defined "megamarketing" as: "The strategically coordinated application of economic, psychological, political, and public relations skills to gain the cooperation of a number of parties in order to enter and/or operate in a given market."

He proposed that gaining access to blocked markets requires executives to address new multiparty marketing problems. In normal marketing situations, the skillful use of marketing's traditional four Ps—product, price, place, and promotion—can create a cost-effective marketing mix that appeals to customers and end users. In "megamarketing" situations, however, Kotler suggests that executives must add two more Ps—power and public relations. Power is a "push" strategy in winning multiparty support, and public relations is a "pull" strategy.

"Megamarketing" clearly requires marketing executives to utilize the skills of corporate public relations and public affairs with professionals and lawyers. Public relations relates to marketing in two different but complementary ways—one in straight-ahead promotional planning, the other in blocked-market situations:

- Marketing public relations (MPR), used in normal marketing situations to influence consumers, is an important component of the four Ps strategy, specifically supporting promotional efforts to facilitate a transaction.
- Corporate public relations (CPR) is used in "megamarketing" situations to influence nonconsumer publics in order to gain market entry. Together with the use of power, CPR adds an important new component to a six-P strategy in blocked markets.[5]

Using the two additional components of power and corporate public relations leads to a third strategy we call "pass" strategy that is useful in today's increasingly complex marketing environment. It allows marketers to make their way past the gatekeepers in order to enter certain markets and to overcome or neutralize opposition.

PR's role is to devise strategies and conduct programs that permit the marketer to "pass" the gatekeepers and enter the market. When customers make purchase decisions, they are, in a very real sense, deciding to buy two things: the product and the company. As illustrated in Chapter 4, people want to do business with companies they know and trust. Consumers' trust is earned by providing quality products at a good value. It is also earned by sponsoring activities and identifying with causes that demonstrate the company's appreciation of the consumer's patronage.

Marketers' Social Responsibility

Another vital element in pursuing a successful "pass" strategy is related to the company's position on a variety of issues that are of concern to both gatekeepers and the consumers who share their views. The role of both corporate and marketing public relations advisors is to define these issues for management, to recommend action, and to communicate that action to the appropriate publics.

CPR professionals act as the corporate eyes and ears, identifying and assessing the present and potential impact of these issues on the company's ability to achieve its objectives. Since the profitable sale of its products is a primary objective, the analysis and influence of senior public affairs officers and counselors should exert a critical effect on the company's marketing efforts.

Using Push, Pull, Pass

In writing today's marketing plans, marketers must consider all three strategies (see Exhibit 5.1). "Pass" strategies involving company policy are primarily the function of

Exhibit 5.1. PUSH, PULL, PASS Public Relations Strategies

Strategy	Target	PR Type	Tools
PUSH	Sales force Dealers Distributors Retailers	MPR	Trade shows Trade publicity Reprints Publications
PULL	Consumer/ End user	MPR	Media events Media tours Story placement Product placement Teleconferences Exhibits Web sites Demonstrations Sampling Surveys Newsletters PSAs Symposia Publications
PASS	Gatekeepers Public interest groups Government Community leaders Other influencers Consumers as Publics	CPR MPR	Assessing issues Advising action Communication Charity tie-ins National sponsorships Local sponsorships

CPR, while branded, trust-bonding programs, along with "pull" and "push" marketing strategies, are the responsibility of MPR.

Some products will succeed by pursuing an aggressive "pull" strategy alone. But, as retailers exert ever-increasing influence over the marketplace, equal attention must be paid to "push" strategies.

The "pass" strategy we suggest comes into play with society and media attention intensifying not only on product safety and efficacy but, as has been demonstrated, on the corporation's response to critical issues facing the society at large. Marketing public relations can, and should, play a part in all three and work in concert with corporate public relations when corporate policy issues are at stake.

6 Circumstances for Success: The Harris Grid

In an address in Sydney, Australia, legendary public relations counselor Daniel J. Edelman, chairman of the largest independent public relations firm in the world, contrasted the roles of advertising and public relations:

... public relations has the unique advantage of presenting the message in the context of the day's news. The story is told in greater depth. ...

My experience over these many years has demonstrated to me that, in proper circumstances, and when handled expertly, public relations can often be the best and most cost-effective marketing technique. Here are some, but certainly not all, of these circumstances:

1. There's a revolutionary, break-through type of product—one that can make news.
2. The company is new or small. There's little, if any, money available for advertising.
3. Television isn't available for regulatory reasons. For example, distilled spirits cannot advertise on network television in the US
4. The environment is negative and has to be turned around quickly.
5. When generating new excitement about an existing product.
6. When a company is having difficulty distributing its product.
7. When advertising is well liked, but fails to build brand recognition.
8. When a product takes time to explain.
9. When you cannot advertise your product to consumers.
10. When established companies or brands are aligned with a cause.[1]

Where MPR Works Best

MPR can work especially well in certain circumstances and for certain product categories.

Books

An author can visit dozens of cities for media interviews for less than the cost of a single ad. Public relations is particularly effective in selling nonfiction books. Autobiographies of famous figures have been especially aided by well-orchestrated PR campaigns and celebrity media tours. First-day sales of former President Bill Clinton's book, *My Life*, exceeded those of any nonfiction book in history, not only in the US, but also in England, France, and Japan. Sales were driven by Clinton's appearances on virtually every top-rated news and interview show from "Oprah" to "60 Minutes" on CBS to NBC's "Today" to CNN's "Larry King Live" and on the cover of magazines like *Time*, which was granted rights to run advanced excerpts.

Cars

Americans have long held a love affair with the automobile, and the media have been willing matchmakers. The story of Ford's Mustang is a classic (see Chapter 3). In the 1980s Ford achieved 50 percent brand awareness and orders for 146,000 Taurus automobiles before they were advertised or seen in dealer showrooms. Similarly, the 1990s saw the successful PR-driven introductions of the 1998 Volkswagen Beetle and Chrysler's PT Cruiser. The latest big car news is hybrid cars. Toyota was first on the market and in the news with its Prius, and Americans were lining up for the cool electric cars when the Prius became the favorite of Hollywood stars.

Technology/Consumer Electronics

The New York Times devotes an entire section called "Circuits" to the latest new technological products. *Newsweek* has its "Tip Sheet." *The Wall Street Journal*'s "Personal" section relates to business readers as consumers and regularly reviews new tech products. All the major metropolitan newspapers have experts who test and review new hardware, software, and consumer electronics in a manner once reserved for automobiles. Tech products are covered by the general media, especially men's magazines, and are seen on TV, especially around the holiday season. For example, exposure of Apple's iPod on network television made it the hottest gift item of 2004.

Fashion

Paris creations, once the stuff of movie newsreels, are now seen regularly, along with the latest US and international fashions, on the network morning shows and often on network and cable shows like "Entertainment Tonight" and "Access Hollywood." Those who really want to be in the know read *Vogue, W,* and a host of general interest women's magazines that regularly feature fashion. The trendy clothes and shoes worn on the popular HBO sitcom "Sex and the City" were sought after by singles. The introduction of "The One and Only Wonderbra" surpassed all expectations and sold out the entire first shipment on the first day, causing retailers throughout the country to order and promote the line with news-making events. Wonderbra not only became the stuff of comic monologues and sitcom laughs; it became the number one push-up bra in America.

Food Products

Food publicity has long been a staple of MPR. The major food companies provide a flow of recipes, serving suggestions, and new product news to magazines and newspaper food editors. Some of the most successful food publicity programs offer consumers ideas for using products as cooking ingredients. For example, Tabasco Sauce and Campbell's Soup have been especially successful in developing and promoting recipes using their products. Similarly, anniversary celebrations of favorite brands like Jell-o's 100th won big coverage in print and on TV and provided an opportunity to introduce new flavors and varieties.

Diet Foods

Americans are the most diet-conscious people in the world. They read all they can about what to eat and what not to eat. From well-publicized low-fat food products, like Nabisco's Snackwell Cookies to an entire range of products containing Procter & Gamble's fake fat, Olestra, consumers have chased the promise of healthy eating. The advent of low-carb cures like the Atkins and South Beach diets led to a parade of low-carb products and launched the Nutritionals brand of the once-controversial Dr. Robert Atkins. His media savvy was an important factor in making his *Dr. Atkins New Diet Revolution* the best-selling diet book of all time.

Sports and Fitness

Health and fitness magazines, like *Prevention*, and the general-interest media offer advice to the stay-fit audiences and feature the latest exercise equipment, hiking gear, and bikes. A popular new breed of men's magazines, like *Men's Health* and *Maxim*, combine fitness with sexual advice. The fitness boom gave rise to the athletic-shoe explosion. The latest shoes from Nike, Adidas, and others are seen everywhere, especially on TV sportscasts. Nike's Fitness Bra was introduced on the global telecast of the World Cup when a US soccer star celebrated her country's victory by whipping off her jersey and exposing the bra.

Pills

Pharmaceutical companies once confined their communications activities to reaching doctors and healthcare professionals. Now they spend big bucks to reach consumers directly with messages about new and existing products, for both prescription drugs and those moving from prescription to over-the-counter. Because of burgeoning consumer interest in health-related news and especially in drugs that treat personal medical problems, the major media have greatly expanded their coverage of medical subjects. The networks and TV stations in major markets all have medical reporters, many of whom are themselves doctors.

Consumer print media have followed suit with health columns and more health features, and a new category of newsletters from the Mayo Clinic, Harvard Medical School, and others has prospered. The antidepressant Prozac became the first pill to make the cover of a newsweekly when in 1987 *Newsweek* proclaimed it a breakthrough drug for depression. A year later, knowing a good thing when they found one, the magazine ran a cover on another pill, aspirin, proclaiming the long-time painkiller a "wonder drug" in preventing and treating heart attacks. As a result, a great many Americans take an aspirin a day.

Special Interest Products

Golfers, tennis players, and skiers, shutterbugs, computer nerds, hunters and fishermen, and other devotees devour specialized magazines devoted to their interests. They absorb everything they read and discuss it with fellow enthusiasts and others who look to them for product information and advice. Marketers of computers, accessories, software, and new consumer electronic products consider major media coverage, glowing reviews, and even product placement more important than traditional advertising. Callaway became the leading golf club manufacturer in the world when the pros began using the memorably named Big Bertha driver. Other brands got into the act when the networks began to cover golf matches weekly during the season.

Multi-use Products

The promotion of Arm & Hammer Baking Soda became a marketing classic by devising new ways to use a very old product as a refrigerator refresher, sink cleaner, and dentifrice. The public relations programs for Saran Wrap and Ziploc bags similarly promote multiple uses of these products. These uses are of interest to consumers and to media that feature service copy.

Arts and Entertainment

Americans can't seem to read enough about their favorite TV, movie, and rock stars. Newly released movies, CDs, and DVDs are regularly featured and reviewed in newspapers and magazines and on radio and television. The media and the entertainment industry perpetually feed off of one another. Major films make the covers of the newsweeklies and other big consumer magazines and are featured on local news programs and weekly TV shows like "Ebert and Roeper at the Movies." Time Warner's *Entertainment Weekly*, introduced in 1990, reviews and grades the latest TV shows, films, music, video, and print. Morning television is now closely tied to the celebrity-culture boom. Publicity-generated word-of-mouth sells out the really big rock shows instantly, precluding the need to advertise at all.

Travel and Tourism

Sunday travel sections of major metropolitan newspapers have expanded their editorial pages to support the growing number of ads for airlines, cruise lines, travel destinations, and travel packages. Travel magazines, like *Conde Nast Traveler,* search out the next hot spot and are targets for public relations firms specializing in travel and tourism. There are opportunities to gain exposure on TV newscasts (e.g., the wildly popular travel feature "Where in the World Is Matt Lauer?" on NBC's "Today Show") and a host of special interest publications that cover such subjects as food, art, golf, fishing, scuba diving, and hiking.

Fads and Trends

The media has always fed fads. In 1958, publicity, including a musical-production number on the popular Sunday night "Dinah Shore Show," convinced 30 million Americans to buy a three-foot-diameter plastic ring called a Hula Hoop. While the hoops were at least good for hip exercise, there was no accounting for the 1975 fad that caused a million people to part with $4 for an ordinary stone named Pet Rock. In 1989, Batmania hit the world and persons wearing Batgear were seen everywhere, including on TV, acting as walking advertisements for the summer's big film, *Batman,* followed, the next year, by Turtlemania—the Teenage Mutant Ninja Turtles. What is "in" is what is news. Where to go, what to do, what to wear, what's in and what's out, what's hot and what's not. As this is written, we are especially interested in such products as plasma TVs, digital cameras, cell phones, laptops, iPods, and portable DVD players. By the time you read it, a host of new products will have captured consumer attention driven by media hype.

The Harris Grid

The first edition of this book displayed a grid to help marketers determine where public relations works best. As has been shown, certain product categories are more newsworthy than others and lend themselves to a news approach. Other product categories are generally not newsworthy enough to justify coverage from the media and are required to "borrow interest" by identification with something that is of greater interest to the target market. That grid has been updated and now defines products in terms of their interest to target consumers and their potential interest to the media, that is, their newsworthiness.

- The upper left quadrant (A) consists of those products that are of high interest to both the consumer and the media.
- The upper right quadrant (B) is of high interest to consumers but lower interest to the media.
- The lower left quadrant (C) is of lower interest to the consumer but not the media.
- The lower right quadrant (D) is of low interest to both the consumer and the media.

Exhibit 6.1. The Harris Grid

	High Media Interest	Low Media Interest
High Consumer Interest	**A** Consumer Electronics Cars Entertainment	**B** Beer Soft Drinks Athletic Shoes
Low Consumer Interest	**C** Razors Cranberry Juice Aspirin	**D** Trash Bags Mufflers Detergents

Of course, within the listing of product categories in each quadrant, some are of higher or lower interest to consumers and media than are others.

Some major consumer product categories have been selected for purposes of illustration. By looking at products (and sometimes the companies that make them) in this way, marketers can select the most appropriate MPR strategic option. Clearly, products in the A quadrant should conduct high-visibility product campaigns. When there is no product news, but the product is of high interest to consumers, as in quadrant B, a sponsorship strategy enhances the brand image. Products in the C quadrant should recognize that the product might not be enough to carry the story alone. This may require new news about the product to generate media exposure.

When the product reaches the maturity or decline stages of the product life cycle, as in quadrant D, there may be no new news about it. This recommends that a borrowed-interest" MPR strategy be employed to link the brand with a public service program or special event that will attract target consumers.

Exhibit 6.2. MPR News Strategy

	Product Category	Product-Publicity Opportunity
(A)	Consumer Electronics Cars Entertainment	iPod Toyota Prius *Spiderman*
(C)	Razors Cranberry Juice Aspirin	Technology Breakthrough Urinary infection protection Heart-attack prevention

Strategic Application of the Harris Grid

In the high-media-interest, high-consumer-interest quadrant (A) are the announcement of a consumer electronics product, such as iPod, the introduction of the first hybrids or other breakthrough cars, and the release of a blockbuster motion picture.

In the high-media-interest, lower–consumer-interest quadrant (C) examples abound as companies look for new "reasons why" the consumer should buy. For example, Gillette's new MACH3 razor was positioned effectively as a technology breakthrough. Ocean Spray research found that cranberry juice cocktail could prevent urinary tract infections in older women. The Aspirin Foundation of America effectively repositioned aspirin as the new wonder drug that could lower the risk of heart attack and stroke.

In the low-news, high-consumer-interest quadrant (B) companies have followed the "borrowed-interest" MPR strategy. Beer companies heavily sponsor an array of sports events including NASCAR, rock tours, and other events to reach entry-level beer drinkers. They try to produce news-making advertising with memorable punch lines. Some advertisers have even started making video news releases as a matter of course when they develop new advertising in an effort to generate publicity about their latest campaign.

Exhibit 6.3. MPR "Borrowed-Interest" Strategy

	Product Category	Product-Linkage Opportunity
(B)	Beer Soft Drinks Athletic Shoes	Sports/Music Sponsorships/ Advertising Coke Olympic Relay Nike Swoosh everywhere
(D)	Detergent Mufflers Trash Bags	Tide Dirtiest Kids Contest Midas Project Safe Baby Glad Bag-A-Thon

Coca Cola extends its official sponsorship of the Olympics by sponsoring the Olympic Torch Relay, which is well-publicized in every city on the coast-to-coast route. The Nike swoosh is omnipresent on athletic shoes, uniforms, golf shirts, and caps on televised sports events and covers of *Sports Illustrated.*

Then there are those products of low interest to the consumer and even lower interest to the media (quadrant D). A new product or a new and improved model may be the biggest news in a marketer's life, but it may not have inherent news value or be of high interest to the consumer. No one thinks about a car muffler until they need one, but Midas won friends and created store traffic through its sponsorship of Project Safe Baby, a program that offered safe baby seats at cost or on loan to visitors to Midas shops. Similarly, Glad Bags partnered with Keep America Beautiful, Inc. to sponsor the Glad Bag-A-Thon, America's largest litter cleanup in communities across the country.

Using the grid, marketers can plot where their product is located as the first step in MPR planning. In a low-interest category and in the absence of news or credible product benefits, even advertising may have to substitute emotional appeals for product appeals by producing commercials portraying the product in lifestyle situations that targeted consumers can identify with or aspire to. Much of today's advertising is of the "borrowed-interest" variety, designed to grab attention through oddball situations, avant-garde graphics, and attempts at humor. The MPR program should focus on increasing brand-name awareness by identifying the product with something consumers value.

PART II

Planning for MPR Success

The MPR Strategic Planning Process

Today's marketing managers expect to see strategic plans for all of the components of their marketing programs—for media placement, advertising creative development, direct marketing campaigns, and even market research. Each plan follows a basic structure that begins with an overview of the current situation and then sets business-oriented objectives, identifies key targets and the messages, strategies, and tactics to reach them, and ends with some type of measurement to assess the effectiveness of the program and to help set the stage for the next program.

If PR is going to be incorporated into the marketing mix, the marketing director will want to know exactly how the PR plan will fit into the overall marketing strategy and what the return on PR investment will be. This means that to write an effective marketing public relations strategic plan, you must know your organization's overall mission and marketing objectives and have a clear understanding of your industry, the customers you serve, it's the firm's geographic scope, distinctive values, and competitive domain.

The Mission Statement

Often, the firm's written mission statement is a good place to start, but many mission statements are too broadly written to supply the information that the marketing public relations plan will need. Take these well-known and well-respected companies—Johnson & Johnson, FedEx, and Celestial Seasonings. Each uses its mission statement in a different way, and each will play a different role in developing the MPR plan.

Johnson & Johnson

At Johnson & Johnson, a perennial top-10 finisher in *Fortune*'s "Most Admired" list of companies, there is no mission statement that hangs on the wall. For more than 60 years, a simple, one-page document, called, "Our Credo," has guided the company's actions in fulfilling its responsibilities to its customers, employees, communities, suppliers and stockholders. Today, the Credo is available in 36 languages to ensure a shared value system across the company's facilities in Africa, Asia/Pacific, Eastern Europe, Europe, Latin America, Middle East and North America. It is the first item shown on the corporate Web site, and it clearly states its priorities for how it will deal with all of its stakeholders. It begins:

> We believe our first responsibility is to the doctors, nurses and patients, to mothers and all others who use our products and services. In meeting their needs everything we do must be of high quality. We must constantly strive to reduce our costs in order to maintain reasonable prices. Customers' orders must be serviced promptly and accurately. Our suppliers and distributors must have an opportunity to make a fair profit.[1]

This document would be quite useful for setting guidelines for an MPR plan.

FedEx

At FedEx, another "Most Admired" company, the mission statement has a much lower profile and is not so readily available on the company's Web site. It is written more from the investor's point of view and would be far less useful for developing an MPR strategy:

> FedEx will produce superior financial returns for shareowners by providing high value-added supply chain, transportation, business and related information services through focused operating companies competing collectively, and managed collaboratively, under the respected FedEx brand. Customer requirements will be met in the highest quality manner appropriate to each market segment served. FedEx companies will strive to develop mutually rewarding relationships with its employees, partners and suppliers. Safety will be the first consideration in all operations. All corporate activities will be conducted to the highest ethical and professional standards.[2]

Celestial Seasonings

Celestial Seasonings, the archetypal 1960s company, transformed its mission into a roadmap for how it operates and wants to be known. Of the three, it is perhaps the easiest to use for developing an MPR plan. From its mission statement, it is clear that some form of social marketing will need to be incorporated, and a tie-in with a health benefit would be a useful strategy. The mission, which, like Johnson & Johnson's, is prominently placed on the corporate Web site, reads:

> Our mission: To create and sell healthful, naturally oriented products that nurture people's bodies and uplift their souls. Our products must be:
> - superior in quality
> - of good value
> - beautifully artistic
> - philosophically inspiring
>
> Our role is to play an active part in making this world a better place by unselfishly serving the public. We can have a significant impact on making people's lives happier and healthier through their use of our products.[3]

All three mission statements would help define the tone and focus of a marketing public relations plan, but legwork still must be done to define the specific goals and values of interest for the present plan and to identify the specific business objectives that management is currently pursuing, including profitability, sales growth, market-share improvement, risk containment, innovativeness, reputation, and so on.

The 7 Steps of an MPR Plan

The elements of a good marketing public relations plan are the same as those in any good business plan. The Whalen 7-Step Strategic Planning Process (see Exhibit 7.1) incorporates all of the steps found in any good strategic plan, but it is particularly useful because it enables the user to apply all seven steps to the overall marketing plan as well as to each individual promotional program, whether an advertising plan, a public relations plan, a trade show exhibit, even a simple brochure. From an integrated marketing perspective, this makes it easy to fit each program together to ensure that the right objectives are being pursued as well as focusing on the right targets. Using one consistent process for each promotional element also makes it easier for management to compare the programs and assess the value of each.

The seven steps are:

1. Situation Analysis, which includes the up-front research stage.
2. Setting Objectives, including long-term business objectives and shorter-term communication objectives.
3. Defining Strategy.
4. Identifying the Targets.
5. Creating Messages to address each target's needs and interests.
6. Identifying Tactics, including timelines for implementing them.
7. Evaluating the effectiveness of the plan.

The steps of the Whalen 7-Step Strategic Planning Process follow a logical progression and are written in a circular pattern because no marcom plan really has an absolute beginning or end. This is an important element of the planning process, since marketers rarely begin at "ground zero." Both the marketer and the target audience are starting from some place. People have an idea of what your brand is about even before you formally communicate a thing, and your plan will want to enhance those ideas or change them, depending on the current situation.

Every plan should begin with an analysis of the current situation. This provides a benchmark or touchstone for you to measure against when you reach the end of the campaign cycle, which you define in some way. As time passes the situation will change. That change will be your standard of measure. Hence the seventh step is actually the first step in an ongoing cycle. The new situation created by a previous phase of a campaign will also require changes in its objectives and strategies, and hence the cycle begins anew.

Exhibit 7.1. Whalen's 7-Step Strategic Planning Process

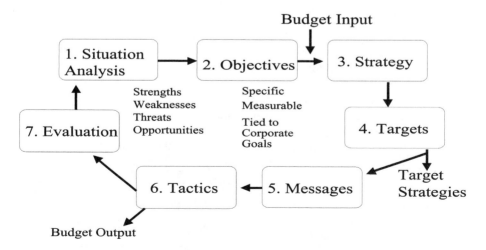

This is true even for new product launches: Your brand may be new on the scene, but your targets will be familiar with your competition or with a substitute product, so there is an existing situation to contend with.

Writing the Plan

Marketing public relations plans must be written in clear, concise language that fits the format of the marketing plan. While some public relations jargon and description of public relations mechanics may be necessary to explain the plan, remember that most of the people reading it are not public relations experts. They are marketing experts or business managers who want to know that the plan is based on sound research, that it supports marketing and business objectives, that it can be executed in a timely manner with a reasonable amount of resources, and that its results can be measured. They will not wade through a tome or listen to an unending list of tactics.

Whether presented by an in-house MPR staff or an outside agency, the plan is typically presented orally in 60 to 90 minutes, including questions and answers, so time constraints require that the plan be focused, concise, and easy to understand. A "leave-behind" is nearly identical with the oral presentation but contains additional information and detail necessary to support the recommendations, such as an Executive Summary and a Conclusions section. Exhibit 7.3 at the end of this chapter incorporates all elements that belong in the "leave-behind." Note, however, that most "go" or "no go" decisions are made on the effectiveness of the oral presentation and the ability of the presenters to defend their MPR recommendations.

Step 1: Situation Analysis

This first step in the MPR strategic planning process includes a research phase, but the level of research will be determined by your timeline and budget constraints. Your goal in this section is twofold:

1. Define the problem that your plan will try to solve.
2. Do a SWOT analysis. This means identifying your brand's strengths and weaknesses, which are usually internal to your organization, and to uncover any threats and opportunities that might arise from external sources. The threats discussion nearly always includes a competitive assessment, unless there is a separate competitive assessment written into the situation analysis.

Much of the work in assessing the current situation can be done through a review of existing marketing and business plans, existing research reports, a review of media coverage about your industry, your organization and your brand, as well as media coverage of your key competitors. In addition, you will likely want to conduct some informal, one-on-one interviews with key executives from sales, marketing, legal, engineering, operations, and finance, as well as outside consultants and agencies that might have done research for your organization. Depending on the need for confidentiality, you might also consider interviewing some of your key customers, distributors, and editors who cover your industry. Questions you might want to ask include:

- What's happening now in this industry that could affect us in the future?
- What might the financial impact be if this is not addressed?
- What is the product?
- What are its benefits to the consumer?

- What is its price and how does it compare with the competition?
- What is the primary market for the product?
- What are the secondary markets?
- What are the channels of distribution?
- Who are the key influencers that should be reached?
- If an existing product:
  —What is its recent sales history? What is its share? What are sales projections? Where will new sales come from?
- If a new product:
  —Where will the product be introduced? What are plans to expand distribution? Where will it be sold? (Geography) When will it be sold? (Seasonality) What are the competitive products? What is the market share of each entry? What are benefits of each? What are positioning strategies for each? What are advertising and promotions for each? What environmental factors impact marketing?

Research in MPR planning. Perhaps the greatest change in marketing public relations relative to past practice is the use of research in the planning and evaluation stages. Today's MPR programs must be grounded in research about the marketplace, the product category, and the consumer.

Increasingly, research is also being used to test MPR messages and is also beginning to be employed to test tactics such as the credibility of spokespersons and the effectiveness of PR materials. Testing can be done under simulated market conditions prior to launch or can be conducted in the field under real market conditions.

Using secondary research. Before conducting any primary research, you should always first conduct secondary research, which means finding existing reports and information that show what is already known about your market. Primary research can be expensive and time-consuming and the expense cannot always be justified in a low-budget MPR campaign.

Existing internal reports are typically the best place to find secondary data, but there are many sources of published materials and other sources of secondary data on your industry and targets, some of which are available for free on-line. Search engines, such as Google and Yahoo, have dramatically improved the quality of a secondary data search.

In addition to on-line searches, many public relations firms today conduct their own demographic, psychographic, and media research since both their message and their media recommendations may complement rather than supplement advertising. In addition to using secondary research to define primary and secondary consumer audiences, MPR places particular emphasis on examining those individuals, groups, or organizations that influence the target audience. These influencers are often overlooked in general marketing plans. (See the discussion later in this chapter on sources of secondary information for psychographic and demographic profiles of targets.)

Finally, secondary research is used to draw a picture of the competitive environment. The components of this environment that may have significant impact on marketing the product include the natural environment, the sociocultural environment, the political environment, the technical environment, and the economic (marketplace) environment. This phase includes examination of events, trends, and constituent demands that could affect marketing.

Consumer product usage data. Simmons and MediaMark Research (MRI) databases provide important demographic and media usage data on thousands of brands. Both of these suppliers of syndicated marketing data conduct surveys of more than 20,000 consumers every year to determine their product usage (heavy, medium, and light) and to determine their demographic characteristics (gender, income, education, family size, geographic region, etc.) and their media consuming habits by magazine, television programs, and radio station preferences.

These databases are particularly useful for understanding current customers, especially loyal and heavy users, regarding the following kinds of questions:

- What else do they buy?
- What media do they use?
- Where do they live geographically?

Conducting primary research. If, after all secondary sources have been exhausted, more information is needed, it is time to conduct primary research. There are two kinds of primary research: qualitative and quantitative research. Qualitative research is rich information gathered from a small number of targets using such techniques as one-on-one depth interviews, focus groups, or ethnographic observations in people's homes, offices, or retail outlets. This type of research, often referred to as "exploratory," can yield a very useful understanding of what motivates your targets and how their daily lives might intersect with your product. This type of research can be undertaken fairly quickly, and valuable insights can be obtained with as few as 20 subjects. The downside to this type of research is that you cannot use statistical analysis to project the results of this type of research onto your target population with any degree of confidence. This type of research will, however, help in the development of some hypotheses that quantitative research might later test.

Quantitative research is research that, if sampling is done correctly, can be projected to the broad target population. This research uses statistical analysis to predict the responses of your target population based on the responses of a much smaller sample. Typical quantitative methodologies include surveys, experiments such as market tests, and using existing purchasing data and other customer information to predict future consumer behaviors. Caution is warranted with this type of research, since mistakes can be made when convenience samples (those drawn nonscientifically) are used instead of probability samples (where each member of the sample has a known probability of being selected). When this occurs, the results are not projectable to the target population, but the statistical data is often presented as if it were. If quantitative research is undertaken, it is critical that you employ research experts who can help ensure a statistically valid sample and research instrument to avoid serious misinterpretations of the results.

Use of media metrics and databases. Public relations people can also make use of content analysis of data banks that retrieve articles and broadcast news stories that have appeared about the company, the product, the category, and the competition in the media. These same sources can be used to gain information that supports proposed tactics within programs. For example, the MPR plan may call for the selection of an expert spokesperson. A databank search will identify experts who have written books and articles or have been quoted in the media on the desired area of expertise.

One of the most popular of these data banks is Lexis/Nexis. Lexis provides legal citations, and Nexis, the news arm of the business, is the world's largest full-text database and can provide access to millions of articles from local, national, and international newspapers, broadcast transcripts from major television and radio networks, wire services, magazines, and trade journals. It also has company and industry dossiers on more than 35 million public and private companies. Another frequently used database is Dow Jones News/Retrieval Service.

In recent years, a number of media metric firms have sprung up to provide analysis of media coverage by industry or by whatever criteria the client states. Firms such as Biz360 provide the software and a "dashboard" of the things that clients wish to search for and contracts with media databases such as Nexis to provide the content from print media. Firms such as TV Eyes provide real-time audio and video monitoring of radio and television mentions of your brand or your competition, or the specified topic of interest. The client then conducts the analysis of coverage in terms of tone, trends, and ranking of mentions. Other firms, such as Delahaye, K.D. Paine, Competitive Insights, and TextAll, will do the analysis for the client and provide useful charts and graphs to track such things as your CEO's "Share of Voice" on a particular issue or your brand's "Share of Mind" with regard to number of brand mentions for a particular product category.

Clarke Caywood, an associate professor in Northwestern's IMC graduate program, also serves on an advisory board for Biz360. In his lectures often cites the following examples of companies that have used this type of media metric data in developing their MPR plans:

- Dell Computer monitored its management team's public statements on a daily basis to see if they were on message.
- Harley-Davidson, which has had over a billion "hits" in media vehicles and Web sites, used the service to help define and monitor its PR success.
- A large law firm assessed media coverage in target regions to assess its global potential.
- Potbellies sandwich shops looking to launch new restaurants into new cities used the service to analyze local opportunities and its competitors.
- VeriSign used the service to keep a pulse on new privacy issues and trends to protect its customers.

How detailed should the situation analysis be? It all depends on how complex the situation is and how much money is being asked for. A request for a large MPR budget will likely require a fairly detailed explanation of the targets, the problem at hand, and the threats and opportunities to be addressed. The level of detail provided might also be influenced by the knowledge and experience of the key decision-maker on the plan and how much research is available from the overall marketing plan or advertising plan.

The main thing to keep in mind is that the situation analysis is a snapshot of where the firm is today. It sets the stage for the rest of the plan, but it does not offer recommendations.

Step 2: Objectives

Objectives must be specific, measurable, and tied to business goals, which means that Step 2, Objectives, and Step 7, Evaluation, are inseparably linked. An MPR plan should never include an objective in Step 2 that does not have a way to measure it in Step 7.

It is useful to separate objectives into long-term business goals and shorter-term communications objectives. The longer-term goals are those things that the entire organization is striving for—or at least the entire marketing organization—not just the MPR team. These brand objectives are defined in terms of units shipped, sales, profit, market share, etc. The MPR strategies and tactics should always be written with these business goals in mind, but they may not always have an immediate or measurable impact on them.

For example, an MPR program that raises brand awareness or educates consumers about a product feature could be logically expected to have a positive impact on unit sales and revenues over time, but it would be difficult to show the immediate correlation between them. As time passes, it would become easier to tie the two together, but even then, a number of other promotional activities, such as advertising and direct marketing, will have taken place and the overall impact of each on unit sales and revenues may be hard to separate from each other. The key is to be sure that the MPR activities have some logical connection to the overall marketing and business goals. In the past, too much PR emphasis was placed on attendance at special events or the number of media mentions obtained, regardless of whether they delivered the intended messages. When management cannot see the direct connection with business goals, they will be less likely to value MPR and even less likely to provide the resources to support MPR activities.

The intermediate-term objectives, more fairly called "Communication Objectives" or "MPR Program Objectives," are the things that the MPR team can and should be accountable for. It would not be fair to hold the MPR team accountable for achieving the business goals, such as a particular sales objective, when that is the responsibility of the entire sales and marketing team. Communication objectives typically fall into two types:

- *Output objectives* can be measured immediately, but they have a more tenuous connection with business goals. They may include an assessment of the quality of materials produced, the number of television placements and print clips achieved, and the number of attendees at a function, the number of media inquiries generated, or even staying within budget or on time. While these are far less important to the overall marketing strategy, it is important to track and measure output objectives. They will keep the MPR campaign on target and provide ongoing feedback to the MPR team to determine if any mid-course corrections are necessary. These objectives often must be accomplished before the outcome objectives can be achieved.

- *Outcome objectives* raise awareness, change attitudes, and persuade consumers to take action. They may also include such things as number of hits on a Web site, calls to an 800#, requests for information, and specific mentions of brand messages in the media. In short, these hits have an obvious connection with the business goals, and they can be traced directly to the MPR activities.

The key MPR questions to ask within the Objectives section are:

- What are we trying to achieve?
- How will we know when we've achieved it?
- How do MPR program objectives support marketing objectives?

Step 3: Strategy

The Strategy portion of the plan sets the tone of the campaign and provides a broad overview of the MPR plans that will address the objectives. Without some budgetary guidelines that give a reasonable expectation of available funds, the MPR team could waste a lot of time developing financially impractical strategies. A discussion of budget-setting methods is provided at the end of this chapter.

Just as MPR objectives must be sharply defined as they relate to marketing objectives, the decision to utilize MPR is a strategy in itself and should be explained as it relates to the overall marketing strategy. A comprehensive marketing plan should also explain how the various marcom tactics being used support each other. A publicity effort might be used, for example, to bring attention to the advertising campaign, or advertising might be used to promote attendance at a sponsored special event. The MPR plan, like the advertising plan, must show how MPR strategies support marketing strategies and must explain why the tactics proposed are on-strategy.

Questions often arise about how to distinguish a strategy from an objective or a strategy from a tactic. It is useful to remember that *strategy* and *tactics* come from military terminology. Strategy is the broader concept that might help us win the war (the long-term objective). Tactics include all the logistical plans to accomplish the strategies.

Far too many public relations plans state something like "obtain widespread media exposure" as a strategy, when that is really an MPR objective, and not a very specific or measurable one at that!

Exhibit 7.2 helps to distinguish between marketing goals, MPR objectives, MPR strategies, and MPR tactics. That chart is adapted from one created by Diane Witmer in her book, *Spinning the Web*,[4] where she provides some excellent comparisons of these concepts.

MPR clients as well as IMC students are often mystified by the distinction between a *strategy* and a *tactic*. Suffice it to say that many MPR tactics can become MPR strategies if they become the central organizing theme of the MPR plan.

For example, years ago Parker Pen developed a self-liquidating book on international gift giving called, *Do's and Taboo's Around the World*.[5] It was full of useful tips on customs surrounding gift giving in various countries. Of course, it highlighted the appropriateness of pen-and-pencil sets as a "can't miss" gift in just about every country. As far as we know, it was a simple tactic used by Parker Pen's marketing department. But think of the possibilities of using that book and its theme of international gift giving as a strategy instead of just a tactic. It could spark an unlimited number of ideas for marketing strategies and tactics including an advertising theme on the many ways pen-and-pencil sets can be presented in international settings, a sales promotion contest where customers send in stories of their most interesting or embarrassing gift-giving experiences, a brochure that could be used as both a trade show premium for

Exhibit 7.2. Writing Goals, Objectives, Strategies and Tactics

Term	Definition	Example or Rule of Thumb for a Fictional Skin-Care Product
Marketing Goals	The business goals that the entire marketing organization is trying to achieve.	These can be intermediate-term or long-term goals and are often in financial terms, such as increased sales revenues, but could also be in terms of market share, product trial, or some other measurable goal.
MPR Objective	The specific communications goals that the MPR plan is trying to achieve, and for which the MPR team should be held accountable. Both outcome and output objectives should be identified. **Outcome objective**: those things that can directly help achieve the marketing goals; **Output objective**: those things that measure the amount and quality of the activities being undertaken.	They answer the question: 'What are we trying to accomplish with our MPR plan that will help us achieve marketing goals?" **Example of an outcome objective:** Conduct a public relations campaign that will increase target awareness of our products skin-enhancing benefits by 15 percent by year-end, as measured by a pre- and post-awareness survey. **Example of an output objective:** Generate positive media coverage in at least 25 percent of the key media aimed at our targets by year-end (a list of target media to be identified).
MPR Strategy	The broad plan of attack to help us achieve our MPR objectives. There are typically just a few MPR strategies recommended.	MPR strategies answer the question: "How can we achieve the MPR objective?" They include things like who to target, how to position the brand, the tone of the campaign, and key message points to emphasize. For example: • Target young professionals. • Focus on beauty instead of health. • Equate the tanning of skin with the tanning of leather.
MPR Tactics	The specific plans of attack for each of the MPR strategies. There are usually several MPR tactics that flow from a single MPR strategy.	These answer the question, "What are the specific things we need to do to make the MPR strategy work?" Examples: • Kicking off the campaign during "fashion week" in a major fashion center such as New York or Milan. • Using an older model whose skin looks 20 years younger than it is to tout the importance of blocking the sun's rays. • Creating press releases with interesting ways that woman have historically tried to keep their skin looking young. • Providing beauty secrets and fashion tips on the Web site.

Source: Diane Witmer, *Spinning the Web: A Handbook for Public Relations on the Internet* (New York: Addison Wesley, 1999), p. 91.

distributors and a media tool that provides ten key things to consider before deciding on a business gift. It could also lead to MPR tactics such as a helpful Web site on international gift giving and an article on the most appropriate way to wrap and present gifts in different cultures. The firm could also conduct some simple research—say at a busy airport—on business people's knowledge of international customs. The results would likely catch a great deal of media attention. The ideas for exploiting this theme just seem endless.

The point is that the original book idea could remain a simple tactic among many other tactics to help stimulate pen sales, or it could become a strategy from which a large list of tactics could be generated. Many other ideas might be considered a strategy or a tactic, depending on how they are implemented. For instance, a trade show in the b-to-b world could become one simple venue for promoting a new product, or it could become the entire focus of a lengthy campaign that includes creation of a video, a poster, a set of new brochures, a live product demo, a press conference, and a research venue to learn about customers needs. The trade show could be the starting point for the use of all of these materials over a year's time, or it could simply be one stop along the way. A test for whether you consider the idea a strategy or a tactic is to think about how many other tactics could stem from this idea. If a number of strong, creative ideas spring to mind, it is more likely a strategy than a tactic.

While media exposure is still at the heart of most MPR strategies, public relations is clearly operating from a new depth of understanding of the marketing process. Product publicity may have once been a seat-of-the-pants business with ideas pulled from the sky and stunts staged to "get ink." Today's MPR planning is becoming ever more sophisticated and its strategies have the ability to lead entire marketing efforts.

Step 4: Targets

In traditional marketing strategic plans, identifying the target is often put before strategy development because the prevailing thinking (for traditional packaged-goods targets) is that all advertising dollars should be concentrated on reaching the market that represents the best return on investment. Therefore it is critical to first identify the target in very specific terms, such as: a married woman between the ages of 25 and 49 who has a high school education and family income of $30,000, keeps house, raises kids, and watches television. The strategy for reaching this specific target would then be developed.

Since MPR can reach additional targets at lower levels of spending than advertising, the MPR plan should also strive to reach secondary consumer audiences, opinion leaders, trade audiences, and the like, not just the principal target. Once these primary and secondary targets have been identified, the Target section of the plan should identify key traits of each of these targets and possibly add new information and insights about them, such as psychographic data indicating a concurrent or alternative public relations approach to reach the same market.

Questions you would want to ask regarding your targets include:

- Who are our publics?
- What do we know about them?
- How many are they?
- Where are they?

- What motivates them?
- What do we want them to know?
- How should we communicate with them?
- What do we want them to do?
- What types of messages will persuade them?

Lifestyle and demographic research. Many sources of demographic and geographic information about various target groups are available and can be found in many places, but MPR people are becoming more focused on understanding consumers' lifestyles, values, and interest.

The most commonly used lifestyle classification system is VALS2, a psychographic segmentation tool by the research firm SRI International, in use in its current state since 1990 and updated slightly in 2003. The VALS2 system was developed from a large study of the US population that divided adults into eight segments based on similarities in their values (beliefs, desires, and prejudices) and their lifestyles—hence, the acronym, VALS. People are placed in a segment based on their responses to a survey, which measures consumer resources and their motivations. The segments are loosely based on Maslow's hierarchy of needs and consist of Survivors, Makers, Strivers, Belongers, Experiencers, Achievers, Thinkers and Innovators. To see a sample of the survey and get specific descriptions of each of the segments, go to *http://www.sric-bi.com/VALS/presurvey.shtml.*

In an early and successful application of VALS research, Merrill Lynch switched its advertising from depicting a herd of bulls charging across the prairie to a single bull in various settings. (One ad depicted the bull walking alone through an empty Wall Street, and another had it walking calmly through a china shop full of glass cases and displays.) The ad described the single bull as a "breed apart." Merrill Lynch changed its original ads after reviewing the VALS segments. It was felt that the herd was consistent with the VALS segment known as "belongers," who are traditionalists content to follow others and are unlikely to be heavy investors." But Merrill Lynch wanted to appeal to "achievers," the VALS segment characterized by independent thinkers who see themselves as individualists and above the crowd.   The result? After changing the ads from a herd to a single bull, Merrill Lynch's advertising had a much greater impact on consumers, and its market share went up.

VALS has also been used by a number of public relations counseling firms to define audiences, develop strategies, and select media targets. A classic PR example is when Burson-Marsteller used the data to help the National Turkey Federation encourage turkey consumption throughout the year instead of just at Thanksgiving and Christmas. Specific messages were targeted to three VALS groups through the media they used. For Survivors, the message stressed bargain cuts of turkey that could be stretched into a full meal. For the highly traditional Belonger group, the message focused on serving turkey the year round. For the higher-income, better-educated Achievers, innovative recipes and gourmet cuts were featured in communications.

Yankelovich MONITOR. The Yankelovich MONITOR® has been studying the American consumer since 1971. Yankelovich works with Fortune 500 firms across industries utilizing syndicated attitudes, values, and lifestyles in combination with consulting to help them:

- *Know* what consumers feel, think, believe, and do.
- Understand the *why* behind the what.
- Discover the *opportunities* emerging trends reveal.
- Apply these insights to your marketing efforts and *improve your bottom line.*

The Yankelovich MONITOR defines lifestyle segments in terms of neotraditional values resulting from a synthesis of the traditional values of the 1950s with the newer values of the 1970s.

Geodemographic data. Claritas also provides useful databases that combine lifestyle issues with specific demographic data and the neighborhoods where targets live. Sometimes referred to as "geodemographics," it is based on the concept that "Birds of a feather flock together." The two most popular are PRIZM and MicroVision. Both can be searched using zip codes. PRIZM is a database of US neighborhoods in 62 clusters and 15 social groups. MicroVision uses the zip + 4 to identify 48 segments and 9 social groups. To explore these further, go to Claritas at: *http://www.claritas.com/.* It also has a UK sister organization at: *http://www.claritas.co.uk/.*

Ethographics. Another database identifies targets based on their religious interests. Called "Ethographics" it is available from PerceptNet, which can be found at: *http://www.perceptnet.com/pn4/homepage.htm* . While probably less useful in marketing consumer goods, this database can be extremely useful for nonprofits looking for donations and in political PR campaigns.

Demographics. For pure demographic data on targets, the US Census Bureau and Statistical Abstracts are the best sources, available at: *http://www.census.gov/main /www/subjects.html* and *http://www.stat-usa.gov/.* Demographic and psychographic information can also be found in past issues of *American Demographics* magazine. An index of articles can be found at: *http://www.inside.com/default.asp?entity= AmericanDemo*

The media. Another target that MPR plans must take into consideration is the Media. While they are not consumers of the product and are sometimes considered just a "vehicle" for getting information to key targets, they are most definitely an influencer and so belong in the list of targets to be addressed.

In addition, since most MPR programs are media centered, most MPR plans include a media placement plan. The plan should describe the means for disseminating useful information to selected target media and, for important stories, to identify specific types of media for exclusives. For example, it is fairly common on major new product launches to offer first access to the story to just one of each of the various types of media—one morning news program, one evening news program, one national newspaper, etc.

The cost of developing the media plan is professional staff time, which does not rise incrementally with each media contact. An MPR media placement plan should not be confused with media buying, which paradoxically is also sometimes called media placement in advertising circles. MPR placement is the result of selling ideas to the media, not buying media space. The advertising media plan details how advertising dollars will be spent to achieve optimum reach and frequency against the target audience.

The MPR media plan might include mass media like network television and national magazines. But it will also be likely to include a wide variety of specialized media vehicles to reach primary and secondary target audiences and media to carry the story to the local level, for instance, media directed specifically to opinion leaders and trade audiences and "created media" like newsletters, service booklets, teaching or program materials, and audiovisual aids.

With the rise of databases in marketing, it is critical for MPR professionals to maintain an up-to-date database on key media. The database should include the types of stories the media covers and which it doesn't. (Nothing angers an editor more than receiving a media pitch or press release for a product or service that has nothing to do with the editorial content of the medium.) The database should also include deadline times and dates, contact information for a range of editorial staff, preferences for how each likes to receive PR materials (by e-mail, fax, Web site, etc.), and some references to any recent stories covered about your firm or your competition.

Step 5: Messages

Meaningful, persuasive messages cannot be developed for your targets until you have developed some deep insights about them. That is why target research is critical to any successful MPR plan. Once an insight is found, you will understand your targets' needs and interests, what motivates them to use your product or your competitors' products the way they do, and what their values are. Then you are ready to develop specific messages for each target group.

Creating specific messages for each target is not inconsistent with creating a common message across all targets (IMC). For example, when Ford came out with its "Quality is Job One" message a few years ago, the concept of high quality and limited defects resonated across all target groups. But the message–that high quality is critical—was important to different groups for different reasons—to employees and to customers as well as to suppliers, government regulators, and a host of other groups.

The key is to gear the message toward the benefits of the product or service for each target, not to focus broadly on product features available to all. It is also important to discuss the solutions that the innovation will create, not provide useless details about the firm. (No one cares that the company is 100 years old, but they do care if the vast amount of experience the company has over its competition gives it a significantly higher-quality rating or faster delivery time.)

A typical consumer marketing campaign usually has a single message that gives the consumer a reason to buy the product. While the MPR message might include common copy points with the advertising, those points probably won't be transmitted by the media in the same words used in the advertising. Nor is it possible for the MPR program to be built around a selling slogan. This is a critical difference between PR and all other marketing communications functions. While advertising puts all of its firepower behind a slogan or single selling point, the MPR program may redirect different strategically correct messages to audiences differentiated demographically, psychologically, or functionally (in the case of opinion leaders and trade audiences).

Public relations is generally dependent on the news media or other third-party endorsers to carry the message to these groups. Other approaches lack the credibility that occurs when a neutral third party presents the information.

Also the same media that MPR is working for a free product endorsement is also being considered by the advertising department for paid ad space. The news media is very sensitive to giving away "free advertising" and insists on the information being news worthy and objective. Fluffy slogans belong in ad copy and must be paid for. This is not to say that the MPR message cannot support advertising, but it cannot emulate an ad campaign that depends on sloganeering, imagery, or emotional appeals like "Coke is it," Nike's "Just do it," or Chevy's "Like a rock." MPR cannot use slogans like Target's "Expect more, pay less," but it can generate stories that give consumers reasons to shop at Target.

Step 6: Tactics

The Tactics section of the plan details the methods that will be employed to achieve media coverage. For example, it describes such media and tools as one-on-one media interviews, media tours, news conferences, press kits, and video news releases necessary to support the MPR effort. The section might also recommend events, sponsorships, and other tactics designed to reach target audiences directly rather than through the media. Media created to support the program (often called collateral), such as printed materials and audiovisual aids are also described here. The variety of MPR tactics, as we will see in Chapter 11, is as broad as the imagination of the people charged with creating and implementing the program.

Some of the key questions you might ask in preparing the Tactics section include:

- What program elements will be used to reach each target market group?
- How will each of these programs be implemented?
- What materials will be required?
- What is the media plan?
- What is the timetable?
- How much will it cost?
- Who will be responsible for implementing it?
- Will a PR firm be used? If so, how will it be selected?

Tactical implementation must be spelled out in detail, accurately budgeted, and developed into a functional timeline. Rough drafts of recommended approaches for some of the key tactics are useful. Some agencies will offer some creative ideas for the look and feel of press kits and brochure covers as well as overall campaign themes or logos.

Step 7: Evaluating the Results of MPR

The public relations plan should always include an evaluation component to measure how well the program's success in meeting its objectives. Marketing management might place greater or lesser emphasis on measurement depending on which is more important to them, the need to justify MPR spending, or the limitations of the research budget. Some marketers build in a research component to specifically measure MPR effectiveness. Others include measurement in a plan to evaluate how well the overall marketing plan works. Still others prefer to concentrate MPR dollars on program planning and execution and evaluate its effectiveness by clip count, "big hits," or "gut feel." Chapter 14, "The Bottom Line: Measurement and Evaluation," provides a detailed explanation of the many ways that an MPR program and many of its component parts can be measured. Here, we outline the key elements of the evaluation process.

Traditionally, if public relations results were measured at all, it was in terms of numbers of clips obtained, total circulation of print media coverage, and TV and radio audience size. Circulation of print media has largely been replaced by "reader impressions," an estimate of total readership of the publication, including pass-along readers (readers who get the publication, usually without paying for it, from a paid source; i.e., the publication is "passed along"). These figures are either provided by the publications themselves (found in Standard Rate & Data Service—SRDS) or calculated by an arbitrary formula.

These are measures of "outputs" only and are not related to marketing or business objectives, which is one of the reasons that PR efforts have often been ignored or underbudgeted. The good news is that PR measurement has started to become much more sophisticated and, as is discussed in Chapter 14, is using many more measurement tools and formulas.

In a 1999 study of more than 100 companies from 13 different industry sectors by the Public Relations Society of America entitled, "Best Practices in Measurement," it was determined that 88 percent of the respondents included measurement and research in their communications budgets, and 30 percent of them have in-house research and measurement staff designation. In addition, clip counting has become more sophisticated and exacting in recent years. Organizations such as Biz360, Cymfony, and traditional clipping firms such as Burrells and Bacons have developed techniques and technology to measure media coverage quantitatively and qualitatively. Firms such as Competitive Insights, Delahaye, Textall, and K.D. Paine will conduct content analysis that can determine the use and treatment of specific messages, placement location within the publication, use of photos or charts, and geographic coverage.

Outcomes vs. Outputs

As discussed in Step 2, objectives should be categorized as outcome or output objectives, and their evaluation should be reported as outcomes or outputs. The method for distinguishing the two was set down in "Guidelines and Standards for Measuring and Evaluating PR Effectiveness," developed by Walter Lindemann for the Institute for Public Relations. According to that report:

> Outputs are usually the short-term, or immediate, results of a particular PR program or activity. More often than not, outputs represent what is readily apparent to the eye. Outputs measure how well an organization represents itself to others, the amount of attention or exposure that the organization receives.
>
> Outcomes measure whether target audience groups actually received the messages directed at them . . . paid attention to . . . understood . . . and retained those messages in any shape or form. Outcomes also measure whether the communications materials and messages which were disseminated have resulted in any opinion, attitude and/or behavior changes on the part of those targeted audiences. . . . [6]

Today, the most commonly used outcome measurement technique is a pre- and post-test where a sample of the target audience is surveyed before and after a campaign to determine changes in awareness, interest, and purchase intention. A variation is tracking polls that measure opinion before, during, and after the campaign.

Focus groups are being used for all dimensions of research and evaluation: in the planning stage, to test message appeals, and also to evaluate the effectiveness of program components. Other techniques borrowed from advertising and market research are now being used by MPR, including day-after recall. Participants are asked to watch a specific TV program on which a company spokesperson is to appear. The next day they are called to determine whether they remembered seeing the spokesperson, recalled the message, and were more inclined to try the product discussed. A variation is the mall intercept in which a group of qualified target consumers is asked to view a videotape of a talk show on which the spokesperson appeared. Participants are asked to play back the messages they heard and tell whether what they learned would interest them in buying the product. These results are measured against a control group that did not watch the program.

Another research method borrowed from advertising is the use of matched markets to measure a program's affects on awareness and also on sales. Two markets are matched for similarity in all characteristics except the presence of the MPR program. While it is difficult to isolate consumers in test communities from all non-PR stimuli, and while matched market tests are expensive to conduct, the tests can prove valuable not only in assessing the value of public relations but in determining the right marketing mix before the product is rolled out or taken national. For example, the Campbell "Soup is Good Food" campaign worked best in a California test market where PR and advertising were used in tandem; neither moved the needle in matched markets where they stood alone.

In some of the most direct measures of MPR outcomes, Bank of America and Miller Brewing Company have both recently found ways to measure their media activities against sales. Bank of America used Biz360 to combine media relations with customer data to measure how PR can drive new customers to the bank and drive the bottom line. Miller Brewing used Delahaye to create a proprietary weighted metric to measure the quality of the news and the circulation of its traditional media to determine which brand or brand programs were effectively being portrayed, which spokespeople were being quoted and which journalists covered Miller compared to its competitors. "By doing this, Miller was able to demonstrate PR's effectiveness by providing a direct correlation between the PR activities and an increase in the volume of beer sold."[7]

Some key questions to ask in evaluating a program include:

- How did we do?
- How well did we meet MPR objectives?
- Did we reach the right people?
- How many people?
- What was the cost per impression?
- Did we increase awareness?
- Did we interest consumers in the product?
- Did they buy it?

- How do we know we were successful?
- How will we measure results?
- How much money is there to evaluate results?
- What did we learn that would make the program better?
- How can the program be changed to be even more effective in the next phase?
- Should we change it?

MPR Budgets

No discussion of MPR strategic planning could be complete without a discussion of budgets. In the past, public relations was far too often an afterthought: underbudgeted and misunderstood. Far too many product managers neglect to adequately budget for MPR from the outset. Because the media placement achieved by a good MPR program does not have to be paid for, some mistakenly believe that MPR is "free." While it is true that the *media coverage* is free, MPR is very labor intensive and often requires special events, hospitality functions, and other activities that may come with a sizable price tag. Improper budgeting leads to internal conflicts, inadequate support, and inadequate performance.

In addition, public relations people have long complained, with some justification, that they are called in too late, after marketing plans and budgets are finalized. They rightfully contend that they can significantly contribute to the development of a truly integrated marketing plan in which advertising, promotion, and public relations are assigned complementary roles that work together to achieve marketing goals.

When budgeting for a campaign and using a PR agency, budgets are usually divided into two categories: (1) staff and administrative costs and (2) out-of-pocket expenses. Staff and administrative costs are based on estimated staff hours required and the individual hourly rates charged for each agency person involved. It would not be unusual for about 70 percent of the agency budget to be for staff and administrative costs.

If the work is being done in-house, only the out-of-pocket expenses would be estimated and budgeted, along with a 10 to 15 percent contingency for unexpected expenses. The department staff expenses are usually budgeted separately as part of the department's overhead. Some notable PR successes have been achieved at a relatively small cost (under $100,000) when compared to the millions typically spent on advertising. However, the larger the PR budget, the more sophisticated the PR campaign can be and the more opportunity there is for conducting up-front research and post-campaign evaluation.

Setting a budget for PR will typically take one of four approaches, and all are fairly subjective:

1. **Total funds available:** Some percentage is allocated. Often this is done while also budgeting for advertising, sales promo, etc.—often based on a percent of sales which might range from less than 1 percent for business-to-business and over 5 percent for a consumer goods product. Once the total promotional budget is set, some portion is allocated to PR.
2. **Competitive necessity:** A comparison of your competition's budget is used. The number is matched or exceeded.
3. **Surplus over expenses:** This is a fluctuating number that ensures that the

Exhibit 7.3. Elements of the Written MPR Plan

I. **Executive Summary**
   This is a one- or two-page summary of the entire plan, outlining what is proposed and why, what it is intended to accomplish, and what it will cost. The summary gives management a roadmap of the elements of the program, stripped of their details.

II. **Situation Analysis**
   A. **The Product**
   B. **Target Markets**
   C. **Competitive Environment**
      This section should include information on market share and explanation of share changes, geographic differences, and a description of competitors' promotional programs. "Megamarketing" factors that block entry into markets should also be discussed here.

III. **Marketing/Business Goals**
   This section reviews objectives and strategies set by marketing management.

IV. **MPR Recommendations**
   A. **MPR Objectives**
   B. **MPR Strategies**
   C. **The MPR Message**
      A key theme that gives the consumer a reason to buy the product and then gets specific to address each target's needs and interests.
   D. **MPR Tactics**
      This is the guts of the program, that will be used to support the strategies stated above. The section consists of:
      1. **The Media**
         Most MPR plans include a media plan that describes the means for disseminating useful information in selected target media.
      2. **The Program**
         This section spells out the specific tactics that will be used to deliver the product message to the target audience.
      3. **The Timetable**
      4. **The Budget**

V. **Evaluation**
   Broken down into short-term "output" measures of MPR activities and longer-term "outcome" measures that reflect business goals, such as increased sales and profits, and intermediate-term marketing and communication goals, such as increased awareness, improved attitude, or increased inquiries about the product.

VI. **Conclusion**
   If the plan is being sold to management, it offers an opportunity not only to restate why the program will work, but, in the case of competitive presentations by PR firms, why the firm should be chosen for the job. In asking for the order, the firm will likely try to demonstrate why it is best qualified for the assignment on the basis of experience, expertise, proven record of results, dedication, and fit with the client-company culture.

VII. **Appendix**
   This is where you would put any supporting materials for your plan:
   - evidence of your research,
   - summary data charts that clarify your points,
   - samples of competitors' promotional materials, and
   - any creative elements that you choose to include in your plan, such as logo ideas, drafts of preliminary press materials, brochure layout, designs for press kit covers or premium items, etc.

organization breaks even. You only spend the profits, so you may spend more or less over the year as you determine the financial status of the organization over time.

4. **Zero-based budget**: This—the most strategic method of budgeting—requires you to set your objectives first and then develop communications tactics to meet those objectives and develop a specific budget for each tactic. The objectives and tactics are prioritized. Funds from a predetermined budget are then allocated to the projects in priority order until all of the funds have been assigned.

Target Marketing: From Demographics to Lifestyle

Target marketing is the practice of identifying the specific behaviors and characteristics of key target groups and developing specific messages and promotional programs aimed at motivating them to take action. Segmentation, the core process involved in targeting, is the process of disaggregating large groupings of information about customers and marketing targets and re-aggregating it into smaller, more homogeneous, targetable groups. It began as a way to emulate the old-time shopkeeper's personal knowledge of individual customers. Advancements in database automation have made it possible for marketers to micromarket in increasingly smaller segments, approaching that mythical market "segment of one." To do this effectively, one typically needs to identify who they are, how many they are, and gain insight into their demographics, lifestyles, and, most importantly, their needs. This is not an easy task and can consume the majority of a PR team's planning efforts for a campaign. But it is time well spent, since the persuasiveness of a campaign will depend on how relevant the message is to those who receive it.

MPR and Target Marketing

For traditional marketers, the steps of segmenting, targeting, positioning, and branding are well known and used often. But for some traditional public relations practitioners, these are revolutionary ideas. Not only does a typical PR campaign rarely target specific consumer groups, but small staffs and even smaller budgets have kept some public relations practitioners from even targeting specific media outlets—favoring, instead, the mass distribution of press releases and pitch letters to everyone on their mailing lists, regardless of interest or past usage.

But, luckily, a growing number of marketing public relations experts have ably demonstrated just how effective MPR can be when properly targeted. Some would argue that they have always targeted key audiences, but may not have labeled it as targeting or micromarketing. Public relations management consultant Al Croft has suggested:

> Many PR practitioners have been successfully communicating to smaller, precisely defined audiences for some time. The disappearance of mass market magazines and the shrinkage in the number of major metropolitan newspapers, coupled with the appearance of a plethora of special-interest, limited-audience publications were early warnings that practitioners had better rethink the media and the approaches available to reach and influence audiences.
>
> As knowledge, sophistication and competence grew, practitioners learned that it was both possible and economically efficient to reach fractured, special interest audiences through a variety of new media and techniques. In addition, they found that "product positioning" was as practical as through mass advertising. Using PR—primarily publicity and special events—to reach micromarkets and

generate both product awareness and positioning has led to innovative approaches.[1]

The New Model for Target Marketing

The traditional marketing tug-of-war has been between retailers and manufacturers. Manufacturers have used on-line product registrations; Web site activities, such as games, contests, and lifestyle information; as well as traditional mass marketing and national advertising to talk directly to consumers, creating the type of customer "pull" discussed in Chapter 5. Retailers, on the other hand, have gained a significant advantage over manufacturers in gaining access to sophisticated customer information through scanners of bar codes on packages and credit card or customer loyalty programs, though most of them have not made very sophisticated use of that information.

This is all changing, however. The huge UK grocer, Tesco, has recently found a few key purchasing patterns in the millions of bits of data from their Clubcard records and, using what they call "share of basket" data, have identified approximately 50 specific target groups that now get customized offers that address their specific needs and interests. According to Clive Humby, a principal in DunHumby, the data-mining firm behind Tesco's Clubcard success, Tesco's market share went from 16 percent when they began implementing the system about nine years ago to 27 percent today, making it the No. 1 grocer in the UK. In addition, their customer loyalty and satisfaction scores have gone up concurrently. A recent article in *Promo* Magazine[2] reported that Tesco has been able to use the Clubcard to launch a bank, a telephone service, and a Web site that rivals *Amazon.com.uk,* and that "a handful of sub-clubs now cater to niche audiences, from new mothers to wine lovers." In 2004, the U.S grocery chain, Kroger, hired DunHumby to set up shop in Cincinnati to help them do the same thing.

As more retailers figure out how to mine the data that they have on their customers or as they form ever larger, more powerful stores, the balance of power will continue to shift away from the manufacturer. Already, the huge national and global chains such as Wal-Mart, Home Depot, Lowes, Borders Books, Barnes & Noble, etc., can now control the supply of products from beginning to end. As manufacturers (or publishers, in the case of the booksellers), even those as large as Procter & Gamble, rely on these retailers for the bulk of their sales, they have begun to lose control over how their products are priced, distributed, and promoted. If a mega-store retailer chooses not to carry a particular line, it would take a massive amount of marketing effort on the part of the manufacturer to create enough "pull" with consumers to encourage the retailer to change its mind.

Of all the large retailers, Wal-Mart has without a doubt had the most dramatic impact on how consumer goods manufacturers do business. According to Don Schultz of Northwestern University and Agora Marketing Consulting, in the future "There are going to be two types of retailers: Wal-Mart, which focuses on supply chain, squeezing costs out and competing on price and location, and Tesco, which competes on customer knowledge and relationships. There won't be any in between."[3]

Segmenting, Targeting, Positioning, and Branding

An effective target marketing effort requires that you know the difference between the key concepts of segmenting, targeting, positioning and branding, and use each to your firm's advantage.

The Segmenting Process

Segmenting is the process of dividing the market into subsets of consumers with common needs or characteristics. Secondary data sources are used to identify key segments, which can be based on demographics, such as age groups, gender, or income level; geographics, such as regional variations in taste or climate; product usage, such as heavy, loyal users; or situational factors, such as those who buy the product as a gift or for special occasions only. Segments can also be based on ethnic differences or differences in lifestyle and interests. However you choose to segment the market, your goal is to identify how many people fit each segment, project the growth of these segments and potential revenue streams, and gain an understanding of where your competition's strength is with each segment.

A growing practice in market segmentation analysis is to mine existing customer data to determine their lifetime value to the organization. Companies have begun to learn which customers are profitable to serve and which are not so profitable. In a *Wall Street Journal* article entitled, "Analyzing Customers, Best Buy Decides Not All are Welcome,"[4] the retailer explains that its best customers are those who "snap up high-definition televisions, portable electronics, and newly released DVDs without waiting for mark-downs or rebates." They label these their "angels." Their "devils" are their worst customers—people who load up on the promotional "loss leaders," who apply for rebates, and who return merchandise for advertised discounts after scouring the Internet for rock-bottom prices and holding the firm to its lowest-price pledge. The retailer estimates that about 20 percent of its current customers fall into the "devil" category and are costing the firm important profits. This will become an even more critical factor over the next few years as Wal-Mart moves to provide similar electronics at lower prices than Best Buy and Dell Computer moves to provide higher-end, more customized products to the less price-sensitive shoppers. Best Buy worries about falling into the same "unprofitable middle" that Toys "R" Us fell into.

To lure its "angels," Best Buy put a marketing strategy in place in 100 of its 670 stores that improves its merchandise availability and provides more appealing service. To deter its "devils," it culled them from its direct marketing lists and cut back on promotions and sales tactics that tended to draw them.

In addition to mining existing data to help retain the best customers, it is also important to identify and acquire new customers who reflect similar behavioral patterns as your best customers. To find these, you must first uncover and gain insight into the various market segments available and determine if they fit into a consumer group already identified by market researchers in terms of their demographics or psychographics, such as Baby Boomers, Bobos, Early Adopters, Empty Nesters, Gen X, Gen Y, and DINKYs. (See Appendix A for definitions of many of these segments.) It is important to note, however, that targets may fit into multiple groups, and their assignment is often arbitrary. However, early classification into one or more of these groups may help in finding existing data about them and in developing insights into what motivates them.

But true insight will come from observing them in their natural surroundings and talking to them first hand, studying their buying behaviors, and uncovering their needs and interests.

A Word of Caution About Segmentation

In her book, *Hitting the Sweet Spot*,[5] Lisa Fortini-Campbell discusses the demographic and psychograpic segmentations available through the secondary sources cited in previous chapters and then warns:

> . . . it's often easy to fall into the trap of thinking that the research segments take the place of people themselves . . . to stereotype people and believe that they *are* "belongers" or "achievers" rather than realize that these are simply labels for grouping consumers with varied characteristics according to what they seem to have in common.

For that reason, it's still best to get to know your customers as individual people before you try to segment them. If you do it that way, you're a lot less likely to make the critical error of oversimplifying them.

The Targeting Process

Once you have identified some useful segments, you can select a target or group of targets from among the segments that you believe your firm can effectively reach and for whom your product offers a unique benefit. The targets selected offer the most opportunity to your organization because of their size and purchasing power, their potential for growth, or because they are an untapped niche that your competitors have ignored.

Before deciding on the "right" targets, you should undertake some secondary and primary research into these target groups to learn about their lifestyles, interests, and consumption behaviors. As Fortini-Campbell points out, face time with them is critical. Ideally, that would include unobtrusively observing them in retail situations, spending time with them in their homes or work environment, listening to their stories about what excites them and what frustrates them, and pulling a group of them together to interact to see if there is a common theme among them. The goal is to gain an insight about them that will help you develop a brand message that will create an emotional connection with your targets.

Developing a Positioning Strategy for Each Target Group

Positioning is often referred to as creating a unique selling proposition or a distinct image for the product in the mind of the consumer that sets it apart from all other brands in the category. Some common positioning strategies and some branding ideas that followed them are:

- by product difference:
    —Made on premises, hand-crafted by a single artisan, etc.
- by key attribute:
    — Quality, selection, product features (avoid positioning on price, however).
- by users of your product:
    — People who love to sew, barbeque, etc.
- by usage:
    — Ball Park Franks for backyard BBQs.

Exhibit 8.1. Typical Positioning Statement

The typical positioning statement takes the form:

> For: (behavioral target)
> Who: (have the following unique customer characteristics and category motivation)
> Our product is a: (describe the product/brand)
> That provides: (key benefit based on insight)
> Unlike: (relevant competitor)
> Our product: (key point of differentiating relevance)

- against a category:
  —"There's only one lite beer . . . Miller Lite."
- against a specific competitor:
  —Avis: "Because we're Number 2, we have to try harder."
- by historical place or geographic locale:
  —Beck's beer as an authentic German beer.
  — The "Bogart Collection" by Thomasville Furniture.

Any advertising slogans or public relations message points should come directly from the positioning strategy. But be careful here. People often mistake promotional slogans for positioning statements. A good positioning statement should lend itself to a good slogan, but it needs to be more than *just* a slogan. It is the overarching theme against which all advertising, public relations, and direct marketing activities should be checked. A silly PR stunt may achieve media coverage, but if that stunt is counter to the positioning strategy to project a warm, sophisticated product image, the stunt may have damaged the product positioning rather than supported it.

Branding and Positioning from an IMC Perspective

Some general guidelines to differentiate the two related but different concepts of branding and positioning are that we tend to think of the brand as something fairly tangible that the firm owns. It has a look (a logo or trademark, a product description, a recognizable package); it has an underlying message (a tagline or an advertising slogan). It has value or "brand equity"—the "goodwill" listed on the balance sheet. It can be bought and sold. It is more closely associated with the product or service it defines than with the company that owns it (i.e., Kraft Macaroni and Cheese will be basically the same in the consumer's view whether RJR/Nabisco, Nabisco Holdings, Altria, or the Acme Corporation owns it).

The brand's positioning, however, is owned by the customer. It is the place in the customer's mind where that brand fits. It is closely associated with reputation. It connects the brand to the internal needs of the customer. It reflects how highly regarded the brand is, how much value it is perceived to provide, and what benefits it will deliver. It also includes a mental mapping of the brand in relation to other brands of that product or service and with substitutes for that product or service. It is very much associated with the consumer's view of the company that owns it. It is the positioning that an IMC campaign needs to address, although it does so through associating the brand with key insights about the consumer's needs.

An interesting and controversial concept is that a firm may own a strong brand while having a relatively weak positioning. Microsoft Windows and Wal-Mart may be such brands. They are incredibly valuable with a very strong market share. They are very profitable because they have standardized their products and services to a point where huge economies of scale can be achieved in production and distribution. They are also the standard by which their competitors are measured. But neither brand is highly regarded in terms of ethics, nor are they considered the highest quality or the most innovative. Based on this assessment, an IMC approach would suggest these brands are very vulnerable in the future and that their primary focus should be on improving their reputations with strategic, integrated marcom endeavors, especially public relations.

Conversely, it is possible to have a weak brand with a very strong positioning. Apple's MacIntosh brand fits this scenario. Macs have less than 5 percent share of the personal computer market, yet its customers are extremely loyal. The company is generally considered to be very innovative and ethical, and the Mac system is generally rated as higher quality and more user friendly than Windows. An IMC approach would suggest that a firm in this situation has a great deal of potential but that general marcom is far less important than strategic alliances with highly profitable suppliers and targeted customers, building infrastructure to support these alliances, and developing creative distribution outlets that would give them a unique advantage over larger, but slower competitors. The success of the iPod may be the launching pad that Apple needed to become a major player again.

The ideal scenario is to have both a strong brand and a strong positioning. Highly regarded firms such as Cisco Systems and Intel fit this category. These firms have large market shares, their stocks trade at very high multiples, and public opinion is generally favorable. An IMC approach for these firms is a constant monitoring of internal and external environments and to use strategic marcom to stay ahead of any potential risks. This might include internal feedback mechanisms to monitor employee satisfaction, ongoing competitive analysis that acts as advance radar for new competitive product launches, and issues monitoring to stay ahead of regulatory or consumer advocacy initiatives.

Tactical Approaches to Targeting

The use of limited-audience, special-interest media to reach target audiences has become a valuable asset to public relations, but that is only part of the story. Localization and regionalization, long accepted as standard operating procedure by public relations practitioners, are accelerating as marketing management becomes sensitized to the value of reaching consumers where they live.

Media tours and desk-side briefings are increasingly delivering more localized messages. Special events are held in popular high-traffic locations. Tie-in sponsorships are often made with local radio stations and newspapers. Participation in local festivals is on the rise. Company floats appear in local parades. Cause-related programs are designed to benefit local institutions and organizations. Local chapters of national public service organizations often provide the arms and legs that assure the success of company-sponsored programs. Local franchisees speak for the company in their communities. Local customers are invited to and entertained at local appearances of company-sponsored sports and arts events.

The programs cited here represent hundreds of marketing public relations programs directed to audience markets of high current interest to marketers, that is, women, youth, senior citizens, etc. The dramatic growth in target marketing to multicultural segments has grown to such an extent in recent years that an entire chapter is dedicated to it in Chapter 9.

Heinz's EZ Squirt Ketchup: Targeting Kids

In 2000, H.J. Heinz Corporation launched "a new wacky ketchup that will not only come in the color of spinach, but will also sport a new plastic bottle designed especially for children."[6] According to Heinz spokesperson Casey Keller, "The core idea is to give kids more control and fun over their food." He noted that children already consume about five billion ounces of ketchup each year but that the new color and hourglass bottle shape would be easier for them to grip and also give kids the ability to dispense ketchup in an ultra-thin stream that allows them to draw figures or even write their names.

The original plan was to leave the color alone and just change the bottle; but, according to Deb Magness, senior manager marketing communications for Heinz North America, after gathering input from more than 1,000 kids by going into schools and homes, and conducting focus groups with kids, they discovered something else: kids not only wanted a more accessible bottle, but they also wanted a different color. Several colors were tested, and green turned out to be the kids' favorite.

The product launch drew lots of media attention. Interestingly, *ABCnews.com* found it intriguing enough to conduct a poll and found that adults were not taking to it very well. The poll found that a little over 50 percent said that the green ketchup is "just plain weird."

"From a public relations standpoint, we made a decision to announce the launch of the ketchup prior to its release in order to gain momentum," Magness said. "We wanted to generate consumer awareness and excitement."[7] They definitely achieved that goal, with media mentions in every major news outlet. But it remains to be seen if the product itself will hold up to parental resistance.

Pillsbury's "Cooking for Two": Targeting Empty Nesters

Pillsbury recently decided to target many of the 78 million baby boomers in the US who are now becoming empty nesters. They did it with a tie-in with AARP (formerly the American Association of Retired Persons) at its National Event and Expo in Las Vegas in 2004. It is the first time the firm had ever targeted this market segment, and its focus is to help empty nesters adjust to cooking, buying, and organizing meals for a smaller household. The program is titled "Cooking for Two" and features Pillsbury's line of Oven Baked frozen dinner rolls and biscuits.

The marketing approach was truly integrated. Pillsbury launched a new TV advertising campaign featuring empty nesters who are experiencing new freedom and opportunities to experiment with new tastes. But the company put most of its efforts into various public relations activities including new "Cooking for Two" information on its popular consumer Web site, *www.pillsbury.com*; a "Cooking for Two" monthly electronic newsletter; and a public relations program featuring baby boomer and Olympic figure skating champion Peggy Fleming.

The company's activities at the AARP National Event included a booth highlighting

Cooking for Two tips, demonstrations and samples, plus a Cooking for Two presentation featuring soon-to-be empty nester Peggy Fleming and Pillsbury test kitchen expert Lynn Vettel. The AARP event also included advertising in *AARP The Magazine* and participation in AARP The Magazine Road Show.

Clorox Pen: Targeting Young Do-It-Yourselfers

An interesting product development for the 90-year-old Clorox Company came about in an effort to reach younger consumers and breathe new life into the product category, but it was PR agency Ketchum that helped the company recognize that the uses for its new Clorox Bleach Pen could go beyond conventional laundry and household chores.

After extensive research among target consumers and finding that bleach-users' biggest fear is accidental splashing, the PR team predicted that teens and other young users would have a love affair with the controllable and easy-to-use pen. While the Clorox Company conducted primary pre-launch research to validate the "bleach-in-a-pen" concept, Ketchum conducted a media analysis to confirm that the do-it-yourself (DIY) trend was topical and relevant for the new product positioning. Ketchum also polled its own internal trendsetters (employees who mirrored target audience demographics) to determine of the new bleach pen would resonate with DIY audiences. Based on these insights, Ketchum then commissioned research with a teen audience to validate the strategy and found a very receptive audience to the product.

The PR program that followed had a budget of $350,000 and the following three objectives: surpass initial media benchmarks of 21 million media impressions, generate a 25 percent aided national consumer awareness level of the Clorox Bleach Pen, and communicate the brand's value proposition and differentiating message "bleach you can control" in 85 percent of placements. The key strategies that were followed were:

- Created a visually compelling press kit to break through the media clutter including a coffee-stained hankie with a big note that simply said, "Try me," and a bleach pen.
- Conducted "see for yourself" desk-side briefings in New York with magazine new product and home care editors using various stains on a t-shirt.
- Targeted media outreach to traditional and non-traditional editors with customized creative topics—such as holiday events and "party fouls permitted" positioning.
- Used a 17-year old teen consultant to validate the concept of the pen as a DIY (do-it-yourself) tool and to review all press materials, Web site content, and graphics to be sure the message was correct for the younger audience.
- Created a special *cloroxbleachpen.com* micro site to deliver project ideas, tips on how to use the pen, and downloadable designer stencils.
- Created a separate press kit for targeting media aimed at teens and included a tiny denim bag so editors could create their own designs.

The results of the campaign were phenomenal. All of the objectives were surpassed with first-year sales of 10 to 15 million units, surpassing original projections by 75 percent. Interestingly, initial buy-in from the trade was slower than expected, but orders exploded after PR placements began to appear. Media impressions exceeded 96 million, surpassing the objective by 350 percent, including hits on every major TV network and in *Good Housekeeping, Redbook, Parents, Real Simple,* and major newspapers across the country. *Business Week* named the Clorox Bleach Pen one of its Best Products of 2003, and the product became a runaway success for Clorox.[8]

Cadillac: Targeting a Younger Audience

After years of lowered sales due to a stodgy image of the Cadillac brand among luxury car buyers and an aging traditional customer base, Cadillac has regained traction with a younger target. According to an article in the *Chicago Tribune*,[9] sales were up 10 percent in 2004, which was on top of an 8 percent gain in 2003, helping Cadillac pass Mercedes to rank third among luxury car brands. It was ranked fifth just three years earlier. The newspaper reported that just four years earlier Cadillac's average buyer was 63, which dropped to 58 in 2004. But more importantly, when asked by a research firm which brands they would like to buy, the average age of those who aspired to a Cadillac was 25, lower than other luxury car brands and lower even than the average age of those who aspired to own a Toyota, which was 28. Five years earlier, the same research found that Cadillac's average was in the low 40s.

What created such a dramatic change? Partly a redesign of the product in the early 2000s—especially the introduction of the CTS, an entry-level luxury sedan with edgy styling, and the Escalade, a full-sized SUV. In addition, Cadillac has significantly improved its quality image, which was typically cited as a reason younger buyers rejected the car in the past. In 2004, Cadillac scored better in three different J.D. Power vehicle dependability studies than BMW and Mercedes, its two main European rivals.

But it is GM's marketing program that gets most of the credit for the turnaround. The marketing has been an integrated mix of edgy advertising and youth-oriented MPR tactics. Its advertising campaign included a television commercial featuring a car smashing the words "Luxury and performance don't mix," with the words disintegrating into a million pieces that resembled a futuristic movie about outer space.

The MPR tactics were aimed directly at a younger target. Instead of using their traditional PR vehicle of sponsoring golf tournaments, the Cadillac marketing team cultivated hip-hop artists to include their style of Cadillac in music videos. They also promoted the use of the Escalade among high-profile athletes and forged a relationship with heavy-metal rocker, Robert Plant, who attended a PR event at General Motors' headquarters and autographed the hood of a Cadillac CTS in 2002. The connection with Plant was because of the use of the Led Zeppelin rock anthem "Rock and Roll" in another series of television commercials, one of which featured Cadillacs kicking up dust at a country club instead of collecting it. Marketing guru, Art Spinella, was quoted in the article saying, "It was a brilliant stroke to use Led Zeppelin. Now you just hear a few bars [of their song] and you instantly think of Cadillac."

Targeting Today's Consumer

Regardless of which target group is being pursued, many "futurists" suggest that they all share a common set of characteristics as they become part of the current networked economy. Melinda Davis, founder and CEO of the Next Group, works with scholars, artists, researchers, policy makers, etc., to get a line on what the future will hold for customers of such firms as AT&T, Corning, L'Oreal, Merck, and Viacom. She outlined some of her insights about the future of marketing in her book, *The New Culture of Desire* (Simon & Schuster, 2002), and Bill Breen summarized them in a *Fast Company* article in 2003.[10] Paraphrases of some of the key points from the article follow:

1. Marketers must sell ideas about how their products can help today's consumer assume another identity, either an aspirational self or helping them with their fascination for dividing themselves into multiple, virtual identities as a way to handle an increasingly complex, chaotic world. The implication of this for marketers is that each customer is actually many customers fitting into multiple segmentation models.

2. Because of all the relentless internal commotion caused by a glut of information and the clutter of nonstop advertising messages, today's consumers seek meaning through narrative and archetype. They long for stories that help them uncover the mysteries of their lives and give them opportunities to interact with the products through on-line movies, novels, and games.

    Brands that have been successful at this are: BMW, Bulgari, the contemporary Italian jeweler and watchmaker, and many action movies that have games that are available before the movie is even released. These practices are perfect for MPR since Davis suggests that "the long tale is the new sound bite; narrative has more teeth than slogan." She explains the phenomenon as if she is a PR pro herself: "Today, we see life as a choice of spins: It's the journey that gives us pleasure. Purposeful deception will always spell disaster, but pleasurable spinning is a road to success."

3. Peace of mind has become the ultimate consumer good, which means that marketers must become healers. Worldwide turmoil has turned many of today's consumers from collectors of things to seekers of "a safe, happy home" and "peace of mind." Marketers who find ways of connecting to the consumer's need to heal will stand out from those still touting their product's features.

    The health and beauty industry is the most obvious place to see this strategy in action with bubble baths sounding like spa treatments, shampoos with names like Herbal Essences, and body lotions and perfumes promoted as aroma-therapy. Other consumer goods are getting in on the act, with firms such as Pepsico promoting drinks with names like Zen Blend and Karma, and Celestial Seasonings naming one of its herbal teas "Tension Tamer," with a tag line that it "works approximately six times faster than psychotherapy."

4. Besides peace of mind, people desire a sense of importance. They want to matter in a world where it's easy to get lost or become invisible. Davis cites the trend *luxe populi* as "the quest to stay visible in an increasingly invisible world by becoming one of the 'important people.'" She suggests that Emeril Lagasse and Martha Stewart have helped to fuel this trend by creating a new elitism and peddling a prestige lifestyle to the masses.

    Davis thinks Target has taken hold of this trend and run with it, suggesting that Target "has seized onto the notion that art is a badge of status. Target has introduced a new department called Framed Art. At *target.com*, you can buy a framed Van Gogh, Picasso, or Monet print for between $100 and $200. One of the categories for Framed Art is Over the Sofa. You get your furniture at Ikea, and then you go to Target and buy your Picasso to hang over the sofa. And the next day, you tell your friends at the hairdresser's all about it: 'I just bought a Van Gogh. I found it on-line. I'm an insider.'" She suggests that marketers have to know how to make their products seem like "trophies of elitism" and how to make their customers feel like they are "players in the precincts of privilege" for them to connect with today's consumers.

5. Finally, marketers need to align with someone that consumers respect and look to for advice—"a Yoda—to show us the way, to tell us what to do and ultimately what to want." Oprah Winfrey has become this person of late, with her book club and "favorite things" segment of her TV show and in her *O Magazine*. Davis suggests that Richard Branson is "being a kind of Yoda of hip commercialism," with his Virgin Atlantic Airways, Virgin Records, and now even a Virgin alternative bridal store. *Amazon.com* tries to be this Yoda by using recommendations from like-minded shoppers. Brand extensions and private labeling do the same thing, they tell the consumer that anything in this line is OK, it will meet your "hip quotient" or your quality expectations.

Appendix A Sample Segmentations

Baby Boomers: A consumer classification that describes people born in the US between 1946 and 1964, labeled the "Me Generation" as members came of age in the liberal years of the 1960s and 1970s, when terms such as "free love" and "recreational drugs" came into usage. Despite this label, they are known for their strong work ethic, even being called "workaholics" by their younger, Generation X, counterparts in the work environment.

Regardless of what you call them, their sheer numbers and demands for products are driving all sorts of trends, from clothing boutiques in people's homes to customize television programming. "Boomers are going to change the way we think about the aging process and how we treat people over 65," says Steve Gillon, author of *Boomer Nation: The Largest and Richest Generation Ever, and How It Changed America*:[1]

A recent *Red Herring* article[2] discussed how the boomers are affecting the $145 billion medical devices market:

Living longer is no longer the goal. Living longer, while looking and feeling young, is now baby boomers' big wish—and the market's command. As more than one-quarter of the US population, 40- to 60-year-olds represent huge potential profits for successful treatments.

Indeed, boomers have long driven the life sciences industry, which includes medical devices and biotechnology. Medical devices—including stents that keep arteries open and a pacemaker-like stimulator from Cyberonics that prevents epileptic fits—are moving beyond life-threatening health conditions to address enhancement, restoration, and feel-good benefits.

They currently have the highest disposable income of all the consumer groups, and the book *Mass Affluence* cites researchers John Havens and Paul Schervish of Boston College's Social Welfare Research Institute, to predict that $71 trillion will pass from the US baby boomers to their off-spring between the years 1998 and 2052.

BoBos: Short for "bourgeois bohemians," a consumer psychographic group made popular by David Brooks in his book, *Bobos In Paradise*. According to the book, "Bobos are the new upper class and are an unlikely blend of mainstream culture and 1960s-era counterculture." Their purchasing behavior is described as follows: "They sip double-tall, nonfat lattes, chat on cell phones, and listen to NPR while driving their immaculate SUVs to Pottery Barn to shop for $48 titanium spatulas. They tread down specialty cheese aisles in top-of-the-line hiking boots and think nothing of laying down $5 for an olive-wheatgrass muffin."[3]

DINKY: An acronym for a consumer group made up of couples that have "double income, no kids yet." They are couples that are married or cohabiting who have not yet had children (or who do not intend to do so) and typically fall between the ages of 18 and 45. DINKYs have both demographic and psychographic characteristics and are thought to be less affluent than Baby Boomers or Empty Nesters, but their double incomes often make them a more affluent target than singles.

Early Adopters: This is one of the most sought-after groups by marketers. The term comes from the theory of Diffusion of Innovation put forth by Everett Rogers in 1962[4] and is still popular today. The theory suggests that new products and new ideas follow a predictable pattern of adoption across the population. The theory predicts six categories of adopters that fall into a normal (bell-shaped) curve that distributes the population as follows: Innovators (2.5 percent), Early Adopters (13.5 percent), Early Majority (34 percent), Late Majority (34 percent), and Laggards (16 percent). Marketers and PR professionals are typically interested in finding and communicating with the Innovators and Early Adopters, since they tend to be opinion leaders who influence others. They also are more likely than any other group to pay the high price of the newly introduced product, even when all the bugs have not been worked out of it.

Empty Nesters: A consumer group made up of couples who are parents, but who no longer have children living at home. Early Empty Nesters (aged between 50 and 64) are characterized as having relatively high disposable incomes and are thought to spend lavishly on rewarding themselves. Late Empty Nesters (aged 65 years and over) have more limited budgets, leading to a greater emphasis on value in consumer goods purchases. See DINKYs for information about their younger counterparts.

Gen X: Short for "Generation X" this is a consumer group that was born between 1964 and 1981 (although there is disagreement about the exact dates). It is the group just below the Baby Boomers in age and was initially refereed to as "Slackers" because they did not exhibit the same workaholic tendencies as their predecessors. Significantly smaller in numbers than their Boomer predecessors they also tend to be more conservative in their politics than Boomers.[5]

Gen Y: Short for "Generation Y," this is a consumer group that was born between 1981 and 2001. They were initially referred to as Millennials because the majority of them were becoming young adults just at the turn of the new millennium. They are also sometimes called "echo boomers" because they are typically children of Baby Boomers and their numbers reflect a similar type of population explosion that occurred with Boomers. Gen Y members tend to be more liberal in their politics than Gen X and have some environmental interests in common with their Boomer parents.

Seniors: Despite the Baby Boomers reluctance to enter the "senior" world, by 2025, Americans who are over age 65 will make up nearly 20 percent of the population. The current median age is now 35.2 years, up from 32.8 years a decade ago. The average life expectancy in the US is 74 for men and to age 79 for women. In the US, heads of households aged 55-plus control about three-quarters of the country's total financial assets.[6]

The older segment of this category is, however, going through serious life changes, with deteriorating health, loss of spouses, and declining income. Most of these people can vividly recall living through the Depression of the 1930s and WWII in the 1940s, with its rationing and product shortages. A recent book by David Solie, *How to Say It to Seniors: Closing the Communication Gap With Our Elders,*[6] tries to help the Baby Boomer children of this group understand what this group is experiencing as they grow older and to learn patience with the elderly and their propensity for repeating stories, obsessing about details, and postponing decisions. He says, "In a society bent on staying young and moving fast, we might not understand the process or have much patience for it, but the elderly have two main tasks: to maintain control over their lives as much as possible and to discover their legacy."

YoCo, or Young Cosmopolitans: This is a new demographic group made up of US Urban Youth. They are multicultural and multi-ethnic, or what some call, transcultural. YoCos are a group that is increasing in size and influence and spreading across cities both large and small.

In explaining how the group was named, the American Marketing Association said, "As the Greek roots of the word 'cosmopolitan' imply, YoCos are truly 'citizens of the world.' In today's diverse urban landscapes, they gather experiences that cross old cultural, ethnic, and racial boundaries as easily as they breathe." [7]

The organization suggests that marketers must adopt a new lexicon and understanding of the urban experience and recognize that freedom is at the heart of the modern urban experience. In looking at this new group, it is interesting to contrast them with the young urban professionals (Yuppies) who dominated the marketing scene twenty years ago.

Yuppie: (spelled Yuppy in the UK): This is a marketing segment first popularized in the 1980s that stands for "young upwardly mobile professional person." It describes people between their early twenties and late thirties, generally of the middle-to-upper class. Yuppies tend to be fresh from graduate school and hold a job in the professional sector and follow all the latest trends. They live in cities, work in well-paid occupations, and enjoy a fashionable lifestyle. Yuppies are thought to be more conservative than the preceding hippie generation. While the psychographic segment is still used today, the term is used most often in a derisive way to describe "a young person who lives in a city, who spends a lot of money doing fashionable things and buying expensive possessions; i.e., "They're just a couple of yuppies with more money than sense." Yuppies tend to be white, but there is another classification, Buppie, to describe a black Yuppie.

With the search capabilities of the Internet and the tightly targeted media channels today, it is becoming increasingly possible to target just about any special needs or special interest group.

9 Targeting Multicultural and Global Markets

In an article entitled, "Five Simple Rules for Launching a Multicultural Strategy,"[1] Gina Rudan, director of multicultural and international markets for *PR Newswire*, points out that the general market is shrinking as multicultural markets have grown, but that only a few companies have begun to tap into these virtually untapped markets. She suggests that those who have strategically targeted these groups have found that there is $1.3 trillion in spending power (based on the combined spending power of African-Americans, Hispanic, and Asian-Americans) and a target base of 88.2 million people, or 30 percent of the US population. The principles of segmentation and targeting discussed previously apply for these market as well.

As with traditional groups, a common mistake marketers make when segmenting is to look at an entire culture, such as the Hispanic community in the US, and treat it as a single target market. This approach fails to recognize the vast differences in lifestyles, customs, needs, and interests among different Hispanic groups, such as recently immigrated Mexican-Americans and third generation Mexican-Americans or the differences among Hispanic-Americans from Mexico, Cuba, or Guatemala living in California, Florida, or New York.

As Chapter 8 pointed out, public relations is uniquely capable of creating programs segmented to discrete demographic as well as geographic and psychographic characteristics. In recent years, greater attention has been focused on programs directed to minority markets, many of which possess growing purchasing power. The rise of marketing consultants in these areas has been accompanied by the growth of public relations specialists in these markets, with counterparts in corporations and advertising and public relations agencies.

Growing Multiculturalism

Non-Hispanic whites made up 69 percent of the US population in 2000. That number is steadily falling and is expected to be below 50 percent by 2050, according to a special report on the growth of diversity in the US, published in *PR Tactics* in August 2004, which also says that nearly one-third of Americans now come from a mix of other racial and ethnic groups, primarily black, Hispanic and Asian. The report states:

> The Hispanic population alone more than doubled from 1980 to 2000. Both the Asian and Hispanic populations are expected to grow by more than a third between 2000 and 2010. Meanwhile, there are a rising number of multicultural Americans and a wide range of diversity within racial and ethnic groups. Add the aging of the baby boomer generation, and you have a recipe for the most diverse society in the country's history.[2]

Though he shocked and upset some people when he said it, Tiger Woods put a very human face on all of the statistics pointing to a multicultural America. When interviewing him, Oprah Winfrey asked him if it bothered him to be referred to as an African-American golfer. He responded that, yes, it did because he didn't consider himself as Black or African-American. His father was half Black, one quarter American Indian and one quarter White, and his mother is half Thai and half Chinese. He had invented a word—Cablinasian—to describe his heritage: Caucasian, Black, (American Indian) and Asian.[3]

These changes will have, and are already having, a profound effect on marketers hoping to reach these increasingly diverse target groups. *PR Tactics* reported on two trends that appear to be taking hold:

- A greater retention of native languages and customs. While America has been known as the melting pot, it may be becoming more of a "salad bowl" due to the relative ease that immigrants now have for staying in touch with their homelands and members of their ethnic community through the Internet, increased native-language media outlets, and relatively inexpensive travel home.
- There is a potential for America to become "Balkanized," as ethnic groups take on unique characteristics and become more separate from each other. Marketers will either target these differences or find the common ground that makes an American unique among all other nationalities in the world, regardless of race or ethnicity.[4]

"Some companies adapt products by creating ethnic-specific brands, while others focus solely on niche positioning. These markets can be tapped in a variety of ways, but most multicultural marketing practitioners employ a few universal rules," Gina Rudan says:

1. Integration is key. Integration of the PR and Advertising functions is particularly important in multicultural marketing, since there is often a blurring of the roles in ethnic media.
2. Do your research. Demographic, psychographic, and sociological information are needed to adequately prepare for the planning phase. Understanding the cultural nuances of a market is critical as is gaining an understanding of your segment's relationship with your product. "Build your lists and identify the appropriate media contacts," Rudan advises. Common requests from these journalists are the same as from mainstream media: Know what I cover, know my reporting deadlines, and know my work prior to reaching out to me."
3. Cultural connectivity is crucial: The ability to reach a consumer through their cultural contexts such as values, community, religion, lifestyles, sexual orientation, class, country of origin, degree of acculturation, and language. Rudan suggests that "the goal is to connect in an intimate way with both communities and individuals simultaneously through effective cultural context," and then to maintain an ongoing connectivity.
4. Perception is reality: How firms interact with an ethnic community on a daily basis helps to shape that reality for members of the target group. Cause-related marketing, discussed in greater detail in Chapter 21, is an important strategy in shaping this reality. Rudan warns: "The best way to conduct these efforts with credibility is to partner with national or local ethnic organizations. . . . These organizations can help you develop an effective program. They can also help in identifying a spokesperson—preferably one who is bilingual for the

Hispanic and Asian markets—who can champion and be a voice for the initiative. Ethnic media love covering cause-related campaigns."

5. Partner with the experts. Rudan's last piece of advice is to hire an agency that specializes in multicultural services. They will know what obstacles need to be overcome and have resources available that, otherwise, might take too long to track down. There is a service guide to help locate such an agency called, "The Source Book of Multicultural Experts," published by Multicultural Marketing Resources, Inc., available at *http://www.multicultural.com/experts/*.[5]

Hispanic Market Public Relations

Any company that wants to grow in the future will have a hard time doing it without the Hispanic market. So say any number of experts in target marketing. According to *The Wall Street* (citing The Association of Hispanic Advertising Agencies and TNS Media Intelligence/CMR),[6] in 2004 the top companies targeting this group with major advertising expenditures were:

Lexicon Marketing—$222.5 million
Procter & Gamble—$169.8 million
Sears, Roebuck—$119.1 million
General Motors—$93.4 million
Univision—$92.8 million
PepsiCo—$85.7 million
World Vision—$66.2 million
McDonald's—$64 million
Ford Motor Company—$56.8 million
Toyota Motors—$56.4 million

Betsy Spethmann, writing for *Promo* Magazine[7] cited additional useful statistics about this market from the US Census Bureau:

The US Census first recognized Hispanics as the largest US minority in 2000. The birth rate mirrors immigration: half the new population has moved to the US, the other half was born here. 'Hispanics' national purchasing power . . . is projected to reach $1.3 trillion by 2020.

- 46 percent of the US foreign-born population is Hispanic
- 11 percent of Americans (28 million) speak Spanish at home
- 21 million Spanish-speakers live in the South and West
- 7 million live in the Northeast and Midwest
- The top five states for speaking Spanish at home: New Mexico, Texas, California, Arizona, Florida

Spethmann says that some of the geographic patterns are changing, however:

The traditional six markets—Chicago, Los Angeles, Miami, New York, San Diego, and Texas—are only part of the story now. The fastest-growing Hispanic markets lay outside that grid. Fifty percent of Hispanic-Americans live in California and Texas, but some population pockets are surprising. Atlanta, Denver, Phoenix, Las Vegas, Portland, Seattle and towns in Utah, North Carolina, South Dakota and Arkansas have grown quickly as Hispanics migrate for factory or heavy-labor jobs.

Advertising Age[8] reported that 54 percent of Hispanics are bilingual but prefer to speak Spanish, 19 percent are bilingual but prefer to speak English, 14 percent are bilingual and have no preference, only 9 percent speak only Spanish and 4 percent speak only English.

Nevertheless, the increase in Hispanic populations has been accompanied by the rise of Spanish-language media. This includes hundreds of Hispanic newspapers and a proliferation of Spanish television and radio stations. Radio is said to be the medium most commonly used among younger, bilingual Hispanics, and Hispanic radio stations in New York, Miami, and Los Angeles successfully compete against mass market stations for top ratings. In addition, three Spanish-language TV networks, Univision, Telemundo and TeleFutura together air about $2.4 billion worth of Hispanic television advertising. *Advertising Age*[9] breaks down their 2002 ad revenues as:

- Univision: $1,508 million, which incidentally, is higher than the ad revenues of the WB, UPN and PAX networks combined
- Telemundo: $774 million (owned by NBC TV)
- TeleFutura: $85 million (owned by Univision)

Spethmann says that, while marketers generally buy media in the Top 10 markets, "some are mulling the Top 20 markets because the group is growing so quickly." She points out that Spanish-language media continue to multiply, with new 2004 TV launches including ESPN Deportes, History Channel en Espanol and Telemundo's bilingual sibling, Mun2 (that's Mun Dos). She also noted:

Si TV, an English-language cable network for Hispanics, launched in February 2004 to 7 million homes with plans to be in 10 million homes (via cable and DISH) by yearend. The network targets young Latinos who mostly speak English, but want Latino programming: Si TV also expects to draw non-Hispanics who like Latino pop culture.[10]

Hispanics are brand conscious and brand loyal. That is why virtually every consumer product company is trying to get a piece of the action. Most of them know to align themselves with causes that matter to Hispanics. According to Schiffman and Kanuk,[11] here's what sets Hispanic markets apart from other US markets:

- Prefer well-known or familiar brands.
- Buy brands perceived to be more prestigious.
- Are fashion conscious.
- Historically prefer to shop at smaller personal stores.
- Buy brands advertised by their ethnic-group stores.
- Tend not to be impulse buyers.
- Increasingly clipping and using cents-off coupons.
- Likely to buy what their parents bought.
- Prefer fresh to frozen or prepared items.
- Tend to be negative about marketing practices and government intervention in business.

Beer Companies Targeting Hispanics

In 2004, Coors Brewing Company began airing, for the first time, Spanish-language TV ads on general market media in key markets like Dallas and Los Angeles. They also began a joint promotional effort, running advertising spots supporting Coors Light's sponsorship of the 2004 Chivas Summer Tournament, a soccer tournament between Mexican teams.

Miller Brewing signed a $100 million deal with Univision Communications, the largest Spanish-language broadcaster in the US, in October 2004. *The Wall Street Journal* said of the deal, "It is a further sign of brewers' eagerness to target Hispanics as one way of countering sluggish volume growth and reduced beer drinking among aging baby boomers."[12] *The Journal* went on to say:

> Equally important, 75 percent of the Hispanic population is under 45 years old—a prime age group for beer consumption, according to Mintel, a marketer-research firm in Chicago. What's more, Hispanics are the most brand-loyal demographic among beer consumers.

In 2004, Labatt and USA's Tecate and Dos Equis brands also undertook major marketing efforts with the Hispanic community, integrating their advertising, sales promotion, public relations, and joint marketing efforts with other brands. Spethmann explains:

> Tu Musica del Verano ("Your music of summer") gives a $5 rebate on a 12-pack of Tecate and a CD from Virgin Megastores. Consumers sample tunes from EMI Records' Latin music division at listening posts in Virgin's 21 stores at *www.cervezatecate.com*. Radio, supermarket P-O-P and Virgin ads support it, and EastWest Creative, New York City, handles.[13]

Procter & Gamble Targeting the Hispanic Community

Procter & Gamble has been among the most aggressive marketers to the Hispanic community. In addition to sponsoring a number of sporting events, especially soccer, which is the number-one sport among Hispanics, the company has also sponsored community activities such as special events and floats in parades for Cinco de Mayo (May 5), which celebrates the victory by Mexico in its war of independence from France. The global marketer has also used cause-related marketing very effectively with this community.

A Burson-Marsteller program from several years ago involved commissioning a popular muralist to direct over 100 children to paint an original mural depicting Hispanic family life at the Fiesta Y Cultura Children's Festival sponsored by Pampers. Another Pampers MPR program, in conjunction with local hospitals at key Hispanic festivals, was Centro Pampers, sanitary diaper-changing centers, where women could join a mothers' club and receive product literature, coupons, and samples.

Two recent caused-related MPR programs involved P&G's partnerships through its Avanzando con tu Familia community outreach program to the welfare of young people. It partnered with the Hispanic Scholarship Fund (HSF) to increase scholarship funds available and The League of United Latin American Citizens National Educational Services Centers (LNESC) to expand the LNESC Young Readers Program.

MPR and the African-American Consumer

The 2002 US Census Bureau estimates that African-Americans currently make up nearly 13 percent of the US population and, as such, are the largest racial minority in the US. They have a purchasing power of $575 billion, so marketers seek them out through the $1.3 billion in advertising, promotions, and events targeted to them through such media as Black Entertainment Television (BET), several radio networks that include Sheridan Broadcasting and National Black Network, and longtime leading publications like *Ebony, Jet, Essence,* and *Black Enterprise* to reach black audiences.

Schiffman and Kanuk[14] warn that, like the Hispanic market, this group is often mistakenly treated as a single target group with uniform consumer needs:

> . . . in reality, they are a diverse group, consisting of numerous subgroups, each with distinctive backgrounds, needs, interests, and opinions. For example, in addition to the African Americans who have been in the US for many generations, there are Caribbean Americans, from such places as Jamaica and Haiti, who have recently immigrated to the US. Therefore, just as the white majority has been divided into a variety of market segments, each with its own distinctive needs and tastes, so, too, can the African American market be segmented.

Reflecting this new targeted approach to what used to be considered a target in and of itself was the launch of the magazine *Savoy.* This publication, which caters to young professional African-Americans, was recently at the center of a recent bidding war between Time Warner and two smaller publishing concerns. According to the *Chicago Tribune,*[15] the publication grew its circulation in just three years to more than 80,000 loyal readers "eager for a lifestyle magazine focused on careers, personal growth and entertainment rather than on such other fare as celebrities and pop music." The median household income of its readers is $56,000. Seventy-two percent have attended college, and 55 percent are males.

Another target within this ethnic group are African-American children and their families. The Borders Group, parent of Borders Books and Music, is interested in targeting this group as it expands its store locations into urban centers. It has employed a number of MPR activities, all using the common theme of "literacy," to target young, urban ethnic groups, especially African-Americans. Here are just a few of the activities cited on the corporate Web site:[16]

- Targeting urban families of various ethnic backgrounds with young children, Borders has actively supported Reading Is Fundamental, the nation's largest children's and family literacy organization and has raised more than $2 million for the organization through various programs over the past several years.
- Targeting urban teens, Borders provides support for The WritersCorps Youth Poetry Slam League, a program dedicated to helping at-risk youth succeed by encouraging them to articulate their thoughts and feelings in the form of poetry at competitive performance poetry slams.
- Targeting African American would-be writers, Borders supports The Zora Neale Hurston/Richard Wright Foundation for their Legacy Awards and other programs and services that the foundation offers to Black writers.

Since the late 1960s, creation of advertising that targets the black consumer market has been part of the marketing plans for many consumer-driven corporations like McDonald's, Coca-Cola USA, and Ford Motor Company. Astute marketers at these and other companies have long understood the importance of developing segmented marketing strategies. It is not unusual, for example, for leading consumer brands to receive over 50 percent of their market share from sales to African-Americans, who are very brand-loyal consumers. Some examples follow.

Canadian Mist's "Fashion for Mist Behavin'"

In the 1980s Canadian Mist undertook what is now a classic MPR campaign that was targeted to the African-American community. Since alcoholic beverage advertising is prohibited from television and outdoor billboards in some states, reaching the African-American as well as the general market is a difficult task. PR can be especially important in positioning the product and reaching the African-American consumer in a meaningful way.

Burrell Public Relations did it through the creation of "Fashion for Mist Behavin'," a showcase of African-American fashion designers that celebrated the contributions African-Americans have made to the world of fashion. The show presented some of the hottest creations of both established designers and up-and-coming talents.

During the 1989–90 season, "Fashion for Mist Behavin'" traveled to seven key markets and in each donated all the show's proceeds to organizations benefiting the African-American community. After three years, Canadian Mist contributions totaled more than $200,000. The recipient organizations were profiled in the show's program brochure, which also highlights the designers, including the hometown talent of designers from cities on the tour.

Since the show was a benefit for local nonprofit organizations, public service announcements (PSAs) were used to promote the show on local television. Press kits were localized for each market, and local radio and television talk shows provided extensive coverage. In addition to the coverage of the event, pre-publicity was gained in each market during the search for local models, which gave the show interesting local appeal.

McDonald's Celebrates Black History Month

Through the years, McDonald's Corporation has created a series of Black History Month programs and continues them through today. It has provided educational materials to schools on "Black History Through Art" and "Black History Through Music," as well as a film on the life of Dr. Martin Luther King. In 1988, the company created "McDonald's Black History Makers of Tomorrow," a program that honors outstanding Black high school juniors who demonstrate leadership, character, exceptional scholarship, and "the potential to become Black history makers of the future." In 2002, it launched a year-long, multitiered Black History campaign called "365 Black."

In 2003, McDonald's USA received the Rainbow PUSH Coalition's PUSH-Excel Corporate Partner Award for outstanding contributions to African American youth. PUSH founder, the Rev. Jesse L. Jackson, cited several factors in selecting McDonald's for this award—including McDonald's longstanding commitment to the African American community, employing and training African-American youth, and the diversity of its national suppliers and Owner/Operators of McDonald's US restaurants.

In accepting the award, McDonald's USA president, Mike Roberts, pointed to the company's heritage of diversity. "Our founder, Ray Kroc, used to say 'None of us is as good as all of us.' Today—that spirit is integral to everything McDonald's does—and we believe it keeps us relevant to our customers and to our employees."

McDonald's Corporation has also been recognized by the National Urban League, National Black Caucus of State Legislators, endorsed by *Fortune* Magazine as one of the "Top 50 Places for Minorities to Work" and recognized by *Working Mother Magazine* as one of America's Top 10 employers for diversity, showing that its commitment to the African-American community goes much deeper than just target marketing.

Procter & Gamble Targets Future African-American Employees and Suppliers

In an interesting twist on minority MPR campaigns, Procter & Gamble has developed a scholarship program to attract minority students into the chemical sciences and has funded a training program to encourage the establishment of more minority-owned supplier firms.

For the future employee scholarship program, P&G has contributed $100,000 to the American Chemical Society's Scholars Program to help academically gifted minority students with financial need to pursue college studies related to the chemical sciences. The company says its support of the program is to emphasize the importance of diversity as a strategy toward a stronger workplace.

P&G's Supplier Diversity Program

Supplier diversity is another fundamental business strategy for P&G, according to A.G. Lafley, P&G Chairman of the Board, President and Chief Executive Officer. He notes that is not just a targeting or relationship-building exercise, but fundamental strategy for the company's future success. He outlined the thinking behind the program in a recent P&G press release.[17] In it, he said:

> Diversity is the uniqueness that everyone—from suppliers to employees to corporate officers—brings to fulfill P&G's Purpose, Values and Principles.
>
> We will continue to expand and build our supplier diversity results. We are also asking our major suppliers to help us meet our long-term objectives by significantly increasing their supplier diversity efforts as well. Supplier Diversity is no longer an issue of social conscience. Our very future depends on capturing and retaining the loyalty of a growing consumer market audience. This is one of the ways we achieve our goals.

The Asian-American Market: MPR Opportunity

While marketers have targeted Hispanics and Blacks for special attention, only a few have directed programs to the Asian-American market. Yet, as *The Wall Street Journal* has pointed out, "Its population is younger, more affluent, and more quality conscious than the US as a whole, and it is one of the fastest-growing minorities in percentage terms."[18]

According to the *Journal,* marketers have been reluctant to go after this market for a number of reasons:

Many say Asians will see and respond to ads in regular publications or on television. Some companies say they haven't yet researched the market, or think it's too small to bother with. Still others cite the diversity among Asian-Americans.[19]

According to the 2000 US Census Bureau, about 12 million Asians live in the United States, and it is the fastest growing American minority group (on a percentage basis). This is a dramatic increase from 1988's Asian American population of under 7 million. Schiffman and Kanuk[20] report:

Six different ethnicities make up about 88 percent of the Asian American population and they are expected to grow at nearly 5 percent by 2005: Chinese (2.5 million), Filipino (1.9 million), Indian (1.7 million), Vietnamese (1.12 million), Korean (1.1 million), and Japanese (797,000). Because Asian Americans are largely family oriented, highly industrious, and strongly driven to achieve a middle-class lifestyle, they are an attractive market for increasing number of marketers. Indeed, about 60 percent of Asian Americans have incomes of at least $60,999 and about 50 percent hold professional positions.

In his recent book on the future of advertising, [21] Joe Cappo has predicted that while Asians still make up less than 2 percent of the total US population, their total numbers will double in the next 20 years, and, by the middle of the twenty-first century, Asian-Americans will have as large a share of our population as Hispanics have today.

Asian-Americans present marketers with an ethnically diverse and highly regionalized market. About 35 percent of all Asian-Americans live in California, and another 40 percent are concentrated in four other states: Hawaii, New York, Illinois, and Washington.

The Asian-American emerging market presents both advertising and MPR opportunities. In addition to the general media that Asian-Americans and other ethnic groups are exposed to, the number of magazines, newspapers, and television and radio stations directed specifically to Asian-Americans is expected to grow, providing marketers with new niched advertising media and publicity outlets. Sponsorship of Asian-American events such as the annual Chinese New Year Parade in San Francisco provides other promotional possibilities. The parade attracts more than 300,000 people as it snakes through Chinatown to the city's financial district, and it is telecast in San Francisco, Los Angeles, and Honolulu on Chinese-language television, offering sponsors of floats and commercial spots an opportunity to reach an even larger audience.

"Ethnic Diversity" Doesn't Reflect Kids' Lives

A 2004 study undertaken by Viacom Inc.'s Network and Cultural Access Group and released by the Nickelodeon Network found that, while the US currently has the most ethnically diverse generation of kids, they are growing up in predominantly segregated environments, despite their sharing of a common pop culture.

The study, which tapped into the lifestyle, attitudes, and mindsets of African-Americans, Asian, Hispanic and White children between the ages of 6 and 14, found that while children in the US, regardless of ethnicity, had common interests and activities—the Internet, radio, television, and value for their families—"they tend to be growing up in homogeneous enclaves where they don't have contact with peers from other ethnicities."[22]

Interestingly, the study found that African-American children had "the most positive sense of self, being more likely than any other ethnic group to see themselves as influential." The study also found that Black "tweens" (between the ages 9 and 14) were significantly more likely than others to believe that they make people laugh, that peers pay attention when they talk, and that others try to be like them.

Other interesting findings from the study were that, despite the stereotype that Asian parents were the strictest with their children, they weren't, at least in terms of unsupervised activities. Instead, that distinction fell on the African-American community. The study found that:

- Their African-American counterparts set a higher threshold for their children's independence than any other group, particularly boys. More African-American parents believe that it's appropriate for their sons to go to the movies without adult supervision only when they are 18 years old, or to stay out with friends until midnight when they're 22.
- Ethnic background—rather than socioeconomic status—influences how much money parents give their children. Overall, 55 percent of children in the US receive weekly allowance. White children get the smallest—an average of $9.20. Asian children receive the highest allowance, $13.70, and are expected to perform the fewest chores in exchange.
- Asian families do have high academic expectations, however. Some teenage Asian children reported in discussion groups that their parents wanted them to study instead of work during the summer. More Asian kids—79 percent—said they worry about doing well in school.[23]

Global Opportunities—An Intersection of Corporate & Marketing PR

While the topic of global public relations could (and should) be the topic of an entire book, there are a few things that those practicing marketing public relations should keep in mind as their companies and their brands potentially become global icons and as the means to communicate corporate actions become faster and easier to distribute and retrieve worldwide.

Organizational Factors

A few years ago, the International Advertising Association (IAA) prepared a study about Global Best Practices in advertising and integrated marketing communication.[24] The study's key concepts still fit in today's world.

First, the role of the CEO has changed over time. Today's global best practice firms have a highly engaged CEO who is personally involved in major brand strategy decisions.

Second, the communication systems being used by these firms are increasingly becoming global in their infrastructure, allowing immediate and shared access to information by key constituencies around the world.

Third, more of these firms are moving toward a form of hybrid branding and marketing structures where centralized firms are looking for ways to incorporate local adaptation, and decentralized firms are finding ways to have tighter integration and regional oversight. Many of these firms have two- or three-tiered systems where global headquarters determines the broad strategic direction and the regional or local groups execute the regional or local strategies and tactics. Many of these firms differentiate *branding* as the broad global function and refer to advertising and public relations as something only executed on a regional or local level.

Agencies have been increasingly trying to mirror their client's structure by providing local services on a global basis and providing a broad array of marketing communications services—from creative and more traditional advertising services to direct marketing, public relation, media buying and research services. This has led to the ever-increasing series of agency mergers and acquisitions that we've been seeing for a number of years. The companies that have undertaken the majority of these deals started out 10 or 15 years ago announcing that they would operate just as holding companies for their acquisitions and allow their acquired firms to continue to operate "as is" as long as they made stringent profit projections. Today's acquisitions are very different and will create a number of interesting challenges as the parent firms try to leverage the strengths of their acquisitions and position themselves as truly integrated firms.

WPP Group, under the guidance of chief executive Martin Sorrell, is arguably the most integrated of all of the large agency holding companies. The $5.72 billion firm (2004 revenues) is now a collection of more than 100 advertising, public relations, and direct marketing agencies. According to *Fortune* Magazine:[25]

> One key to WPP's success has been Sorrell's ability to get disparate parts of his sprawling empire—ad agencies like Ogilvy & Mather and J. Walter Thompson; media strategists such as MindShare; and direct marketers such as Wunderman—to work together to woo clients. Sorrell and other consolidators have been talking about synergies in the business for years, but for the first time, there's evidence that having a wide array of services under the WPP umbrella is an asset rather than an organizational and managerial headache. Indeed to win HSBC's ($600 million global marketing campaign), Sorrell put together a team from across WPP instead of relying on one agency to make the pitch.

The Golden Workshop: Ideas for a Global Future

A few years ago the Arthur W. Page Society posted the proceedings of its "Golden Workshop,"[26] which addressed the global issues facing the public relations field in the new millennium and the impact on corporate leadership and the structure of the corporate communications role and function. Some of the key findings from that conference were:

- Globalization will impact every aspect of the PR chief's work.
- Analysis of competitive factors demonstrates that going global is not a question of choice. It is a necessity. Leading corporations, in most business sectors, that do not become increasingly global, will fail. The choice is globalize, or demise.
- Numerous US corporations are already global in most respects, with vast operations in many countries. Such firms as Coca-Cola, Johnson & Johnson, American Express, J. P. Morgan have multinational top management teams, organizational approaches that make no distinctions between US and international, and investment strategies that see vast, long-term, non-US outlays.
- Most leading US corporations, however, are still dominated by US operations and considerations, although all have international business links of diverse

and numerous kinds. They are corporations where defining characteristics include:
—top managements with only modest international experience;
—most employees, suppliers and customers are US-based;
—most investor and financial relationships are US-based;
—most issues of governmental affairs are related to the US agenda;
—the PR department is overwhelmingly composed of US nationals with little non-US experience; and,
—the PR agenda is dominated by US issues and audiences.
• But, a global business paradigm is in the ascendant almost everywhere now. In relative terms, the US will play a decreasing role in each of the above described areas.
• Corporate leadership must now plan marketing strategies that are interrelated with the rest of the world.
• As more American companies go global, they find most of their employees lacking the background, the understanding, even the interest necessary to be truly effective.
• While multilingual fluency may not be the set criteria for hiring tomorrow's corporate PR chief, it is probable that CEOs will increasingly seek PR advisers with a broad and firm grasp of the global environment. They will want to feel assured that their PR advisors are presenting them with speeches for foreign audiences, and tips on foreign cultures, that avoid embarrassment because of cultural insensitivity.
• More importantly, CEOs will want PR chiefs at the top management table who have something of real value-added to contribute to strategic discussions on international challenges, especially in crisis situations.
• Going global also means establishing a reputation of excellence on a global level.
• The growth of the Internet, the evolution of global media entities (CNN, News Corporation, The Financial Times, Dow Jones, etc.), and the rapidly increasing integration of financial markets and institutional investor communications across national borders, means that PR chiefs can swiftly talk to many audiences in many countries in a uniform way from a single base. It sounds efficient. Yet, can PR continue to be centralized, or seek a new form of centralization, in a corporation where almost all business areas are enjoying unprecedented decentralization?
• There are no simple answers. Some functions may need to be centralized, or, at a minimum, that there will be a need for a head office capability to act globally on urgent PR issues. At the same time, it may be the case that the overall corporate forces of decentralization leave the PR chief with few organizational choices.

Global Outreach

The challenges of operating in a global environment are many, and there is not always a clear distinction between the corporate public relations function, the marketing public relations function, and even local or regional public relations functions in international settings. But despite this, a global public relations presence is critical to a firm's international success. It does not really matter which function takes the lead, as long as the issue is addressed and the messages are coordinated within the organization for timely response and message consistency.

Using Procter & Gamble as an example, here are just a few examples of the dozens of its global outreach programs that it reports in its annual social responsibility and corporate contributions reports.[27] The following examples from its Web site show how public relations has been used on a global level to solve a local problem while enhancing the company's reputation and improving its marketing opportunities for its brands.

Saving Children's Lives through Clean Water in Haiti. A new water purification product developed by Procter & Gamble was launched in November 2004 in Haiti, where diarrhea is a major killer of children under five, by an initiative funded by the Global Development Alliance of the US Agency for International Development (USAID).

PUR, Purifier of Water, was launched by the Safe Drinking Water Alliance, a public-private partnership created to increase access to safe drinking water by low income people which is comprised of P&G and three nonprofit organizations: Population Services International (PSI), the Johns Hopkins University Bloomberg School of Public Health's Center for Communication Programs (CCP), and CARE. The Alliance is also implementing safe drinking water projects in Pakistan and Ethiopia.

P&G in China. At the start of the millennium, when P&G was entering the rapidly growing China market, it focused on relationship-building and charitable contributions. The company already had a number of well-known brands in China's consumer product market, such as Ariel washing powder and Rejoice shampoos, and in 2000 the company launched its new Ariel Stain Bleach with an anti-bacterial component into the Shanghai market.

As part of the product launch, P&G used a cause-related strategy that gained considerable attention in China. In partnership with the China Charity Federation, the company launched the Ariel Caring Collection Activity in the four Chinese cities of Beijing, Shanghai, Guangzhou and Chongqing to collect and wash donated clothing to remove common laundry germs before giving them to people in need.[28]

Another cause-related project in China that has garnered much public support for the company and its brands has been its involvement for more than eight years with Project Hope. In that time, the Company has contributed nearly $2 million and thousands of hours in volunteers' time. These resources have helped build and staff 100 P&G Hope Schools, benefiting more than 50,000 poor children who would otherwise not have access to education.

P&G Canada and Assistance Dogs for Kids. In a classic MPR example, P&G Canada is building on an 11-year relationship of Eukanuba Brand Dog Foods supporting the MIRA Foundation. MIRA is a Montreal-based assistance dog organization that was the first in North America to provide assistance dogs for children.

Eukanuba Dog Foods introduced the *Salute to Assistance Dogs* program, reaching out to Canadians, especially children, who could benefit from the partnership of an assistance dog. These marketing PR or corporate PR activities, however you see them are critical part of P&G global business strategy. As the Arthur Page Golden Workshop proceedings suggest:

The degree to which a corporation enjoys a high reputation has a direct impact on its ability to gain entry to new foreign markets, to find the best joint venture partners, to win the confidence of governmental authorities, sources of finance, suppliers and customers. Reputation management in the global arena is a bottom line competitive issue. It has to be a top priority for the CEO.[29]

And, we might add, it already is a top priority for public relations professionals.

10 Reaching a Critical Audience: Internal Branding

Scott Davis and Michael Dunn, authors of *Building the Brand-Driven Business*, [1] suggest that a brand-based corporate culture provides tangible reason for employees to believe in the company, allows employees to understand how they fit into the corporate "big picture," and instills a sense of pride in employees. As consumers, we see the truth of this observation every day: We are motivated to seek out a product because we saw an ad, read a positive review of it in a publication or were swayed by a direct mail piece. We may, however, contact the company and be put off by an employee who is apparently having a bad day or just plain doesn't care. It's a lost sale that all the smart marketing in the world cannot get back.

But an internal branding program can. As Marc Drizan, director of the 2003 Extending Your Brand to Employees Conference,[2] put it:

> A strong brand is a valuable asset that if leveraged well can increase the value of your company. It can increase customer loyalty, revenues and stockholder value. Historically, brand equity was viewed as an externally delivered strategy. However, it is the employee who ultimately delivers the brand promise to the customer. Given this apparent gap between the delivery of external and internal brand, senior leaders are seeing the importance of a systematic approach to brand management that aligns corporate and employee branding for successful delivery of the brand promise in the marketplace.

The numbers bear this out. Some studies have shown that marketing efforts, including MPR activities, will be wasted if internal audiences are not properly addressed. For example, Juliet Williams, a communications consultant in the United Kingdom,[3] has conducted research that shows:

- 40 percent of all marketing effort is wasted once customers encounter a firm's employees.
- 68 percent of customers who do buy from a firm, will not come back because of something that those employees did or did not do.

In their book, *Internal Marketing*, Varey and Lewis[4] cite similar findings. They found that 41 percent of customers are more likely to buy or not buy again because of the way employees treat them.

To address this important issue for marketers, one must first understand the common terminology. *Internal branding* is a term that has gained momentum in the last few years and is used by some enlightened marketers to indicate the importance of employees in the overall marketing equation. It involves educating employees about brand positioning and promotional strategies, ensuring that they buy into the strategies, are trained about the brands, and have the resources they need to provide the customer experience that has been promised. The concept is also being embraced by some human resources departments to be sure that employee communication programs, incentives, and motivational efforts help employees feel that they are a valued part of the brand experience.

Internal marketing is a similar term that has several different meanings, depending on who is using it. For some, it means the same thing as internal branding. For others the meaning is very different and means selling a product, service, or idea to employees. For the purposes of this book, we use the terms *internal branding* and *internal marketing* as interchangeable and consider both to be based on the simple premise that because customers will inevitably come into contact with employees, it is important that the employees know and understand what the brand stands for and communicate that to the customer. Making that happen, however, is not as simple as it sounds, and at least part of the responsibility for doing so should fall to those practicing marketing public relations.

The Internal Branding Process

Internal branding is the process of bridging the chasm between those who interact with the customers directly—primarily the sales and marketing functions—and the rest of the organization. Its goals are to make all employees feel ownership in the customer experience and to motivate them to do their best work to help the organization achieve its marketing and financial goals. Two important hallmarks of internal branding are:

1. Educating all employees about the brand promise being made to customers—which means keeping all employees informed about marketing strategy and promotional efforts *before* taking any of them to the outside world.
2. Helping employees understand their roles within the organization and how what they do can have an impact on the customer's experience with the brand.

Doing this requires a great deal of coordination among departments, especially between human resources and marketing. A growing body of evidence indicates that firms with a strong interaction between these two functions are more likely to attain their marketing and financial goals. In one study, Piercy[5] suggested that the ideal Marketing/HR partnership should help achieve the following:

- Realignment of the training processes with customer issues.
- Reinforcement of employee ownership of the customer service encounter through an appropriate organizational climate.
- Tracking of both customer and employee satisfaction through regular surveys and feedback.
- Establishment of linkages between customer satisfaction measures and training.

These activities, along with the appropriate measures of employee performance against financial goals, make up the internal branding initiatives being employed throughout forward-looking organizations around the world. Exhibit 10.1 shows Ahmed and Rafiq's[6] interpretation of the complete marketing function for these firms. It illustrates how, in addition to the traditional external marketing activities and the customer loyalty programs that dominate most marketing activities, there is a function aimed at motivating employees and integrating customer messages to them.

Exhibit 10.1. The Complete Marketing Process

Source: Ahmed and Rafiq, *Internal Marketing* (London: Butterworth-Heinemann, 2002). p. 139.

Obstacles to Internal Branding Efforts

According to Rodney Gray, an employee communications consultant in Sydney, Australia, the first obstacle to overcome is a lack of awareness on the part of many corporate executives about the importance of internal audiences to the bottom line. "Many executives can't see how (internal) communicators 'add value,' " he says.[7] But perhaps a more important obstacle to internal branding is using the wrong communication tools to reach internal audiences. Gray suggests that "many (internal) communicators concentrate on the wrong things by continuing to focus on traditional communication tools," such as electronic newsletters. He says, "These have been shown repeatedly to have little impact on satisfying employees' overall communication needs, and are of questionable value in facilitating necessary organsational [sic] changes."

So what does work? According to Gray, who conducted a statistical analysis between types of communications employed and employee satisfaction with the organization's communication activities, "helping the CEO and senior executives improve their relationships with the workforce is far more likely to improve employee satisfaction with communication than, say, working on the intranet, e-mails or publications."

These findings are very similar to those uncovered by an extensive study by Patricia Whalen of internal communication tools used during mergers and acquisitions.[8] The study found no reduction in conflict between the merging firms when formal internal communication tools, such as intranets, employee newsletters, posting banners and slogans, etc., were used alone. Nor was there any improvement in the deals' outcomes. However, conflict was reduced and outcomes improved when those firms also employed a high level of informal communication tools—such as cross-training, informal

Q&A sessions in common areas, sports teams whose membership drew from across functional and management boundaries, creating directories to make it easier to find and contact counterparts in other parts of the organization, and managers just walking around and having impromptu conversations in the hallway.

So, a significant part of the internal branding effort has not only to keep employees informed about the latest external branding plans, but to encourage management to communicate the importance of these plans directly and through as many informal means as possible.

The Payoff for Employee Involvement

There can be a huge payoff for companies that learn to involve all employees in their marketing efforts and to increase employee commitment. A "Human Capital Study" [9] undertaken by the consulting firm Watson Wyatt found that US business units that scored in the top half on employee involvement compared with units in the bottom half, have seen the following rewards:

- 86 percent higher success rate on customer satisfaction
- 78 percent higher success in safety ratings
- 70 percent higher success in lowering employee turnover
- 70 percent higher in productivity
- 44 percent higher in profitability

Firms with "high commitment" levels from employees had 112 percent three-year returns to shareholders compared to firms with "low commitment," which had 76 percent three-year returns.

Another study with important implications for management was presented in November 2004 at the Forum for People Performance [10] by Dr. James Oakley, assistant professor of marketing at Purdue University's Krannert School of Management. "The Impact of Employee Attitudes on Market Response and Financial Performance" links employee satisfaction and engagement to the profitability of satisfied customers. "The study's central objective was to understand the drivers of employee satisfaction and quantify the downstream effect on customer satisfaction and financial performance," Oakley said.

Whose Job Is Internal Branding?

Since corporate public relations is often responsible for employee communications in general, it is a logical extension of the public relations function to have those handling marketing public relations take responsibility for communicating brand values to employees to help motivate them to deliver brand values to its customers.

However, internal branding is not the primary responsibility of MPR. It is primarily the responsibility of corporate management and ultimately falls under the responsibility of the Human Resources Department to be sure that employees' activities and incentives are aligned with the firm's goals. Careful coordination between corporate PR, MPR, and HR is critical to the success of internal branding. But the process can be a subtle one and hard to define.

Don Schultz elaborates in a recent article entitled, "Live the Brand": [11]

One of the interesting things about gaining internal brand support is that it's either uppermost in the minds of senior management or it's totally ignored. . . . Living the brand is not something management can get employee to do, no matter what the experts say. Living the brand is something employees have to want to do. It's their belief in the company, the leadership, the products and services, the future, and their part in it."

The Fish Story: Seattle's World Famous Pike Place Fish Market

The Pike Place Fish Market is a great example of a firm that has embraced the importance of employee involvement to a point where it has actually become more famous for its internal branding activities than for the products it sells. It has become world famous without buying a single advertisement. Its owner, John Yokoyama, has relied entirely on the enthusiasm of his employees to create a word-of-mouth "buzz" about the market. Soon news crews started showing up, and books were being written about the place. He now uses a fairly sophisticated Web site to convey his "fish philosophy" and occasionally even sell some fish! In his own words, here is John's story:

How We Became "World Famous"[12]

The first step for us at Pike Place Fish was to decide who we wanted to be. In one of our early Pike Place Fish meetings with Jim (our coach from bizFutures), we began an inquiry into "who do we want to be?" We wanted to create a new future for ourselves. One of the young kids working for me said, "Hey! Let's be World Famous!" At first I thought, "World Famous . . . what a stupid thing to say!" But the more we talked about it, the more we all got excited about being World Famous. So we committed to it. We added "World Famous" to our logo and had it printed on our shipping boxes.

Then, after a while, we asked ourselves, "What does this mean—being world famous?" And we created our own definition. For us it means going beyond just providing outstanding service to people. It means really being present with people and relating to them as human beings. You know, stepping outside the usual "we're in business and you're a customer" way of relating to people and intentionally being with them right now, in the present moment, person to person. We take all our attention off ourselves to be only with them . . . looking for ways to serve them. We're out to discover how we can make their day. We've made a commitment to have our customers leave with the experience of having been served. They experience being known and appreciated whether they buy fish or not. And it's not good enough just to want that—it takes an unrelenting commitment. We've made it our job to make sure that experience happens for every customer." To us, being 'World Famous' is a way of being. You can't manualize it. It gets created by each one of us, newly every time. It comes out differently for different people. It also depends on who the customer is . . . how they react. It's about taking care of people. We're always on the lookout for how we can make a difference in people's lives.

Originally we wondered, 'How are we going to become world famous? We don't have any money to advertise!' Jim told us we didn't have to know how to become world famous. . . .

Except for our Web site, we've never advertised. Without spending one penny, we've received more media exposure than many large companies that spend tons of money in advertising. All of this is the result of our continuing to come from our vision and be true to our commitment to make a difference for people—to be 'World Famous.' Our story is really a great testament to the power of commitment. We create intentions and commit to them. We never know how the results are going to show up. So, while it's true that we've intended everything that has happened, the events seem to come 'out of the blue.' Change really happens as Jim says, 'Naturally, just out of who you're being.'

People want to copy us—to do what we're doing. We keep telling them, 'Your success isn't in doing what we do; it's in discovering your own way. Don't do what we do—we made it all up . . . do what inspires you . . . make it up! . . . JUST BE IT. Your challenge is to 'just be' who you want to be . . . for free . . . just because you said so.

Procter & Gamble's Employees Living the Brand

Another example of a company that encourages its employees to live the brand is Procter & Gamble. One of the tools it uses is employee volunteer activities, and it proudly showcases them in its 2004 Contributions Report, proclaiming how its "employees are touching lives and improving life with their time and talents around the world."[13] A few of the examples it mentions:

In Belgium, a group of enthusiastic P&G employees and retirees spent a day at Les Salanganes, an organization that provides food, housing and necessities for children in need. In Indonesia, more than 100 employees volunteer their time and skills to help keep a center operational to provide health and nutrition services for more than 900 children and expectant mothers each month. They also make financial contributions to the center. Some of the program highlights include:

- Training locals to run the center so they can open more facilities in local villages.
- Providing free medical services to children.
- Establishing a library for all 26 elementary schools in the area.
- Constructing a public sanitation facility to provide safe water.
- Providing health and hygiene education to students.
- Promoting active lifestyles by coordinating athletic competitions.
- Providing scholarships for poor and disabled children to attend school.

In Korea, P&G employees participated in community service work in celebration of the 15th anniversary of doing business in Korea. Instead of having a party, employees put "Touching Lives, Improving Life" into action by doing volunteer work. Employees' volunteer activities included bathing and feeding disabled children as well as cleaning up a charity center. Employees coordinated a charity auction a few days before the volunteer day, where products donated by employees were sold.

McDonald's Chipotle Employees Living the Brand

In an article aimed at CEOs entitled "The CEO Refresher: Developing a Brand Centric Supply Chain," Thomas Marlow used the Chipotle chain as an example of employees who enthusiastically represent the brand: [14]

> A great brand that comes to mind for me is that of McDonald's Chipotle restaurants. What a great concept! Steve Ells, Founder & CEO, certainly embraced the philosophy of keeping things simple. Chipotle has great customer service, healthy and tasty food, a great atmosphere and a guacamole recipe that speaks of perfection, all at a reasonable price. The sense of teamwork found behind the counter would put the national football league (NFL) teams to shame. Their advertising concept reflects the "keeping things simple" idea as well with plain white backgrounds and clever and eye catching phrases. In a nutshell, what defines Chipotle is the consistency of service, from the cashier to the cleanliness of the bathrooms to hog farmers extraordinaire who collectively make up the "Porkutopia" who raise the free range pork to make their Carnitas tacos and burritos. I frequent Chipotle at least once or twice a week and I've never once known them to falter in their service. Chipotle is a company I defiantly brag about to my loved ones, friends and colleagues and say, "Hey, let's go eat at Chipotle."

This level of service and commitment from employees is no accident. McDonald's has invested a great deal into employee training, especially English lessons for its many non-English speaking employees. It also invests in cultural training for managers and employees alike, so they can better understand each other's needs and concerns. The result has been an increase in promotions among the line workers, and a highly motivated workforce.

Starbucks Employees Living the Brand

Marlow also ranks Starbucks as among the best in motivated employees:

> Truly successful companies seem to have every employee believing in, and being direct representatives of the "dream," if you will, the dream of a creating a great company. A great brand, that fuels the entrepreneur's motivation to work hours into the night and on through the day. Howard Schultz, Chief Global Strategist, Starbucks Coffee, has been able to achieve this throughout the Starbucks organization. He and his employees have developed and embraced the dream and vision of the Starbucks brand since he took over the company in 1987. Believe it or not, a barista behind the counter at a southern California store was the one that came up with the famous Frappaccino drink.
>
> I won't speak for all of us, but I believe that most adult humans gathered in the 48 states, and many abroad, have come to depend on that particular jolt of morning pick me up that Starbucks has shaped into their own unique "blend." Sure they have good coffee, but that's not what Starbucks is really serving. Starbucks serves up a great customer experience, a place to meet with friends before the Friday night movie or a place where business deals take place, as well as a good cup of coffee.[15]

How to Build This Level of Employee Enthusiasm

Don Schultz asks the all-important question, "How do you get this type of living, breathing, enthusiastic support from employees, channels, and other stakeholders? . . . A lot of it comes from leadership—people like Michael Dell, Herb Kelleher, and the late Sam Walton." But there are other important factors:[16]

> The other thing that builds the employees' desire to live the brand is reputation. Companies that have strong reputations for doing business the right way with their customers, suppliers, associates, and channels build this kind of culture and enthusiasm for living the brand.
>
> Another important element is trust, built up over time, that the company will "do the right thing." It will care for its customers. Care for its employees. Care for the communities in which it operates. Care for the environment in which it sells and markets. Care for others, not just itself and certainly not just for its senior managers.

A number of icons have fallen or at least become shaky recently—Enron, World-Com, Arthur Andersen, and a number of pharmaceutical companies with major product recalls, to name a few. All of these focused on the external brand—what was being touted to investors and customers. This is not to say that they did not have strong corporate cultures, but it would be interesting to explore their internal branding efforts to see how much of those efforts were directed toward protecting the customers' interests versus selling customers a bill of goods.

So we come full circle to the opening assertions of Scott Davis and Michael Dunn:[17] a brand-based corporate culture provides tangible reasons for employees to believe in the company (beyond its stock price), allows employees to understand how they fit into the corporate "big picture," and instills a sense of pride in employees. The marketing value in all this is that "the power of employees who are truly engaged as brand advocates is difficult for competitors to replicate,"[18] and, therefore, it provides the brand its one, true competitive advantage.

# MPR Tactics A to Z

The tactics that can be employed by MPR are limited only by the practitioner's imagination and ability to execute. In this chapter we will describe just a few of them that are frequently used to gain media and consumer attention for new and established products and services.

AWARDS have been used by sponsors to honor the worthwhile and the simply interesting: for example, best-dressed or best-coiffed.

In the 1980s, Blistex, Inc., of Oak Park, Illinois, manufacturer of lip-care products, conducted a public relations program designed to create a preference for its products by positioning Blistex as "the" authority on lip care. Blistex's Beautiful Lips Contest was a publicity feature that was perennially popular with both the print and broadcast media. Each year, "the lip-care experts" at Blistex selected a dozen people with the "World's Most Beautiful Lips." Photos of the winners and their citations were distributed to newspapers across the country, and the contest was covered extensively by radio and television. The popularity of the Beautiful Lips Contest resulted from combining names that made news with humorous citations. The Chicago Bureau Chief of the Associated Press told a meeting of the Publicity Club of Chicago that "Beautiful Lips is the kind of feature we are looking for," reminding his audience that AP must judge 600 to 800 stories a day. Because of the selection of foreign winners, the Beautiful Lips awards were featured in media all over the world, and company executives were interviewed by media in England, Canada, and Australia. The company's president received an article from one of the most widely circulated magazines in Japan from Blistex's Japanese distributor, with a note stating: "These kinds of PR activities are a great help for the brand."

BIRTHDAYS AND ANNIVERSARIES are a tried-and-true way to bring attention to your product.

OshKosh B'Gosh celebrated its centennial by conducting a search for the oldest bib overall.

Jell-o's celebration of its 100th birthday and made front-page news and all the TV networks. The company used the occasion to introduce a new flavor on a popular daytime talk show, publish a book, *Celebrating 100 Years of Jell-o*, and unveil a Jell-o exhibit at the New York Historical Society Museum.

Harley-Davidson celebrated 100 years in business in 2003 with a massive gathering of more than 250,000 bikers in Milwaukee, where the company is headquartered. In a front-page story, *The New York Times* described it as "a huge, choreographed event that turned the company's hometown into a sea of roaring motorcycles, hard rock bands, scruffy beards, leather vests, chaps and bikinis, and, of course, all products Harley."[1]

BLOG (short for *Weblog*) is a Web site for which an individual or group generates text, photos, multimedia files, and/or links.

BOOKS AND BOOKLETS of the consumer-friendly variety, such as General Mills' *Betty Crocker Cookbook* and Maytag's *Encyclopedia of Laundry*, have been published by consumer product companies for years. Scores of self-published recipes, helpful homemaker tips, and "how-to" booklets are published and offered to consumers every year by manufacturers.

Something new in book endorsements appeared in 2002, when well-known novelist Fay Weldon was hired by a famous jeweler to author a book called *The Bulgari Connection*. Her contract called for her to mention Bulgari jewelry at least a dozen times.

CONTESTS AND COMPETITIONS ranging from the serious to the whimsical, from the Pillsbury Bake-Off (discussed in Chapter 3 on Classic MPR) to Tide's Search for the Dirtiest Kids, are a good way to involve the public with the brand.

To celebrate the 50th anniversary of the largest-selling laundry detergent, Procter & Gamble staged a contest to find the Dirtiest Kid in America. The contest and the final event, a Stain-a-Thon in New York's Central Park, were widely covered in the broadcast and print media. They also provided a platform for the company to introduce a new and improved formulation of Tide.

IBM famously pitted Garry Kasparov, the world's greatest chess player, against a computer named Deep Blue. The match was front-page news and the stuff of late-night TV monologues. In addition to the billions of media impressions it generated, the final day's match was covered live on an IBM Internet site, attracting one million viewers. It was the largest audience that had ever visited an event on the net.

CHOTCHKES, otherwise known as trinkets and trash, are widely used in public relations to entice press and public alike.

Billions of T-shirts, sweatshirts, sweaters, caps, aprons, umbrellas, tote bags, and more are walking promotions for brands and branded sponsorships. So popular are these chotchkes that the sale of branded merchandise has become a miniature profit center for many companies. The Hard Rock Cafe is world famous because of its T-shirts.

Hardly a person leaves Anheuser-Busch's Busch Gardens theme parks without becoming a walking advertisement of his or her favorite A-B brand by buying a Budweiser, Michelob, or Busch cap, jacket, sweatshirt, or T-shirt.

Harley-Davidson shops are devoted exclusively to selling a wide variety of Harley-Davidson merchandise.

CHARACTERS AND CRITTERS have been endearing companies to consumers for decades.

Company characters, like Ronald McDonald, the second most-recognized figure to the children of the world (outranked only by Santa Claus), the Campbell Kids, Mr. Clean, the Energizer Bunny, Morris the Cat, and Ernie the Keebler Elf are highly visible and personalize a company to consumers. Costumed actors portraying these characters appear at events sponsored by the brand and frequently make store appearances. In 2004, Advertising Week was celebrated with the first five advertising characters inducted into a new Madison Avenue Walk of Fame. The winners selected by a national consumer election were Planters' Mr. Peanut, Kellogg's Tony the Tiger, the Aflac duck, the Pillsbury Doughboy, and the M&M's guys.

M&M/Mars sent its costumed M&M characters on a national media tour to generate consumer interest and media coverage of a consumer poll to select a new color M&M. They appeared in malls and supermarkets and at events like the Super Bowl and Mardi Gras in New Orleans. The live exposure and tremendous media coverage caused more than 10 million consumers to call or fax their votes.

Of all the vast array of promotional vehicles and programs used by Anheuser-Busch to carry the Budweiser name and colors to the public, the most famous are the Clydesdales. To celebrate the end of Prohibition, the promotional-minded August Busch, Jr., hitched up a team of Clydesdale horses and delivered a case of Budweiser to President Franklin D. Roosevelt. Since then, reports *The New York Times*, "the Clydesdales have been transformed into a highly visible marketing force for Budweiser. . . . The big horses have become one of the best-known corporate symbols in the world."

Today the company maintains three hitches, in St. Louis, in California, and in New Hampshire. Each appears in more than 100 parades and county fairs a year in response to requests by Anheuser-Busch's 950 wholesalers. The company says it cannot come close to accepting the thousands of appearance invitations received each year for the Clydesdales. Wherever they do appear, however, they are backed with advance publicity, feature stories, and local event coverage.

ENDORSEMENTS can also be helpful in brand building. Many brands have capitalized on third-party endorsements from respected organizations that support their market positioning. The endorsement of Crest toothpaste by the American Dental Association propelled the brand to category leadership. The dancin' California Raisins were greeted by mayors of major cities, where they entertained children at hospitals and consumers at supermarkets.

Personal endorsements, especially those of the unexpected kind, make news:

- Hollywood stars, such as Tom Hanks, Harrison Ford, and Cameron Diaz, thought it would be cool to arrive at the internationally televised 2003 Academy Award ceremonies in their new hybrid Toyota Prius cars. The car was quite a switch from the usual limos and elite sports cars. It was suitably high-tech, looked great, and made a statement about alternative sources of energy. It was no accident; Toyota handed out their hybrid electric cars to Hollywood stars to get attention from the fans and the media. *USA Today*, *People*, "Access Hollywood," "Entertainment Tonight," and "Good Morning America" all ran stories that picked up on the PR campaign theme, "On Oscar night, it's not what you wear, it's what you drive."
- Weight Watchers made news by hiring Sarah Ferguson, familiarly known as "Fergie," the former Duchess of York, as a spokesperson.

- Phoenix sheriff Joe Arpaio, who bills himself as "the toughest sheriff in America," asked to be the first customer at a new suburban Krispy Kreme doughnut shop. After downing his doughnut, the sheriff exclaimed before the TV cameras, "These doughnuts are so good they should be illegal." The company was so successful in getting publicity for its store openings that when the company went public, the prospectus noted that Krispy Kreme had been featured on more than 80 television shows.
- On the other hand, Jared Fogel became one of the best-known commercial spokespersons by shedding hundreds of pounds through exercise and a diet of low-fat Subway sandwiches. Fogel, who once weighed 435 pounds, was discovered when an article was written about him in the Indiana University daily student newspaper. The story was picked up by other newspapers and magazines. The Subway people read a story about Jared in *Men's Health* magazine, and they interviewed him and shot a test commercial, which led to his role as Subway's spokesperson in a long-running advertising campaign.
- Athletic endorsements are as old as the hills. We expect jocks to endorse cars, cereals, and sports gear in advertising, but they gain greater credibility when a celebrity athlete can talk to the media about how a product made a real difference in his life. The great golfer, Jack Nicklaus, who had been sidelined from play for a year, told the *Today* show audience that a Stryker ceramic hip replacement device had relieved his pain and enabled him to return to championship play. Similarly, Coach Dan Reeves, who suffered a heart attack while coaching the Atlanta Falcons, became the spokesperson for Zocor, a cholesterol-lowering medication, on how to prevent and survive heart attacks. After the respective publicity launches, Nicklaus and Reeves appeared in advertising. Coach Mike Ditka, a tough guy in any man's book, made news when he told us how he "stays in the game" by using Levitra, an erectile dysfunction pharmaceutical.

EXHIBITS range from the permanent exhibitions in high-traffic locations like Walt Disney World's Epcot Center and Chicago's Museum of Science and Industry, to traveling exhibits, such as Campbell Soup's soup tureen collection and Bally Corporation's exhibit of lottery memorabilia to interactive exhibits in shopping malls.

When Chicago's Field Museum of Natural History acquired the largest and best-preserved Tyrannosaurus ever found, McDonald's opened the McDonald's Fossil Preparation Lab, which let visitors watch experts work on the massive preparation project. The company also traveled two life-sized casts of Sue throughout the country and the world.

FAN CLUBS, once the province of entertainers, now encompass the fans of products ranging from Barbie Dolls and Mustangs to Harley-Davidson motorcycles. Fan paraphernalia typically includes membership cards and certificates, brand-merchandise offers, newsletters, and booklets. Periodic fan club meetings keep interest high and generate publicity and word-of-mouth.

Harley-Davidson enthusiasm has elevated fandom to cult status. The company created the Harley Owners Group in 1983. It now has thousands of members, who receive a monthly magazine, all manner of pins and patches, and participate in state and national "Hog" rallies.

GRAND OPENINGS can range from plant tours and ribbon-cutting ceremonies for the opening of locally franchised restaurants or stores, to black-tie galas run by department stores to benefit charities.

HOTLINES have proliferated with the advent of 800 and 900 telephone lines. One of the best-known is Butterball's Turkey Hotline, which has answered thousands of calls from consumers looking for new and better ways to prepare turkey dinners and has become Butterball's principal marketing tool.

JUNKETS are used to bring the media to the story. They often include trips to out-of-town locations to attend special events, new product introductions, or to tour new facilities. While all-expenses-paid trips were once prevalent, today, most national media assign reporters and pay their way for "must-cover" events.

More than 500 journalists were among 2,500 guests who attended the unveiling ceremonies for Windows 95 at Microsoft's headquarters in Redmond, Washington. Interviews with Bill Gates by the TV networks and print media were beamed to media all over the world.

MEDIA TOURS in person or on TV via satellite are frequently conducted by marketers to maximize exposure for new and established products in key markets. The spokesperson may be a company executive or a celebrity endorser.

Food companies have effectively used spokespersons, often a famous chef or celebrity who can prepare dishes on the shows they visit. The media favor products that can be demonstrated on TV, such as high-tech devices, consumer electronics, or videogames.

The media tour is almost always used by publishers to bring attention to new books. Authors of current affairs books vie to appear on national news magazine and interview shows like "Hardball," "Sixty Minutes," "Larry King Live," "Charlie Rose" on PBS, and "Book Chat" on C-SPAN, in addition to major market media.

A popular variation of the live major market tour is the satellite media tour, in which dozens of pre-arranged appearances for the spokesperson are consecutively booked with media outlets in target markets. The guest executive or celebrity talks directly with a local TV reporter. These feeds often incorporate a video news release, especially with an exciting and demonstrable new product.

MIDNIGHT MADNESS helped make Windows 95 a success for Bill Gates when it went on sale in stores at midnight.

Scholastic, the US publisher of the Harry Potter books, encouraged hundreds of bookstores to hold midnight madness events for each new book of the phenomenally popular Harry Potter series. The publisher provided guidelines on how to run an event that had kiddies lined up, dressed up in wizard attire, to be the first on their block to buy the latest installment and maybe appear on television. Harry Potter midnight madness was widely covered by local TV and newspapers from coast to coast.

MUSEUMS. In 1990 the Coca-Cola Company opened a freestanding three-story museum in Atlanta called "The World of Coca-Cola." The museum, which is visited by as many as a half-million people a year, houses more than 1,000 items of memorabilia, exhibits, movies, a high-tech fountain that shoots a stream of Coca-Cola 20 feet in the air, and what the company calls "the most remarkable Coke sign ever created."

When it opened, *The New York Times* pointed out that "the Coca-Cola museum is the latest—and perhaps most ambitious—example of the growing use of corporate historical exhibits as promotional tools." *The Times* said that "seeking fresh ways to reach an advertising-bombarded public, companies are converting themselves into nothing less than tourist attractions through a confluence of marketing, education, and entertainment."[2]

Binney & Smith maintains a Crayola Crayon Hall of Fame that attracts thousands of visitors to the company's headquarters in Easton, Pennsylvania. When the Spam Museum in Austin, Minnesota, opened, it was covered by NBC anchor Tom Brokaw and a host of media who were there to celebrate the event. The museum featured more than a dozen Spam exhibits, a conveyor belt that keeps cans of Spam forever circling overhead, a video theater that plays Spam commercials, and even a classic Monty Python sketch that pokes fun at the product. The sketch inspired a Broadway musical called *Monty Python's Spamalot*, which opened in 2005 and won several Tony awards.

NEWS RELEASES, or feature stories written in ready-to-use journalistic style, are the basic tool of public relations. Releases distributed to newspapers are often still called press releases. They are the basic building block of a press kit, which includes other materials, such as fact sheets, backgrounders, bios, CDs, and photos. News releases may be delivered in person or handed out at new conferences or press parties. They can also be mailed, transmitted for a fee by outfits like The Business Wire, or e-mailed directly to journalists. Today, most reporters prefer to receive news releases by e-mail.

NEWSLETTERS are used to communicate news and keep products, places, and personalities top-of-mind among consumer and trade audiences. In recent years, many hardcopy newsletters have been replaced by on-line newsletters. Companies build mail and e-mail lists from in-pack buyer questionnaires, visitors to company exhibits and events, people who write for booklets offered in publicity, and 800-number callers.

PODCAST distributes audio and video programs over the Internet. The term was devised to describe the technology used to transfer content from Web sites to consumers using iPods—thus the term *pod*—or other devices such as mp3 that support the audio technology.

PRODUCT PLACEMENT in movies and on television shows has become a miniature industry, ever since Reese's Pieces achieved a remarkable sales boost when the candy was featured in the smash hit movie *E.T.* The marriage of brand names and Hollywood films has a long history. But marketers really took notice when an extraterrestrial visitor called E.T. took a fancy to Reese's Pieces in one of the top-grossing films (and, subsequently, videos) of all time.[3]

While some companies may provide products free and take their chances that their brands might end up on the cutting-room floor, the trend has been toward so-called "back-end promotions" incorporating PR and advertising. Companies may pay promotional-consideration fees for critical product placements in films with big box office potential. Others provide promotion of the film in pre-release product promotions and advertising in exchange for product exposure in the film. This exposure is critical to the success of the film since the box office fate of most films is decided on the first weekend of release. In the movie business, however, there are no guarantees of success, and a product promotion may die with the film.

Product placement has become more pervasive in television as 30-second commercials become less effective and networks look for ways to give advertisers more exposure within the context of entertainment. Despite much criticism, product placement is likely to be here to stay, not only because advertisers are looking to supplement their network television buys, but also because it saves studios money and helps them promote pictures. Also realism requires it. In portraying real-life situations, actors drive brand-name cars, shop in real stores, eat and drink brand-name products, and wear brand-name clothing. Their kitchen and bathroom shelves are not filled with Brand X products. Generics did not sell in the supermarket and don't work in the movies on TV.

PUBLIC SERVICE PROJECTS identify brands with the concerns of consumers as individuals and members of society at large. Some of these programs bring people closer to products by relating the sponsor to issues that consumers care about.

America's largest organized litter cleanup, the Glad Bag-a-Thon, is sponsored by Glad Wraps and Glad Bags in cooperation with Keep America Beautiful affiliates. In every market, citizens are mobilized to clean up sections of their city by collecting trash in Glad Bags. The public relations effort encourages civic and community leaders to organize their constituencies to support the program. The program is endorsed by mayors who pitch in collecting trash, and the Glad Bag-a-Thon is almost always covered by local TV and newspapers.

PUBLIC SERVICE ANNOUNCEMENTS (PSAS) are used by companies and trade groups to identify themselves with subjects and issues of interest to the public. Widely used on both radio and television, they link commercial sponsors with good causes, ranging from literacy to fire safety to pet adoption.

RADIO TRADE-FOR-MENTION CONTESTS generate frequent on-air product mentions, which are traded for prizes provided by the manufacturer.

A twist on this theme is the remote radio broadcast where the on-air personalities run a contest that takes them and a number of listeners to an exotic locale where they broadcast every day. When Pat worked in the mobile satellite communications industry, she helped organize a number of these events on cruise ships, on remote islands, and other locales that needed some high-tech support for the broadcast. They continue to be popular events with opportunities for tie-ins with local travel agencies, airlines, auto dealers and the like.

ROAD SHOWS can make headlines, attract trade interest, and generate marketplace excitement. They are a trademark of the automotive industry, and are often used for what they call "long-lead" media—usually magazines that must obtain the story several months in advance of the publication date in order to meet production deadlines. But they can also be very effective in promoting coverage of a new car launch with national and local media:

> The road show is still alive and well in the twenty-first century. In 2004, Mercedes Benz USA conducted a two-month, 12-city road show to showcase its cars to consumers and the media. In each city, the company set up three test tracks, one for off-road SUVs, one for convertibles and roadsters, and one for "Driving Thrills." The "Driving Thrills" track included simulated icy roads, twisty corners, and sand. A Mercedes spokesperson told *PR Week* that the event was designed to "put cars in a lifestyle environment so people can see how the cars reflect their lives." Mercedes erected a "lifestyles pavilion" at each event with home-design products, fashions, and cutting-edge technology that complemented the cars. The company sent out 800,000 invitations to consumers and created the inevitable Web site, where consumers could register to attend the event in their city.[4]

RESEARCH conducted by trusted institutions can generate excitement about new products and generate new news about old products. News of a study conducted by Harvard Medical School that revealed that Ocean Spray Cranberry Cocktail Juice could prevent urinary tract infections generated publicity in consumer media and caused a sales surge, opening a new market for Ocean Spray among older women. News about new benefits of using aspirin appears with frequency as findings from new research are published. Research undertaken on behalf of any organization can become the subject of media coverage. This is discussed further under "Surveys."

SAMPLING of products is a longstanding weapon in the marketing arsenal. New products are mailed to residences in selected zip codes, given away in stores and on street corners, and packed with established products.

> MPR sampling is designed for a different purpose. Sampling (or in the case of high-ticket items, loaning) products to reporters has long been standard public relations practice. Increasingly, public relations has provided samples to other opinion leaders and taste makers.

> Another function of MPR sampling is to gain visibility. Having the right product in the right place at the right time will result in trial and start word-of-mouth endorsement. It can also offer an opportunity to reach a larger audience if a strong publicity angle can be created around the sampling occasion.

> In 1981, millions of people got their first taste of the new sweetener NutraSweet in, of all things, a gumball. They were given away at high-traffic events like state fairs. In the first year, nearly 3 million people wrote the company for a free sample sleeve of four brightly colored NutraSweet-sweetened gumballs. Gumballs became the brand's signature and the one thing that everyone identified with NutraSweet.

> Halls Cough Suppressant Tablets, a 60-year-old brand, is the number-one-selling brand in the US and the world. With the exception of new flavor additions, there is very little news about Halls. Warner-Lambert set out to create news about Halls

Cough Suppressant benefits. The company distributed a survey to 2,500 patrons at three leading symphony orchestras to determine the most distracting audience noises encountered during symphony performances. Whispering, coughing, and sniffling ranked first, second, and third, respectively, followed by rattling of candy wrappers, humming along, and constant moving about in one's seat. Publicity about the survey was released in conjunction with an innovative anti-noise campaign launched at the onset of the concert season. In an effort to create "Silent Nights at the Symphony" during winter's cough-and-cold season, Warner-Lambert began providing complimentary wax-wrapped Halls Cough Suppressant Tablets to patrons of major symphony orchestras. In an article about the Chicago Symphony Orchestra season, music critic John von Rhein of *The Chicago Tribune* wrote:

> Perhaps the most intriguing item on the press release heralding the 98th Chicago Symphony Orchestra season is the news that Warner-Lambert now will provide free cough lozenges to those attending Orchestra Hall performances. The lozenges, available in five flavors, will be wrapped in noiseless wax paper and dispensed in all lobby areas. Warner-Lambert has performed a similar service with other orchestras across the nation and reports considerable reduction in coughing noises during concerts. Any way you unwrap it, this is a historic boon to musical mankind. Cough-free Copland! Low-noise Lizst! Silent Schubert! The prospects are endless and tantalizing. If the idea clicks, Warner-Lambert will have earned the deathless gratitude of the silent majority of subscribers, not to mention the long-suffering performers on stage."[5]

STUNTS have been employed by the entertainment industry to bring attention to their attractions since P.T. Barnum's day. They are frequently used by companies to introduce new products. M&M/ Mars bathed the Empire State building in blue to announce the winner in a widely publicized promotion to select a new color M&M. The same building was bathed in the red, yellow, blue, and green of the Windows 95 logo on launch day. The worldwide celebration of the new millennium on New Year's Eve in New York's Times Square featured the lowering of a specially designed Waterford Crystal globe, an event that was seen on television around the world.

A mega-stunt that made headline news was the giveaway of a new Pontiac G6 car to every member of the studio audience of daytime TV's top-rated *The Oprah Winfrey Show*. To launch her 19th season on television in 2004, Oprah surprised her audience of 276 people by presenting each of them with a box containing the keys to a new car. The entire audience followed Oprah to the studio parking lot, where they found their cars wrapped with huge red ribbons. Pontiac, a division of General Motors, designed the G6 specifically with women in mind. When they learned that the season premiere show was built around the theme of "dreams come true," Pontiac marketing officials contacted the show, offering the mass car giveaway. Messages on *Oprah.com* and summer telecasts of the show identified viewers who desperately needed new wheels. Both the show and Pontiac were after big publicity, and they not only got front-page newspaper stories and news magazine articles, but also extensive television news coverage on all the national and cable news network stations that carry the show and those that don't.

Coverage included 700 print stories and 600 broadcast news stories, which gener-ated the equivalent of more than $100 million in advertising time and space. The cost of the cars was a small price to pay for the kind of exposure with its target audience that Pontiac gained for a new model car.

Sometimes, however, stunts can go bad. When the president of Rival Dog Food appeared at a press event to introduce a new doggie meatball, the president ate one, but the dog refused. The story, as reported by the Associated Press, appeared in hundreds of papers.

SURVEYS not only provide marketers with valuable consumer information, but they also give MPR programs quotable material favored by the news media. Surveys on fashions, favorite foods, and lifestyles are widely publicized.

Orkin even releases an annual survey on cities where termites eat the most wood. Survey results, supported by charts and graphs, are a staple of USA Today, the na-tion's only national newspaper, and are frequently reported by newspapers and network newscasts.

When research in the cruise industry undertaken a few years ago to learn what passengers knew about making telephone calls to and from a cruise ship, some of the more interesting and controversial findings became the subject of a press con-ference at a major travel industry show that ultimately generated dozens of na-tional news articles, including a front page story in the travel section of the Sunday New York Times. The sponsoring firm's shore-to-ship telephone traffic more than doubled within a few months following all the publicity.

SYMPOSIA, SEMINARS, AND TELECONFERENCES are sponsored by companies to discuss trends, reveal research, and stimulate discussion related to the company's products and consumers. These events have been especially effective in introducing new pharmaceu-tical products and revealing new research extolling the benefits of the sponsor's products.

VEHICLES, including hot air balloons, sailing ships, planes, trains, and racing automo-biles, are rigged up by companies to gain visibility for their brands. The granddaddy of them all, the Goodyear Blimp, always seems to appear where the action is.

J.K. Rowling, author of the Harry Potter books, toured her native England aboard a train called the "Hogwarts Express" to meet the fans and the press on the publi-cation of her third book in the series.

The United States Postal Service outfitted a train called the "Celebrate the Cen-tury Express" to visit 100 US cities on an eighteen-month journey across the country. The train housed a restored railway post office, an exhibit car displaying stamps and historical displays to promote the post office, and a series of "Cele-brate the Century" stamps that portrayed historical highlights of the twentieth century, decade by decade.

Kids who grew up in the 1950s recall the time they saw a 23-foot, four-wheeled hot dog come down the street in their hometown. The first of Oscar Mayer's fa-mous Weinermobiles hit the streets of America in 1936, and subsequent models visited hundreds of US cities until the late 1970s, leaving behind memories and a bit of marketing Americana.

In the 1980s, the company used the last drivable vehicles for two anniversary tours. They were so successful in attracting attention and headlines that the company brought back the Oscar Mayer Weinermobile "by popular demand." A fleet of Weinermobiles still tours cities across America.

The revival of the Weinermobile was tagged by the company as "a return to family values and traditions and a familiar link between parents who remember the Weinermobile and their children who are seeing it for the first time." The tour has been updated in a number of ways through the years. Little Oscar, the company's goodwill ambassador who escorted earlier Weinermobiles to such activities as parades and grocery-store openings, retired and was replaced by Oscar Mayer "Hotdoggers," selected from hundreds of graduating college seniors who compete for the jobs. Their job is to drive the sleek, futuristic-looking, new Weinermobiles, "painted weiner-red with a splash of mustard-yellow on a lightly toasted bun," around the country; hand out balloons, stickers, and buttons; and make special appearances at promotional events, charity functions, festivals, parades, picnics, ball games, and nursing homes.

The premiere of the 2005 musical *Monty Python's Spamalot* featured a visit from the world famous "Spamobile" and free cans of Spam to the first 100 ticket buyers.

VENUES where events are staged could enhance the news. Walt Disney Company is particularly adept at selecting such locations. The company held a mass preview of *Pocahontas* for 100,00 lottery winners on four giant screens at a free-by-invitation event in New York's Central Park. A few years later, Disney company invited 2,000 people to preview the action film, *Pearl Harbor* at an open air theater set up on the deck of a nuclear aircraft carrier at the real Pearl Harbor in Hawaii.

VIDEO NEWS RELEASES (VNRs) are short, pre-packaged news stories created for television. They are used to transmit newsworthy product news and event sponsorships to television networks and stations both in edited and extended (B-roll) form, allowing users to customize or localize their reports. Most local TV stations now use VNRs regularly. VNRs, which were once shipped or delivered live to TV stations and networks are now mostly downloaded from a satellite downlink. Some marketers also send audio news releases to radio stations on tape.

WEB SITES have become the standard means for individuals, organizations, companies, venues, government, and non-government agencies to transmit a wide variety of information to on-line visitors twenty four hours a day. The Web is used in MPR to provide information about products and services and event sponsorships. Web sites have become a principal source of information both to consumers and the media.

The Butterball Talk-Line Web site, for example, receives millions of hits every year from consumers who need cooking help.

Most company Web sites today house recent news releases, press kits, pictures, and commercials, as well as general and historical information. Companies use the Web to stage on-line interviews and media conferences. Much advertising includes a Web address where consumers can get more information than can be crammed into an ad. Network, public television, and local newscasts typically refer viewers to their Web sites for additional information on subjects in the news.

Web sites have become a mainstay of the entertainment industry where they are used not only to hype films or live events, but also to entice consumers to participate in promotional offers, contests, and games. The Web played a key role in the success of *The South Beach Diet*, one of the best-selling diet books of all time. *The Wall Street Journal* reported: "Do an Internet search for 'low-carb diet' and, chances are, you'll come up with a link to 'The South Beach Diet' Web site." The paper reported that "the Web blitz is one of several unconventional marketing techniques that helped transform 'South Beach' from a regional diet to a national juggernaut. The diet got one of its most unusual boosts from an aggressive Web campaign that has persuaded hundreds of thousands of dieters to join an on-line community."[6]

WEEKS, MONTHS AND DAYS are used by companies and trade associations to focus consumer attention and provide media with a reason to feature their products. Tom Harris's first public relations assignment was to promote National Hot Dog Month. "Chase's Calendar of Events" lists hundreds of special days, weeks, and months.

Here's a sampling of national months that promote food products:

- January is both National Soup Month and National Hot Tea Month.
- May is National Egg Month, National Hamburger Month, National Salad Month, and National Salsa Month.
- June is National Frozen Yogurt Month, National Candy Month, and National Iced Tea Month.
- In October, National Pasta Month, National Pork Month, and National Caramel Month is celebrated.

12 Getting Coverage in Traditional Media

Corporate executives will often notice a positive story about a competitor and ask PR for similar coverage, as if it were merely a matter of picking up the phone and demanding equal time. In fact, it's part art, part science, and, in today's media world, part magic. For every one of the "wizards" who consistently "get ink" or "get a media hit," countless others have limited success. They may blame the media's lack of interest or the product's lack of news appeal for the failure. That might be partially true, but the process of getting free media coverage can be made easier and more productive with an understanding of the nature of traditional media and the motives behind its key players. In this chapter, we discuss how the media landscape has changed over the past 15 years and provide some tips for effectively targeting and reaching this media.

The Changing Media Landscape

The proliferation of new technologies and media options over the past decade has greatly complicated advertising decision-making, but it offers tremendous opportunities for public relations. These opportunities could hardly have been imagined a few decades ago when the big three television networks dominated all forms of mass media and such well-established national magazines as *Life, Look, Collier's,* and *The Saturday Evening Post* faded from existence because they found it impossible to compete with television. As they disappeared, so did many opportunities for product publicity.

It is a very different competitive landscape today. Magazines are back with a vengeance—even *Life* has attempted a comeback—and the "big three" TV networks have now become the not-so-big seven—ABC, CBS, NBC, Fox, WB, UPN, and PAX. Or, perhaps it is more accurate to say, "the big 4 and not so big 3." *Advertising Age*[1] lists the advertising revenues of the seven English-language broadcast networks as:

NBC: $6,403 million
CBS: $5,405 million
ABC: $4,488 million
Fox: $2,960 million
WB: $ 857 million
UPN: $ 468 million
PAX: $ 224 million

Public relations focus has broadened to permanently include cable TV and the many new opportunities to pitch one of the growing number of 24/7 news channels such as CNN, Fox News, CNBC, MSNBC, the Bloomberg Financial Network, and even the Weather Channel. These programs have huge "news holes" to fill every day and are more open to featuring a company's news story, with its product as the "star," than the broadcast news programs with such limited time slots.

On the print side of the landscape, daily newspaper readership continues to decline. The Newspaper Association of America reports that fewer than 54 percent of all adults read a weekday newspaper on an average day and 63 percent read a Sunday newspaper on an average Sunday in 2003.[2] To address this loss in traditional readers, the newspapers have created new venues for readers, such as on-line versions of the paper that continuously report throughout the day for the most current news coverage. Like cable news programs, these on-line versions often have the same need to fill large news holes. Many daily newspapers have also introduced new, targeted versions of their papers aimed at younger readers or suburbanites. Some have added weekly supplements to focus on entertainment or home improvement, while others, such as the *Chicago Tribune*, now distributes its colorful, tabloid-size *Red Eye* to commuters and college students who seem pleased with its easy-to-read news synopses and heavy focus on entertainment news.

Magazines have also experienced major changes over the past few years. According to Jeff Bercovici of *Media Life* Magazine:[3]

> While total magazine circulation, which rose steadily for decades, has finally begun falling, helped along by the proliferation of competing content on the Internet and cable TV, readership of 171 continuously published titles increased 5.3 percent among adults from 1998 to 2002, according to a new report by (Media-Mark Research, Inc.—MRI).
>
> That's faster than the 4.4 percent growth of the US adult population during the same period, according to MRI, which based its report on an analysis of more than 26,000 at-home interviews, conducted annually. The magazine study attributes the improvement to increases in the average number of readers per copy, or pass-along readership.

New Media Habits and Multi-tasking

One of the most significant changes in media habits over the past decade has been the phenomenon of multi-tasking—using multiple media at the same time. According to Forrester Research,[4] today's media consumers typically split their attention whenever they use any form of media. Four out of five television viewers are doing something else as they watch. A majority of Web, print media, and radio consumers act similarly.

Citing similar findings, the Media Center at the American Press Institute[5] found that three quarters of US television viewers also read the newspaper at the same time and that two thirds of television viewers go on-line while watching TV. Twenty percent of newspaper readers say they also read Internet news blogs as a news source. In many ways, this is great news for public relations, because it provides many more opportunities to get company messages across. It is not such good news for advertising, since brand managers may not want to pay the same high advertising rates for viewers who are only marginally focused on their programs and commercials.

Other Media Habits of Interest

According to the 2004 edition of the Veronis Suhler Stevenson Communications Industry Forecast,[6] media supported by consumers (through paid subscriptions and direct purchases) continued the trend of taking market share away from media supported by advertisers. The change is driven by increased time spent with the Internet, home videos, and videogames as well as multi-tasking.

Other areas experiencing growth included the entertainment field, fueled by strong growth in the DVD segment and interactive entertainment segments, in many cases extending revenues from full-length feature films by creating interactive video games based on them.

One of the most dramatic changes in the media landscape over the past decade has been the decline of the importance of network news. While network television had an exclusive hold on 95 percent of TV viewers through the late 1970s, that percentage was cut by more than 50 percent as cable TV found its footing in the late 1990s. Nowhere was this felt more than in the once venerable network TV newsrooms. In 2002 *The New York Times Sunday Magazine* did an extensive piece on the declining power of the network TV anchors and predicted the "coming disappearance" of the evening news.[7]

But despite these declines, the collective audience for the three nightly newscasts is still larger—at 30 million viewers—than that of most prime-time entertainment programs—24 million for a top-rated sitcom. And they continue to turn a profit. According to the *Chicago Tribune*,[8] evening news is still a cash cow, with each of the big three evening news broadcasts generating more than $118 million in ad revenues in the first nine months of 2004. That article ultimately concluded that "network news will be around as long as networks are around."

But regardless of their long-term health, they have become a difficult target for achieving public relations mentions, especially since the 2001 attack on the World Trade Center. This difficulty is partly due to a more somber approach to the news and growing criticism that the news programs had allowed too much sensationalism and fluff to invade the programs. But it is also due to commercial pressures that have shrunk the newscasts' editorial time to 18 to 19 minutes, from 21 to 22 minutes 15 years ago, putting pressure on them to only cover the most important news stories of the day.

Morning News Opportunities

The other bastion of public relations mentions on broadcast TV has historically been the morning news programs, which have always been a better target for MPR campaigns than the evening news, because they are four times as long (two hours compared to a half hour), and their formatting has always leaned more toward softer news than their evening counterparts.

So pervasive were MPR product placements in television—especially the morning news programs—that in the late 1980s *Advertising Age* commissioned Northwestern University's Medill School of Journalism to find out how many "free plugs" occurred during the average broadcast day. Students viewed tapes of consecutive 24-hour-broadcast days of each of the Big Three networks, recording every brand mention they heard or saw. In a single day of programming, they found 818 instances of a recognizable product or mention of a brand or corporate name. News programs accounted for 360 (44 percent) of the brand-name inclusions; variety shows had 199 mentions; and news features, 117. The greatest number of mentions of products and brands came during the early morning news programs, that is, NBC's "Today," ABC's "Good Morning America," and "CBS This Morning" (as it was then called).[9]

Today, these morning news programs are still important targets for MPR activities, but they have changed significantly over that past few years. Although their collective viewership remains significantly below that at the evening news, in May 2004, *The New York Times*[7] reported that the audience size for these programs was growing as the audience for the evening news programs has been shrinking: NBC's "Today" with 6.3

million viewers; ABC's "Good Morning America" with 5.1 million viewers; and CBS's "The Early Show" with 3 million viewers. In addition to their increased audience numbers, their profits were way up, making them secure elements in the broadcast TV lineup for years to come.

But while this should be positive news for public relations practitioners, these shows, too, have seen a significant decline in public relations placements over the past few years. The reasoning, however, is very different than for the evening news programs.

These morning news programs have become the primary vehicles for capturing promotional synergies from the ever-growing business of media mergers and acquisitions. NBC is owned by General Electric, ABC is owned by Walt Disney Company, and CBS is owned by Viacom. All three of these companies own a wide array of other media outlets—cable TV networks, publishing companies, radio stations, record labels, movie studios, theme parks, etc., and in the early days of the acquisitions they were criticized by investors for not taking advantage of the logical opportunities for cross-promotion. They are criticized no more—or at least not by investors.

It is a significant challenge for a public relations person to pitch a story angle to any of these programs today, because there is little room in the line-up after featuring the latest cast-off from the previous evening's reality TV show, featuring the musical artist from its parent firm's record label, hyping a book being published by one of its sister companies, or featuring the actors of one of its related film deals.

In one blatant cross-promotion in the spring of 2004, "Today" showed a lengthy excerpt of an interview that Katie Couric would be doing on "Dateline NBC" later that night. The persons being interviewed were fellow NBC employees—the cast of the popular NBC sitcom "Frasier," which happened to be broadcasting its final episode later that week.

This practice of cross-promotion is not without its critics. Media analyst Tom Wolzien, at Sanford C. Bernstein & Company, told the *New York Times*, "The question is, at what point do you start turning off the audience by doing too much pandering?"[10] But while it remains to be seen whether the morning news programs will start toning these efforts down in the future or increasing them, the challenge for public relations professionals hoping to crack into the line-up is to make their story pitches fit the style and format of the program, make the story angle truly unique, useful, or heart-warming, and offer them as exclusives, or at least, morning exclusives, which seems to spark the competitive nature of their producers.

Other MPR Opportunities in Television

Despite the challenges of broadcast television, the fragmentation of the television audience has wide implications for marketing public relations. The options for exposure have been increased numerically, and the changing nature of television programming has led to greatly expanded opportunities. Independents and cable have all expanded time slots for reality-based programming, as have affiliates in non-network time.[11]

Inexpensive-to-produce, non-scripted programs, particularly talk shows that command large audiences, are made to order for guests to discuss product-related subjects. Local TV news outlets are another opportunity for product mentions. Since advertising on local news programming is the major source of station income, news programming has been extended with noon news, afternoon news, and expanded early evening news.

With more time available, stations are supplementing hard news coverage with more 'lighter side of the news" interviews and features. A company-sponsored guest preparing a recipe on the noon news or a brand-sponsored event covered on the evening news is not unusual.

Cable TV Opportunities

The cable networks have opened major opportunities for marketing public relations. This is particularly true of CNN (Cable News Network), which created 24-hour news coverage in the 1980s and quickly expanded into an international version. It is now one of the most widely watched news networks in the world. CNN and ESPN (Entertainment and Sports Network) are seen in virtually all 73 million cable households. Moreover, CNN has expanded into a huge franchise of networks consisting of:

- CNN International
- CNN Money
- CNN Airport Network
- CNN en Espanol
- CNN Radio
- CNN en Espanol RADIO

The news services can also be downloaded to hand-held digital assistants and mobile telephones for up-to-the-minute news.

There are many other cable networks are of interest to public relations practitioners, including Bloomberg Television, a 24-hour business and financial news channel that targets serious investors via 10 networks in 7 languages, reaching more than 200 million homes around the world. CNBC (Consumer News and Business Channel) from NBC is another important new outlet for product news as is NBC's joint venture with Microsoft, MSNBC.

One of the great advantages to getting a product placement hit on one of these 24-hour all-news programs is that they regularly repeat certain features, so there is a much greater chance of a product message being seen multiple times a day by whole new audiences. This is particularly true of CNN's Headline News and the stories that run on its Airport Network. In addition, there are times that some of the partnered networks will share resources and staff, so a story that appears on MSNBC or CNBC could find its way onto the NBC network if it is considered compelling enough.

Several features of cable programming distinguish it from broadcast television; the most important are that cable television can carry more bandwidth, that it can better control who can or cannot receive a signal than broadcast television can, and that, because it does not use the public airwaves, it does not have the same FCC restrictions on adult-oriented content such as nudity and strong language.

The greater bandwidth allows for 10 to 20 times as many channels as broadcast TV, and now 100 channels or more are now the norm for most cable operators. The bandwidth also allows for coding signals and having decoding equipment in the homes to enable subscription-based premium channels and pay-per-view services. Because it is a paid service—with charges based on the number and perceived quality of the channels available—audience numbers tend to be smaller, so entire channels can be dedicated to more specialized programming (such as gardening, animals, food, and specialized sports).

This has a positive side for both advertising and public relations. Advertising costs are significantly lower than for most broadcast programs, partly because of the smaller number of viewers per channel, but also partly because it is supported by paid subscriptions. And, in addition to the lower cost, advertisers are able to pinpoint their targets by sponsoring much more specialized programming, compared to the mass appeal programs on most broadcast stations.

The public relations opportunities are also wide open on these specialized cable channels. Much of the programming is done as inexpensively as possible, so the producers of the shows seem to be very agreeable to blatant product placement. Home improvement shows are not the least bit shy about sending people out to The Home Depot to pick up supplies, asking a crew member to "Swiffer" the furniture (while prominently holding the package of dusters in front of the camera), or walking around in every episode drinking a large cup of Starbucks coffee. The Food Network seems to have a very large segment of programming every week made up almost entirely of video news releases and full-length glamour pieces on how a particular food is made or giving its history. Since these placements are paid for, they are walking a fine line between advertising and PR, but, as was mentioned in Chapter 2, the growing use of TiVo and other digital video recorders that are able to bypass commercials will only serve to increase this type of programming in the future. (There is an interesting footnote to the TiVo story. Beginning in March 2005, TiVo users will begin to see static pop-up ads when they zip through TV commercials—perhaps a logo for an advertiser or a message about the product.)

Booking a TV Guest Appearance

One of the most reliable ways to place a person into a news story is to include them in a video news release where they have had time to rehearse and put their comments on tape. Sometimes this is done as part of a Q&A session provided at the end of some B-roll (background) footage. The spokesperson might also be the subject of a satellite media tour, (Chapter 11 on MPR Tactics) where several prearranged remote appearances, via satellite video conference, are consecutively booked with media outlets in target markets. The spokesperson talks directly with a local TV reporter (or sometimes with a producer who serves as a stand-in and the reporter's questions are later edited in).

Placing someone live on a news program is much more difficult and can be risky, since there is no guarantee that the reporter will stick to agreed-upon questions in advance. But despite the risks, there are plenty of individuals who hope to gain such an appearance, and television producers now routinely conduct pre-screening interviews to determine if they will make good on-air guests. Unfortunately, some of these pre-screens do not take place until the executive is already in the studio ready to go. According to MediaChannel founder and executive editor Danny Schechter, in an interview with the *Journalists Speak Out* newsletter,[12] here are some of the things spokespeople should keep in mind:

1. "It's not your job to be objective." That's the reporter's job. Your job is to get your point across.

2. "Know your role, and play only that part." Usually there is a pro and con side being presented, and you are being asked to represent one of those sides. If you want to remain in a neutral, middle camp, you probably should not be going on air.

3. "Swallow your pride." Many of the news reporters have huge egos and are looking for someone to dominate. If you want to be on the show, you'll need to back down and appear to be non-threatening (at least in the pre-interview).

4. "Simplify, simplify, simplify." Television is not a good medium for presenting complicated ideas. You should be able to condense the issues into a few easy-to-understand points and have some simple examples to illustrate them. The 30-second sound bite rules in television.

5. "Be as opinionated as possible" If they are asking you to be on a show, it is to present your opinion quickly and aggressively.

Opportunities in Radio

According to the Radio Advertising Bureau, 99 percent of all US households own a radio and 78 percent of all adults listen every day.[13] Over its history the medium has taken a complete 360-degree turn from when the commercial medium began in the 1920s. It began as a predominantly national medium, but by the 1960s had become very much a local medium, and to a great extent, it still is.

However, many local radio news programs have been cut, and there has been a proliferation of nationally syndicated programs distributed to radio stations around the country, in a similar manner to the way broadcast television is provided to local affiliates. Today, most radio stations are owned by one of 10 media companies. *Advertising Age*[14] reported the following radio advertising revenues for these top 10 firms:

Clear Channel Communications	$3,717 million
Viacom	$1,859 million
Walt Disney Co.	$ 579 million
Westwood One	$ 421 million
Entercom Communications Corp.	$ 391 million
Citadel Broadcasting Corp.	$ 310 million
Radio One	$ 296 million
Hispanic Broadcasting (Univision)	$ 257 million
Cumulus Media	$ 253 million

While there are MPR opportunities on all stations, the trend has been for FM stations to program music because of its greater fidelity and availability of stereo. AM radio has become a news, sports, and talk medium, offering abundant opportunities for guests to deliver product-related messages. There are also targeted radio opportunities, such as Hispanic Radio and stations aimed at urban youth. Other tactics are discussed in Chapter 11 on MPR tactics.

While not available for advertising, public radio receives support from both listeners and corporations who wish to reach upscale audiences by identifying with such quality programming as National Public Radio's news programs—"Morning Edition," "Weekend Edition," and "All Things Considered"—which reach more than 5 million listeners a week. These and other network and local public radio programs also offer opportunities for coverage of sponsored events and spokesperson interviews

The Next Wave: Satellite Radio

The technology has been available for more than a decade to deliver satellite signals to individual vehicles, but the subscription levels were too low to be commercially viable until very recently. It was the marketing success of "On-Star," General Motors' satellite-based vehicle-tracking and emergency service and other up-scale car manufacturers' satellite services have prompted more auto companies to offer the satellite radio option. The subscription service costs $10 to $13 per month and offers more than 100 channels of mostly commercial-free music, news, sports, and talk. Consumers can also purchase a satellite-ready radio unit and the necessary antenna hardware themselves at retailers such as Best Buy and RadioShack.

In 2005, the only two licensed companies to provide the satellite radio service were XM and Sirius. By early 2005, XM had over 3.1 million subscribers compared to Sirius's 1 million. But that will likely change. Sirius created headlines when "shock jock" Howard Stern signed a multiyear contract beginning in January 2006, with 12 million loyal listeners, as well as exclusive rights to all National Football League programming. The future of the medium seems assured and now offers public relations professionals another couple of hundred radio channels to pitch with MPR messages.

Opportunities in Newspapers

Trends in newspaper publishing favor marketing public relations. According to the Newspaper Association of America (NAA), newspapers remain one of the most relied-upon mediums for news and information, and they continue to innovate and expand the ways in which they reach consumers. The association reports that in 2003 there were 1,456 daily newspapers published in the US, 787 of them morning papers and 680 of them evening papers, with 917 of the dailies publishing Sunday newspapers each week, and another 6,700 weekly newspapers published, primarily "alternative" press, weekly shoppers, or suburban newspapers.

In addition to the traditional printed newspaper product, today's newspapers are delivering content through various channels including the Internet, mobile devices and niche publications. Newspapers benefited from improvement in the overall economy in 2003 as advertising expenditures returned to positive territory.

Sunday newspapers offer special MPR opportunities to reach readers who have more time to read on weekends, as well as those who do not usually read daily newspapers. Because they contain more advertising, Sunday papers have more editorial space to fill. The trend has been to include more feature material, opening up increased public relations placement opportunities.

Additionally, marketing consultants have influenced daily newspapers to include shorter, lighter articles and to publish lifestyle sections. *USA Today*, heavily influenced by television news style, has become a major outlet for public relations material, including new product introductions, sponsored events, and surveys. The proliferation of weekly suburban, community, and special-interest newspapers increases the number of print media options that figure in many a marketing public relations plan. Weeklies offer an additional benefit in that they stay in the house and are read throughout the week.

The one obstacle that newspaper publishers will need to address in the future is the declining readership of younger people. According to Michael P. Smith, Managing Director of Northwestern University's Media Management Center,[15] there are some common threads to all of the research relating to declining readership among young people:

- Young people feel a disconnect from the issues and stories that dominate news and excite journalists—stories of conflict and details of intricate governmental policy.
- Young people see the daily newspaper as elitist and not relevantly reflecting their interests or the lives of people they know.
- Young people see most news coverage as dark and bleak, filled with gloomy reality and an unpromising future.
- Young people see the news as full of political spin and hidden agendas, and, therefore, they are distrustful of the messenger.
- Young people see too much moralizing in the newspaper. In America, young people feel as if the newspaper is preaching to them.
- Young people say that newspapers are too complex, too big, too unwieldy and difficult to understand.
- Young people say that there is no sense of fun, energy or innovation in newspapers. Some refer to newspapers as a deadwood medium.

As a result of these attitudes, newspapers face a very tough future unless they can prove that there is much more to newspapers than what the young people perceive.

And many newspapers are taking action to stem this tide. Here are just three international examples:

- In Japan, the number 2 daily—*Asahi Shimbun*—is the number 1 newspaper delivered to cellular telephones. It has more than 1.2 million subscribers to the newspaper who get it sent to their phones.
- In France, four daily age-specific newspapers have a combined circulation of over 200,000 readers each day, some as young as five and the oldest at age 16.
- In Guatemala, *Nuestro Diario*, which did not exist five years ago, has become the number 1 circulation daily in the country by carving out a middle-market niche.

Magazine MPR Opportunities

Product exposure in consumer magazines is of immeasurable value to marketers. According to an MRI magazine readership study, readership growth in the top 171 continuously published magazines was fastest among women and people over 35, but it increased in other categories as well.

Magazine titles have proliferated because publishers have targeted their products to niche audiences and special interests. The industry's ability to segment its market to reflect the changing trends and interests of society has facilitated the growth of consumer magazines. The implications for public relations are vast. Opportunities to reach consumers in publications focused on their particular interests have exploded. Cosmetic and fashion marketers have long known the value of editorial exposure in the fashion books. Carmakers have aggressively sought the editorial endorsement of *Motor Trend* and *Car and Driver*. Travel-destination marketers now have a half-dozen monthly publications, including *Travel & Leisure* and *Conde Nast Traveler*, available to portray their destinations in words and four-color pictures to well-heeled travelers. In addition, there are hundreds of niche magazines, from *Golf Digest*, to *Fitness*; from *Photography* to *Tennis* and *Bicycling*, there is a publication aimed at every interest imaginable. There are even new shopper magazines, such as *Lucky*, that have expanded the concept of an annotated catalog.

The advent of the computer has given rise to a major new category of consumer magazine. The typical airport newsstand offers more than a dozen titles like *PC World and PC Magazine* to computer buffs. Users of Apple's Macintosh computer even have their own magazine, *MacWorld*. Like the carmakers, high-tech hardware and software companies value, and eagerly seek, the editorial endorsement of these publications for their products.

The list goes on and on, niche by niche, providing news, features, pictures, and product reviews to eager readers and influencing their purchasing decisions. Following the success over the past 20 years of city and state magazines, such as *The New Yorker* and *Chicago Magazine,* which cover new product stories on restaurants and entertainment, regional publications like *Southern Living* and *Sunset* have emerged, devoted to special-interest regional subjects.

Another development that has grown in the 1990s is the computerized process known as "selective binding." Based on subscriber demographic information, computers are now able to instruct binding machines to include special sections based on the individual reader's demographic profile.

Marketers can effectively employ MPR to reach retail decision-makers through articles about new products, new promotions, new sizes, new packaging, new store displays, new advertising, and new public relations programs in trade publications. Retail buyers, whether at the headquarters, regional, or store level, read the key trade books to keep up on what is new in their product category. A feature story on a successful promotion, or a byline by a vendor's marketing director, can also influence the buyer's decision to stock the item and the manufacturer's strategy to "push" the product through the distribution system.

What Makes News

To address these opportunities for marketing public relations within the traditional media of broadcast and cable television; radio, newspapers; and consumer magazines, it is critically important to understand what motivates the reporters and "gatekeepers" within these media and to understand the fundamental difference between the goals of PR people and the media.

In simplest terms, marketing PR people are looking for free, positive media coverage about their organizations and brands. The media, on the other hand, are looking to sell publications or increase broadcast ratings by providing useful and/or provocative news stories that catch their audiences' attention. They also want to avoid being "spun"—being used or manipulated by PR people into providing free advertising (paid advertising pays the media's salaries).

The media are not opposed to doing stories about interesting things an organization is doing, but only if it meets a "news" criteria and won't appear to be a "fluff piece." To avoid this, they will often seek to include other organizations—sometimes even competitors—in the story, and they will often look for an opposite point of view in order to keep the story "objective." (PR people are often chagrined when this happens, and are hard-pressed to explain to their clients or management how the story they developed and pitched for the express purpose of highlighting a unique ability of the client, ended up as a round-up article that equally featured all the key industry players' abilities.)

Anyone who has taken an introductory journalism course knows that being "balanced and objective" is the credo of all good journalists. Therefore, it is a fact of life that news reporters will likely look to broaden PR story pitches, so it is a good idea to plan for this in advance and have some ideas for ways to feature other organizations in the story and to line up people outside your organization who would be willing to provide input to the story. In addition, PR pros who want to succeed in their media relations efforts would be well served to learn their media's needs and interests and the types of stories they are most likely to cover.

PR professionals also need to know how those media define "news." While it will vary by publication and broadcast outlet, there are some common criteria that most reporters look for, and controversy and drama lead the list. PR people sometimes reduce the criteria down to the single phrase, "If it bleeds, it leads," but serious reporters are open to many different story ideas as long as they are newsworthy. Exhibit 12.1 lists eight news values and some ideas that marketing PR professionals should keep in mind as they plan their MPR campaign strategies. If the stories being pitched do not address at least one of these news values, then it will be unlikely to be of interest to the news media.

Pitching Traditional Media: Some Suggestions from the Pros

Once there is a news angle for the product, it will need to be pitched to the media. The editor of the newsletter *Bulldog Reporter*[16] offers this insight for successfully pitching the media:

> Use E-Mail. Forget snail mail, faxes, and even the phone; most journalists prefer PR pitches via e-mail. The most common, but, unfortunately, the least effective, approach is simply to write a "one-size-fits-all" press release and mass e-mail it to every known reporter and editor in the universe. With the low cost of e-mail distribution and the ease in acquiring media distribution lists, this lazy approach is being used far too often. The consequence is angry editors who treat all press releases from the offending company as "spam."
>
> So how do you keep your e-mail pitches out of the e-mail trash bin? Some pitches are eagerly anticipated and acted upon quickly. What makes them different? First is a useful subject line that explains what the topic is about. NOT: "News from XYZ company." Second, the pitch or release is relevant to this publication's audience, addressing at least one of the following: It refers to something timely within the industry. It asks a question that really begs for an answer. It ties the product or the company in with a hot trend. It refers to a controversy that the product or company can help resolve. More often than not, it shows how the trend is affecting other companies or products too—the PR rep doesn't get greedy with the story.

Exhibit 12.1. Important News Values

Timeliness
>Announcing when it happens
>Linking to current events and holidays
>Linking to ongoing issues: i.e. healthcare, safety, and current trends

Prominence
>Celebrities
>Quoting well-known people

Proximity
>Local angles
>Citing local authorities and involving local celebrities

Significance
>The value of the deal and its impact on an industry or community
>Ability to affect many people

Unusualness
>The largest, smallest, or weirdest anything has the potential to make news

Human Interest
>Anything that touches the heart. Some media successes:
>>80-year-old grandmother graduating from college
>>10-year-old boy wanting to put his grandparents' home on map
>>Disabled vet using your product
>>Executive with unusual background

Conflict
>Provide a contrary point of view to a common issue
>Challenge the status quo
>Find a fun way to create open competition with a person or organization

Newness
>Introduction of new technologies or new application of the technology
>New uses for old products

Other suggestions for pitching the media:

1. Keep the pitches short–something that would easily fit on a Blackberry.
2. If you do pitch over the phone, don't script the pitch or use rookies. Use people who are in the know. The person doing the pitching needs to be able to explain the product and answer questions beyond the immediate release.
3. Plan for the questions you don't want to receive because, odds are, those are the exact questions you will receive.

To pitch lifestyle mainstays like *LIFE Magazine,* the *Bulldog Reporter*[17] suggests:

1. Pitch into your target's editorial mission—and know when it has changed. "It's sounds so obvious—but look at the publication or outlet you're pitching," he says. In *LIFE*'s case, "That means we want to hear ideas that zero in on weekend topics—things readers deal with in the 48 hours before they go back to work," he continues. "For example, we've now got a 'Sunday Dinner' page, where we profile a cook or chef who can share a quick recipe. We also have a

weekend projects page—how to plant a tree, hang a picture or do anything that's fun, creative and domestic."

2. Think visually. The best human-interest stories can be told with a picture. "We're still photo driven," shares Shapiro. "So in our case, think visually if you're pitching an idea."

3. Pitch beyond "just the facts." Find your story's "emotional quotient." "The anatomy of a great *LIFE* story, for example, starts with emotional appeal," says Shapiro. "We want people to feel something—so ideas need to be emotionally resonant."

4. Provide access. Everybody loves the "inside story." "The 'backstage pass' component to our coverage is key for readers," Shapiro believes. "I don't think we're alone in this. Everybody in the media wants behind-the-scenes access. Keep that in mind when you call," he advises. "For example, this latest issue features rare and exclusive photos of the pope as a young man looking like a beatnik. Most PR people can't do that—bring a rare shot of the pope. But the point is to show us a different side of your story, company [or product]. Behind-the-scenes stuff is golden to anybody in the press."

5. Work your way up. Good ideas rise to the top. "I'm sure it's the same elsewhere, but my rule to PR people is, 'Don't call me directly,'" says Shapiro. "I got 125 mails from PR people the day the new *LIFE* came out. I told them all to take me off their lists—and to look at the masthead as a pyramid. Start at the bottom with your ideas. If they're good, the reporters will pass them on to their editors. That's why they'll listen to a phone pitch or read a PR e-mail—their job is to find something golden and to send it upstairs." His point? "Good stories trickle up. Trust the process—and don't try to circumvent it."

The Next Generation of Media

While traditional media will continue to be the chief focus of MPR for the foreseeable future, there is a growing trend toward what is sometimes called "user-generated" media. It can be a little disconcerting to public relations professionals who have grown their careers in public relations, and who have developed relationships with members of the traditional media, to see the exponential growth of this type of media, where it is rare to have any personal relationships.

Internet-based media will be discussed in greater detail in Chapter 13. They include personal Web sites, discussion board comments, digital clips that are passed via e-mail with comments attached, and blogs—weblogs that can be as simple as a personal diary or as complex as a full-blown on-line magazine, complete with graphics, guest authors and feature stories.

These new media now exist in the millions and their content is generated by individual opinion leaders on-line, making it very difficult for public relations professionals to track what they are saying, let alone influence them. A recent *Advertising Age* article reported that there are up to eight million blogs on the Web and some 14 to 20 million people read blogs today. These numbers will only get larger over time, so it is essential that the public relations industry finds a way to reach them effectively. They will continue to grow as an important force in the media landscape.

Getting Visibility On-Line

Its importance is a fact of modern life. Today 442 million people worldwide and 167 million people in the US alone—two-thirds of the US population—are using the Internet, and those numbers are growing daily. Internet access spans every age group and, in some, approaches 100 percent penetration.[1]

Today, the technology is being used to rapidly reach very specific and targeted audiences, provide up-to-the-minute information during crisis, save on printing and mailing costs, obtain real-time feedback from customers and other key constituencies, and reach out to thousands of journalists that would otherwise be impossible to address through traditional means.

The Impact on MPR

While this revolution in technology has changed the way business is done across the board, two significant changes have had a basic impact on the practice of marketing public relations.

The first has been in how press releases and other media materials are developed and distributed in pursuit of MPR objectives. The traditional text-only printed press release distributed via the postal service (or faxed in more recent years) has all but disappeared. Today's releases are typically in a multimedia format distributed via e-mail and posted on corporate Web sites. They have links embedded in them to expert sources and other support materials. Pictures can be clicked on for retrieval in various file sizes and resolutions, artwork for corporate logos and product graphics can be captured, and many include a streaming video link with a product demonstration and quotes from corporate executives. The result is a more complete picture of the product or service being distributed that can be digitally archived for later retrieval.

The second significant change is in the wide array of media that MPR professionals can now target. As discussed in Chapter 12, nearly all forms of traditional media have some form of Internet component. Nearly every newspaper has an on-line version that updates stories as things change, so there is usually a second chance to correct a misstatement or provide additional information. Online stories are sometimes open to providing links and additional company information not available in the original story. Unfortunately, however, these on-line stories rarely have the audience that they do in the traditional vehicle.

In the broadcast world, most news programs also have an on-line component offering similar features. Some programs, such as PBS' "Frontline," have created very interesting interactive sites associated with their programs and have actively encouraged viewers to visit them before the program, during, and in follow-up. Some talk shows, such as "Oprah," do the same thing and encourage viewers to go on-line after the show to learn more about the books or products that she featured or to take a quiz. Live news programs often encourage viewers to go to the Web site during the show to ask a question or to take a poll. These types of interactive and integrated approaches to media will only continue in the future.

Media Relations Then and Now

Public relations' role in the groundswell of Internet enthusiasm during the early 1990s was primarily to hype the fledgling companies and to get them ready for an IPO (Initial Public Offering). The order of the day for most PR agencies working for these firms was to pump out daily press releases for pick-up on search engines such as Yahoo. There seemed to be a direct correlation between the amount of news reported about these firms and their stock prices, so the new wunderkind CEOs became big supporters of the PR function, but only as far as it could generate interest in the company's stock. Little importance was placed on using the technology for creating a dialog that would help organizations know their customers better or develop a deeper relationship with them. As a matter of fact, in those high-flying days, "customers" were mentioned far less often than "shareholders" and "investors." People were getting rich from venture capitalists and IPOs without making a single product sale, and everyone wanted in on it.

By the time the dot.com bubble burst at the start of the new millennium, the investment world had finally figured out that on-line shopping sites could not survive without the infrastructure behind them to ship product in a timely manner, bill securely, handle returns, and deal efficiently with customer service issues. They also found that the predicted advertising revenues for the new on-line media never materialized, because readers found increasingly ingenious ways to block the annoying pop-up ads being foisted on them. Media investors also found that all of the free access to the same information previously only found in the traditional media was reducing parent publications' overall subscription rates and newsstand sales.

Although it was a hard lesson to learn and many of the billions of dollars invested were lost forever, today's Internet business model is much saner, and the technology is being used for much more customer-friendly activities than hyping the stock price.

In addition, the new technology has changed the concept of media relations for the better. Just ten years ago, a reporter wanting to write a story about a company's most recent global marketing activities, and who wanted to prepare for it in advance had many hoops to jump through to obtain recent press releases, read through the annual report and most recent financial statements, and browse through product photos and literature. He or she would have had to call the firm during regular work hours, find a PR person who was available, and have that PR person put them in touch with someone who actually knew what was going on in global marketing. Then the reporter would have to request copies of recent press releases, photos, and brochures and have them mailed, which could take a week or longer to arrive. If the reporter later had questions or wanted to get a pithy quote from a company executive, he or she would have to repeat the entire process—during regular work hours of course.

But if you were a reporter in 2005 looking to do a similar story about Coca-Cola's marketing plans, in less than 30 minutes you would have been able to pull together just about everything you needed for your story at 10 p.m. on a Saturday evening without speaking to a single person at the company.

For example, you would have gone to Coca-Cola's corporate Web site at: *www.cocacola.com* and gone to its electronic Press Center to find a complete index of all press releases for the past three years, sortable by topic, with access to full-text copies. You also would have found several recent speeches by Coca-Cola executives from around the world, a photo gallery with dozens of shots of corporate executives, product logos, people from all over the world using Coca-Cola products, and various news events featuring Coke products or people. You would have also found a number of video clips featuring interesting events and charitable activities that the company supports worldwide and found that within the past six days the company had issued a number of press releases directly related to the global marketing story you planned to write.

Disintermediation of the Media

Another important benefit of sophisticated on-line press centers such as Coca-Cola's is that they allow customers, shareholders, and other interested parties free access to the same information that used to be available only to the news media.

Opening on-line press rooms to the public has helped firms get their messages past media gatekeepers. Traditionally, the news media controlled the information that a firm's important stakeholders were able to see. Companies' public relations professionals would issue press releases that contained the exact information that they wanted to convey to these stakeholders, but the reporters and editors who received these releases might never publish them and would certainly alter them if they used them at all. In the past, the only way to ensure that a key message would be delivered exactly as intended was to pay to have it delivered directly to each stakeholder or to buy advertising space in a wide array of media that the stakeholders used. Otherwise, the PR professionals had to accept the fact that the news media had the last say over the messages they were trying to convey.

Today, PR professionals have the ability to go directly to their targets using a variety of methods—the most common of which is posting their messages on their firms' Web sites. To ensure that the information is seen, many firms have found ways to attract key targets to their Web sites on a regular basis by providing special features and content that is of interest to them.

The newest method for directly communicating to target audiences is "podcasting," which is a method of publishing audio programs via the Internet, allowing users to subscribe to a feed of new files (usually MP3s). While the term comes from the combination of "broadcasting" and iPod, the targets do not actually need to use iPods or any portable player to receive the information.

According to Wikipedia, the free on-line encyclopedia, Podcasting is distinct from other types of on-line media delivery because of its subscription model, which uses a feed to deliver an enclosed file.

> Podcasting also enables independent producers to create self-published, syndicated "radio shows," and gives broadcast radio programs a new distribution method. Listeners may subscribe to feeds using "podcatching" software, which periodically checks for and downloads new content automatically.[2]

Blogs and Key Influencers

Weblogs, or "blogs," have become an extremely popular tool for micropublishing on the Web. They are individual diaries, discussion groups, or bulletin boards posted by individuals on the Internet that feature opinions and the latest news in a particular area of interest—or at least what is of interest to the Blog owner. These devices are proliferating exponentially—some reports suggested that in 2005 there were more than 10 million blogs and 40,000 new ones joining them every day. This makes it extremely difficult for PR professionals to stay up on who is writing about their firms and how they are being criticized or accused of wrong-doing.

For example, one popular technology blog, *www.slashdot.org*, on a single day in late 2004 carried articles on Apple Computer, NASA, AMD, Yahoo, Intel, and IMB, as well as a broad discussion on the advisability of free wireless Internet connections in San Francisco, as well as two computer open-source code discussion groups on LINUX and Unix. On the same day, another popular blog, this one focused on pop culture, *www.plastic.com*, ran stories on the tobacco industry in Europe; fantasy sports team activities featured on ESPN, CBS Sportsline, Yahoo, and the BBC; a story about a major glitch in Toshiba's flat screen TVs; and a critical article about mainstream broadcaster news anchors.

For many younger and tech-savvy individuals, these and similar blogs are their principal sources of news about the world. Therefore, the people who put these blogs together and keep them running are very important influencers in the marketplace. In addition, their importance to PR practitioners increases, because blog owners tend to read each others blogs, so misinformation can spread rapidly from one blog to another.

Some marketers to younger audiences have begun to take advantage of these blogs. Some have used "guerilla marketing" techniques and have hired teens or other influencers in key target markets to start their own blogs or to respond to a number of other's blogs to build interest in a new movie or the latest fashion trend. Some have been quite successful in creating "buzz" for their sponsors, and these are discussed in greater detail in Chapter 19, "Experiential Marketing—Building Buzz, Placing Products." Most of the Hollywood movies with teen story lines distributed in the past couple of years have used this technique with some degree of success. But using deceptive bloggers not only raises ethical questions. There also is serious risk to the organization if the targets learn of the deception—that the comments posted were not personal opinion, but were placed by a marketing firm. If that happens, the good "buzz" could potentially turn to very bad buzz very quickly. In PR terms, it would be equivalent to readers of what they thought was an objective product critique learning that they were reading something written by someone on the company's payroll.

This is not to say that firms should not create their own blogs, but they should be up front with who the author is. Microsoft has actually hired bloggers and encouraged employees to respond to inaccurate blog posts. Their comments have generally been well received and are often considered more credible because of who these commentators are.

E-fluentials®

PR agency Burson-Marsteller has attempted to plug into the mindset of influential Internet users, which it has called, *e-fluentials*, by creating a Web site *(www.efluentials.com)* and a viral marketing blog, *http://blog.efluentials.com/*. The *e*-fluentials are a group of online "movers and shakers" who shape the opinions and attitudes of their peers on-line and offline. According to the Burson-Marsteller's Web site, the PR firm "uses its proprietary *e*-fluentials research to help clients identify their influential stakeholders on-line" and "create positive relationships with *e*-fluentials among their customers and target new *e*-fluential audiences to generate buzz about a new product, enhance customer loyalty and manage issues." [3]

Clients can tap into this key group of influencers by using Burson-Marsteller's proprietary algorithm and research expertise. Based on a quiz that visitors to the *e*-fluentials site can take *(www.efluentials.com/quiz)*, some of the key characteristics of these powerful on-line influencers include regular participation in the following activities:

- Participate in chat rooms.
- Post to bulletin boards.
- Post to newsgroups.
- Post to listservs.
- Send e-mails to companies.
- Send e-mails to politicians.
- Send e-mails to well-known news and media companies (e.g., *Time*, *Newsweek*, CNBC).
- Make friends on-line.
- Make business contacts on-line.
- Provide feedback to Web sites.
- Forward news and Web site information to others.

As part of its on-line public relations services, Burson-Marsteller offers to identify clients' own set of *e*-fluentials and assist them in earning their on-line influencers' support for promotional campaigns.

Burson-Marsteller recommends this six-step approach to help clients reach the right target of influential stakeholders:

- Step 1: Think of several audience groups that would find your products/services appealing— movie aficionados, conference attendees, donors to charities, etc.
- Step 2: Find ways to draw attention to your products and services. Organize events, find partners and send out incentives to their customers, offer freebies.
- Step 3: Generate a list. Ask people to sign in to receive continued news and product/service updates from you.
- Step 4: Think of criteria that would indicate an opinion leader in your industry or niche area. Do they write back to the media? Do they donate money to charities? Do they give speeches or just get asked for advice?
- Step 5: Invite your list members to take a short poll. Ask questions to identify those who might be opinion leaders.
- Step 6: Engage those you identified as opinion leaders in future marketing activities.

Tracking and Pitching the Blogs

In its July 2004 newsletter, *The Gauge*[4] Delahaye Medialink reported that "of the more than four million blogs created via popular blog-hosting services such as LiveJournal and BlogSpot, more than half were published by individuals between the ages of 13 and 19. Two-thirds had not been up-dated in two months." Delahaye suggests that one way of finding the important blogs is to monitor journalist blogs, and analyze any relevant entries alongside more traditional media coverage in its media analyses.

The Web site *www.cyberjournalist.net* lists dozens of journalist blogs or personal Web sites. If there are journalists you're working with or who may have some influence over your company or client's reputation, it probably makes sense to track their blogs as well. As for the less mainstream blogs that post original news, track the ones that cater to your target audience and have gained a critical mass of visitors Blog search tools, which can help you find relevant sources, include *Bloglines.com, Feedster.com* and *Daypop.com.*

Mark Vangel, senior account director for Delahaye, advised: "I've always been a proponent of analyzing Internet discussions in order to understand and address the concerns, opinions, and desires of your target audiences. The millions of non-journalist blogs are a means of tracking this consumer 'buzz.' But don't waste your time, budget, and resources with sites that update only monthly and receive a handful of visitors. Build a list of sites that have gained a following, using Google and a blog search resource like *Feedster.com*,"[5] he said.

Regarding how to pitch the relevant blogs, B. L. Ochman, the on-line journalist and Internet marketing consultant, provided these suggestions to the *Bulldog Reporter's* e-zine: *Journalists Speak Out on PR*:[6]

- Make the pitches short, smart and striking e-mails. "Nobody wants to get a pitch that everybody and his dog has also received." She also notes that bloggers are particularly skeptical of hyperbolic or overly commercial releases."
- Write more casually than to traditional media. She suggests addressing bloggers by their first names and never using formal address such as "dear editor."
- "Get straight to the point and underscore your news value or your expert's credentials up front."
- "Be a regular. Let the blogger know you've at least looked at the blog, and see if you can find something nice to say about it."

Creating Your Own Blog

More and more companies are forming their own blogs to put out their point of view and connect with customers in cyberspace. The consulting firm BeTuitive Marketing[7] predicts that Blogs will replace e-mail newsletters because it empowers the recipient. The messages are pulled in by the reader, so they are never rejected by spam filters or caught in bulk e-mail folders. The firm launched its own blog in mid-2004 and reports that it experienced these benefits:

- Because they are updated on a regular basis, search engines are in love with blogs.
- BeTuitive has appeared in the top 10 Google searach results under many terms and phrases because of our blog messages.
- Blogs are very nonthreatening due to 100 percent of the permission being in the recipients control.
- We are driving traffic to our Web site from our blog, which is turning into sales leads.

Ochman suggests that before launching their own corporate blogs, PR pros should check out the following models and ideas first:

- Bold Career Blogs (*http://www.boldcareer.com/blog/*)—which includes a useful on-line assessment tool.
- Hammock Publishing (*http://rex.weblogs.com/*)—a blog by CEO Rex Hammock which focuses on the magazine industry and custom publishing.

- DaimlerChrysler—which uses blog intranets, where managers discuss problems and keep a record of their solutions.

Corporate Web Sites and MPR Strategies

In addition to managing the corporate press center and the content of the internal corporate intranet site, public relations people are often asked to write and manage the content of the Web site used by the sales and marketing functions because public relations professionals typically are strong writers and are often former journalists who know how to report all the relevant facts and get to the point quickly. Smart MPR practitioners also incorporate Web activities for nearly every strategy they employ. Most of these add little cost, and add a level of sophistication that will help increase the visibility and effectiveness of the traditional MPR strategy or tactic:

- If an invitation to an event is mailed to customers and the media, an e-mail follow-up should be undertaken and an on-line RSVP provided.
- If a brochure is printed, an on-line version with the most up-to-date information should be posted and kept updated.
- If a live event is held, a Webcast of it should be posted for those who cannot attend (and if money is tight, then a streaming video of it can be posted after the fact).
- If an event covers multiple locations—a boat race, a cross-country road trip, a touring exhibit, etc.—then an on-line map, showing current and past locations and planned locations for the future, should be posted. If the subject of the tour is a vehicle or vessel, then equipping it with GPS (a satellite-based Global Positioning System), will allow real-time tracking of it.
- If a celebrity or technical expert is hired to host an event or hold a public forum, then their picture and biography should be posted on the Web site, along with any product tips, recipes, or inside stories that would help to make them come alive.
- If a contest is held, the rules should be posted on-line and the winners featured. Copies of their winning essays, photographs, or ideas should be posted as well.
- If the MPR campaign generates coverage in well-known media, the actual broadcast clips (if permission is granted) or quotes should be posted, along with recognizable symbols of the media (the mastheads of well-known newspapers or magazines such as *Time, Newsweek, Business Week, Parade,* etc. or photos of the media figures who delivered the story (Dan Rather, Jay Leno, Regis Philbin, etc.).
- If the results of a survey are used to generate media coverage, the full survey should be posted with all the key findings highlighted at the beginning.

Making Your Web Site Work for MPR

Knowing how people read Web sites can be the first step in an effective Web strategy. Eyetrack III[8] research undertaken by the Poynter Institute's Estlow Center for Journalism & New Media, and Eyetools shows that text, not photos, grabs readers' attention first on-line; that people do typically look beyond the first screen; and that horizontal navigation is more effective than vertical navigation.

The *PRInsite* Newsletter,[9] citing a 2003 Web usability report by the Nielsen Norman

Group entitled "Designing Web sites to Maximize Press Relations," provides ideas for improving the design of PR areas of corporate Web sites to keep journalists from leaving the PR sections too quickly:

- Provide a link to press information on the corporate Web site's home page or in the About Us, or About [company name] section of the site. Name the link one of the following: Press, Press Information, Press Room, Media Information, PR, Public Relations, Newsroom or something similar.
- Provide press releases and links to news articles about your company on your site. Label internal press releases as such, and external news items as such. Many companies make the mistake of labeling press releases as "news," which is confused with external news items. (Also be sure to include contact information on archived releases.)
- Enable users to re-order the list of press releases based on date and topic, if possible. Do this by assigning general categories to each release.
- Make it possible and simple to search press releases and archived press releases only, independent of the rest of the site.
- Provide recent and archived annual reports for your company in an easy-to-find section. In addition to the printable PDF file, provide an HTML version that can be quickly navigated without additional software.
- Provide information about the company's socially responsible and philanthropic efforts, and make it easy to find. If such efforts are impressive, it can swing a reader to view your company more favorably. Give thorough information about actual, tangible activities. Do not provide only filler text with marketing information, such as "We care. . . ."
- If your company is having a difficult time; or a representative at your company, or a product has somehow been recalled, remiss, or otherwise broken the law, acknowledge this in some way on the corporate Web site. Consider linking to news articles that have been particularly fair to the company, or that focused on the positive aspects of the situation.

Dan Gillmor, *San Jose Mercury News* tech columnist, who posted an open letter to "PR People" on his blog, *weblog.siliconvalley.com/column/dangillmor,* advises: "I think the press release page of a company (Web) site should have its own RSS feed. PR people will have a better shot at having journalists like me read their headlines if they do this:"[10]

RSS (Really Simple Syndication or Really Simple Script) is a file format that most weblogs have in place. It allows software of various kinds to read content from a variety of Web sites, all on one screen, without having to surf to each of those sites. It uses a newsreader or news aggregator to check for new blog postings or other Internet source material and scan it for material of interest. It then creates a folder that lists all of the sites with RSS feeds, and each file in the folder can be opened and read without going through an Internet browser. It controls for spam, since it seeks out information, but does not allow for it to be "pushed" onto the recipient without the recipient requesting it. Marketers find it useful because the feeds steer clear of e-mail filters, and they are non-intrusive. They don't require users to click into an e-mail application and then the message itself to access information.[11]

He provides these other tips to enhance the on-line PR experience:

- Provide more links. The most important feature about weblogs is links. PR people should be open to posting links to other sites, even those unfriendly to the firm. "If there's something wrong with the article, then post a rebuttal next to it on your site. The more you can help journalists get a full context, the better," he says.
- Find and read blogs in your space. "Any reporter with a brain is reading the weblogs," says Gillmor. It is important to "follow what's going on and being said about your company."
- Pitch blogs in your space. "There are examples out there of blogs doing better journalism than most print pubs," he says. For example, he warns high tech firms, "If your company or client makes gadgets and you don't pitch Gizmodo—you're missing an important opportunity."

Other Issues Affecting Web Site Usage

Locating your site is critical to its success. Think through every possible key word search and pay the major search engines such as Google, Yahoo, and MSN to have your site listed when those words come up. Periodically check those key words to see if you can find your own site easily through a search engine.

Make sure that your Web site URL is posted on all printed materials—on stationery, business cards, at the bottom of the address on a brochure, and in your advertising. Ask employees to post it as part of their e-mail signatures.

Keep the site up-to-date and accurate. If any information is out of date or has obvious inaccuracies, all of the rest of the site becomes suspect. Someone should be assigned on a daily or, at a minimum, weekly basis to check content for old news that can be eliminated and new information that should be added. The person responsible for updating the content should periodically send out requests for updates from the rest of the organization and set up an in-box for collecting corrections that need to be made.

Add current photographs of people in action to accompany news articles and add photos to biographies and other places where people are mentioned.

Be sure to include a keyword search on your home page and always provide for an e-mail option for the visitor to contact you with questions. Send an automatic reply message to acknowledge receipt of the inquiry and provide a custom reply within 24 hours whenever possible. Track the response time for the person assigned to answer these e-mails.

Use Web-tracking software to find out how many hits your site gets on a daily basis and track the places where visitors leave your site to determine if there are weak spots.

The Downside of the Web

"A good rumor will always have a life of its own. But on the Web, even the dimmest one can grow quicker, uglier and more embarrassing than a zit on a teenager's forehead. But thanks to the increasing sophistication of data-extraction technology offered by a host of Web intelligence agencies, corporate PR is sharpening its surgical-strike capability: the power to extinguish a rumor as soon as it's born."[12]

—Aparna Kumar, reporter for *www.wired.com*

In addition to the wide array of opportunities for public relations, the Web has also opened up a new avenue of "media"—former employees and bloggers with axes to grind, as well as unions and special interest groups sometimes disguising themselves as unhappy customers. A very popular site, *www.vault.com*, gives employees and former employees (usually unidentified or disguised) a forum for discussing rumors and assessing management. Another primarily focuses on rumors of layoffs and bankruptcy, but will occasionally mention product failures and rumors related to marketing campaigns.

These sites are regularly monitored by traditional media looking for a good story. They also seem to be monitored by late-night comedy writers looking for a funny story. In addition, certain Web sites, such as the Drudge Report and the *Smoking Gun.com*, track down rumors and try to uncover corporate and political secrets before the general news media does. These sites' accuracy on past stories has made them a common source for traditional news media to check early and often.

14 The Bottom Line: Measurement and Evaluation

Evaluation should be the final step in any MPR activity and the first step in assessing the new situation as the next cycle of the MPR campaign begins. The point of evaluating the activities is to see if the needle has moved toward your goals and to see if any mid-course corrections are necessary. Even more important, the measurement activities provide for greater accountability for the MPR efforts. The two main questions they answer for management are:

- Were our efforts a success?
- Was the value of what we achieved worth what we spent?

Evaluation tools also help managers make better strategic decisions. They enable managers to take quick, short-term "pulse-taking" to get instant feedback and to make immediate tactical changes or strategic adjustments. And they also allow for more effective planning at the start of a campaign and longer-term measurement of the campaign's outcomes.

In a seminar at the PRSA's 2004 International Conference,[1] Clarke Caywood, a Northwestern University IMC professor, provided some fascinating case histories showing how today's public relations evaluation methods have now progressed to the point that:

- Dell can monitor media messages from its management team on a daily basis to see if they are on message.
- Harley-Davidson, with over a billion "hits" in various media each year, can still define and monitor its PR success.
- A large law firm can use worldwide coverage of legal issues to assess its global potential.

Smart marketers measure a variety of things and report progress along the way, not just at the end of a campaign. If you only report media coverage achieved, the results could be disappointing—especially at the end of the first cycle. You may pique the curiosity of a major media outlet to run a feature story, but it may not be published for six months—and it will be even longer before that article influences anyone to purchase your product.

Measuring Outputs

Short-term measures of an MPR campaign include:

- How many releases were written.
- How many reporters attended a media event.
- How many articles were generated by a press mailing.
- How many gross impressions were generated by the media coverage of a story.
- How many hits the Web site generated.

Although it is important to measure "outputs," measuring outputs alone will not justify an MPR budget or convince management to put more money into PR for the next phase of the marketing activities. This can only be done by measuring the impact of the campaign's outputs and then measuring the outcomes against initial goals and objectives.

Media Metrics: An Impact Measure

Increased and increasingly sophisticated computerization has made it possible to measure outputs in terms of "impact." Just a few years ago, the best we could do was create a clip book of articles and perhaps do a simple content analysis that counted key message points and brand mentions. Today any number of computer tools and/or measurement firms provide a strategic analysis of the coverage you achieve and compare it to the coverage that your competitors achieved.

The array of tactical quantitative and qualitative measures of media coverage includes:

- Quantitative
  —Share of Voice
  —Media name, date
  —Reporter
  —Spokesperson quoted
  —Favorability of mention
  —Extent/Prominence of mention
  —Key message appearance

- Qualitative
  —Tone
  —Message communication context
  —Positioning on issues

One of the biggest advantages to this type of analysis is that it lends itself to graphical display, which puts PR on similar ground as the other marketing functions for the first time ever. Exhibits 14.1 and 14.2 are graphics that can be easily developed with this new type of media metric.

Advertising Equivalency

Within the marketing function, another often-used measure of the media coverage of an MPR campaign is called Ad Value Equivalency (AVE), a fairly controversial practice of measuring PR performance by comparing the cost of reaching the total media impressions achieved by articles placed by the PR efforts versus the cost of paying for those same placements as paid advertisements. Typically it is calculated by obtaining the ad rates for the amount of space that the articles took up and adding them together. Often the PR program costs are subtracted from the total and then compared to the same calculations for an advertising program. In most cases, the PR programs will appear to be significantly more effective than paid advertising.

Part of the controversy around this practice deals with how much of an article should be counted when calculating the equivalent ad cost. If a 20-inch article appeared in *The Wall Street Journal*, but only one line referred to the brand, some would still count this as the equivalent of a 20-inch ad. Also, what if some or part of the article was

Exhibit 14.1. Example: Positive Media Exposure Years 1 & 2

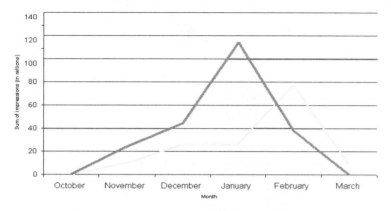

Exposure by month, in impressions

negative about the brand or also featured the competition? On the plus side, some marketing experts such as Phillip Kotler have suggested that the third-party endorsement of a media article actually makes the mention more valuable than an ad.[2] Some will take positive articles and multiply them by 3 or 5 times the ad value because of this factor.

Some of the modern media measurement firms, such as TEXTALL and Biz360, are able to automate the process quickly and set whatever parameters the client wants to measure, but most PR professionals and academics oppose the use of Advertising Equivalencies in PR measurement because it can be so misleading. (PRSA Silver Anvil judges usually look unfavorably on firms that include AVE in their evaluations sections of their campaign submissions.)

However, within an IMC setting, or marketing in general, it is difficult to completely omit this type of measurement, since marketing managers tend to think in terms of advertising costs, etc. If the AVE measure is used, it should be carefully explained and should never be the primary method of measuring a PR program's success.

Special Events and Other MPR Metrics

In addition to media metrics, it is useful to measure the effectiveness of special events and trade shows. The less strategic approach is to report the attendee levels of events (a measure of output), but putting the attendance into a metric that compares the attendance with the size of the target audience or the number of targets that attended does more to measure "impact."

The equations in Exhibit 14.3 provide some ways to measure these activities. To do so, however, requires that the show management can provide an accurate breakdown of the show's attendees, and the client has a mechanism for tracking and identifying the number of people who stopped by its exhibit. Many shows provide electronic badges and wands to facilitate the capturing of this information.

Measuring Outcomes

Outcome measures are those results that make a difference to the bottom line of the organization. Firms are not in business to produce brochures or press releases. They want

Exhibit 14.2. Measure Tone of Coverage vs. Competition

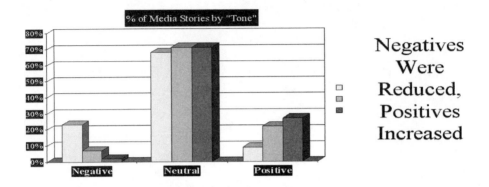

Negatives
Were
Reduced,
Positives
Increased

to sell products or services, and they want their marketing efforts to have a direct impact on those goals. Most outcome goals look to improve the numbers that drive business. They could include a(n):

• Increase in awareness
• Increase in preference
• Increase in purchase intent
• Increase in customer loyalty
• Share of positioning

The ultimate outcomes are increases in revenues and profits. Even stock price increases may, at times, be attributed to an MPR campaign if it generated a high level of media attention. Public relations can most definitely help to achieve these important objectives, but finding measures to prove that PR made a difference can be challenging. Occasionally, the PR efforts are done in isolated target markets with all else remaining the same in other markets, so it is reasonable to attribute to PR any bottom-line improvements in the target areas.

This was the case with a major community relations MPR campaign undertaken by Ball Park Franks in the mid-1990s. The firm partnered with the Points of Light Foundation for a "Clean up a ball park" contest and volunteer activity in five urban areas of Cleveland, Charlotte, Miami, Los Angeles, and Philadelphia. It followed immediately after the very successful national advertising campaign that featured Michael Jordan, with the tagline "Michael Jordan is buying a ball park." Sales and market share were up nationwide following that campaign, but they were up significantly higher in the five cities where the MPR campaign also ran. This was a rare instance where PR could comfortably take credit for an increase in revenues.

Return on Investment (ROI)

One of the most important outcome measures in an MPR campaign is some form of Return on Investment (ROI) calculation. Don Schultz, a professor at Northwestern University's IMC program, has published a number of articles extolling the virtues of ROI measures, the most important of which is the credibility it gives to communications efforts. This is because business people talk in financial terms and expect to receive reasonable returns on their investments in plant and equipment. Marketing and communications folks lose credibility when they expect management to spend millions of dollars for advertising and sales promotion activities without any real proof that they are working.

Unfortunately, in an integrated campaign, it is very hard to separate the individual contributions of each of the communications tools, so developing an ROI for your MPR efforts can be problematic. However, we provide here a common ROI formula for those who are able to isolate their PR efforts and believe they can measure their contribution separately.

For example, if a firm spends $30,000 on an MPR activity that generates $300,000 in additional revenue, its profit contribution would be $270,000 (which is the increased revenue attributable to the MPR, less the MPR costs). The simple ROI is calculated as follows:

$$ROI = \frac{\text{Incremental contribution to revenue} - \text{MPR Costs}}{\text{MPR Costs}} \times 100$$

Example: A $30,000 MPR activity that yields $36,000 in additional revenue would have a 20 percent ROI:

$$ROI = \frac{\$300,000 - 30,000}{\$30,000} \times 100 = 900\% \text{ ROI.}$$

A Word of Caution

We provide this formula with two caveats: First, it is a simplistic calculation at the very least. It is commonly used within the marketing function to compare the returns of various communications tools. But this ROI cannot be compared to the ROIs calculated with more sophisticated financial measures, such as cost-of-capital and internal-rate-of-return figures, that a chief financial officer would insist upon before investing in a tangible asset.

Second, regardless of what the formula suggests, public relations people should be careful about taking too much credit for the revenue generated. Most consumers don't make their minds up to purchase a product based on a single exposure to an article about your product or service. If you ask a woman what influenced her make the purchase, she may mention the last exposure she can recall. Perhaps it was your great Web site or an article praising the usefulness of the product, or perhaps it was her best friend talking about how she has heard nothing but good things about the product since it came out. But more likely, it is the combination of these exposures that caused her purchasing behavior.

Also, even if the MPR campaign can be tracked by its contribution to revenues and profits, and even if there is no significant change in other marketing activities to dilute MPR's impact, be careful here. It is almost impossible to hold everything else stable, and there are many things that can happen in a market that affect revenues and profits—most of which are not under our control. After a fabulously executed MPR campaign, there might still be no change at all in revenues. Or worse, sales could actually go down during the period. If MPR was the only activity added to the marketing mix, it could be blamed for the decline.

How could revenues drop in a period of high MPR activity? Quite easily. A competitor may have beefed up its advertising or promotional efforts. The product or service quality may have dropped during the period. The sales force may have lost an important member of the team, or a distributor may have had a significant decline in service.

There are many things that affect sales and profits, and it is impossible to measure how much worse things might have been without the positive MPR efforts.

Softer Outcome Measures

Let's face it. Not everything we do in public relations has a revenue or profit goal—at least in the short term. Obviously, an MPR goal will be to increase sales or, at least build the brand, but often in the early stages of an MPR campaign, the initial goals may be to simply build awareness or to drive people to a Web site. Some of the things that MPR is best at are those things that take time or complement the more direct revenue-generating activities of the rest of the marketing department. These tend to be "softer" outcome measures that cannot or should not be measured against a direct dollar figure. Some of these outcomes include:

- **Relationship Building:** that critical goal of all of today's marketing activities, but very difficult to measure in dollars. It can, however, be measured with surveys of customer satisfaction, attitude, and loyalty. It can also be measured qualitatively with focus groups, depth interviews, and discussions with key influencers such as the sales force or distributors.
- **Awareness:** This measures things like recall of your brand's important attributes or associating your brand with an good cause or positive experience. Awareness is often achieved through repeated exposure to key message points. It encompasses the first steps in the traditional AIDA marketing model, where PR is critical in generating the Attention and Interest for the product, but is less influential in the stages closer to the actual sale: Desire and Action. Therefore, it often does not get the credit for generating the sale, although the sale would not have occurred with out it. Survey techniques with aided and unaided recall can help to gauge how well an MPR effort educated targets about key messages.
- **Attitude:** An often-misunderstood construct, attitude is a learned predisposition to act favorably or unfavorably toward a brand or object. There are those in marketing who discount the value of measuring attitudes because older research failed to find a direct correlation with purchase behavior. But today's research shows that there is a strong relationship between attitudes and more direct behaviors such as sending away for more information and conveying sentiments to friends and family. But one must recognize that a positive attitude will not always result in a purchase, since there are other determining factors such as product availability, price considerations, and personal circumstances that may preclude the purchase. For example, a college student may have a positive attitude toward BMW, but not the means to buy one. A free-lance writer may have a positive attitude toward Macintosh computers, but

Exhibit 14.3. Some Exhibition & Event Metrics

- **Attraction Efficiency =**

  $$\frac{\text{Number of Attendees from Target Audience who Visited Booth}}{\text{Size of Target Audience at Event}}$$

- **Contact Efficiency =**

  $$\frac{\text{Number of Attendees from Target Audience who Visited Booth and were Contacted in Booth}}{\text{Number of Attendees from Target Audience who Visited Booth}}$$

- **Conversion Efficiency**

  $$\frac{\text{``Effective'' Number of Leads (adjusted for quality)}}{\text{Number of Attendees from Target Audience who Visited Booth and were Contacted in Booth}}$$

---

may buy a PC because it is more compatible with his clients. The key point to remember when measuring attitude is to ask multiple questions that would uncover those things that might interfere with the purchase behavior. It is also advisable to ask multi-part questions that not only explore how well a brand is perceived on particular attributes, but also measures how important those attributes are in the purchase decision: For example, the responses to the following two questions could be multiplied together to find a better attitude measure than just asking about the brand choice:

—A watch that is easily recognized by others is:
Very bad –3 –2 –1 0 +1 +2 +3 Very good

—How likely is it that a Rolex watch will be readily recognized by others?
Not likely –3 –2 –1 0 +1 +2 +3 Very likely

- **Feedback:** PR can be a very useful tool for generating dialog with key influencers, but it is very difficult to put a dollar figure on the value of that dialog. One can, however, measure the number of responses received, suggestions offered, or on-line surveys completed.

- **Trust Bank:** Discussed in Chapter 4 more fully, a trust bank is that "benefit of a doubt" when things go wrong that a customer or government regulator might give your firm because of years of building a strong reputation for doing the right thing. This one is almost impossible to measure directly, but it might be useful to find examples of firms that did not head off a crisis, and use their dollar losses to show what might have been. For example, it is estimated that in 2000 when Bridgestone/Firestone was forced to recall 6.5 million tires due to the poor handling of its product crisis, it lost hundreds of millions of dollars in sales and endured plummeting stock prices. In addition, it still faces lawsuits that will easily be in the billions of dollars of losses. It is not easy to measure the *absence* of a crisis, but giving some dollar figures for organizations in your field that poorly weathered a crisis can be very enlightening to management trying to place a value on strong public relations activities.

Budget Issues That Limit MPR Measurement

The best way to prove the effectiveness of the MPR activities—especially in achieving those "softer" objectives like awareness and attitude—is to conduct surveys or other analysis before beginning your campaign and then follow up with an identical survey after the campaign. This is commonly referred to as a pre-test, post-test. It significantly increases the validity of your measurements. Otherwise, you are faced with the possibility of reporting that your awareness levels after the campaign are 40 percent among your target group, but have no idea if 40 percent is a good measure or not.

However, it is not easy to get the budget for this type of measurement, which, on the surface, may seem to be totally self-serving. If its goal is simply to prove that the MPR campaign worked, it mainly benefits the MPR manager, who is likely to get a nice pat on the back and a larger budget for the next campaign.

Research is expensive, and with MPR budgets traditionally so much lower than advertising and sales promotion budgets, many managers feel it is wasteful to allocate the precious PR budget with this type of self-serving measurement. Unlike advertising campaigns that may be risking tens of millions of dollars if they are not right, MPR budgets can easily be a fraction of a typical advertising budget, so there may be little perceived risk if the PR campaign is ineffective. Therefore, measuring them may be considered less important.

In addition, for some, there is an open acceptance that public relations will always work on some level, so there is no need to try to prove that it worked. It just seems intuitive that reading positive stories about your product or service written by neutral third parties will favorably influence customers and potential customers some time down the road, so measuring the effect is simply a self-serving activity. But as long as public relations pros allow themselves to be lulled into thinking that they cannot or should not measure the outcomes of their efforts, they will be forever relegated inadequate budgets and a limited role within the marketing function.

One of the more practical ways to get a research budget for MPR measurement is to make sure that the research has value beyond measuring the success of the campaign.

When Pat Whalen was with the Communications Satellite Corporation (Comsat) in the early 1990s, she managed to get a large MPR research budget approved for the cruise market by establishing a number of critical objectives for the research. While one of the goals was to create a pre- and post-test benchmark for the awareness levels of cruise passengers and travel agents about satellite communications on the high seas, the research also served a number of other marketing and public relations purposes. It was these other purposes that justified a fairly large budget and allowed for in-person passenger intercepts at the Ft. Lauderdale cruise terminal over several days and telephone interviews with several hundred travel agents. When completed, the research did the following:

- It allowed some fun questions about favorite foods and ports of call that were later turned into freestanding press releases that got Comsat's name widely associated with the cruise industry.
- It allowed for customer feedback on the types of communication services they would like the company to develop and became useful input for the product development and engineering teams.

Exhibit 14.4. Trends in Measurement

Clarke Caywood has identified the following 11 trends and predictions for the future of media relations measurement (MRM):

1. Research opportunities will increase for PR and PR connected to business analysis as the percent of program costs decrease for data systems.
2. Increasing liability risk for organizations not having full-service metrics and up-to-date information "required by law" (Sarbanes-Oxley, RegFD, NYSE Rules, etc.).
3. Old Robotics and automation lessons from Detroit: Re-educate yourself and your staff or fail to be relevant.
4. New agency/corporate/consultant positions as Data Advocate and Analyst.
5. Inventions of more "killer" applications in media metrics including predictive metrics, ROI, breakeven, and causal models for sales and profits.
6. Invention and compiling of databases for non-media based message and data analysis.
7. Short-term and longer-term linkage to CRM to demonstrate marketing and financial power of PR.
8. With technical skills and analysis to sell, the Consultancies will lead.
9. For PR or others, databases will capture and recapture measurements of risk communications, issues management, competitive threat, financial fragility, government involvement.
10. The decline in the value and credibility of traditional media will expand the reach of PR measurement.
11. PR will become much more than a media-based profession.

Source: Clark Caywood presented at the PRSA International Conference in New York, Oct. 25, 2004.

- It provided input from cruise-only travel agents, who ultimately became the primary distributors of pre-cruise communications materials for passengers. It also allowed them to volunteer to be added to a direct mailing list, which added hundreds of key contacts that no one else in the industry had.
- It provided insights into what passengers knew and didn't know about the service that later became the driving force behind an FAQ pamphlet and a worldwide telephone directory of cruise ship telephone numbers. These unique materials were then direct mailed to travel agents and used in press materials that caught the attention of major travel media and generated dozens of articles, including a front page story in the Sunday Travel section of the *New York Times* and a nationally syndicated article by a travel writer for the *San Francisco Examiner*.

The research would never have been approved if its only goal was to measure the effectiveness of the MPR campaign, but it certainly did fill that need.

Summary

In measuring your MPR activities, make sure that you've started with clearly defined objectives and that for every objective there is a measurement. Measure those things that you did (the outputs) as well as the impact that those thing had on your targets. Then measure the things that your targets did (the outcomes):

- Outputs—Did you get the coverage you wanted?
- Impact—Did your target audience see the messages? Did they believe the messages?

- Outcomes—Did audience behavior change?

Other things to remember when measuring an MPR campaign include:[3]

- Identify your measurement plans before the campaign begins.
- Create benchmarks pre-campaign to measure against post-campaign.
- Build measurements into the design whenever possible.
- Develop special PO boxes and 800 numbers if necessary to track responses.
- Do quantitative analysis whenever possible.
- But remember that not all events or exhibits are intended to directly create a sale.
- Fit the measurement tool to your objectives.

PART III

Using Marketing Public Relations

Introducing New Products

Marketing public relations can be used effectively throughout a product's life cycle, but its best-known use has been and continues to be in the introduction of new products. Marketers also understand that the news of a new product must precede the advertising break. Products that are newsworthy to the media and of high interest to the consumer (reporters are consumers, too) have the best potential for maximum exposure. Once the consumer sees the advertising, the product is no longer new to the media. The operative word is *new* because *new* means "news." The business of the news media is to cover the news and the business of marketing public relations planners is to orchestrate programs that persuade media gatekeepers to make room for new products. Marketing expert Jack Trout believes that the general rule of marketing today is that PR comes first, advertising second. In his book *The New Positioning*, Trout writes, "PR plants the seed. Advertising harvests the crop." [1]

Al and Laura Ries, authors of the best-selling book *The Fall of Advertising and the Rise PR,* claim that you can launch new brands with public relations only and that a brand must be capable of generating favorable publicity in the media or it won't have a chance in the marketplace. They cite Starbucks, Microsoft, Intel, *Amazon.com,* Yahoo!, eBay, Palm, Google, PlayStation, Botox, and Blackberry as examples of marketing successes that have been PR successes, not advertising successes. The Rieses counsel their marketing clients to launch new marketing programs with publicity and switch to advertising only after the PR objectives have been achieved.[2]

Toyota Introduces the First Hybrid

Toyota's spectacular success in introducing its hybrid gas-electric car the Prius is a case in point. It used PR for the pre-launch and soft-launch phases in the US to get attention before any advertising or traditional marketing began.

The company gained huge media attention by getting celebrities to drive and praise the Prius to the news and entertainment media. A number of top Hollywood stars were seen by millions on TV arriving at the Academy Awards in a Prius Toyota, which then won the endorsement of environmental groups and maximized media attention because of the car's increased fuel economy. Print coverage included articles in *People*, *USA Today*, and an Associated Press story that appeared in hundreds of newspapers. Television coverage included segments on "Access Hollywood," "Entertainment Tonight," and "Good Morning America." The story was also covered in on-line media including AOL and Yahoo! News.

The public relations effort was so effective that a traditional hard launch with massive media advertising was unnecessary.

Updating Nostalgia: The New Beetle

When a product is truly newsworthy, marketing public relations can drive a successful integrated marketing campaign, one that delivers a one-two punch with publicity building excitement about the product and receptivity to the advertising that follows.

In 1998, Volkswagen had buyers standing in line for the new Beetle long before the break of advertising. As a direct result of massive coverage in print and broadcast media, there was 65 percent awareness of the new Beetle months before the advertising broke or anyone had seen the car. When the car was introduced to the media, Volkswagen and its public relations firm Ruder-Finn were able to generate more than 900 national and local television segments about the Beetle in the first week alone.

Every major newspaper in the country featured the new Beetle, many of them on their front pages. The new Bug's success story made the cover of *Business Week* before it hit the showrooms, the magazine crediting it for launching a "nostalgia boom." VW staged a love-in to introduce the Love Bug to 300 journalists from around the world. Young women in tie-dyed T-shirts handed out daisies and peace medallions in a psychedelic rock hall. The new car is equipped with a bud vase, a reminder of the flower-power days of the first Beetle. So was the press kit, which was downsized to represent the small car of the era.

Three days after its unveiling at the North American International Auto Show in Detroit, the new bug took New York City by storm. The network news targets were carefully selected for the launch. Extensive launch morning coverage was assured on NBC's "Today Show." The car was placed outside the network studio in New York's Rockefeller Plaza where crowds of people gathered daily for a chance to see the show's stars, Katie Couric, Matt Lauer, Anne Currie, and Al Roker and be seen on network television. The new Beetle was featured on every half-hour break. Footage of the classic '60s Beetle was shown, and Matt Lauer, who owned one, fondly talked about it while interviewing a VW executive.

The evening news TV target was "The CBS Evening News with Dan Rather." The veteran anchor introduced a segment that found correspondent Harry Smith boarding a new red Beetle at Times Square and wheeling around town eliciting applause from consumers and thumbs up from construction workers. Smith reported that the Beetle was a traffic-stopping spectacle that "caused a sensation."

Interest in and enthusiasm for the Beetle drove consumers to VW dealerships. "Many of them were experiencing VW for the first time, according to Steve Keyes, VW of America director of corporate communication. Keyes said, "We knew that if we could communicate properly, it would work as a magnet for the whole brand. Our business was up almost 40 percent for the first quarter of 1998 before the first Beetle even showed up. That was our best indication of the power of PR."[3]

The phenomenally successful PR campaign was followed by an excellent advertising campaign that embodied the look and feel of the original VW ads of the '60s. The VW brand's overall sales were up 59 percent for the year, the brand's best performance in a decade. *Advertising Age* named VW Marketer of the Year 1998, but columnist Bob Garfield admitted that "The Beetle would cruise even without fine ads."[4]

The Best a Man Can Get: Product Research Is the Story

The Gillette Company's commitment to finding a better way to shave is paralleled by its commitment to using public relations to build consumer and trade excitement about its products. The first edition of this book described the key role that MPR played in the introduction of the Gillette Sensor Razor, one the most successful new products of 1989. Gillette surpassed even that success with the introduction of the MACH3 razor in 1998. Both capitalized on how Gillette research enabled the company to come up with better products that give consumers a better shave. The public relations effort was so effective that MACH3 had already become the best-selling razor by the time Gillette launched its $200 million advertising campaign.

Eric Kraus, Gillette's vice president of corporate communications, and Porter-Novelli, the company's longtime lead agency, assembled a network of 15 PR firms to introduce the razor in 19 countries in North America and Western Europe. The goal was to make sure that the same product benefits, imagery, and communications strategy were consistent. The tactics may have differed but the message was the same from country to country. The public relations campaign they engineered broke two months before the razor went on sale.

Even though it would not be available at retail for three months, MACH3 was revealed to the media in mid-April for a number of reasons. Retail customers were approached as early as January to secure adequate facings to accommodate the biggest product launch in Gillette's history. However, they were not given any specific product details. Sales reps attending the company's global sales meeting only one week before the announcement were told the big news was on the way. The financial community was primed for the announcement and the product was to be featured at the company's annual meeting a few days later.

The US introduction of MACH3 took place at New York's Hudson Theater, a historic landmark that coincidentally opened in 1903, the year that King Gillette introduced the first safety razor. Gillette said the new three-blade technology would provide men with a closer shave in fewer strokes with less irritation and be "a quantum leap in shaving technology." The company announced that it would back MACH3 with a $300 million marketing program, the largest and most comprehensive in the company's history and previewed commercials that used jet planes and sonic booms to reinforce the product's position as a high-performance, technologically advanced brand.

The event was attended by 81 media representatives from a broad range of national and international print and broadcast media. Gillette set up a full schedule of one-on-one interviews with a team of its executives representing management, consumer research, manufacturing and marketing, all of which were completed in time for the second major event of the day, an early afternoon meeting attended by more than 100 financial analysts.

The planning paid major media dividends. The next day, *The Wall Street Journal* headlined "Gillette Finally Reveals Its Vision of the Future and It Has 3 Blades." The next week *Time* magazine ran a feature on "The Men Who Broke MACH3: For razor scientists at World Shaving HQ, the face is the final frontier." An Associated Press photo of the razor ran in scores of major national and international newspapers. A seven-page *The New Yorker* story reported on the development of "The Billion-Dollar Blade" that the magazine said "should be the most popular razor in America by the turn of the century."[5] It was.

In keeping with its focus on technology, Gillette created both a consumer Web site and a journalist-only Web site dedicated to the launch of MACH3. Reporters visiting the site could browse an on-line image gallery, download and order product and lifestyle photography, sample B-roll footage and the new advertising campaign as well as all press releases, backgrounders and fact sheets. There were 140 interviews arranged during the following week.

Gillette employed word of mouth as well as word of media. The company knew that opinion leaders who received the first MACH3 would trumpet their excitement about the product. A select group of 200 VIPS received this message from Gillette. "Tomorrow, you will experience the shave of your life. Save your shave until the arrival of a special delivery from the Gillette Company and be one of the first men in the world to experience the next generation of shaving." Razors were sent to sports stars, entertainment personalities and political leaders who were the first to try it. This generated buzz and resulted in some big media hits. David Letterman even shaved with a MACH3 on his popular late night show on CBS.

Gillette's CEO Alfred M. Zien told Reuters that "PR led the way in this product introduction, not only in generating awareness about MACH3 but also creating intense media that helped fuel sales. This is a heck of an achievement and we've done it without a penny of advertising."[6]

Viagra Breaks a Taboo

High on our list of "MPR's Greatest Hits" is a little blue pill that became one of the world's most popular pharmacuticals. The flawless public relations plan not only pushed a pill. It opened up discussion of a subject that had previously been taboo in polite conversation and was never mentioned in family media—erectile dysfunction.

Pfizer introduced Viagra with a public relations campaign that was so successful that in its first month on the market it had generated two billion media impressions and caused doctors to write a million prescriptions. According to the Chandler Chicco Agency, which managed the public relations effort for Viagra, the launch of the drug broke every record and set new standards for communicating and marketing a blockbuster drug that the media called the first of the "lifestyle drugs."

The pre-introduction publicity was so effective that by the time Viagra was approved by the United States Food and Drug Administration on March 27, 1998, thousands of men had booked appointments with their urologists months ahead. Doctors were said to have bought rubber stamps so that they could churn out prescriptions more rapidly. Upon receiving the good word from the FDA, Pfizer called an instant press conference to deliver a message that was heard around the world. Within 48 hours of approval, the Viagra story had generated more than 850 million audience impressions. It was covered extensively by virtually every major print and broadcast news channel.

The company enlisted and media trained an army of 150 spokesdoctors and company officials to respond to the onslaught of medical and media inquiries. To make sure that they were all on the same page, Pfizer produced a communications briefing book that, in effect, explained "Everything You Have Always Wanted to Know About Erectile Dysfunction But Were Afraid to Ask." The agency's top priority was to ensure balanced reporting of the key messages through all channels—internal spokespeople, physicians, patients and third-party resources.

The impact of the public relations campaign was news in itself. The lead of a *Business Week* cover story proclaimed "Viagra. Viagra. Viagra. TV shows are interviewing ecstatic customers. Newspapers and magazines are analyzing its cultural implications. Internet chat sites are spreading info on how to get it. Bars and cocktail parties are buzzing with jokes about."[7]

Viagra had captured 98 percent of the market before any advertising support kicked in two years after the initial publicity blitz. In the first five years on the market, Pfizer sold a half billion Viagra pills. Viagra had annual sales of $1.7 billion by the time competitive products Levitra and Calais came on the market. The product had inspired more than 60,000 news stories. Studies have shown that millions of Americans get their news first on late night network comedy shows. Viagra had become a monologue mainstay. Jay Leno, star of NBC's "Tonight" show, alone delivered 944 Viagra jokes.

Star Wars: Who Needs Ads?

For months, it seemed that every conceivable newspaper, news show and magazine on earth had dutifully reported every tidbit of information they were fed by Lucasfilms about "Star Wars: Episode I—The Phantom Menace." With nothing left to say on the eve of the opening, the media finally got around to reporting the story behind the all those stories.

The "Star Wars" media relations campaign was extraordinarily effective. It made advertising virtually unnecessary. It orchestrated a year-long campaign that peaked at show time. It parceled out bits and bytes of information to every imaginable print and broadcast media outlet, tailored to the specific editorial interests of each. It revealed the trivia but not the plot in print and on TV and out there in cyberspace. It effectively replayed "Star Wars" greatest hits to build extraordinary interest in the "prequel" among cultists and the new market kids alike. It had fans lined up for days and weeks to be the first on their block to see it. It set a weekend record and was so effective that fans saw it over and over again before the rest of the general public were ready to brave the crowds.

The publicity machine was in full gear when a two-minute trailer of the film was released six months before the film opened. The media reported that hordes of fans paid $7.50 to see the preview and skipped the feature film. The drumbeat continued, reaching a crescendo in the days leading up to the grand opening. In every city where "The Phantom Menace" premiered, newspapers, radio and TV interviewed diehard fans who camped out days, sometimes weeks, before the very first midnight showing. Those reports convinced the uninitiated that the new "Star Wars" was no mere movie but a can't-miss event that comes around every couple of decades.

Newsweek did its own content analysis and devised a fascinating chart showing how key messages showed up in major takeouts in *The New York Times, Vanity Fair, In Style, Wired, Time,* "Sixty Minutes" and *Premiere* (which for the first time devoted an entire issue to one film. They found that "biggest movie ever," "digital backlot," "Hollywood rebel," "cool offices," "single dad," "3 adopted kids," and "not a recluse" and, of course, exclusive photos appeared in them all. In its cover story "Ready, Set, Glow!" *Time* admitted that every magazine except *The New England Journal of Medicine* had already displayed "Star Wars" on their cover. They included magazines as diverse as *Vogue, GQ, Popular Mechanics* and *TV Guide,* which didn't even bother to explain what "The Phantom Menace" had to do with television. Media in overseas markets where the film would premiere were likewise saturated with Star Wars stories. The French magazine *Elle Decoration* contained an "exclusive" six-page spread on the design elements of the film.

The Star Wars team capitalized on use of the new media. There was the official "Star Wars" Web site, of course, but the Yahoo search engine listed 1,185 other sites devoted to "Star Wars." So much "Star Wars" stuff was floating around in cyberspace that newspapers like The *Chicago Tribune* published their top Web picks. *TheForce.net* was getting 20,000 hits a day when the film opened and *countingdown.com* offered a second by second countdown to showtime. Associated Press reported that Apple Computer's Web site, the host of the 25-megabite file containing the film trailer, had been downloaded 8 million times, pointing out that that was equal to downloading the entire printed collection of the Library of Congress 20 times!

Then there was all that publicity surrounding "Star Wars" toys, video games, soundtracks and enough books (visual dictionaries, sticker books, cross-sections and a novelized Phantom that became an instant best seller) to create entire departments at Target, Borders and Barnes & Noble stores.

When "The Phantom Menace" finally opened, *Advertising Age* ran a story with a most unusual headline for the leading trade publication of the advertising business: "Star Wars: Who Needs Ads?" It reported: "Because of the publicity and general public awareness of the film franchise, marketing executives said the awareness level for 'Star Wars' is at the highest levels ever for any movie since this type of data has been compiled. National Research Group, used by movie studios to predict box-office results had put awareness level at 96 percent." [8]

Those awareness scores translated to box office bonanza. "The Phantom Menace" passed the $200 million mark faster than any other film in history at the time and became one of the biggest and most profitable films of all-time. *Advertising Age* columnist Scott Donaton speculated that " 'The Phantom Menace' will hit profitability at an earlier box-office threshold, in part because George Lucas spent so little money on advertising and marketing. Lucas was able to save those pennies because he got tens of millions of dollars in free publicity." [9]

Tempest in a B Cup : Accidental Exposure?

When Clark Gable, reigning king of the movies, took off his shirt to reveal his bare chest in the 1934 film "It Happened One Night," sales of men's underwear shirts (the nerdy kind with the straps) plunged. When Brandi Chastain whipped off her jersey after scoring the winning goal for the US Women's soccer team in the 1999 World Cup, baring her Nike Inner Active Encapsulated Racerback sports bra, sales of Nike sports bras skyrocketed. Some women just couldn't wait a few weeks to buy the new bra and "Nike's older model sports bras just flew off the shelves," according to Kirk Stewart, Nike Vice President of Communications. Quite a wonderful word picture and a great way to reduce inventory and make way for the one everyone wants.

Some cynics claimed the bra-baring was, as one *Newsweek* reader claimed, "shamelessly orchestrated." Not so, said Stewart. Brandi's exuberant gesture was "totally and completely spontaneous." [10]

Soccer fans were not all that surprised. Sports bras are much in evidence in health clubs, gyms and jogging paths, so why all the fuss about Brandi's gesture?

To reprise the scene: after two hours of the hard-fought scoreless encounter between the US and China, victory or defeat came down to a single penalty kick. Ninety thousand fans at the Rose Bowl, a record for a woman's sporting event, were swept up in the drama of the moment. *Newsweek* reported: "As frenzied fans roared, she whipped off her shirt and waved it at the crowd before being buried in celebration by a pile of her team mates. 'I didn't hear any noise. As soon as the whistle blew, I just stepped up and hit. I just sort of lost my mind.'" She called stripping down to her black sports bra "momentary insanity."

The picture of Brandi kneeling in her swoosh-marked bra and shorts appeared on *Newsweek's* cover story. *Sports Illustrated* also picked the Brandi bra shot for its cover. *Time* followed suit with its cover story "What a Kick!" *Time* said of Brandi's act, "Hey, her name is Chastain, not Chaste."

Among the fans in the stands was Katherine Reith, Nike Senior Manager of Communications, who told *The Washington Post*, "We had no idea. I was totally flabbergasted and I started screaming even louder if that's possible." Far from planning it, she determined that branding the bra would be inappropriate amidst the excitement of America's thrilling victory. Despite her efforts to play it cool, the picture of Brandi's victory gesture captured the excitement of the occasion so well that it instantly appeared across the globe. On Sunday, the AP bureau in Portland, Nike's hometown, called Katherine to inquire if Brandi's bra was a Nike. Katherine decided it was time to identify her company as the source of the now-famous bra. She called *USA Today* and left a message for the business editor.

The next day, the paper squeezed in a short story headlined "Chastain insanity." The item revealed for the first time the bra was indeed a Nike Inner Active bra and that Nike had fitted the team with them and other gear a month before the match. *USA Today* followed up Monday's brief with a cover story on the impact of the event on Nike's bra business the next day. It quoted corporate identity expert Allen Adamson of Landor Associates who said, "It's a moment in sports that will always be etched in our minds. That 10-second piece of film is all Nike needs to sell more bras than it can produce." The article reported that Brandi and some of her teammates had been, in fact, on an advisory committee of women athletes that had given Nike feedback about its bra during its development. Nike had brought 20 women athletes from sports as diverse as basketball, track and soccer to the Beaverton campus to give them feedback on the line a year earlier.

The *USA Today* story revealed all the particulars about the Inner Active sports bra. In addition to its own 2 million plus readers, *USA Today* is closely watched by reporters and editors throughout the USA. Nike's phones were ringing off the hook as reporters from newspapers, radio and television checked in. The story was a natural followup to the main event that made America feel so good. The World Cup story morphed into the B Cup story.

Brandi and her teammates celebrated with fans at Nike Town in New York, an event that was covered by "Entertainment Tonight," among others. Fox News channel got so carried away that it reported "Everybody in the country is going to want one." On the "Today Show" Matt Lauer introduced "an uplifting story about sports bras," Katie Couric displayed "the picture that had become the lasting image of victory," and correspondent Jonathan Alter commented "the most visible sign of defiance against male oppression was burning your bra. Women's liberation in the late 1990s—the most visible sign of achievement is showing your bra. Well, your sports bra, anyway."[11]

Hundreds of newspapers ran the AP story with this lead, "Brandi Chastain may have created the best known new undie since the Wonderbra when she doffed her jersey after delivering the winning kick at the Women's World Cup." *Chicago Tribune* marketing columnist, George Lazarus, reported that while the Nike swoosh had 97 percent awareness, Chastain's dramatic gesture did more for the brand in less than 15 seconds than any dozen pro basketball stars did this year in the post-Michael Jordan NBA era."[12] As *The St. Louis Post Dispatch* put it : ". . . , Nike got a free commercial with 40 million viewers watching on television."[13]

Nike's efforts in April to introduce the Inner Active line to long-lead women's, girls and sports media were paying off. Just as the bra and the entire Inner Active line was delivered to stores, longer-lead publications like *Sports Illustrated for Women, Self, Golf for Women, Weight Watchers, Jump, Heart and Soul, YM, Cosmo Girl*, and *Teen People* checked in with their explicit third-party endorsements.

Just how powerful was the impact of the event out there in the world of retail reality? *Women's Wear Daily*, the bible of the retail trade, proclaimed, "The exposure of the Nike Inner Active sports bra worn by US Women's Soccer star Brandi Chastain is expected to boost the popularity of the category at stores nationally."[14]

Two-Buck Chuck: The Wine That Everybody's Talking About

With an estimated 10,000 plus labels competing in a static market, the Charles Shaw success story is one for the books. A good wine at a great price that brought hordes of new wine buyers into the market. The phenomenal sales success and earned media played the key role for brand beloved by headline writers as "Two-Buck Chuck." The stories said that a good bottle of California Chardonnay, Sauvignon Blanc, or Merlot could be bought for $1.99.

Longtime California wine publicist Harvey Posert says that *Wines & Vines* had the story first, printing a short item on a staff tasting where Shaw was preferred over a $67 Chardonnay. Posert used that magazine item to interest consumer media in the story and to document the quality and value of Charles Shaw.[15]

Charles Shaw first became known as the "fundraiser's wine." A *Los Angeles Times* executive became curious about the brand when he kept seeing it at charities. As a result, a story about it appeared in the paper early December 2003. The *Times* story was the tipping point. The timing couldn't have been better. As the holidays approached, people moved from buying bottles to cases. The *Times* story was reprinted by newspapers all over the country. That, in turn, led to national media coverage of Charles Shaw in print, broadcast, and on-line media. Many Americans became aware of Chuck when the hosts of NBC's "Today" show did a blind taste test of the brand with a quartet of excellent wines and found it to be as good or better than high-priced labels. That was one of seven network newscasts that together with Reuters and Associated Press wire service stories introduced "Two Buck Chuck."

Stacks of Charles Shaw cases were piled near the checkout counter of Trader Joe's under a sign that says "The wine that everybody is talking about" and moved out in a parade of shopping carts. Most of the stories quote unsolicited consumer comments.

Posert says that since Bronco Wine Company executives rarely talk to the press, the stories mostly quoted consumers. Some of the best consumer responses were posted in Internet wine chat rooms and were provided to the traditional news media, adding credibility to the story. In fact, it was a Trader Joe's employee in a chat room who gave Charles Shaw the nickname "Two Buck Chuck."

Charles Shaw has never been advertised. Why bother when every media person interested in wine has read about it, tasted it, or heard about it. The most talked-about name in wine had only been on the market for less than a year when it became famous because of publicity.

In his book *Spinning the Bottle*, Harvey Posert wrote, "The Charles Shaw phenomenon demonstrates some ideas about public relations—concepts relating to the public's interests—and publicity, skill in handling the media."

"First, be an early example of a trend. These days, good wine does not have to be expensive. We're making good wine all over California and many places overseas. Media jumped on the negative news of the glut.

Second, take a leadership position. The Franzia family of Bronco Wine Co. had been successful at grape growing, producing, distributing and marketing, building brands known for quality and value.

Third, make a dramatic statement. As bulk wine prices fell, an efficient wine operation like Bronco could work with a niche retailer like Trader Joe's to market good wine profitably at $1.99.

Fourth, look for a positive industry slant to the story. At that price, wine is being bought by the occasional wine buyer and served to the very occasional wine drinker, helping to bring in new customers to an industry which spends little to increase consumption."[16]

The result was the kind of third-party endorsement that brands dream of.

Botox: Let's Party

By the time the FDA approved Allergan Inc.'s Botox for treating frown lines, many Americans had already been to a Botox party—on NBC's "Today" show, that is. The show's co-host Katie Couric winced when a doctor injected the stuff in the face of a Beverly Hills matron. But the ladies seemed to be having a wonderful time.

The otherwise sedate *Wall Street Journal* ran two stories on approval day: a soiree story in "Marketplace" and a news story in their new "Personal Journal" section. *The Journal* attended a Botox party in Redmond, Washington, calling it "a Tupperware party with needles" because a hostess invited her friends over for an afternoon of wine, cheese . . . and Botox. It reported that Botox parties, complete with invitations, injections, and hors d'oeuvres, had spread from coast to coast. After signing a consent form, the party-goers would file, one by one, into a back room with the doctor for a "15-minute treatment." Doctors had been using Botox for some time to remove facial wrinkles, but when the FDA approved its use for the relief of frown lines, the media smiled.[17] *Newsweek* got so excited that it expanded its coverage to a nine-page cover story: "The Business of Botox."[18]

With publicity like this, Botox became a household name even before Allergan began to run its $50 million advertising campaign. Allergan said it did not support Botox parties, but there were few frowns at the company on the day when the FDA said OK—not with the stock up $3.80.

The Botox story illustrates the classic integrated PR-advertising one-two. Botox garnered three-quarters of a billion media impressions before the $50 million "ask your doctor" ad campaign hit in 24 magazines from *People* to *The New Yorker*. The ads promoted not only a toll-free information-line but a Web site listing a network of Botox cosmetic physicians. All the marketing components were in place to make Botox the next billion-dollar drug.

Botox became a natural for late night comedy monologues. Even *New York Times* columnist William Safire took time out from world affairs to discuss the politics of Botox, concluding with this story:

> Rose, a woman recently widowed, begins to spend her inheritance on a complete makeover—new face, new hairdo, new figure, new clothes. Killed by a speeding bicycle courier as she steps out of a beauty parlor, Rose stands before God's great judgment seat and says: "For 50 years I scrimped and saved, and the minute I'm on my own it's all over. You call that justice? The booming voice from on high replies in amazement: "Rose—is that you?" [19]

Harry Potter: An International Success Story

Young Harry Potter fans lined up long past bedtime on September 8,1999, to pick up their hot-off-the-press first day copies of *Harry Potter and the Prisoner of Azkaban,* the third installment of the most phenomenally successful series of books, children's or adult, ever published in the English language. The first two, *Harry Potter and the Sorcerer's Stone* and *Harry Potter and the Chamber of Secrets,* had sold well over 2 million copies in the UK and 5 million more in the US, and both were still flying high on the adult bestseller list when *Azkaban* arrived in America. More than 30,000 books had already been ordered on the Internet from Britain by Potter fans who couldn't wait a month for the US edition. Advance orders made it number one on Amazon's US site weeks before it was published. *The Wall Street Journal* reported that more copies of *Harry Potter and the Prisoner of Azkaban* were sold in its first week than any title since the paper initiated its book index in 1994. The week *Azkaban* was published Harry scored an unprecedented trifecta. The new title was number one, *Chamber* number two and Sorcerer number three on *The New York Times* best-seller list. By that time, Harry had become an international phenomenon. He had been translated into 27 languages in 130 countries.

How did Pottermania get started? *Business Week* reported that Scholastic Inc., the US publisher, "started a word-of-mouth campaign months before the first book was released, circulating early copies to influential critics, librarians, children and 'our own universe of big mouths,'"[20] a universe that surely included all the news media heavyweights. Since then, the Cinderella story of author J.K. (Joanne) Rowling has been repeated in hundreds of stories in print and on the tube. It is the rags-to-riches story of an unemployed, unpublished divorced mom who wrote out the first book in longhand in an Edinburgh coffee house while her baby daughter napped. "Sixty Minutes" profiled the author at the now-historic table where she jotted down the first Harry ideas on an napkin. J.K.'s story is the stuff that Hollywood dreams are made of.

Harry was again the hottest story in publishing and the marketing public relations story of the year in 2000. You knew that Harry Potter had arrived when no-nonsense political reporter Sam Donaldson skipped the politics on ABC's "This Week" and put on Harry specs to read from *Harry Potter and the Goblet of Fire.* On the same day, "Sunday Morning on CBS" carried an interview with J.K. Rowling aboard the Hogwarts Express. The old-fashioned steam engine-powered train was described in a *New York Times* report from Oxford, England. "It's the centerpiece of a publicity stunt timed to celebrate and feed the frenzy stirred by the latest in the series, published to great hullabaloo today. The train's itinerary is to trundle for four days from book signing to book signing at railway stations large and small where the Harry Potter aficionados await a glimpse of the person that gave them their hero." [21] Harry became the lead news story on the "Today" featuring a Katie Couric interview not with Rowling but with *Newsweek* editor Malcolm Jones who had been awarded an advance exclusive interview with Rowling. In what must have certainly been a first in newsweekly history, a fictional character made the cover in two consecutive issues of *Newsweek.* "The Return of Harry Potter!" was followed by a cover story "Why Harry's Hot." [22]

Like its predecessors, *The Goblet of Fire* became the fastest-selling title in history overnight. It joined the first three Harry Potter books *The Sorcerer's Stone, The Chamber of Secrets* and *The Prisoner of Azkaban,* which all still remained on the *New York Times* best-seller list.

Goblet was embargoed until midnight of the release date. The title, the plot, the cover design, even the length (734 pages) were all kept secret. The publisher swore that the "don't open until midnight" rule was not a marketing ploy. Midnight madness was covered by every local and national print and broadcast medium on both sides of the Atlantic. Rita Clifton, CEO of the British brand consultancy Interbrand, compared the Harry Potter campaign to the launch of a new car. "There is quite an obsessive secrecy. All the news is kept under strict control. And you create a sense of expectation and anticipation." [23]

The first weekend Amazon shipped 375,000 copies and made national television news. Barnes and Noble had sold more than 850,000 books in its stores and on its Web site. Independent booksellers ran costume parties, served witch's brew, got plenty of local media attention, and sold record numbers of books. When it became clear that the initial US printing of 3.8 million copies would immediately sell out, a second printing of two million more copies went to press. Scholastic, the US publisher, decided to translate Rowling's English prose into American. They changed Mum to Mom, jumper to sweater, post to mail and lorry to truck. Crumpets inexplicably became English muffins. As all Potter fans know, the first book in the series, published in Britain as *Harry Potter and the Philosopher's Stone,* was changed to *Harry Potter and the Sorcerer's Stone* in this country.

J.K. Rowling, by then the world's most popular writer of children's books, was runner-up to George W. Bush, the newly elected President of the United States, as *Time's* 2000 "Person of the Year." At the time, her four Harry Potter novels had sold a phenomenal 76 million copies. Her books became so popular that *The New York Times* submitted to the demands of authors and publishers and moved them from the main fiction best-seller list to a new children's book category (despite the fact that a good many of Harry's devoted readers were grown-ups.) Assisted by a pull-out-the-stops public relations push, Harry IV, a.k.a. *The Goblet of Fire,* sold over 45 million copies in the US alone. The success of Harry became especially newsworthy because so many kids are taking time out from TV and computer games to devour a 734-page tome.

Following the Hogwarts express book-signing tour in the UK, Rowling did a summer tour of North America, designed to make herself available to young readers, culminating in a reading to 10,000 people in the Toronto Sky Dome.

The movie version of the first book *Harry Potter and the Sorcerer's Stone* was released in November 2001 with fanfare comparable to the books. Hollywood was not to be out-hyped by the book business. Harry's US publisher, Scholastic Inc., and *USA Today* ran an essay contest on "How the Harry Potter Books have Changed My Life." Product spin-offs for the first film included, in addition to the inevitable Hogwarts school sweatshirts, Harry eyeglasses, baseball caps and board games, intriguing items like Everyflavor Jellybeans. With the release of subsequent movies in the series, the worldwide hype paralleled that of the books upon which they were based.

Time magazine, which ran its first Harry Potter cover in September 1999, featured Harry on its cover again in June 2003. This cover photo was of a dozen grinning kids wearing Harry specs and eagerly awaiting the release that week of *Harry Potter and the Order of the Phoenix.* The angle this time was "The Real Magic of Harry Potter: What the World's Most Popular Series Says About The Secret Lives of Children." [24]

Countdown clocks in Times Square and countless book stores., costume parties, midnight madness, ballpark promotions in four major league baseball stadiums and news embargoes resulted once again in massive media coverage. That was all part of an overarching marketing campaign for "Harry Potter and the Order of the Phoenix." The publisher distributed 3 million bumper stickers, 400,000 buttons, 50,000 window displays and 24,000 stand up posters. They sent more than 150,000 "event kits" to bookstores packed with materials and party planning suggestions that even covered how to handle long lines of impatient fans.

J.K. Rowling, once a single welfare mom, was now wealthier than the queen of England. She bypassed the traditional book tour this time but she appeared before 4,000 British and Irish children in London's famous Albert Hall to answer their questions and read from the book. Ten US children who won an essay-writing contest run by Scholastic joined these kids, chosen by ballot. The event was webcast around the world. *Phoenix* zoomed instantly to the top of the best-seller list, quickly selling out the first printing of 8.5 million copies of the nearly 900-page book, the biggest press run in book publishing history. The fifth volume of the phenomenally successful series not only made history in the USA, breaking all publishing records. It was simultaneously published in English in Europe and Asia, much as *Harry Potter and the Goblet of Fire* was published simultaneously around the world.

In Europe, the marketing wizards behind Harry Potter books came up with a new way to excite readers, get publicity, sell books, and help the homeless. Two weeks before the release of the German language version of "Phoenix," the first entire chapter appeared in 19 street newspapers in Germany, Austria, and Switzerland. The newspapers are sold by the homeless in subways, shopping districts, and bars presumably frequented by moms and dads. Homeless vendors got to keep a buck. As a result, Amazon had received 150,000 advance on-line reservations from readers in these countries. It took a thousand postmen working overnight to deliver two million copies to bookstores.

The Wall Street Journal reported that by the time *Phoenix* was published, the four previous Harry Potter books had sold more than 200 million copies in 55 languages spanning more than 200 countries. Their success was part of a precisely orchestrated worldwide marketing campaign driven by public relations.[25]

Paul Newman and McDonald's: A Healthy Partnership

Legendary actor Paul Newman was on hand at McDonald's restaurant in New York's Times Square when McDonald's launched new Premium Salads because McDonald's was also announcing a linkup with Newman's Own, Inc. Under an exclusive alliance, the new salads featured Newman's Own all-natural salad dressings. Newman himself served salads with his dressings to media and invited guests. The event and related media relations preceded advertising and was alone responsible for driving awareness of the product and the alliance.

McDonald's introduced three premium salads nationally. The new entree salads, which featured with seven types of fresh lettuce and warm chicken, were California Cobb Salad with Newman's Own California Cobb Dressing, Caesar Salad with Newman's own Creamy Caesar Dressing and Bacon Ranch Salad with Newman's Own Ranch Dressing.

The new product announcement attracted additional media attention because of its social responsibility dimension. Paul Newman donates profits from Newman's Own products to a variety of educational and charitable causes, which meant that McDonald's was helping the recipients of Newman's generosity by purchasing the salad dressings for its 13,000 US restaurants from Newman. Both brands came to the partnership with notable social responsibility records. McDonald's supports Ronald McDonald House Charities and more than 180 Ronald McDonald Houses around the world, which provide a home away from home for families with seriously ill children.

USA Today, one of hundreds of newspapers to carry the story, reported that Paul Newman has tapped a new, if unlikely, Sundance Kid as his partner: "Ronald McDonald."[26] Ronald was indeed on hand and shown with Newman on TV network newscasts. At the press event, B-roll footage was shot, edited, and fed to TV stations nationwide and an AP photo was transmitted to print news media. Desk-side interviews were conducted with top consumer and business publications,

In the first month, the launch of Premium Salads generated more than 180 million media impressions with more than 200 television broadcasts, 1,000 radio broadcasts, and 300 stories in print. Since there was no national or local advertising support, McDonald's was able to isolate the public relations impact on sales. The day the *USA Today* article appeared, McDonald's shares rose 21 cents on the New York Stock Exchange. During the week of and the week after the national PR events, McDonald's registered a 10 to 15 percent increase in average unit volume. The company made headlines in the financial media when in the introductory month, McDonald's showed the first increase in 14 months because of the demand for new salads.

McDonald's sold 150 million premium salads in the first year. The company benefited at the cash register because the average check for someone buying a salad is double that of a typical bill. *BusinessWeek* was so impressed that, in an article titled "McDonald's: Fries With That Salad," they stated, "Today's $3.99 salads are doing more than boosting profits. They're letting the company recast its image as a place where folks can really get a healthful bite to eat." [27]

What's "It?": A Triumph of Teaser Publicity

A masterful teaser public relations campaign that ran throughout most of 2001 built widespread interest in a product identified originally on ABC's "Good Morning America" only as "It." The "What's 'It'" guessing game engaged millions of people at office water coolers, cocktail parties and cybercafes. The revelation of the identity of "It" was meticulously orchestrated by the PR firm Burson-Marsteller. Exclusives were granted to one national newspaper, one major newsweekly, and one TV morning show. *The New York Times, Time* magazine and "Good Morning America" were selected. A teaser segment on GMA a few days before the unveiling primed great curiosity not only among the show's viewers but scores of other media who were compelled to cover the story.

The strategy to target three key media outlets paid off handsomely. The Segway personal transporter was revealed on "Good Morning America" by the inventor Dean Kamen, and the show's hosts Diane Sawyer and Charles Gibson were seen giddily gliding about New York's Bryant Park on "It." The Segway story dominated GMA, appearing on all eight of the show's 15-minute segments for a total of 24 minutes of air time. This exposure generated 1.9 million visitors to the show's Web site, prompting a return appearance by Kamen two days later to answer the most frequently asked questions about Segway. The inventor then reappeared later that week on the PR program's network of choice on "Prime Time," ABC's news magazine.

The exquisitely orchestrated public relations campaign offered a magazine exclusive to *Time*, which ran a 7-page color feature called "Reinventing the Wheel." The story asked the overarching question "Could this thing really change the world?" Inventor Kamen had no doubts.[28]

Segway was also featured on page one of the prime newspaper target *The New York Times* and that was only the beginning. More than 2,300 print articles appeared and more than 1,000 broadcast segments were devoted to the invention. The value of the more than 800 million impressions generated by the PR campaign would be the equivalent of $21.5 billion in advertising space.

One cautionary note, however: While there is little doubt that this was one of the most effective uses of public relations to launch a new product ever, in some ways, it may have been too successful. Sometimes the snowball effect of mass media attention on a product can be take the beneficiary by surprise. And that surprise can destroy a company's infrastructure—sales and distribution networks, adequately staffed toll-free telephone lines, and a sufficiently powerful company Web site able to handle massive numbers of hits—isn't in place. Putting the PR efforts too far in front of the actual product launch can have diminishing returns. This was somewhat the case with the Segway launch.

In October 2002, a full year after the initial PR blitz, a high-tech writer, Michael Garfield, reported that the company still did not know when the products would be ready for purchase, despite already having 65,000 orders pending.[29]

A recent meeting with Dean Kamen and his staff provided me with no additional tips. I would have loved to walk away with the secrets behind the gyroscope-based machine. Even better, I could have scooped the world if I found out WHEN and HOW the Segway HT will come to market. Alas, the only thing I walked away with was walking itself (they didn't let me take a model home with me).

. . . The company is still trying to decide how to sell the machines to the public. I figured anyone would be able to walk into a Sears or Best Buy and roll right out with one. But from the talk around the meeting table, the final route may be to copy the distribution model of cars, trucks and motorcycles—dealerships.

That might not be a bad decision as long as the salesmen don't wear plaid pants or have you wait to close the deal as they go inside and talk to their manager.

While the public clamored unsuccessfully to find the product, many municipalities, including the city of San Francisco, moved to preemptively ban it along with motorized scooters, which had become the bane of many a pedestrian. With no user base in place, there was little opposition to the ban and little a company so thinly stretched could do about it.

The company was not ready to roll out a full national marketing program until late June 2004, when they announced the availability of "new collateral materials, dealer showroom displays, a product video . . . and a regional TV campaign with over 12,000 commercials appearing over a 10-week period in major metro areas where we have strong dealer representation."[30]

What two enterprising authors of the book, *Marketing Without Advertising*, Michael Phillips and Salli Rasberry, suggested that Segway should have done was:[31]

Distribute the first few hundred machines to athletic groups, like college polo teams or soccer teams and pay them to develop games with the device.

Offer a few hundred more, around the country, to some bicycle clubs, skate boarders, extreme sports stars and surfers. Let the young, adventurous people in our society, who are not behavior bound, find new, useful and most importantly, *fun* roles for the Segway.

Once some useful, fun roles and models are visible, then we would set up a distribution network that parallels the new Segway usage patterns. If snowboarders are the first people to love the Segway and use it, then use the snowboard distribution channels.

Hypothetically you would go to snowboard shops, set up retail outlets, and in the same location, create rental companies so people can try out the Segway before they buy. Definitely create repair shops, in the same location, so people know that the device can be repaired quickly and locally.

With this marketing plan, Segway would succeed very rapidly. No engineering mind, just an open commercial mind.

16 Maintaining Brands and Making Advertising News

The role of marketing public relations in introducing new products is widely accepted by marketers, and PR is almost always an integral part of the total introductory marketing effort. Its use in growing brands, sustaining mature brands, and supporting declining brands is less universally understood. In fact, public relations programs can and do support products in every phase of the product life cycle. While MPR may lack the ability of reminder advertising to reach the consumer with measured frequency, it can often surpass advertising with its greater reach. Advertising media budgets for many mature products are reduced or eliminated altogether when the company puts its advertising muscle behind new product entries. As a result, many marketers rely on promotion techniques, like direct marketing offers, couponing, and freestanding inserts (FSI), whose immediate sales impact is measurable but whose long-term effect on the brand franchise may be detrimental.

Marketing public relations, on the other hand, provides marketers with the opportunity to extend the reach of advertising and to capitalize on the credibility factor to build brand loyalty. The role of MPR in relaunching, revitalizing, repositioning, and sustaining mature and even declining brands may be ultimately of even greater value to the company than the quick and dramatic hit that can be achieved in publicizing new products. Maintaining and building the brand franchise is a role for which marketing public relations is particularly well suited because of the variety of tools and tactics that it can apply.

Marketing public relations rarely stands alone. It is most effective when it works strategically with advertising and promotion in integrated marketing communications campaigns. It can complement advertising in mass media by reaching discrete or specialized demographic, psychographic, ethnic, or regional audiences with specifically targeted messages. On other occasions, MPR might complement consumer advertising by influencing influentials who, in turn, influence the consumer.

MPR can be used to supplement the advertising campaign by carrying the same message to the same or different markets, and it can also be used to test marketing and positioning concepts. Public relations pioneered the fitness walking concept that became The Rockport Company's total marketing thrust and the basis of its advertising. Likewise, Campbell Soup Company developed the healthful eating concept as a public relations program before it became the national advertising campaign.

This chapter discusses two ways in which public relations supports existing products:

- Making new news about old products.
- Making the advertising the news.

New News About Old Products

One of the best ways to make old products newsworthy is to discover and promote new uses or new consumer benefits. MPR has been used extensively by major marketers and industry groups to generate new news about old products to keep them at top of mind and relevant to consumers' changing needs and expectations.

Aspirin: The Wonder Drug

In 1986, Alka-Seltzer, which contains aspirin for pain relief and an antacid for upset stomach, publicized a study that showed that one Alka-Seltzer tablet a day reduced the incidence of MI (myocardial infarction, or heart attack) by 51 percent in patients with unstable angina.

Another study showed that second heart attacks were reduced by 21 percent and overall mortality by 15 percent as a result of taking aspirin. Then, a study published in *The New England Journal of Medicine* in 1988 revealed that aspirin could help prevent first heart attacks. In the study, more than 22,000 physicians over the age of 40 took one Bufferin (buffered aspirin) every other day while another group of physicians took placebos or fake aspirin. At the end of 57 months, those healthy men taking aspirin had 47 percent fewer heart attacks.[1]

Within hours after the news of *The New England Journal of Medicine* story was reported by the news media, one aspirin maker beamed a video news release to hundreds of television stations by satellite uplink. Bufferin, Anacin, and Bayer flooded magazines and television with advertising identifying their products with cardiovascular health. Bayer even issued a "calendar pack" reminding users to take a tablet every other day. Sales of aspirin increased 25 to 30 percent in the month following the publicity.

New studies continued to document the health benefits of aspirin. By the millennium, Americans were taking 29 billion aspirin tablets a year, 26 million a day just for heart health. New news about aspirin continued to make headlines in the new century. In March 2003, a six-column headline in *The New York Times* stated "Aspirin Can Lower Risk of Getting Precancerous Polyps in Colon, 2 Studies Find." It reported, "For the first time, researchers have shown in the most rigorous kind of studies that they can reduce the risk of developing colon and rectal polyps, the precursors of almost all colon cancer, with aspirin." The studies had been published in the prestigious *The New England Journal of Medicine*, a principal source of medical news for the mainstream news media.[2]

A year later, the equally prestigious *Journal of the American Medical Association* reported a study that found taking an aspirin a day could ward off breast cancer. In its "TipSheet" page, *Newsweek* commented, "If you're already taking the little wonder drug for heart problems, it's nice to know there may be an added benefit."[3]

Category MPR

The strategy of generating new news about old products can be used effectively both by branded products and entire product categories. Trade-group MPR programs that generically promote the benefits of their product categories provide excellent examples. The theory is that, simply, a rising tide benefits all the boats.

Some of the most successful public relations campaigns have been those conducted by food trade associations and grower groups to keep their products in the news, at top of mind, and relevant to consumers. One of the most successful has been the Florida Citrus Commission program, which has produced more than 1,000 percent growth in Florida-orange consumption since the program began 50 years ago.

Some trade groups run advertising and public relations programs in tandem, but as advertising costs have risen, most have come to depend almost entirely on the power of public relations to carry news about their products to the consumer. A couple of million dollar MPR budget can buy a lot of awareness for the category because the programs are perceived by press and public as "noncommercial." Editors who resist using brand names have no problem running stories about California avocados, Idaho potatoes, or Florida oranges.

In the late 1970s, the American Frozen Food Institute and the National Frozen Food Association formed a joint effort to promote the benefits of frozen foods. Their public relations firm, Golin/Harris, created an industry-wide information program called FACT, the Frozen Food Action Communications Team. Tom Harris served as its executive director for five years. The mission of FACT was to correct misconceptions about the quality of frozen foods and to promote the acceptance and use of frozen foods for all meal occasions both at home and when eating out. Through broad educational initiatives and an immediate response program, FACT gained extensive print space and TV time to tell the positive story of frozen foods. The program was credited by *Frozen Food Age*, the industry's leading trade publication, with reversing a decline in frozen-food sales.

As the industry improved the quality of frozen foods and the attacks subsided, FACT was able to move from a defensive to a promotional position. An MPR program sent gymnast-actress Cathy Rigby to major media markets to extol the virtues of frozen foods and to prepare recipes using frozen foods on local talk television shows. Food editors from the top newspapers and women's magazines were taken on a tour of California farms where vegetables were harvested and frozen at the peak of freshness. They were served dishes prepared with frozen foods by the chefs at famous restaurants, causing the editors who were previously wedded to fresh vegetables to take a fresh look at frozens.

Pets Are Wonderful: Expanding the Market

In most instances, the objectives of the trade-group public relations programs are straightforward: to increase consumption by telling the positive product story, to increase "share of mind" awareness, and to give people persuasive reasons to try or to buy more of the promoted product category. The Pet Food Institute faced a different problem. Per-capita consumption of dog and cat food was steady, but there was a decline in pet ownership. The objective, therefore, was to increase the number of pets owned. By so doing, the market for the sale of pet food could be expanded. The underlying assumption was that, as the market grew, each of the supporting manufacturers would share in a bigger pie. The industry is, of course, highly competitive, and the battle for market share is backed by multimillion-dollar brand-advertising campaigns.

The approach taken by the Pet Food Institute and its public relations counsel, Golin/Harris, was to address pet acquisition rather than sell pet food. The program, in fact, assiduously avoided even the most generic references to what to feed pets. The program was called Pets Are Wonderful (PAW), and its sponsor was a nonprofit public service organization called the Pets Are Wonderful Council.

The marketing objective of the Pet Food Institute was to sell more pet food by creating more canine and feline mouths to feed; the public relations objective was to persuade people to acquire a pet. The public relations strategy was to communicate the benefits of pet ownership to a principal target market of families with children at home.

If the decision to acquire a pet were plotted on a grid, it would probably fall between a rational, thoughtful, considered decision and an emotional decision, where feelings make the difference. In either case, the decision to acquire a pet is a matter of high involvement. The PR strategy was expressed this way: to communicate the joys and rewards of pet ownership. Here are a few of the tactics that worked to communicate these messages. The joys of pet ownership were communicated through:

- A traveling shopping mall exhibit enabled prospective pet owners to see and touch animals from local shelters.
- "Most Wonderful Pet" contests in cities across the country showcased the importance of pets in their owners' lives.
- National PAW spokespersons, celebrity pet lovers like TV's Betty White, Sally Struthers, and Bill Cosby, appeared in Pets Are Wonderful PSAs and on national television.
- Media spokespersons brought lovable puppies and kittens from local shelters on television talk shows, inevitably resulting in a wave of adoptions.

The rewards (thinking benefits) of pet ownership were also communicated:

- Research was funded in a new field of scientific study called the human/companion animal bond.
- Papers presented at the Human/Companion Animal Bond Conference on such subjects as the importance of pets in teaching children responsibility, in lowering blood pressure, in helping heart-attack victims, and in providing companionship for the aged were widely publicized.
- The exposure included a segment on TV's top-rated "60 Minutes" called "Man's Best Medicine" that was repeated four times.
- A program directed to city dwellers communicated the ease of urban pet ownership.
- A program directed to parents of latchkey children extolled the benefits of coming home from school to a loving pet rather than an empty house.

How do the group know the program worked?

First, unlike many marketing communications programs, the public relations program stood alone. Therefore, measurable results could be directly attributable to public relations.

Second, the program had built-in research mechanisms from the outset. Focus groups were held to determine consumers' views about pet ownership. Media analysis was used to track publicity regionally and measure the incidence of positive, negative, and neutral publicity about pets. The media plan was revised quarterly to overlay certain messages in specific geographic areas. A benchmark national attitude survey was conducted to determine attitudes toward pet ownership and compare them with subsequent studies reflecting attitude change in specific areas addressed by the program. A national survey on the incidence of pet ownership was conducted annually among 7,500 households nationwide. In 1986, dog ownership increased, marking the reversal of a 10-year decline.

Advertising Makes News

In the absence of real product news, a newsworthy advertising campaign may be equally effective in generating media coverage. Perhaps Apple Computer's startling "1984" commercial is the classic. The commercial, which introduced the Macintosh

Computer, ran only once on network TV during the Super Bowl telecast on January 22, 1984. But once was enough to generate far more in pre- and post-publicity than the equivalent cost of producing and airing the extravagant Orwellian spot. The combination of the spot and the publicity about it sent droves of buyers into computer showrooms. Sales surpassed Apple's most ambitious goals. *Advertising Age* named it the "TV Commercial of the Decade" and said that the spot "created a new genre of commercials—advertising as an event—and transformed the Super Bowl into a venue of choice for campaign launches."

Since then, commercials have been run in TV newscasts reporting on the cola wars, beer wars, the burger wars, and even the bankcard wars, garnering valuable free airtime in the process. Philip Dusenberry, then chairman of the giant BBDO advertising agency, told *The New York Times* that "when you get this type of publicity, it's like somebody coming along and handing you a whole pile of money you didn't have."[4]

Advertising on The Super Bowl: A PR Event

At a cost of $2.4 million to $2.5 million for a 30-second spot for the 2005 game, every news outlet in the country seems to fixate on what a company could possibly say to be worth this outlay of cash. Articles begin to appear six months prior to the game outlining who has signed on and what the new product launches will be. Then during the game, several news agencies do on-line or phone-polling to rate the ads. Of course, this focus on Super Bowl ads began 20 years ago with the now-famous "1984" TV spot launched by Apple's MacIntosh. That was the first time the media began to pay attention to the break-through nature of Super Bowl spots. Today, there seems to be more media coverage of the ads and greater value in the public relations aspect of the event than the actual advertising coverage or the game itself.

One of the most popular ad reviews is *USA Today's* Super Bowl Ad Meter, which began in 1989 to gauge consumers' opinions about TV's most expensive commercials. The paper assembles 136 adult volunteers in Tampa and electronically charts their second-by-second reactions to ads during the Super Bowl. The results are so popular that sometimes they are reported on before the score of the football game. And for several days after the game, articles appear critiquing the ads and interviewing the company spokespeople to determine if it was all worthwhile. Dozens of Web sites capture the ads, allowing people to play them over and over again. Most are archived and can be viewed years later. Bob Garfield of *Advertising Age* has appeared on Good Morning America the day after the Super Bowl to discuss the ads. In many ways, there is greater value in the public relations aspect of the event than the actual advertising coverage.

In an article entitled, "Free Association: More Marketers Seek Out Media Exposure to Enhance Their Traditional Paid Campaigns," *Advertising Age* reported:

> The TV commercial—once the ultimate form of advertising—is just the beginning these days. Increasingly, advertisers are augmenting traditional media schedules with additional exposures, the so-called "free media." . . . Public relations agencies are telling clients that such exposure is as much as four times as valuable as equivalent paid time. . . . Amid concern about the escalating cost of TV time as viewership fragments and clutter cuts an ad's impact, more advertisers are exploring free media possibilities.[5]

In the twenty-first century, users of TiVo-like devices are recording or replaying programming with the commercials deleted. Advertisers are struggling to find ways to keep viewers from zapping their stuff.

Marketing columnist Eleanor Trickett suggests that, "Used well, PR might actually be able to encourage people to seek out their ads during a break or maybe not forward through the advertising at all, producing a happy halo effect for other advertisers. And if the ad is not only available on a good advertiser Web site, but also needed elsewhere on the internet, then you have a way to reach all those people who prefer the internet to TV."[6]

Mary Wells's News-Making Ad Campaigns

The advertising industry has long used public relations to bring attention to their campaigns. Many ad makers today specifically create campaigns to make news. The legendary adwoman Mary Wells Lawrence understood this and created her first pattern-breaking, news-making campaigns in the 1970s with that in mind.

Others did it before, but nobody did it better than Mary Wells. Mary not only made her ads famous, but, in the process, made herself a celebrity. She became the best-known and certainly the most photographed ad person of her time. It didn't hurt that she was very bright, stylish, good looking, and blonde. Mary made international news when she married her client Harding Lawrence, CEO of Braniff Airways.

Mary was as masterful a publicist as she was a copywriter. In her biography, *A Big Life in Advertising*, she recalls that when Lawrence needed "something so big it will make Braniff important news overnight," she responded with "The End of the Plain Plane." She dressed Braniff hostesses in uniforms designed by Emilio Pucci and painted the airline's 707s blue, green, yellow, red, and turquoise. When she invited the international press to a "fly-by," 300 reporters and photographers from around the world covered the event. It put Braniff in the news and on the map. Mary wrote, "In 1966, if you hadn't heard about Braniff, you had to be in solitary confinement. In less than a year, we received more publicity in newspapers and magazines than we paid for advertising in over ten years."[7]

Mary tried to create ads that made news for all of her clients. In the index of her book are 38 references to the press. She recalled launching an offbeat campaign for Benson & Hedges Cigarettes this way: "We staged a public relations reception at the Four Seasons Restaurant. We had invited the press from everywhere and Manhattan's trendiest crowd. Beautiful models in glittering miniskirts served champagne and perhaps a little stardust because people jammed into the movie theater and wouldn't come out. They just watched those commercials over and over again, laughing and applauding."[8]

I'm Lovin' It

Advertisers of the twenty-first century are very much aware of the value of public relations in extending the reach of and excitement about their new ad campaigns. That reach has now gone global. In 2003, McDonald's Corporation, the largest foodservice retailer, announced the launch of its hip and edgy "I'm Lovin' It" campaign in Munich, Germany, in what the company described as "an unprecedented global brand campaign." The campaign was a key part of McDonald's business strategy "to connect with customers in highly relevant, culturally significant ways around the world." The theme and attitude was not only used in advertising, but in crew training, national sponsorships, promotions, and even local street marketing. Larry Light, McDonald's executive vice president and global chief marketing officer, said "It is a multidimensional approach to customers around the world that goes from television sets and computers to our restaurants—and everything in between." *The New York Times* headline was "McDonald's Campaign Aims to Regain the Youth Market."9

The ad campaign created by McDonald's German ad agency, Heye & Partner, was launched at a nightclub in Munich. A battery of executives from the company's Oak Brook, Illinois, headquarters flew there to underscore the global nature of the campaign. They unveiled a two-year integrated marketing campaign that, for the first time, used the same branding message and commercials in all worldwide markets, covering 119 countries. The series of high-energy, adult-focused commercials was designed to reflect the lifestyles and attitudes of contemporary customers and culture. The US spots featured cameo appearances and vocals by pop music superstar Justin Timberlake, who tied in with his "lovin' it live" tour in the US and Europe. Another pop icon, professional skateboarder Tony Hawk, appeared in other commercials, and McDonald's sponsored a 29-city US tour featuring the world's best skateboarders, freestyle motocross, and BMX stunt riders.

The US campaign was kicked off in Chicago, McDonald's hometown, with a lakefront VIP party attended by national and international media. Millions of media impressions were generated by the press conference and premiere party, the Justin Timberlake tour, and a later press conference to introduce new global packaging. In addition to these events, the company used a wide array of publicity techniques, including one-to-one media interviews, an electronic press kit, an audio news releases, commercial reel and B-roll distribution, and an AP wire photo. Sneak peeks of the spots began appearing in high-profile television programs and on the Internet. The publicity primed audiences for the campaign, which debuted on highest-rated fall TV shows, including the Miss America Pageant, the Emmy Awards, Monday Night Football, and the season premieres of the popular sitcoms "Will and Grace" and "Friends."

The new campaign was so important to McDonald's that, in his letter to shareholders in the company's 2003 annual report, Chairman and CEO James Cantalupo commented:

> Our unprecedented worldwide 'I'm lovin' it' campaign—with its contemporary look and sound—has connected with customers in a powerful way. It has created excitement. It is driving sales. And it is bringing the magic back to McDonald's marketing. 'I'm lovin' it' has helped us think differently about how we present ourselves to customers, and we'll continue to use this creative approach to build relevance with our key customer segments.10

He added, "We're proud that the campaign was ranked one of the five best of 2003 by *The Wall Street Journal*, citing an editorial endorsement to support his enthusiasm for the campaign.

The Sock Puppet Takes a Fall

The cover of Al ad Laura Ries' book, *The Fall of Advertising & the Rise of PR*, portrays the *Pets.com* sock puppet dog playing dead. The dog had its day when it was loved by consumers and lauded by marketers. *Advertising Age* called the sock puppet "the first bona fide celebrity to be created in *dot.com* land." The sock was as much a creature of publicity as advertising. The ads were, in fact, so popular that the puppet was profiled in *People* magazine, *Entertainment Weekly,* and *Time* and was actually invited to do guest shots on big TV shows like ABC's "Good Morning America," where the puppet was interviewed by Diane Sawyer.

Everybody loved the advertising, but as the Rieses pointed out, the ads gave pet owners no reason to buy their pet supplies from *Pets.com*. Neither prize-winning advertising nor great public relations could save the company. The demise of *Pets.com* was the result of a bad business plan that killed many a dot com company.[11]

17 Sponsorships and Special Events

Special events are big business. Marketers have turned to special events of all descriptions to cut through mass-media clutter and gain greater brand awareness and loyalty. Sponsorship has soared by billions of dollars over the past two decades. The 20th Annual IEG Sponsorship Report, published by International Events Group, found that marketers in the US and Canada spent $11 billion on special event sponsorships in 2003, and that growth has been paralleled in Europe and Asia, with worldwide sponsorship reaching $28 billion, not including money spent on advertising, promotion, and public relations activities in support of these sponsorships.

Seventeen companies spent more than $50 million on sponsorships in 2003. Ten of them spent more than $100 million. The list was led by PepsiCo, Anheuser-Bush, General Motors, Coca-Cola, Nike, Miller Brewing, DaimlerChrysler, Ford, and McDonald's. By becoming NASCAR's biggest sponsor, Nextel Communications joined the list.[1]

IEG has defined five major categories of event sponsorships. Sports are, by far, the largest category. IEG projected 2004 spending for sports in North America at $7.69 billion, or 69 percent of the total dollars spent on all sponsored events. Entertainment tours and attractions came in second at 10 percent, driven by "music sponsorships which have the potential to cross borders and cultures and impact the youth market." Cause marketing (9 percent), festivals, fairs, and annual events (7 percent), and arts sponsorships (5 percent) completed the list.

Here is how IEG explains the reason for the explosion in sponsorships:

> There is a huge gap between how marketers want to reach people and how people want to be reached. No matter how commercials are dressed up, most people will avoid them if they can. The advantage that sponsorship has over all media is that it is the only medium that gives brands the opportunity to create, enrich, and facilitate engaging experiences, emotions, and ideas. People are hyper-attuned to marketing: they understand sponsors are seeking a commercial return, but because they benefit—as does the property they care about—they appreciate the sponsor's effort, and that appreciation is linked to behavior, such as product purchase. The greater number of experiences—intellectual, spiritual, and physical—to which a brand can provide access, the more effective its marketing will be in sales and profits. [2]

The big sponsors are increasingly moving toward single sponsorships, or "sponsownership," a term coined by Paul Stanley of PS Productions. *Adweek*'s Marketing Week points out that ". . . event ownership can provide a mechanism for generating profit from the event itself while remaining true to marketing objectives."[3] A sponsor who controls the talent can control location, promotion, and such MPR considerations as personal and media appearances.

The Marriage of MPR and Sports Marketing

Recent research shows that editorial coverage can be as effective or more effective than running the sponsor's commercials. Counselor Steve Lesnik, of Kemper Lesnik Communications, advises that a sports marketing program should achieve one or more of the following objectives:

- Drive sales
- Enhance image
- Generate product awareness
- Encourage customer trial
- Gain access to mass media
- Nurture client and/or employee relationships
- Enhance community relations

He says, "As a title sponsor of an event, a company expects, above all else, recognition of the sponsorship by all target audiences including consumers, the media, employees, and other key influencers. It is the responsibility of public relations to help generate that recognition which most often is accomplished through the activities of a corporate information bureau, which plays the lead role in undertaking all communications activities for the marketer. They include creating, developing, and producing all media materials, managing proactive media relations efforts, and responding to media inquiries."[4]

Recent research has shown that "editorial" coverage of a TV sports event can be as effective, or more effective, than running the sponsor's commercials. Lesnik commissioned a research firm to conduct a four-city study to measure public attitudes regarding a company's sponsorship of a series of family-oriented sporting events. Questions were asked of two groups. One group had seen the event as it was shown on TV, including commercials. The people who had viewed the telecast saw the CEO present trophies and make a warm, engaging little talk; heard well-known, credible sports announcers mention the company's name repeatedly in association with the event; witnessed admired international superstars express gratitude to the company and its CEO; and saw the company's logo intimately associated with the event and celebrities. The second group saw the TV show without commercials.

The research found rather conclusively that viewers of the telecast were more likely to respond favorably to questions about the sponsoring company than nonviewers. But in addition, viewers of the telecast who had not seen the company's commercials in the program responded as favorably and, in some cases, more favorably than viewers seeing the program with commercials. Confidence in the company was about 45 percent higher for both viewers who had seen and who had not seen commercials in the program, compared with consumers who had not seen the show at all. Viewers of the program were also more likely to think the sponsor's product "is good for children," an important measure to the sponsor.

On both general and specific questions, viewers exhibited decidedly improved attitudes, which were even better if they had not seen the commercials. Lesnik's conclusion: "This research refutes the old saw that event sponsorship just creates a warm and fuzzy plus or that advertising moves research needles and PR doesn't."

Wheaties and Sports Since 1933

The identification of sports with popular brand names, rediscovered in the 1980s, has been effectively used for decades. One of the pioneers was Wheaties through its association with professional baseball. In 1933, nine years after the cereal was first introduced by General Mills, Wheaties first ventured into the sports world as sponsor of play-by-play baseball broadcasts. That year, too, marked the creation of a slogan that became one of the most popular ever in advertising history: "Wheaties—The Breakfast of Champions."

Wheaties' baseball broadcasts were immensely popular throughout the 1930s. From one station, they expanded to 95, spreading to teams and cities throughout the country. Athlete testimonials were a key part of the "Breakfast of Champions" broadcast package. Wheaties sponsored the first televised commercial sports broadcast on August 29, 1939, when NBC presented a game between the Cincinnati Reds and the Brooklyn Dodgers for some 500 owners of television sets in New York City.

Wheaties' popularity boomed during the 1930s, and the cereal became synonymous with all branches of the sports world. Testimonials by great athletes, such as Babe Ruth, Jack Dempsey, Red Grange, Bronco Nagurski, Otto Graham, Babe Didrikson, Patty Berg, Sam Snead, Ben Hogan, and George Mikan, made Americans aware of the product.

In 1956, General Mills sought a spokesperson to present the Wheaties story. From more than 500 candidates, two-time Olympic pole-vaulting champion Bob Richards, a well-known crusader for fitness, was chosen. The Wheaties Sports Federation was established, with Richards as director. The organization worked closely with such groups as the US Olympic Committee, the US Junior Chamber of Commerce, and the President's Council on Youth Fitness to promote sports and athletic participation throughout the country. The federation produced a large number of instructional and educational films, which were made available free to the public. It also gave direct financial support to such activities as Olympic educational programs and the Jaycee Junior Champ Track-and-Field Competition.

Bob Richards served as product spokesperson from 1956 until 1970. Wheaties has recognized several hundred amateur and professional athletes on the storied orange cereal package, but only eight celebrity athletes have been honored for lifetime achievement and have become spokespersons for the cereal, appearing nationally on Wheaties packages, in commercials, and in TV interviews. Bob Richards was followed by Olympic decathlon champion Bruce Jenner, Olympic gold medal gymnast Mary Lou Retton, baseball's Pete Rose, the late football legend Walter Payton, tennis star Chris Evert, basketball great Michael Jordan, who represented the brand for a decade from 1988 to 1998, and Tiger Woods, the world's top-rated golfer, who began his association with Wheaties in 1998.

The Olympics

Every four years, corporations scramble to become official sponsors of the Olympics. Sponsors paid up to $80 million to sponsor the 2004 Summer Olympics. To get the most from their hefty cost of being the official sponsors of the games, they go to great lengths to extend their sponsorships.

Coca-Cola and the Olympics

Coca-Cola has been continuously associated with the Olympic Games since 1928, longer than any other corporate sponsor. From 1992 through the Athens Olympics in 2004, the company was responsible for selecting more than 10,000 torchbearers and 8,000 escort runners, more than any single organization in the history of the Olympic Games. The company's participation has indelibly identified it with the Olympics in thousands of communities and enabled it to reach millions of consumers live, and these contacts have been multiplied geometrically by those viewing the relay on local TV and reading about it in their local newspapers.

Coca-Cola was the exclusive sponsor of the coast-to-coast torch relay in 1996 and was so omnipresent at the Olympics that summer in their hometown, Atlanta, that many called it "The Coca-Cola Olympics." The company selected 2,500 of the 10,000 torchbearers through promotions held around the world, making it the first time torchbearers from outside of the US carried the flag in this country. Coca-Cola also recruited all 2,500 of the 1996 relay escort runners from high schools on the basis of their athleticism, character, and leadership qualities. That year, the relay covered a record 15,000 miles through 42 of the 50 United States.

The 2004 Olympic Torch Relay was presented by Coca-Cola and Samsung Electronics Co., who were responsible for selecting all of the worldwide torchbearers. It covered 27 countries in North America, Asia, Europe, Oceania, Africa, and South America. The relay route included every city that had ever hosted the Summer Olympic Games. The two companies hosted the first and final legs of the event.

Bank of America Down Under

A year to the day before the opening of the 2000 Olympic Summer Games, Bank of America, the official bank of the US Olympic Committee, launched a massive program to enhance its brand image worldwide. With more than $600 billion in assets, the program began with a spectacular appearance on NBC's "Today" show. Gymnast Mary Lou Retton and track-and-field star Jackie Joyner-Kersee, former gold medalists, appeared live on the show. They were interviewed in front of a 60-foot by 70-foot, inflatable facsimile of the Sydney Opera House, which the bank set up in Rockefeller Center.

The appearance of Mary Lou and Jackie was part of an entire morning of exposure on the network, which would telecast the games in the Unites States. The cast also included a team of painted Aboriginal dancers who made fire by rubbing sticks together. Animal handler Jim Fowler was also on hand with a trio of Australian marsupials, a wallaby, a tiny sugar glider, and a feisty kangaroo named Harry. The "Today" show appearance, and the press conference that followed, kicked off Bank of America's Down Under Tour. The mammoth tour was the centerpiece of a multifaceted effort mounted by the bank in support of its Olympic sponsorship.

The Down Under Tour covered 18,000 miles and hit 48 cities in 21 states for a year, concluding in San Francisco on September 15, 2000—the day of the opening ceremonies of the Olympics in Sydney. Bank of America said it designed the tour to help customers, employees, and communities who couldn't make it to Australia experience the Olympics.

A team of Bank of America public relations officers from every region advanced the tour and built media excitement in every tour market. The story was shaped to have across-the-board appeal to news, sports, and business media in tour cities.

Mary Lou and Jackie were members of a five-person team of Olympic champions enlisted by Bank of America as "associate coaches" who met with Bank of America people across the country to talk about how the ideals of the Olympic movement mirror Bank of America's core values. The Olympians were introduced to bank customers and interviewed by local reporters along the tour route.

The traveling show was an interactive, multisensory exhibit that took visitors on a virtual journey of Australia. Visitors walked through a gateway pavilion accompanied by sights and sounds of past Olympics and made their way into the Sydney Opera House. The opera house had a state-of-the-art, mega-surround-sound, giant-screen theater, where visitors could enjoy a spectacular film produced especially for Bank of America and experience the sites and sounds of Australia, from the Sydney Opera House to the Aboriginal tribesmen in the Outback. "Tour ambassadors" from each of the 10 Australian states were on hand at every tour stop to greet visitors, answer their questions, and demonstrate authentic Australian activities.

Other Down Under exhibits included the Outback Airlines Experience, an exciting, four-minute, interactive adventure, including a journey through the Outback and white water rafting, without the need for vests. The Aboriginal art exhibit featured authentic dot paintings, woodcarvings, musical instruments, and live demonstrations by Aboriginal artists and musicians. For the virtually adventurous, there was the Ayers Rock Climbing Challenge, a mechanical rock climbing experience that enabled visitors to experience the challenge of the climb without ever leaving the ground.

The Down Under Tour Outpost sold US Olympic Team merchandise, items indigenous to Australia, and original Aboriginal works of art, with proceeds going to the US Olympic Team and the Aboriginal Arts Council.

The big show appeared in tour cities on Saturdays and Sundays. The traveling squad was assisted at each stop on the tour by volunteer local Bank of America associates. In each community, there was also a Friday preview event for school children. The bank distributed educational kits to 600,000 children in 20,000 classrooms in every Bank of America market visited by the tour. The school package included a video, color maps, and enough material for a month-long teaching unit. It was all created to celebrate both the Olympic movement and the history and culture of Australia.

MPR Acting Local

The Glenlivet Office Putting Championship

You don't have to sponsor a major event or break the bank to gain involvement, get media coverage, and reach target customers.

The Glenlivet Single Malt Scotch Whiskey brand wanted to dramatically increase brand awareness and consumption among affluent young adults and to nurture appeal to a younger generation of Scotch drinkers. Research indicated that golf is the most popular participatory sport among younger Scotch drinkers. There is a natural connection between golf and Scotch Whiskey, since both have their historic roots in Scotland. To meet the challenge, the brand's public relations firm, Kemper Lesnik Communications, created the Glenlivet Office Putting Championship for the Chicago market. The competition to crown the champion indoor putter of Chicago's business community was irresistible to both companies and the media.

The Glenlivet Office Putting Championship was scheduled for February, enabling young Chicago business people to indulge their love for golf while the weather outside was frightful. From hundreds of companies that registered for the event, 128 were picked at random to compete. Each of them was presented with an engraved wooden box containing four Glenlivet glasses, which served as holes, event golf balls featuring the brand logo, ball makers, official rules and regulations, and, of course, a bottle of 12-year-old The Glenlivet Single Malt, for post-event libation.

The agency set up five-hole competition courses down hallways, around cubicles, and even in the boardrooms of the chosen companies. To drum up media interest, the agency staged a series of pre-tournament events. The kickoff event featured a putting battle between teams from Chicago's two daily newspapers, *The Chicago Tribune* and *The Chicago Sun-Times*. A second media event was held at Monsanto headquarters in the Merchandise Mart on what was billed as Chicago's, and maybe the world's, longest indoor putting green: a one-block-long, 186-yard straight hallway. This event was covered by both CNN and The Golf Channel. Still another pre-championship promotional event was a charity tournament for Chicago-area media celebrities. Glenlivet donated $1,000 to each of their favorite charities and offered $100,000 for anyone who could sink a 60-foot putt.

The champion from each office advanced to compete in the Citywide Finals in the Grand Ballroom of The Fairmont Hotel Chicago. The grand prize winner received a title, a trophy, and a trip to play Scotland's legendary golf courses, St. Andrews and Royal Troon, and, of course, to visit the Glenlivet Distillery.

Media coverage reached consumers not only in the Chicago market, but also in national and international markets. Of the more than 600 spectators who attended the Citywide Finals, most were young urban professionals targeted by the brand.

Sales could be tracked against the previous year, since there was no additional marketing activity in the market during the promotion period. A sales surge of 300 percent could be directly attributed to the excitement the event created in the marketplace. Both on- and off-premise retailers reported significant sales increases.

Gatorade and Sports Performance

In the 1960s, a team of researchers at the University of Florida developed a product that would rapidly replace fluids and loss of body salts brought about by physical exertion. The formula was tested on members of the university's football team. The University of Florida Gators team enjoyed a winning season in 1965 and became known as a second-half team because of its endurance and efficiency. When the Gators defeated their opponents in the Orange Bowl, the losing coach said, "We didn't have Gatorade. That made the difference." The quote was picked up in *Sports Illustrated*, launching the phenomenal sales success of Gatorade and its involvement with sports that continues in the twenty-first century.

Media exposure continues to be integral to Gatorade sports sponsorships. The sight of their pro-football heroes drinking Gatorade from the familiar green cups during NFL telecasts reminds millions of fans of the product's benefits in achieving peak performance. Bob Dilenschneider recalls the public relations agenda that Hill & Knowlton created to make Gatorade a part of the game itself:

> If you want amateur athletes to buy Gatorade because it rehydrates you, show Heisman Trophy winners chugging it down when they have just finished an

eighty-yard dash to the end zone. So, on the sidelines, we put huge chests of Gatorade with the trademark on the chest and added stacks of Gatorade cups. As television added more sideline reaction shots and personal coverage of the players, televised football became a continuous promotion for Gatorade. It was the teams themselves that launched the ritual of dousing winning coaches with Gatorade or ice water from the Gatorade chests.[5]

Gatorade has become not only the official sports drink of the NFL but also the NBA, WNBA, Major League Baseball, US Soccer, and numerous professional, collegiate, and amateur teams and events throughout the world.

Gatorade sponsorships also permeate the college and high school ranks. The company is an official sponsor of the NCAA, providing visual opportunities in all sports, and is the official sponsor of a number of high school athletic associations. The Gatorade Circle of Champions program, inaugurated in 1985, honors state, regional, and national winners in seven sports each year. Administered by *Scholastic Coach Magazine*, it generates tremendous publicity nationally and in each of the markets where local athletes are honored.

Another key to Gatorade's commercially successful identification with sports is the leadership position it has taken in supporting the athletic training community at all levels. The link is important because athletic trainers are responsible for the treatment and prevention of athletic injuries, of which heat illness is the most common. As a result, Gatorade is the official sponsor of the Professional Athletic Trainers Association, the National Basketball Trainers Association, the Professional Baseball Athletic Trainers Association, and the National Athletic Trainers Association. The company publishes media guides annually for the football, basketball, and baseball trainers, providing sports media with biographical information about the trainers of each league team.

The ultimate objective for nearly all of Gatorade's sports-marketing activities is to maintain and extend the product's sideline, courtside, and dugout visibility. This has successfully aligned Gatorade with the product's target users, 12- to 43-year-old physically active males. How well did it work? Gatorade became Quaker Oats Company's number-one selling product and the principle reason why the company was acquired by PepsiCo.

Suds and Sports

The link between the beer business and the sports world is so pervasive today that *Sports Illustrated* ran a cover story on "Suds and Sports." The magazine put it this way:

> Nothing loves suds like a sports fan loves suds. This is an indelible fact of contemporary American anthropology. It is a matter of demographic statistics. It is blessed chapter and verse in US brewers' bibles of marketing and advertising. It is the reason that almost every kind of sporting event, from a rinky-dink hometown road race to the Olympic Games, is played out, as often as not, in an environment of beer slogans, beer signs, beer songs, and beer salesmanship.[6]

Sports have played a pivotal role in the ascendancy of both Miller Beer and Anheuser-Busch. Miller was the seventh-ranked beer when it was acquired by Philip Morris in 1970. With Philip Morris money and marketing know-how, Miller became deeply involved in TV sports and, by the late 1970s, was buying more than half of all beer commercial time on network sports programming. Miller Lite, with its funny, macho, Over-the-Hill-Gang commercials, climbed to second place among all US beer brands. Miller's largest commitment is to motor racing, but, according to *Sports Illustrated*, Miller also puts sponsorship money into a sports potpourri, including tractor pulls, ski racing, NBA All-Star balloting, and the offering of a million dollars to anyone on the pro bowlers' tour who wins a three-tournament parlay called the Lite Slam. Miller gains greater visibility for its NASCAR (National Association for Stock Car Auto Racing) sponsorship by displaying a duplicate of its car in shopping centers and other retail outlets, in an effort to attract crowds and interest in the race.

In 2000, South African Brewers purchased Miller from Philip Morris and changed its named to SABMiller, but the company remains one of the largest sponsors of sports in the world.

In 1977, Anheuser-Busch got into the act in a major way, increasing its share of the national beer market from 22 to 40 percent. A-B, brewer of Budweiser and Bud Light, is one of the leading sponsors of professional and amateur soccer in the world. Budweiser has sponsored every FIFA World Cup since 1986. The multi-tournament agreement with FIFA (Federation Internationale de Football Association) is the biggest sponsorship package in Budweiser's long history of sports marketing. August Busch IV, vice president of marketing, said, "Budweiser is becoming a truly international brand, and our sponsorship of the FIFA World Cup enables us to promote the brand's position as the world's best-selling beer to millions of beer drinkers worldwide."[7]

Budweiser sponsors a variety of motor sports teams. In its first 14 years of auto racing, Bud teams won 36 national and world championships. It is the official beer of NASCAR and of the National Hot Rod Association. It sponsors Dale Earnhardt, Jr., and the BMW Williams F-1 Team, a global leader in Formula One racing.

Bud is also the official beer of the National Basketball Association, Major League Baseball, and 27 of the 32 National Football League teams. In addition to football, baseball, basketball, motor sports, horse racing, boxing, tennis, golf, bowling, and track-and-field events on network TV, A-B sponsors "about a thousand individual events, competitions, and leagues," according to Roarty. They have ranged from the Budweiser US Pro Tour of Surfing and Body Boarding to the Bud Light Ironman Triathlon World Championship in Hawaii. The Triathlon was picked for Bud Light, when it was introduced in 1981, because it fit the desired image of a healthful, low-calorie, but macho, product. The combination of swimming, cycling, and running, new at the time, fit the bill, and the Triathlon has moved from a novelty to a popular spectator and participant sport.

McDonald's Sports Marketing

McDonald's Corporation became a major sports sponsor to help build brand presence and brand preference for McDonald's on international, national, and local levels. McDonald's sports-marketing activities encompass gymnastics, track, figure-skating, golf, and basketball.

The company applies the following screens to evaluate a sports program:

- Does it enhance McDonald's leadership position?
- Does it deliver national TV presence?
- Can McDonald's own it?

- Does it help McDonald's stand out from the clutter?
- Does it provide local extensions?

Since its inception in 1977, nomination and selection to the McDonald's All-American High School Basketball Team has become one of the most prestigious honors for high school players. The team is composed of the top high-school-senior basketball players in the nation. It starts with the naming of the 2,500 most outstanding senior players, nominated by a committee of high school basketball coaches. From this group, the field is narrowed to 25 McDonald's All-Americans. Members of the "Dream Team" have included such greats as Michael Jordan, Ervin (Magic) Johnson, Isaiah Thomas, Kevin Garnett, Carmelo Anthony, and LeBron James. The McDonald's All-American High School Basketball Game is the only event that brings together the best high school players from the East to compete against the best of the West. The proceeds from the game are donated to the local chapter of the Ronald McDonald House, where the game is played. More than $3 million was raised by the first 25 games. In 2002, the company inaugurated the McDonald's All-American High School Girls Game, which is played before the Boys Game in the same venue. Both games are broadcast live on ESPN.

The event guarantees network visibility to McDonald's and offers opportunities for local and regional publicity on sports pages and television sports broadcasts for all players nominated and selected for the boys and girls teams.

As the Official Restaurant of the 2004 Olympics, McDonald's was omnipresent in the athletes' village, the main sports complex, and the press center. Every Olympic athlete, fan, and journalist had to pass by and hopefully stop for a bite at a McDonald's. They were served by a team of McDonald's employees from around the world. The company also gained exposure by signing up a number of Olympians as global ambassadors. Chinese basketball star, Yao Ming, appeared in commercials, as did Ronald McDonald, who was portrayed competing in a variety of Olympic events. The company held a news conference in Athens, in which International Olympic Committee President Jacques Rogge thanked McDonald's for its financial support and praised McDonalds' employees for sharing the Olympic values of hard work and team spirit. Olympian tennis star Venus Williams and swimmer Janet Evans served as rival coaches of four teams who competed to whip up the most Big Macs in three minutes.

NASCAR: America's Favorite Sport

The National Association for Stock Car Auto Racing (NASCAR) is the largest motorsports-sanctioning body in the world with a reported 75 million fans. The best drivers, teams, and cars compete all season long in events that lead to the coveted Nextel Cup. In 2003, Nextel Communications succeeded R.J. Reynolds, the longtime sponsor of what was formerly called the Winston Cup. Nextel sponsors the overall 10-month-long racing series, which includes such major events as the Pepsi 400 and the Coca-Cola 600 race.

In addition to live audiences, NASCAR races are seen on Fox, NBC, and TNT. They attract the second largest sports-viewing audience after the National Football League. A CBS "60 Minutes" piece on veteran racer Richard Petty featured a parade of marketing executives, not only from Petty's longtime sponsor, STP, but such nonrelated products as Gatorade and Heinz Ketchup. All of them agreed that NASCAR sponsorship is one of the surest ways to move merchandise off the shelf. Racing fans are notoriously loyal to the brands that sponsor their heroes. Not only do they buy these products, but they also advertise them on their hats, shirts, jackets, and T-shirts.

NASCAR claims that three out of every four fans will buy sponsors' products—a far higher loyalty rating than fans of any other sport. And sponsors apparently agree. Corporations spend more than $1 billion a year for NASCAR sponsorships and promotions. Companies like Anheuser-Busch, Miller Brewing, Procter & Gamble and Newell Rubbermaid sponsor NASCAR because their research shows that a NASCAR fan is the most loyal fan of all sports. Eric Pinkham, director of corporate event marketing at Newell Rubbermaid, said, "In addition to the valuable on-air exposure, NASCAR lends itself well to the grassroots marketing efforts that are critical to our brand-building efforts. Our race team allows us to take advantage of television, radio, print, and Internet in terms of exposure and publicity, but it also provides us with a show car program at retail locations, which we use to leverage our sponsorship year-round." He said that Newell Rubbermaid can measure incremental business resulting from their NASCAR sponsorship: "Our teams, on a daily basis, focus on brand preference and loyalty, not just brand awareness."[8]

In one of its promotional pieces to sponsors, NASCAR lists 17 most popular methods of sponsorships:

1. Sponsorship of a car
2. Sponsorship of a driver
3. Car-and-driver combined sponsorship
4. Track sponsorship
5. Family-night sponsorship
6. Series sponsorship
7. Single-event sponsorship
8. Lap sponsorship
9. High-performance sponsorship
10. Trackside-billboard advertising
11. Program advertising
12. Prize-money sponsorship
13. Trophy-and-award sponsorship
14. Corporate hospitality-area sponsorship
15. VIP-suite sponsorship
16. Grandstand-section sponsorship
17. "Sponsorship of ironic occurrences"[9]

How MPR Supports Title Sponsorships

With the proliferation of competing television sports events and softening advertising support, the networks that once shied away from plugging an event's sponsor are now offering new opportunities for companies to own title to once untouchable big events. Buying title sponsorship helps advertisers avoid being part of the clutter of 30-second spots. During the college "Bowl" season, viewers have been able to enjoy such postseason classics as the Tostidas Fiesta Bowl, the Nokia Sugar Bowl, and the Federal Express Orange Bowl. The names change every season. Then there are such created-for-sponsor bowls as the GMC Bowl in Mobile, Alabama; the MPC Computer Bowl in Boise, Idaho;

the Capital One Bowl in Orlando, Florida; and the Continental Tire Bowl in Charlotte, North Carolina.

The print media have tended to look skeptically on the practice of title sponsorship linked to the TV ad buy and often drop the sponsor's name in their bowl listings and sports coverage unless the name is inseparable from the event's name. That is why sophisticated users of MPR make certain that they capitalize on sponsorships by planning newsworthy activities around the event.

For similar reasons, ballparks and stadiums are now named for sponsors. Coverage from these venues, whether on television, radio, or in newspapers or magazines, is impossible without identifying the sponsor. The Cardinals have long played at Busch Stadium, but the Colorado Rockies now play at Coors Field and the Milwaukee Brewers at Miller Park. At this writing, the Seattle Mariners play at Safeco Field, the Chicago White Sox at US Cellular Field, and the Arizona Diamondbacks at Bank One Ball Park. But nothing is forever in the name game. The Houston Astros used to play at the Astrodome. They moved to Enron Park in that company's heyday. When Enron hit the skids, they got their energy from Minute Maid Orange Juice. The San Francisco Giants opened Pac Tel Park, but it wasn't long before Pac Tel was acquired by SBC, and the ballpark was renamed for its new owner.

Women's Sports

Philip Morris became one of the earliest title sponsors when it committed Virginia Slims, its cigarette aimed specifically at the young, upscale woman, to sponsor the first women's professional tennis tour. Marketing public relations played a major role in making Virginia Slims synonymous with women's tennis. In those days, before Chris Evert, Martina Navritalova, and Steffi Graff were known to the multitudes, it was essential to introduce the players to the public and to develop excitement about women's tennis as a spectator sport.

The company's public relations firm, Ruder & Finn, designed a program to reach the media with stories and angles of interest that extended far beyond match results and sports pages. The publicity generated during the early years of the Virginia Slims circuit contributed greatly to the gain of popularity and attendance at women's tournaments. The Virginia Slims media guide, published annually and containing tournament results, earnings, and season and lifetime records of all the players, became the encyclopedia of women's tennis and served as an invaluable tool for sports media and the tennis establishment. A kick-off media luncheon was held every year in New York, and a luncheon, hosted by Philip Morris and honoring female athletes, was held in each tournament city weeks before the local event. Charity tie-ins were arranged in each city to create publicity on newspaper pages other than sports pages and to identify the Virginia Slims tour with the local community.

The circuit brought widespread recognition to Virginia Slims entirely through non-advertising channels. Despite the ban on cigarette advertising on television, the Virginia Slims Tournament was covered by network television. Virginia Slims became the pioneer in women's sports marketing, bringing the advertising slogan "You've Come a Long Way, Baby" to life. Billie Jean King says the company lifted women's tennis from stepchild status and helped bring it wealth, power, and prestige.

However Virginia Slims' sponsorship of women's professional tennis came under fire in 1990, when US Secretary of Health and Human Services, Dr. Louis Sullivan, joined a coalition of health groups to protest the sponsorship. He said that cigarette sponsorship of sporting events like Virginia Slims' tennis implied that "smoking is compatible with good health." He called on tobacco companies to drop their sponsorships of all sports events and asked athletes not to participate in tobacco-backed events. Sullivan's pronouncement coincided with his attack on cigarette companies for targeting minorities, women, and young people. Subsequently, Kraft General Foods replaced Virginia Slims after 15 years of loyal sponsorship.

Arts and Entertainment Sponsorships

David Finn, chairman of Ruder-Finn and a pioneer in arts sponsorships, says, "above all, commitment is the key to the effectiveness of a public service program, whether it's corporate- or product-driven. Commitment means being convinced that this is a sound policy for the product and the company, that it's worthwhile for the community, and that the PR and marketing mission is to stay with the project until the best way is found to achieve company benefits."

In his book, *Good-Bye to the Low Profile*, Herbert Schmertz, former Mobil Corporation public relations chief and father of public-television sponsorship, suggests eight more directly self-serving reasons for corporations to be active in supporting the arts and culture:

First, cultural excellence generally suggests corporate excellence. . . .

Second, these discretionary projects offer the opportunity to present your top management not as narrow-minded experts, but rather as corporate statesmen whose concerns go beyond the bottom line. . . .

Third, arts and culture programs enhance the pride of your employees. . . .

Fourth, your company's involvement in the arts provides an excellent opportunity for leadership in the community. . . .

Fifth, the sponsorship of cultural events allows you to entertain important customers at openings, special tours, and similar events where you have the opportunity to introduce important people to other important people.

Sixth, because government leaders often have specific cultural interests and favorite projects, your sponsorship of similar projects and causes provides the opportunity to form useful alliances and valuable contacts.

Seventh, corporate sponsorship of the arts is good for recruiting. . . .

Eighth, in an era when corporations are often criticized for their alleged lack of societal involvement, participation in cultural or arts programs can present excellent opportunities to be involved in constructive social action.

In addition to these principally corporate public relations advantages, arts sponsorships have proved to have equally important marketing benefits.

After fifteen years of artistic and cultural activity, we now find that when we give certain publics a reason to identify with the projects and causes that we have chosen to support, they will translate that identification into a preference for doing business with us.

Schmertz cites a 1982 Mobil public-opinion survey of upscale college graduates in the Boston area. Not only did the respondents identify Mobil with quality programming, but also 31 percent of them said they bought Mobil most often, compared to far lower percentages for Exxon, Gulf, and Texaco. [10]

Schmertz believes that support, like Mobil's sponsorship of "Masterpiece Theater" built brand loyalty, particularly among a growing number of consumers who are highly and deliberately resistant to product advertising. He says that the people in this group are upscale viewers with discretionary dollars to buy, "for example, premium gasoline for all three of their cars."

He points out that it's not only these upscale viewers who consider much advertising infantile, shallow, and misleading. When they watch public TV, pay cable, or rent cassettes without advertising, "it's more difficult than ever for them to sit through product advertising."

As conventional advertising runs up against a growing number of obstacles, corporations are quickly discovering that one alternative to the various problems of traditional advertising is "cause-related marketing," also known as "affinity-of-purpose marketing," which consists of identifying the company with a worthy cause that a high proportion of the target audience happens to believe in. As a result of that identification, consumers reward the company by buying its products or otherwise helping business. In other words, they are choosing to help a third party by doing business with a second party.

After its merger, Exxon-Mobil, the successor company, continued to sponsor "Masterpiece Theater" on PBS, making it the longest-running sponsorship in television history.

Evolution of Arts Marketing

Support of the arts is moving from corporate philanthropy, a CPR function, to arts marketing, an MPR function. Arts marketing is coming of age as corporations learn how to get marketing mileage as well as gain corporate goodwill from its cultural sponsorships.

In a story titled "This Exhibit is Brought to You By . . . ," *Business Week* reported "That museums are hungry for sponsorship dollars is hardly new. What has changed is that corporate America has become bolder in turning galleries into an extension of their own marketing plans." The magazine said that the Field Museum in Chicago rejected two potential corporate sponsors of its Tyrannosaurus Rex Sue exhibit for having "inappropriate marketing plans." The museum secured $8.3 million from McDonald's Corporation and Walt Disney Co. "Among the benefits: the museum's new fossil lab was named for McDonald's, and Disney gained the rights to display a life-sized copy of Sue in its parks." [11]

Philip Morris and the Arts

For nearly 50 years, Philip Morris has been a pioneer in supporting the arts. Its first grant was made in 1958, for an outdoor concert in its hometown of Louisville, Kentucky. Today, Philip Morris has expanded far beyond tobacco to become the world's largest producer and marketer of consumer packaged goods. The Philip Morris companies are one of the leading corporate supporters of arts programs throughout the world.

Former Philip Morris Chairman George Weissman explained the rationale for the company's support of a then-leading edge "Pop and Op Art" exhibition in the 1960s:

How we, at Philip Morris, arrived at our definition perhaps may be constructive. In the early 1960s, we were a small company doing three hundred million dollars a year in the tradition-bound cigarette industry. There were only six companies in the industry, and we were at the bottom of the totem pole. We turned to the arts to provide us with the impulses for new ideas and innovative approaches. The fundamental decision to support the arts was not determined by the need or the state of the arts. We were out to beat the competition. We came to the conclusion that it was no longer possible for business to operate in the old time-tested and traditional manner, and still be successful.

Because we are essentially an industry and a company of creative managers and creative marketers, we had to say to ourselves and to our people that we were open to new ideas, new approaches. At Philip Morris, we began to deal with art, in our case, primarily visual art, that would force us to look at everything in a completely new manner. For us, art was a restless, probing presence to help convert us into a creative mass-marketing organization.[12]

Since "Pop and Op," its first museum exhibition in 1965, the company has sponsored such major shows as the landmark "The Vatican Collections: The Papacy and Art" (its $3 million gift to the Metropolitan Museum of Art was then the largest corporate grant ever given to the arts); the much-heralded "Primitivism in 20th Century Art" (1984); "Picasso and Braque: Pioneering Cubism" (1989) at the Museum of Modern Art, and "Henri Matisse: A Retrospective" in 1992. Philip Morris has also supported a number of African-American art and regional art exhibitions through the years, including the seminal "Two Centuries of Black American Art," in 1976.

Philip Morris is also one of the world's leading corporate supporters of dance in the world. To celebrate the thirtieth anniversary of its support of dance, the company contributed $1.8 million to more than 100 dance organizations and artists in the 2002–2003 season. The company has sponsored the US and international tours of Alvin Ailey American Dance Theater since 1981. In addition to financial support, Philip Morris provides extensive advertising and marketing services to build visibility and new audiences for dance companies and underwrites advertising campaigns for Alvin Ailey tours and for the Brooklyn Academy of Music's New Wave Festival. Philip Morris has supported the American Ballet Theater and Dance Theater of Harlem, the Joffrey Ballet of Chicago, and Hubbard Street Dance Company since the early 1980s.

18 Place Marketing

Virtually every country, state, and city has well-funded tourism and economic development programs in which public relations plays the principle role. Travel and tourism is a specialized public relations practice in both the largest full-service PR firms and those devoted exclusively to the specialty. In their book *Marketing Places*, Philip Kotler, Donald Haider and Irving Rein suggest six tasks in which MPR supports place marketing with examples of each.

1. Assist in the launch of new products. Each time Walt Disney Company adds a new theme park in the Orlando area, such as EPCOT Center or MGM studios, it launches a public relations campaign with press interviews, press releases and special events to motivate people to revisit Orlando and see the new marvels.

2. Assist in repositioning a mature product. New York City had extremely bad press in the seventies until the "I Love New York" campaign began, bringing millions of additional tourists to the city.

3. Build up interest in a product category. As a dairy state, Wisconsin was hurt as consumers switched away from milk, cheese, and other dairy products. The state is helping the American Dairy Association use PR to rebuild interest in the purchase of dairy products.

4. Influence specific target groups. Greece, in its efforts to build up more tourism, implements special campaigns directed to Greek-American communities in the United States to go back and visit Greece.

5. Defend places that have encountered public problems. When parts of the Miami area were devastated by Hurricane Andrew in 1992, the tourist industry feared cancellations by tourists. The public relations departments of southeastern Florida overnighted thousands of faxes, news releases, and videotaped interviews assuring recipients that the damage was limited. The quick response is credited with helping restore business and clarifying misconceptions of the storm's impact.

6. Build the place image in a way that reflects favorably on its products. Atlantic City had a largely negative image as the spectacular gaming centers contrasted with shabby boardwalk shops and slum housing. Donald Trump, owner of Trump Plaza, launched a campaign to reposition the city as the boxing center of the United States. The strategy, which included weekly bouts on ESPN and championship fights on HBO, was meant to capture overnight visitors and big spenders. The boxing events provide story material for every sports section in America and build word of mouth about the appeal of Atlantic City.[1]

Travel and Tourism

Hotels, resorts, cruise lines, and cultural destinations aggressively seek coverage not only in travel magazines and newspaper travel sections but also in a variety of special interest magazines. The Travel Channel on cable television is made to order for travel public relations. There is also an array of television news, talk and entertainment shows that offer unlimited possibilities.

Reality television, led by "Survivor," has transported contestants to a variety of exotic locations. Major tourist destinations vie aggressively to gain a visit from the co-host of NBC's "Today Show" in conjunction with the program's annual "Where in the World is Matt Lauer" feature, which takes viewers to places they always wanted to see.

Ever since motion picture production moved from Hollywood back lots to locations throughout the world, audiences have been introduced to places they might want to see for themselves. Puerto Vallarta was a sleepy Mexican fishing village until Elizabeth Taylor and Richard Burton went there to film *The Night of the Iguana*. The exposure made it a premier travel destination. So did the Cayman Islands when Tom Cruise was lavishly entertained there by *The Firm*. Moviegoers today often stay through an endless list of credits to see where a film was shot in the hopes of finding some special destination for their next vacation.

Promoting Mexican Tourism

The diversity of publicity outlets available to travel and tourism public relations is highlighted by Aaron D. Cushman in his book, *A Passion for Winning*. Cushman's PR firm has a specialized practice in travel and tourism and has represented clients as diverse as Marriott Hotels, the city of St. Louis, and the Mexican National Tourist Council. His description of how his firm handled the Mexico account is a textbook example of how a country can promote itself:

> We used our travel page contacts to make quick placements in magazines like *Conde Nast Traveler* and *Travel and Leisure*. Next we approached syndicated travel columnists who worked primarily out of New York, Los Angeles and San Francisco. In the first three years with Mexico, we organized one national Society of American Travel Writers convention in Mexico City and pre- and post-trips to Acapulco and Puerto Vallarta. Over 250 writers came back with stories and pictures. SATW is subdivided into five geographic chapters and we had two chapters each come to Guadalajara for regional meetings. Our initial approach to encouraging more Americans to visit Mexico was concentrated on travel sections. Then we got talking about peripheral publications and that led to a giant effort toward special interest publications. We began listing areas and they seemed to go on indefinitely. There was tennis and golf, swimming, snorkeling, scuba and fishing. There were beaches, weather, flora and fauna, history on ancient civilizations, history of Jews in Mexico, architecture, archeology, private aircraft, boating, costumes. Food peculiar to Mexico, the unusual insurance and real estate government regulations, silver and gold mining, crafts and even medical publications. Once these categories were reasonably complete, we began fleshing out the numbers of magazines within each category. Our list came to several hundred to be added to our travel list.
>
> We put together a media tour of seven magazine editors from the medical field. When discussing medical questions in Mexico with Americans, all conversations began and ended with "The Touristas." Our gringos (US citizens) were told to fear the water in Mexico and be careful about what they ate. Practically no one was familiar with Mexico's first-rate hospitals and the fact that they had a quality

medical school in Guadalajara. We convinced these editors that they owed it to their readers (mostly physicians) to examine Mexican medical facilities first hand. We were well aware that doctors were among the major traveling groups in the US, and, with modest educational seminars, they were able to write off the expense of a trip. Mexico wanted more medical group meetings, and we felt that the media tour was a step in the right direction.

One by one, we attacked each special interest group of magazines using different approaches. The volume of publicity was overwhelming. The Mexican National Tourist Council had never see such vast coverage, and tourism was up in response."[2]

Municipal Promotion: Milwaukee Salutes an Icon

Sometimes a commercial brand is so identified with its city of origin that it becomes a major tourist attraction. The Coca-Cola Museum in Atlanta is a leading tourist attraction. Motorcycle riders call their Harley-Davidsons "Milwaukee Iron."

Once Milwaukee wasn't so sure about Harley. Bikers were seen mostly as rebels and antisocial drifters, hardly honored guests. Harley-Davidson, started in 1903, was itself going downhill in the 1970s, but as motorcycles became the sport vehicle of choice among bankers, businessmen, and professional men, the company turned the corner. It now has sales of over $4 billion and employs 9,000 workers, with 2,000 of them in the Milwaukee area. So a company that was down and out and a city on the skids are now inseparable. Harley has become so mainstream that the Library of Congress has declared it an American icon.

In the past few years, with the support of another major Milwaukee institution, Miller Brewing Company has built a new major league baseball park and opened a world-class art museum. The Milwaukee Art Museum itself celebrated Harley-Davidson by featuring an exhibit of the art of the motorcycle.

When Harley-Davison celebrated its 100th anniversary in 2003, its hometown Milwaukee, Wisconsin, got in on the act in a big way. A front-page story in *The Chicago Tribune* reported that The Greater Milwaukee Convention and Visitors Bureau estimated the economic impact of the events reached $37 million. Tours and events were also held in four other Wisconsin cities where Harley has plants. It was the largest single commercial event in Wisconsin history.

Milwaukee went full throttle to welcome bikers to town. Weddings and tours were held during the 100th anniversary weekend at Harley-Davidson's headquarters. Free concerts were presented and bike exhibits were set up at Veteran's Park and on the Summerfest grounds at Milwaukee's lakefront. Several museums hosted Harley history and art displays. The whole city is involved, said Anne Gbory-Goodman of the Milwaukee Institute of Art and Design. Her students helped create a photo exhibit of the cross-country rides that led to Milwaukee in recent weeks. 'It's not that they like motorbikes, it's that they're part of the whole thing. It's been community building.' Milwaukee's mayor John Norquist even spent three months learning to ride a "hog" so that he could get into what *The Tribune* described as "a two-hour parade of leather, fur caps, hog masks and feathered boas."[3]

The event attracted 250,000 bikers and as many locals, most of them wearing some items of Harley-Davidson clothing. Vendors sold anniversary pins, T-shirts, caps, duffle bags and teddy bears. The parade on Milwaukee's main drag, featured riders from

England, Ireland, Australia, Switzerland, Israel, England, Mexico, Canada, and Japan. *The New York Times* reported that a chartered jet flew in 300 Japanese bikers and their motorcycles. Bikers rode in on four organized rides from around the country and reporters came from around the world. So a brand that became an icon was celebrated not only on front pages and network news in the United States but also by media throughout the world.[4]

Destination MPR

The notion of "place" is easy to understand in the context of tourism, but it can be equally powerful in other contexts, from retailers to hotels, department stores, and fast food chains. Grand openings that support local charities that engender good will in the community and gain extended coverage in local media are time-honored traditions. In the early days of McDonald's, the new fast food company went all-out to publicize the opening of every new restaurant, bringing in local celebrities and often Ray Kroc, the company's founder himself.

Destination theme parks are, of course, an industry all to themselves. They pull out all the publicity stops to herald their newest attractions. You can count on every new Disneyland or Disney World attraction to be covered not only by the ABC network, which is owned by Disney, but also by the other networks and major print media. Everybody expects the quarterback of the winning team of the Super Bowl to declare "I'm going to Disney World" to the largest television audience of the year.

Legoland California

You don't need to be the biggest or own a television network to use the media effectively to attract vacationers and drive traffic. In Danish, "leg godt" translates to "play well." Back in 1934, Ole Kirk combined the two words and came up with the word Lego to describe the wooden vehicles, animals and yo-yo's he was making. After World War II, the Danish toymaker bought his first plastic molding machine and began producing those colorful "Automatic Binding Bricks" now known the world over as Lego toys. At the turn of the century, more than 200 billion Lego elements and 11 billion Lego and Duplo (those big blocks for little kids) bricks had been created and played with by 300 million people.

Lego is the centerpiece of one of the great marketing showcases of our times: Legoland. The first Legoland, opened in 1968 in Billund, Denmark, the company's hometown, and quickly became the country's most popular tourist attraction outside of Copenhagen. The second Legoland park in Windsor, England, became that country's most popular new attraction, proving that those little bricks are more fun for kids than the crown jewels housed nearby.

The first Legoland in America was built in Carlsbad, California. The 128-acre park is unlike any other theme park. There's no mistaking the Lego-ness of its 40 rides and attractions, which are built entirely of Lego plastic. Kids can run a Lego boat, fly a Lego biplane, or maneuver a Lego helicopter. There's even a tour through an automated factory where Lego bricks are molded, decorated, assembled and packaged. And, of course, before you leave, you can and most likely will stop at The Big Shop, which is stocked with more Lego stuff than any toy store. But somehow all that brand exposure enhances the fun rather than detracts from it. That's the genius of Legoland.

The park is designed to attract kids from toddlers through "tweens." The target group at Legoland California is youngsters age two through 12, according to communications director, Jonna Rae Bartges. More than 1.5 million kids, parents, and grandparents enter the brightly colored gates every year. This is especially remarkable considering the competition of such well-established kid-oriented attractions as Sea World, Disneyland, San Diego Zoo, and Wild Animal Park.

Savvy media relations drove the success of Legoland California. Bartges, a onetime newspaper and TV reporter and publicist for Disneyland and Sea World was recruited to create a "big national buzz" nine months before the park opened. She began immediately issuing weekly newsy one-page releases, appropriately named "Brick-a-Brac" to the media every week. She assigned her four staffers to cover the park like reporters on a beat, coming up with news items of interest.

Bartges began inviting key reporters to the park when it was little more than barren hills, issuing them hard hats and helping them visualize the wonders that were coming. Now insiders, these reporters were brought back every few months for a look-see at what was going on. Bartges decided to eschew the Disney protocol of keeping everything under wraps until the big unveiling. Instead she and her staff developed feature angles for targeted media months before the opening.

She issued the same challenge to reporters that human resources was giving to applicants for "model citizen" jobs—to build a Lego animal in twenty minutes. A reporter from the San Diego NBC station went for it and his story ran on network affiliates in fifty markets. She suggested to the Entertainment Channel that they invite a kid star to preview the park's attractions. The "E" segment featured Justin Cooper of TV's "Brother's Keeper" who had a ball at Legoland with his sisters and a friend.

With a cadre of enthusiast media boosters on board, Legoland set up a "Media Village" in the parking lot for the press three days before the gates opened to the public. The grand opening was covered by 357 journalists and 33 TV stations. Across the country in New York City, the Legoland story was brought to the "Today" show. Lego model makers recreated the New York skyline. Today's cameras zoomed in on a reproduction of the show's famous Rockefeller Plaza venue complete with models of the show's co-hosts Katie Couric and Matt Lauer made of Lego bricks and live fans cheering.

In the first nine months, Legoland California generated more than one billion media impressions, gaining TV and print exposure in all 50 top US markets. With all that coverage, Legoland California began packing them in from all over the state, the country and the world.

Legoland California is composed of six major themes areas—called "blocks," which can be seen from a Sky Cycle where you can pedal your way around the park on an overhead track. You can also take a cruise boat on an excursion of a 1.7 acre man-made lake. The cruise takes tourists past Mount Rushmore, the New York City skyline and the Statue of Liberty, all of them meticulously replicated in Lego bricks. Bartges described Miniland as "a dedication to the ultimate expression of Lego art form." A stroll through Miniland also covers New Orleans, the California Coast, a New England Harbor and Washington, DC., all reproduced at 1.20 and 1.40 scale and animated with cars, trains, people movement and sound. It took 20 million Lego bricks to build Miniland, an attraction that appeals as much to adults as to kids.

Lego is everywhere. There is plenty of opportunity for kids to dream up their own Lego creations. Kids entering The Imagination Zone are greeted by 18-foot giraffes constructed entirely of Lego and a 19-foot Technic T-Rex. The little ones can play and build with big Duplo bricks while the older kids at Lego Mindstorms create things with "intelligent" Lego bricks that have an imbedded computer chip and build robots with computer-controlled Lego Technic models.

Legoland has an ad campaign in California, but it relies largely on its Web site, publicity and word of mouth from satisfied visitors to carry its message across the USA. The Legoland Web site even has a fun way to help the word of mouth along. Kids can choose a picture post card of their favorite attraction and mail it to their friends from Legoland.

The Web site, done up engagingly in primary colors and Lego brick designs, covers all the bases, stakeholderwise. For adults, there is all you need to know about the park, what's there, what it costs, how to get there and how to skip the real lines by buying tickets on-line. For teachers, there is information about education programs for their students. For prospective employees, there is a list of job opportunities at the park updated weekly. For the kids, there are matching games, coloring pages and puzzles and a way e-shop for exclusive Legoland California stuff. For everybody there is a virtual tour where you can visit one or all of 15 virtual locations by finding the attraction of your choice on a Legoland map.

European companies have proved that you can build strong brands without relying on mass media advertising. Marketing guru David Aaker of the University of California, Berkeley, says that US companies would do well to study their counterparts in Europe who "have found that communication through traditional mass media has been ineffective, inefficient and costly." These European companies have discovered "alternative communication channels to create product awareness, convey brand associations and develop loyal customer bases." There's no better evidence that the European marketing model can work in this country than the success of Legoland California.[5]

Dolls R Them

The St. Louis Post Dispatch declared that for families with a girl the American Girl Place "is not just a store, it is a travel destination." Nearly a million girls and women have visited the 35,000 square foot doll and book emporium that has become the hottest retail establishment on Chicago's Magnificent Mile. If there is little girl in your family, you probably know all about American Girl, that phenomenally successful line of books and upscale dolls, doll clothing and accessories that were available until 1998 only by direct mail catalogue or through *www.americangirl.com.* Pleasant Company, the Middleton, Wisconsin, company behind the American Girl, has sold more than 5 million dolls and 61 million books since it was founded in 1986.

Julie Parks, public relations manager of Pleasant, describes the American Girl phenomenon:

> Books are the heart of the collection in terms of what they do for the girls that read them. They are the reason the line has sustained the interest of its audience for so long. You can't buy a doll without a book, but you can buy the American Girl line of books at all major bookstores. You can also find them at most public libraries. We don't think of ourselves as being in the doll business, or the book business or the clothing business or the direct mail business. We're in the girl business.

You don't need to own and dress a doll to participate in the American Girl experience. That's important since the dolls aren't cheap. They go for $84 (with the paperback storybook, $90 with the hard cover.) But that's less than many video games or other disposable toys that may quickly fade away. American Girl dolls, on the other hand, can be cherished for a lifetime or passed on to the next little girl in the family.

In keeping with the character of its line, American Girl Place is a unique retail and entertainment experience that brings the catalog spectacularly to life. It is the only place in the country where girls can see the entire collection on display. The store is stocked floor to ceiling with dolls, doll outfits and "dress like your doll" apparel, all irresistibly displayed and packaged.

Mary Ann McGrath, marketing professor at Loyola University, told *The New York Times* that American Girl Place has taken the shopping "to a new level by melding the idea of a museum combined with a store."[6] *The Minneapolis Star-Tribune* calls it "the Mecca of doll adoration." *The Chicago Sun-Times* calls it "the ultimate American Girl experience."

Little girls who visit American Girl Place know the cast of characters on sight— Felicity, Josefina, Kirsten, Addy, Samantha, and Molly. Each of them has her own story and represents a period of American history. The girls bring their dolls along for lunch at the elegant "grown-up" cafe where they are seated in their own doll-sized booster seats.

When Molly wants a change from her 1944 sweater and skirt, or Samantha from her turn of the century taffeta dress, they can be dressed in very today outfits. They can be clad in a roller blade outfit with helmet and skates and a karaoke outfit, complete with a real sing-along karaoke machine.

In addition to the cafe and all that merchandise, shoppers can visit a historical exhibit, have their pictures taken for the cover of *American Girl Magazine* (circulation 700,000) or attend "The American Girls Revue," an original musical production performed in its own theater with a cast of teen age girls and a five piece band. That is, if you make reservations weeks or even months in advance. *The Chicago Tribune* theater reviewer pronounced it "an appealing musical that is a rich piece of Americana" performed by a cast "brimming with talent" in "an elegant, intimate space where audience members can feel they are part of this celebration of girlhood." [7] The show was written by a couple of real pros, Gretchen Cryer and Nancy Ford, the team that wrote the hit off-Broadway musical "I'm Getting My Act Together and Taking It On The Road." Cryer loved the American Girl books she had read to her granddaughter and suggested the idea of the show to Pleasant Rowland, founder of the company.

The story of Pleasant T. Rowland, a schoolteacher who founded Pleasant Company and created American Girl, is made for media. The company does not advertise and the dolls are sold only through the mail order catalog and at American Girl Place.

Ms. Rowland conceived her dolls as anti-Barbies. But 12 years after she sold her first doll, she sold her company to Mattel, the home of Barbie. Mattel is never identified on American Girl merchandise. Rowland made a rare appearance at the press preview of American Girl Place in her hometown of Chicago. Forty reporters from national, regional and local print and broadcast media were given a pre-opening tour that included an opportunity to sample the food at the cafe and preview the show. The initial wave of media coverage in places like *USA Today* and the AP wire snowballed. The week American Girl Place opened, the company scored what may be an unprecedented publicity coup. American Girl was featured by daytime TV's then two top talk show hosts, Oprah Winfrey and Rosie O'Donnell on the same day.

How good was the pre-opening publicity? By opening day, American Girl Place had taken more than 12,000 reservations for American Girl Cafe and sold more than 8,000 tickets to the show.

A second American Girl Place opened in New York in 2003, allowing little girls on the east coast to have a grown-up lunch with mom, see a real musical review staged just for them, and partake of the complete line of American Girl dolls and books. A front page *New York Times* article was headlined, "It's the Hottest Place in Town, and Dolls Eat Free."[8]

Publicity in the American Girl catalog, rave reviews in the media, and excited word of mouth have attracted families from all 50 states and many countries to American Girl Place stores in Chicago and New York. Their success is likely to be duplicated in other major cities.

Unconventional wisdom. Pleasant Company's program defies conventional wisdom for product publicity. Julie Parks says, "We don't believe that all publicity is good. While we get many requests, you won't see little girls dressed as our American doll characters at parades and other events. We know that girls like to imagine themselves as the characters and we want to make sure they have that opportunity. And we don't proactively seek trade or business publicity."

Another no-no is product placement. The company mostly says no to using American Girl dolls in TV shows and movies, opportunities that any other toy company would die for.

Totally in character, Pleasant held a gala benefit to celebrate the Chicago store's grand opening for the Chicago Public Library Association to support children's programming. The company donated an American Girl doll and a complete collection of 36 books to each of the library's 78 branches.

While Pleasant Company rejects standard publicity techniques, it has carefully crafted a number of public relations programs that connect consumers with American Girl in large, small and medium markets.

The company provides all that nonprofit organizations need to run a successful fundraiser. They can choose from among five different programs to sponsor. The "American Girl Fashion Show" features girls from the local community modeling a seasonal selection of historically inspired and contemporary clothing from the catalogue. There are also "Samantha's Ice Cream Social," "The American Girl Pastimes Party," "Dancing Through Time" and "Josefina's Fiesta." The nonprofits license the rights to produce and present one of these events several times over the course of a weekend. They receive not only a detailed manual and materials but also a mailing list of American Girl customers in their area. There are more than 250 of these events staged every year attracting some 700,000 girls and their moms. The average profit for these fashion shows is $20,000. And for each event, Pleasant Company contributes 5 percent of orders from the American Girl catalogue to the charity.

Building Buzz, Placing Product, and Experiential Marketing

In their 2001 book, *The Soul of the New Consumer*,[1] David Lewis and Darren Bridger contrast the needs and interests of today's New Consumer with a less demanding Old Consumer. They suggest that, while both consumers exist today, New Consumers are the more technologically savvy consumers who are less influenced by mass media and hype and more influenced by "buzz" and the idea that a product is "cool." They break down the key differences in the two consumer profiles as:

Old Consumers	New Consumers
Seek convenience	Seek authenticity
Synchronized	Individual
Less often involved	Highly involved
Conformist	Independent
Less informed	Very well informed

In Search of "Cool" and "Authentic"

Lewis and Bridger cite Malcolm Gladwell, a *New Yorker* magazine writer and author of *The Tipping Point* and "The Coolhunt" to explain how the buzz is generated and the tag of "cool" is come by:

The trick is not to be able to tell who is different but to be able to tell when that difference represents something truly cool. It's a gut thing. You have to somehow know.[2]

Some tricks of the trade for cool hunters—it's good to blend into the background so you can see but not be seen. The gay community is a great place to spot a trend that will become popular later with the straight community. You have to be cool to spot cool.

The interesting trick for people in this profession—the seekers of all things "cool"— is to know "what will be and what will never be in the world of trends, providing manufacturers of everything from paint to clothing accessories with early warning about what colors and styles are set to become fashionable when they are still only being recognized and appreciated by small groups of early innovators."[3]

Buzz Beats Hype

But once a cool hunter has divined that something is, or soon will be, cool, they then often help those manufacturers sell it to the masses, and this is where their risk of "hype" comes in, which we'll discuss a little later. More often than not, "buzz" happens spontaneously. It's a lucky combination of product uniqueness, timing, planning, and serendipity. It is often difficult to duplicate and even more difficult to pinpoint that one specific plan of action that ignited the buzz. It's what happened when McDonald's used Beanie Babies in a sales promotion, and the world went temporarily insane trying to collect them. It's what happened with the Cabbage Patch Kids in the 1980s.

According to Gladwell, it's also what happened to Hush Puppies in the early 1990s.

The casual, brushed suede shoes that had long before gone out of style were about to be discontinued by the manufacturer and replaced by an "active casual" smooth leather shoe. But then some young, hip people in Manhattan's East Village starting hunting them down in thrift stores and in old-fashioned shoe stores and bragging when they were able to wear "an original pair of Hush Puppies." Before long, fashion designers took note and called the manufacturer asking for pairs to be featured in their collections. Fashion stories began to appear about the shoes. The buzz was that Hush Puppies gave you "the coolest feet on the street." Lewis and Bridger, citing Gladwell, reported that "at the peak of the revival, Hush Puppies won the prize as the best accessory at the Council of Fashion Designers' awards dinner at Lincoln Center."

A lesson from this experience is that, first, the buzz got started through informal word on the street—it was not manufactured or hyped. But the sensation grew through the power of the cool hunters who spotted the trend and accelerated its progress through their personal and professional endorsement. In this case, it was "professional mavens" who served as the cool hunters and established the "coolness" of the trend. Lewis and Bridger say that professional mavens are individuals whose job or qualifications give them genuine authority or expertise in a specific area. Fashion designers certainly fit the title, as do film, book, and music critics, restaurant and theatre reviewers, and shopping and consumer consultants on TV or in print. The techie blogs on the Internet have also created a form of fanatical mavens who talk up a particular technology—such as Mac or Linux—to the detriment of less cool operating systems, especially Microsoft. According to the authors, Hollywood celebrities and national sports figures can sometimes be seen as mavens and trigger a cool trend, but they are less influential with today's New Consumers, who prefer to be seen as individuals, than with Old Consumers, who tend to want to run with the pack and be like everyone else.

Lewis and Bridger suggest that today's trend-setting professional mavens seem to get their power of persuasion from three sources: First is their willingness to track down the information that New Consumers want to know, which is that the thing is authentic and has the appropriate provenance or pedigree. Since the birth of the World Wide Web in the early 1990s, most of us have the ability to do this type of research ourselves, but we rarely do it. But since authenticity is critical for the New Consumer, the buzz will stop dead in its tracks if the thing is declare to be "fake" or "inauthentic" by a well-respected maven.

Lewis and Bridger suggest that the second source of power of the professional mavens comes from a natural distrust that New Consumers have when they purchase anything new and unfamiliar. Futurist Faith Popcorn calls it "vigilante consumerism," saying: "We, vigilante consumers, seek substance over style. Truth over packaging. Answers, not press releases."[4]

The third source of power of the professional mavens comes from the glut of products now available in stores and on-line, making it difficult and confusing to know which will meet our needs. There are dozens of models of digital cameras, computers, MP3 players, and the like, and New Consumers are open to having someone they trust tinker with them to determine when they might be appropriate for their own purchase needs. The lesson for marketing public relations, then, is to stay on top of trends related to their industries and enlist the aid of one of these mavens to authenticate their product's legitimacy.

Rubbermaid did this a few years ago, when they commissioned a book on "decluttering" your home by a well-known organizing guru. That author made the rounds of various talk shows and morning news shows plugging her book and also providing a few important tips on organization, a few of which just happened to use Rubbermaid storage bins. She did not hide the fact that her book was underwritten by Rubbermaid. Instead, she embraced that and discussed the logical connection between her skills and a company like Rubbermaid that wanted to learn how to make its products even more useful to homeowners. It did not come across as hype to consumers or to the news media that covered it. Today, a similar technique is used with paid product placements on the various organization and home remodeling cable television programs such as "Trading Spaces," "Mission Organization," "Design on a Dime," etc., when the resident experts whip out a package of Swiffer cleaning products or Clorox wipes. However, these walk a much closer line to "hype" because the usage and connection does not always seem authentic.

Harry Potter and Grassroots Buzz

The incredible success of J.K. Rowling's Harry Potter books in the late 1990s was the result of "authentic" buzz created through a grassroots word-of-mouth campaign via influential mavens rather than through marketing hype. Before the first book was even published in 1997, its US publisher Scholastic Inc. sent out advance copies of the first book about an 11-year-old wizard to critics, librarians, and, most importantly, to children who liked to read. Their enthusiastic comments and recommendations set up a high degree of excitement and expectation around the official publication date that caught the attention of the media, which heightened awareness of the book. The buzz caused the $18 hardcover copies to fly from bookstore shelves, causing further notice and interest. The buzz grew when, to avoid future delays, people started ordering advance copies of the second book from *Amazon.com.uk*, and that company announced limits on what it would ship to the US.

The rest is history. By year-end 2004, the Harry Potter movies, alone, had reaped more than $2.7 billion in revenues. The books and movies continue to be eagerly awaited, and each is introduced with a fanfare of MPR tactics.

Blair Witch Project—The Ultimate in Internet Buzz

The current marketing trend toward creating an Internet buzz began as a result of the phenomenal success of the 1999 film *The Blair Witch Project*. This extremely low-budget movie (reputedly $22,000) grossed more than $150 million at the box office with virtually no promotional efforts, except Internet buzz, making it one of the most profitable movies in history.

But it did not happen accidentally. As Lewis and Bridger explain, the film's co-writer and director, Eduardo Sanchez, was quite clever in making the movie. He used unknown actors, poor quality lighting, realistic hand-held shots, and videotape to keep audiences guessing about whether it was a fictional movie or actual footage that was found by accident. After its first showing at a midnight screening on the first day of the 1999 Sundance Film Festival in Florida, most distributors would have nothing to do with it, and it seemed destined for a quick release to video, if it was released at all. Most were shocked to learn that a small New York-based company called Artisan Entertainment paid $1 million for the distribution rights.

To help build the " real-deal" buzz about the movie, Sanchez set up a Blair Witch Web site that supposedly traced the story back to the eighteenth century and the mysterious disappearance of a group of village children. To navigate the Web site, visitors had to get involved with the story and read academic, unemotional descriptions of such horrors as disembowelment. Word spread, and very quickly the site was flooded with young and very impressionable visitors who firmly believed that the story of the movie was fact. It became a teen quest to find out where it was playing and to go see it. Later, as the on-line debate raged about whether it was truth or fiction, people would go to see it multiple times to try to spot something that would give the secret away.

Viral and Guerrilla Marketing:
The Commercialization of Chit-Chat

Such successes as Hush Puppies, Harry Potter, and Blair Witch have encouraged a new trend of creating "buzz agents" to tout companies and products through a secret underground campaign using hired or volunteer "trendsetters" or "influencers" or "street teams" to execute what are variously called "word-of-mouth campaigns," "seeding programs," "viral marketing," or "guerrilla marketing."

The strategy has gained momentum in recent years because of the growing consumer distrust, especially among young people, of more traditional advertising vehicles. It has also become popular among advertisers who recognize that their commercial messages are being skipped over at record levels evidenced by the increased use of TiVo and other digital video recorders, the rise in commercial-free satellite radio, and computer programs that banish pop-up ads. The strategy also makes sense in light of such research as the 2004 marketing study undertaken by Research and Markets Ltd., which reported that "a growing number of consumers are citing word of mouth as the most important factor influencing their interest in products. With the latest Eurobarometer survey showing that 58 percent of Europeans do not trust corporations, relying on the relative credibility, honesty and impartiality of word of mouth will continue to grow."[5]

In 2002, Sony Ericsson hired 60 actors in 10 cities to accost strangers and ask them: "Would you mind taking my picture?" Those who obliged were handed a Sony Ericsson camera-phone to take the shot, at which point the actor would remark on what a cool gadget it was. And thus, as *The New York Times Magazine* later reported, "an act of civility was converted into a branding event."[6]

Unfortunately, there was a small public relations backlash on this event—especially about the use of hired actors, which Lewis and Bridger would put into the realm of "fake," "inauthentic," and "hype." A new approach to the same strategy was developed using volunteer buzz agents. Some companies have had little trouble recruiting hundreds of thousands of volunteers to perform these new promotional activities without monetary reward. Instead, they receive the "social rewards" of being "in the know," "ahead of the curve," "a trendsetter," "an influencer."

The cover story of the December 5, 2005, issue of the *New York Times Magazine*[7] analyzed this trend in detail and the companies that utilize volunteer "buzz agents" to talk up products to their friends, bring samples to parties, and ask about them in retail stores. Called "The Hidden (in Plain Sight) Persuaders," the article discusses how this new, more structured form of "word-of-mouth" PR and marketing activity has increasingly become mainstream and has been used to promote products such as sausages, books, jeans, perfumes, and teenage beauty products. But the article's author, Rob Walker, concluded that regardless of whether the buzz agents are hired hands or volunteers, "They are all attempts, in one way or another, to break the fourth wall that used to separate the theater of commerce, persuasion and salesmanship from our actual day-to-day life."

The article explains how the process works:

Over the July 4 weekend last summer, at cookouts up and down the East Coast and into the Midwest, guests arrived with packages of Al Fresco chicken sausage for their hosts to throw on the grill. At a family gathering in Kingsley, Mich. At a small barbecue in Sag Harbor, N.Y. At a 60-guest picnic in Philadelphia.

We know that this happened, and we even know how various party guests reacted to their first exposure to Al Fresco, because the Great Sausage Fanout of 2004 did not happen by chance. The sausage-bearers were not official representatives of Al Fresco, showing up in uniforms to hand out samples. They were invited guests, friends or relatives of whoever organized the get-togethers, but they were also—unknown to most all the other attendees—"agents," and they filed reports. "People could not believe they weren't pork!" one agent related. "I told everyone that they were low in fat and so much better than pork sausages." Another wrote, "I handed out discount coupons to several people and made sure they knew which grocery stores carried them." Another noted that "my dad will most likely buy the garlic" flavor, before closing, "I'll keep you posted."

These reports went back to the company that Al Fresco's owner, Kayem Foods, had hired to execute a "word of mouth" marketing campaign. And while the Fourth of July weekend was busy, it was only a couple of days in an effort that went on for three months and involved not just a handful of agents but 2,000 of them. The agents were sent coupons for free sausage and a set of instructions for the best ways to talk the stuff up, but they did not confine themselves to those ideas, or to obvious events like barbecues.[8]

Walker reported that the number of coordinators of these volunteer groups is growing. Key players are: BzzAgent, which currently has more than 60,000 volunteer agents in its network; Tremor, a word-of-mouth operation that is a division of Procter & Gamble, which has an astonishing 240,000 volunteer teenagers spreading the word about everything from toothbrushes to TV shows; a spin-off called Tremor Moms; and other marketers, particularly youth-oriented firms, that have put up Web sites recruiting teenagers to serve as "secret agents."

The marketing practice has now become so mainstream that it has stimulated the development of various professional marketing associations in the field. The two biggest are Word-of-Mouth Marketing Association (WOMMA) in the US and Viral and Buzz Marketing Association (VBMA) in Europe. Both provide networking and learning opportunities to professionals working on viral marketing projects. As an example, VBMA recently hosted an on-line forum called the "cognitive dissidents index" to promote an on-line discussion of ideas among other buzz marketers.

Potential Backlash of Viral Campaigns

Marketers should be warned, however, that despite the growth in the practice of building buzz and the apparent success of the technique, there is serious potential for a PR backlash. The "buzz agent" approach commercializes one of the last trustworthy sources of product recommendations—people's friends—and could potentially taint the traditional word-of-mouth channel.

Walker and, undoubtedly, various consumer advocacy groups, are suspicious of this new approach to marketing. Walker suggests that it may spark the same level of public outcry as the subliminal advertising scare of the 1950s did. He says:

> This idea—the commercialization of chitchat—resembles a scenario from a paranoid science-fiction novel about a future in which corporations have become so powerful that they can bribe whole armies of flunkies to infiltrate the family barbecue. That level of corporate influence sounds sure to spark outrage—another episode in the long history of mainstream distrust of commercial coercion and marketing trickery. Fear of unchecked corporate reach is what made people believe in the power of subliminal advertising and turn Vance Packard's book "The Hidden Persuaders" into a best seller in the 1950's; it is what gave birth to the consumer-rights movement of the 1970's; and it is what alarms people about neuroscientists supposedly locating the "buy button" in our brains today. Quite naturally, many of us are wary of being manipulated by a big, scary, Orwellian "them."[9]

These concerns, plus the ethical issues raised by the fact that the volunteers often do not reveal that they are in some sense working on behalf of the company sponsoring the campaign, should give public relations practitioners some pause about when and how these tactics should be employed. An angry and distrustful public does not make for a loyal customer base. In addition, the Research and Market Ltd. study on viral marketing suggested that the technique "is most effective when promoting experiential, complex, premium, quirky and cool products. Given that most packaged goods products do not meet these criteria, marketers will benefit from devising campaigns that enhance consumers' involvement in general product purchases and their emotional attachments to brands."[10]

But despite these concerns, it appears that the technique will continue to grow in usage, because they appear to have been quite successful to date—stimulating name recognition, enhancing corporate reputation, and increasing product sales—often producing better results than when more traditional PR and marketing approaches have been used

Measuring the Success of Viral Marketing Campaigns

Another important element to consider before executing a viral marketing campaign is how it should be measured. How do you know what sort of awareness the viral marketing campaigns produced? How far did the messages travel? The key to being able to measure viral activity is to decide on the outcome variable beforehand. What does success mean to this user? Is it increased sales? Hits on a Web site? The number of people who show up at an event? Media coverage generated from the event times the number of people who read/watch these media sources? Marketers should tie each step of the viral campaign to a measurable outcome.

Product Placement

Another method for building buzz around a product is in placing it in highly visible situations, especially on television and in popular movies. Paid placements are becoming more common, especially on cable television programs, but not all product placements are paid for. In a now famous episode of the 1990s hit comedy series "Friends," the Pottery Barn was prominently featured in the story line. The writers simply wrote the story featuring the store. One of the characters loved the store's furnishings and the other hated them (although she later changed her mind). But after the episode ran, the store's sales went up dramatically nonetheless.

"The Apprentice" Sparks Record Consumer Interest in Crest Toothpaste

In a more planned product placement, Procter & Gamble featured its Crest Whitening Expressions Refreshing Vanilla Mint Toothpaste on the popular television show "The Apprentice" featuring Donald Trump. In an interesting twist on the placement strategy, contestants were told to create a viral marketing campaign to launch the product in New York City. According to a September 28, 2004, P&G press release:

> Seconds after the newly dismissed contestant of NBC's "The Apprentice" heard The Donald's fateful decree, thousands of consumers got "fired up" themselves and flocked to the *crest.com* website to play armchair quarterback about how they would have launched Crest Refreshing Vanilla Mint toothpaste. With more than 4.7 million hits to the product website, the appearance on the show led to the highest level of on-line interest in a single product launch in P&G history.
>
> The increased Web traffic started immediately after the show aired, with more than 800,000 hits in just two hours. In addition, more than 40,000 samples of the product were requested and more than 20,000 applicants submitted ideas on how they would have created buzz.[11]

The interesting approach combined the placement opportunity with a sales promotion contest. The winners would receive a trip to New York City, tickets to see the live airing of "The Apprentice" finale, and an invitation to attend the VIP after-party, which would most certainly generate additional media interest. According to P&G, its Web site was flooded with 100 ideas a minute in the first 20 minutes after the show ended.

P&G has adopted the product placement strategy for a number of its other product lines. Its Swiffer line of dusters and cleaning products seems to receive the bulk of the placements. Most notably, P&G has become the sponsor for "How Clean Is Your House?," a reality program on cable television where two matronly English ladies dole out cleaning advice to hopeless homeowners whose homes have gotten out of control. They end up using a wide array of P&G products to clean up the place.

Other reality show sponsorships that end up with a large number of product placements are Sears' sponsorship of "Extreme Makeover—Home Edition" and The Home Depot's sponsorship of "Trading Spaces." In both, cast members are constantly seen going shopping in the stores and/or showing up at the site with trucks or boxes prominently labeled with the stores' logos.

"Trading Spaces" and The Home Depot's Do-It-Herself Workshops

In one of the more integrated approaches to product placement, The Home Depot created a PR event in July of 2004 that targeted women nationwide, asking them to "experience the design-inspired adrenaline rush of TLC's hit series "Trading Spaces" at The Home Depot's "Do-It-Herself Workshops." During the free workshops for women, participants had "creative license" as they learned how to enhance their homes' decor through fun design projects previously showcased on Trading Spaces. Workshop topics included how to tile a backsplash, create a stylish tabletop, build a versatile display cube and make a charming headboard out of picket fencing.

Adding more PR value, cast members from "Trading Spaces" joined The Home Depot associates in leading Do-It-Herself Workshop sessions in three cities—Atlanta, Boston, and Sacramento. Kia Steave-Dickerson shared her design expertise with participants at an Atlanta store, Amy Wynn Pastor, one of the show's carpenters, helped inspire women to complete projects for themselves at a Boston-area store, and in California, designer Christi Proctor brought her imagination to clinics in Sacramento.

More Traditional Methods for Creating Buzz

In addition to product placements and related events to building buzz around a product, there are a number of tried-and-true MPR strategies that can generate news about a product or service. (They follow the news values associated with traditional media.)

There are eight characteristics of any story that might make it "news" to a reporter and, therefore, more likely to get coverage: conflict, human interest, newness, prominence, proximity, significance, timeliness, and unusualness. It also doesn't hurt if the story is funny or heart-warming—those are the most likely to end up in a crowded news line-up or get mentioned on a TV talk show.

For example, Glad and Whirlpool sponsored "National Clean Out Your Refrigerator Week." The news value of this take-off on the old chestnut "National [Your Product Here] Week" approach was the lighthearted approach. The press release led with "Have your strawberries gone south? Is your broccoli beyond saving? Is there a suspicious odor creeping from your kitchen? It's time to scrub the shelves, deodorize the drawers, pitch rotten produce and reevaluate your refrigerator."

OshKosh B'Gosh "Search of the Century"

OshKosh B'Gosh followed more of the "unusual" approach tied into a "timeliness" strategy to garner widespread consumer awareness of its 100th anniversary. It relied on the funny and unusual "Search for the Oldest Bib Overalls" and to its status as a world-famous children's wear and adult workwear brand. As part of its tactics, it created a video news release (VNR) with footage that included rare and well-preserved photos, old ads, and price lists dating back to 1895 contrasted with the company's contemporary line of cute kid's clothing, visuals of the company's manufacturing facilities, and visits to the company's new European retail stores.

With a budget of just $32,000, the campaign received media coverage from across North America, reaching more than 14 million viewers, total potential television households of more than 186 million, and achieving an 18 percent increase in market share in a year when advertising spending remained flat.

Warning: The Downside to Too Much Buzz

It is important to note that timing of an MPR campaign is critical to meeting its objectives, as is picking the right targets for the right time. The introduction of the Segway personal transporter was a public relations dream that turned into a nightmare. The product was a true marvel, but the promotion got too far ahead of product development and general infrastructure. But looking at the campaign in hindsight, it also provides a cautionary tale about achieving too great a success in terms of media coverage if the product infrastructure is not in place to support it. By the time the product was built and available in retail outlets, two years had passed and the demand for it had waned.

A more recent example of getting too much buzz too soon involved Blinkx, a fledgling San Francisco-based Internet search company that had a good story to tell and decided to tell it fast and early—too early. The company pursued a few very influential blogs, and before they knew it the buzz began. According to the *Red Herring*:

> Blinkx, almost overnight, started getting a phenomenal amount of publicity. Its name appeared in the *London Times*, the *Boston Globe*, and the *San Jose Mercury News*—all in the span of a few weeks. And that's just print: Kathy Rittweger, Blinkx's co-founder, did interviews for the BBC, CNBC Europe's "Power Lunch," and CNN.[12]

Meanwhile, Blinkx faced the challenge of keeping its media strategy together when Ms. Rittweger started receiving unsolicited phone calls from venture capitalists offering to invest: someone in the company had posted her cell phone number on Blinkx's Web site. Then, she received another call complimenting her on a billboard with a huge Blinkx logo alongside Highway 101, which links San Francisco with Silicon Valley. The sign was news to her.

But because of all the media attention, the company decided to "take a risk and strike while the irons were hot." It released its search tool several months early, trying to stay ahead of the power players such as Google and Intel, who were also being influenced by all the media hype.

Their bet seemed to pay off in the short term, with more than 200,000 people downloading Blinkx's search tool, but long term, product quality (and thus satisfaction and acceptance) was uncertain.

Another challenge Blinkx faces as a result of its media blitz is inflated expectations. Says Ms. Rittweger:

> Our initial plans were a lot more conservative. Back in September last year, at least as far as I know, I didn't think there was such reception in the market for something like what we had created."[13]

Quoting Pat Whalen, *Red Herring* suggested that before companies speak to the media, they should consider how their message will fit into a wider communications strategy:

> Ms. Whalen says that startups too often put tactics before strategy—writing press releases and meeting journalists before thinking about the stages of a coordinated communications campaign. 'Not only do you need to know when and how to communicate, but when not to,' she says.[14]

To be sure, no amount of money could buy the media coverage that Blinkx has received, which helped it acquire customers, interest from investors, and, perhaps, potential buyers. But it remains to be seen whether Blinkx's focus on courting the media will set it on a path to long-term success, or simply represent its 15 minutes of fame.

Experiential Marketing:
Extending the Brand into a Fourth Dimension

The concept of experiential marketing is relatively new. It is the attempt to let the consumer experience the brand promise first-hand and to make the experience more valuable than the actual service being rendered. Joseph Pine II and James Gilmore wrote a ground-breaking article for the *Harvard Business Review* in 1998, explaining the importance of experiential marketing:

> At theme restaurants such as the Hard Rock Café, Planet Hollywood, or the House of Blues, the food is just a prop for what's known as "entertainment." And stores such as Niketown, Cabella's, and Recreational Equipment Incorporated draw consumers in by offering fun activities, fascinating displays, and a promotional events (sometimes labeled "shoppertainment" or "entertailing").
>
> . . . Business-to-business marketers increasingly create venues as elaborate as any Disney attraction in which to sell their goods and services. In June 1996, Silicon Graphics, for example, opened its Visionarium Realty Center at corporate headquarters in Mountain View, CA, to bring customers and engineers together in an environment where they can interact with real-time, three-dimensional product visualizations. Customers can view, hear and touch—as well as drive, walk or fly through myriad product possibilities. "This is experiential computing at its ultimate, where our customers can know what their products will look like, sound like, feel like before manufacturing," said then chairman and CEO Edward McCracken.[15]

These experiences are not only valuable to customers, but they have a real impact on the media that cover these industries. A press release that uses hyperbolic language to describe the luxurious feeling of a spa or the sensuous taste of pure milk chocolate may be scorned by a news reporter who receives it. But invite that reporter to experience the spa first hand, or to visit the new Hershey's "virtual candy factory" that is planned to be opened on Michigan Avenue in Chicago in 2005, and there's a good chance that the reporter will use those words himself.

Pat Whalen described this phenomenon in her work with Comsat, the mobile satellite communications provider. Because the firm's "coast earth stations" with their multiple arrays of huge satellite antennae were located in very remote spots in Connecticut and California, she never imagined that she could entice the general news media to visit or show much interest in the service. But a chance call from an *Los Angeles Times* reporter asking for information about the station convinced her to try a media tour of the two facilities. She was amazed to receive more than 30 acceptances for the visits. There was extensive media coverage, including personal stories from some of the earth station operators who had assisted in bringing Coast Guard rescues to sinking ships or staying on the line with a downed airplane pilot while rescuers tried to find him. The resulting media coverage sent scores of yacht owners and private pilots to the company to learn more about the service.

Bosch Creates Buzz in Holiday Publications[16]

When the Bosch Company undertook a relaunch of a line of small kitchen appliances, the firm had incredible success with the high-profile, large-circulation consumer press that generated lots of buzz for the new product line. Not only did the firm get the pick-up in the consumer press, it got it in the most coveted issues for any retail product—the magazines' holiday issues. How did they do it?

According to Erika Price Schulte, PR Director at Bosch's agency, RiechesBaird, June and July are when editors at mainstream, million-plus magazines do their holiday planning. To that end, Schulte began to invite select editors to a media suite or, rather, "An Exclusive Private Media Preview of Bosch Small Appliances to Launch at Christmas." Furthermore, she said:

> The venue (SoHo Grand) was chosen, in part, as a convenient location, but also because it reflected the character of Bosch products. It is a fairly new hotel with a really strong design element that really complimented the products. It was not cold and austere, but rather modern with a very wrought-iron industrial look that is indigenous to the [neighborhood]. It was a cool place to go in New York and very visually appealing."

Adding to the "exclusive" appeal, Schulte sent limos to transport journalists to and from the event. "It was primarily done for convenience and to make sure things ran on time," she explained. "But the personal attention and location helped set the tone and represent the Bosch brand as a producer of luxury products. We kept in mind, however, that limos and free drinks don't buy coverage. Once there, the products have to speak for themselves."

Neiman Marcus and the Experience of Luxury

The annual Neiman Marcus Christmas catalog is a perennial media favorite, partly because of the outrageous items often listed in the catalog, but also because it exemplifies the Neiman Marcus brand that promises luxury at every turn. A typical story is one that recently ran in *The Wall Street Journal*:[17]

> When Neiman Marcus's limited edition 2005 Maserati Quattroporte went on sale at noon Oct. 14, 2004, all 60 of the $125,000 customized sedans sold out in four minutes. Other extravagant gifts featured in the annual Neiman Marcus Christmas catalog are also selling at an unusually brisk pace, including hand-encrusted crystal versions of Mr. and Mrs. Potato Head, for $8,000 each, and a $20,000 customized suit of armor.
>
> And it is not just the catalog sales doing so well. The Neiman Marcus Group posted earnings of $205 million for its fiscal year ended July 31, up 87 percent over the year before. Its stock price has more than doubled in the past two years, and its average sales per square foot is well above all other department-store retailers. It's most recent quarter posted a 14 percent increase in profits, and the company was projecting another strong performance for the 2004 holiday season.[18]

The story went on to discuss how the luxury retailer has such success selling such expensive items at a time when Wal-Mart's low prices are driving so many other retailers out of business. It quotes Burton Tansky, president of Neiman Marcus, who said the company understands who its affluent customers are and knows how to deliver on their expectations by presenting them with an overall experience of luxury whenever they interact with the company—whether it is shopping at the stores, buying on-line or browsing through its world-famous catalog:

Price is a by-product of the ingredients in the item. We don't set out to buy expensive things, we set out to buy the best designs from the best designers and vendors. It's the quality of the material, how it's made and designed, where it's made, who designed it—all of that comes together and there's clearly a price for that, and it isn't low. Our customers don't seem to mind the price so long as we deliver the quality and all the ingredients that go into the best product.[19]

As long as the media who cover the retail industry have a similar experience of luxury every time they interact with Nieman Marcus, they are likely to continue to position it in this luxury space.

Other Media Opportunities to Experience the Brand

Apple iPods. With the Apple iPod enjoying a strong demand from consumers and high praise from the news media, Apple stores match the Apple brand experience. *Fortune* magazine referred to the stores as "zeitgeist beehives, great places for celeb sitings." The brand experience has always been one of Apple's biggest advantages:

Apple's intrinsic cool factor can't be underestimated either. Being cool isn't exactly something you can plan, but Apple has backed it up with its unique designs, marketing savvy, and cult figure Steve Jobs as CEO. . . . Apple can also afford to advertise and build lush stores because as a seller of premium products, it isn't in a price war.[20]

The Bentley experience. In an effort to increase its exposure to the "right" people, the makers of the $233,000 British automobile have recently taken to hiring "uberstylists" to throw swank soirees at places like the Chicago Museum of Contemporary Art.

"It's an image party," Jesse Garza said to the *Chicago Tribune* social page reporter, Lucinda Hahn, one of the members of the media covering the "Brilliantly British" event. "It's to get the brand in front of a really cool crowd, to get a buzz going about Bentley and not have it be weird and like you can't walk into the showroom," Garza said.[21]

It's a fine line to walk—trying to make the car seem accessible, while also trying to maintain the experience of elegance that Bentleys are known for. But a good start were the strawberries and cream and the new "Moonbeam" colored 2005 Arnage T parked in the museum's main hall where guests could experience it first hand.

Clairol's Try It On studio. As Clairol promotes its newest lines of hair colors, it offers a high-tech way to experience the brand through its Web site at *www.clairol.com.* The site asks visitors, "Ever wondered what you'd look like with a different cut, style or color? At Clairol's Try It On Studio, you can experiment with all three—without the commitment! Just log in to get started. Or if you're not yet a Clairol member, join the fun!"

Savvy reporters covering this industry would likely take them up on their offer, so savvy public relations pros would want to test out the site themselves, making sure that the links all work, that the sign-in is easy, and all the options are available. It would also be important to ensure that the colors brought up on the Web site are true to form and don't oversell the look that is possible to achieve.

For all of these examples, while it is important that all customers have positive experiences with the brand, a smart public relations professional will pay special attention to how the media interpret the experience. As Pine and Gilmore say, "Excellent design, marketing, and delivery will be every bit as crucial for experiences as they are for goods and services."[22] The media have the power to relay these experiences to many customers and potential customers, and so their experiences are truly critical for how the brand will be portrayed to the public.

Business-to-Business MPR

In their book, *Business-to-Business Marketing Research*,[1] Martin and Tamara Block define four challenges of the b-to-b environment that reflect its unique characteristics:

- Derived demand: the motivation for the b-to-b purchase comes from outside the company—derived from your customer's customers' needs and interests.
- Complex buying cycles and buying influences: b-to-b purchases are typically well planned, thoroughly researched, and have many actors involved including members of the department that actually needs the product or service as well as members of a professional procurement department.
- Opportunity for negotiation: Stems from the built-in focus on cost-containment in the b-to-b environment and the fact that most b-to-b selling is done through personal sales contacts.
- Focus on customer service: The competitive vendor mix in b-to-b selling often makes the after-sale customer service activity a key factor in determining if the sale was successful and is likely to be repeated.

These factors, along with the built-in need for information in the b-to-b environment, make it a perfect candidate for an integrated approach to marketing communications. In many ways, these factors make it an even better candidate for the use of MPR than b-to-c environments. There are at least five characteristics of b-to-b firms that make blending public relations into the marketing mix such a logical choice.

1. The relatively small marketing budgets allocated to b-to-b promotional efforts.
2. The large number of trade publications covering b-to-b firms.
3. The intimate relationship that often exists with direct customers, but not with end users of the b-to-b firms' products.
4. The high usage of trade shows to showcase b-to-b product innovations.
5. The relatively small marketing communications staffs in b-to-b firms.

Each of these characteristics will be discussed in depth in this chapter with examples of how b-to-b firms have successfully used MPR in their marketing strategies.

Smaller Promotional Budgets

B-to-b marketing budgets typically are much smaller than those for consumer goods. While budget allocations will vary by industry and company, a general rule-of-thumb is that b-to-b firms tend to allocate about one percent of sales revenues for marketing activities, while consumer goods firms allocate about five percent. B-to-b firms instead spend a much higher allocation on their sales forces than consumer goods firms because b-to-b products are usually far more complex and have very long sales cycles. In industrial marketing, these sales cycles can be two or three years and sometimes even longer. Members of the sales force often become extended members of their customers' firms, helping them with their planning and product design issues.

According to the Center for Exhibition Industry Research (CEIR), a typical breakdown of the b-to-b sales and marketing budget is:

51 percent to Sales
15 percent to Exhibitions
12 percent to Advertising
10 percent to Direct Marketing
7 percent to Public Relations
5 percent to Telecommunications

Although the PR budget is relatively small in the b-to-b world, it is actually a larger percentage allocation than in a typical b-to-c environment and the 7 percent allocated to PR can buy a great deal more exposure for a b-to-b firm than the 12 percent allocated to advertising.

An Active Trade Press

One of the advantages to b-to-b MPR stems from the many trade journals that cover every major industry. They provide an instant forum for explaining new processes, product innovations, new product launches, and even management practices. A trade journal is distinguished from a consumer or business magazine in that it is typically distributed free of charge to members of the industry that it covers, if they meet some specific criteria that fit their target profile. Advertising rates are established based on qualified readership, which is typically authenticated through one of the major audit bureaus: the Audit Bureau of Circulations (ABC) or the Business Publications Audit (BPA).

Readers of these publications are often the key targets of interest to the b-to-b firm. They include customers, potential customers, suppliers, employees, potential employees, and even financial analysts reporting on specific industries. According to the Standard Rate and Data Service (SRDS), in 2004 there were more than 9,300 domestic trade and healthcare publication listings in more than 220 market classifications compared to just 3,000 consumer publications in 85 market classifications.[2]

The editorial staffs of most trade publications consider themselves to be part of the industries that they cover and are, therefore, typically friendlier to companies in these industries, and more understanding of their issues, than the general news media. The trade media are genuinely interested in covering industry topics and events, and their small staffs allow greater opportunity for providing bylined articles and case histories as well.

Relationships with Customers but not End Users

In a recent article in *The Business to Business Marketer* magazine entitled, "What Makes Business-to-Business Marketing Different From Consumer?" Robert W. Bly suggests:

The business buyer needs your product—the actual, physical product, not just its benefits—and wants to spend his money on it. Yes, the benefits are critical. But he needs more than just the benefits or advantages; he also needs the actual product—a fax machine, personal computer, domain name, credit line, pollution control system—itself . . . The consumer wants the benefits your product delivers, but does not want the product itself. Nor does he want to part with his money to obtain it.[3]

This interest in the product or service by the b-to-b customer, along with the high degree of personal selling that takes place, is another advantage of b-to-b marketing over b-to-c marketing. It implies a high degree of knowledge about customers' needs and interests that can only be imagined in most b-to-c environments. (The term *consultative selling* is popular in most b-to-b circles and taken very seriously.). This knowledge provides a certain amount of face time that gives companies access to their customers' manufacturing and marketing plans.

Customer databases are relatively easy to develop and maintain in this environment because of this characteristic. On the other hand, it is not often easy to learn about your customer's customers' needs and interests, and these are the ultimate drivers of demand. They are the critical end users of the product or service, but it is difficult to know who they are or how to reach them. And direct customers are often reluctant to share that information, in fear that their suppliers may someday become their competitors by selling direct.

Public relations is an excellent tool for reaching these unidentified end users. Creating a "pull" for your products by educating the end users can be a very powerful strategic approach to your marketing endeavors. One of the most used b-to-b tactics in this regard is creating case histories about how various end users' problems were solved through the use of a product or service. The trade media are typically open to running these types of stories—especially if they can have access to the end users to enhance the story and to verify their experiences.

Tom Harris was involved in the publication of an article about a security system installation that linked the schools in Boston; the publication was a journal directed to school purchasing agents. As a result of this single placement, Johnson Controls received an inquiry from the Cleveland school system that resulted in the sale of a multimillion dollar installation.

Another useful PR tool is creating the useful "how-to" technical article that addresses some specific problem that a number of end users might experience and which your product or service might solve. These books or articles can have their origins in a number of places, but often they come from internal experts or hiring a well-known expert in the field who has some association with the firm.

Computer Sciences Corporation (CSC), a leading global consulting and information technology services firm, used this approach in 2001 to build sustained visibility for the company's national supply chain and e-commerce practices. It hired PepperCom to promote a book that was being released by two CSC Consulting partners entitled, *E-Supply Chain: Using the Internet to Revolutionize Your Business*. The agency leveraged the partners' expertise and developed a number of useful case histories during the book launch and created university relations and trade association outreach campaigns, including holding seminars and providing free copies of the books.

Hobart Corporation, the world's premier commercial food equipment manufacturer, used a similar technique in 2002, when it started to feel the pinch of niche competitors coming up on its heels. The company decided that it must reposition itself or risk looking like every other equipment manufacturer. Using HSR Business to Business as its agency, Hobart set out to become *the* authority on food industry issues. In addition to seeking out prominent, front-of-the-book editorial opportunities in trade publications that offered Hobart experts a platform for discussing pressing industry issues, an important part of the strategy was to create a new publication—SAGE: Sound Advice for the Food Industry Professional. This was a sleek magazine that provided another vehicle for positioning Hobart as an authoritarian source of industry knowledge and best practices. "SAGE has been a critical component in Hobart's brand positioning, said Dean Landeche, Hobart's vice president of brand marketing. "Bringing together relevant content with the Hobart perspective demonstrates to industry operators that Hobart has something to say on the issues that keep them up at night."[4]

In addition to hiring an agency to develop or launch these types of free-standing books or magazines, there are three common approaches to technical articles that can also result in strong outreach to the end user. The first approach is to pitch it to a trade publication editor, who will assign a staff member or freelancer to write it using materials and technical people you provide to help them.

Another popular approach is to have the article written by a well-known technical expert in your firm or industry, such as the chief engineer or product manager. A PR professional—either in-house or at the PR agency—would then edit the article to be sure it is understandable to a lay person and then pitch it to several non-competing trade journals for publication as a bylined article. The advantage to this approach is that you can be pretty confident of the article's technical accuracy, and there is a greater chance of the article being accepted for publication in multiple trade magazines.

The third approach addresses this problem by having a PR professional or a hired technical writer interview the technical expert to develop the story outline and obtain technical reference materials. Then that writer "ghost writes" the article for the technical expert, who will review it and correct any technical errors before it goes out for publication. The article still appears as a bylined story by the technical expert, but it is often faster and more efficient in the long run to have the initial draft written for him or her, and it still can be pitched to a variety of publications.

Another advantage to having a PR professional write the initial draft of a technical article is that it serves as a training vehicle and makes the PR person that much more knowledgeable about his or her product or service when dealing with the trade media. This is an important distinction from consumer-based media. If PR people are to have any credibility with this media, they need to be able to act as spokespersons on the general technology, and not simply be gatekeepers, forever making arrangements for the media to speak to other more knowledgeable people within the organization.

Many years ago, when Pat Whalen worked in the Components Division of Clark Equipment Company (the inventor of the forklift truck), she worked closely with a team from Burson-Marsteller to "ghost-write" a number of these types of technical articles. They were phenomenally successful, even with such less-than-catchy titles as, "How to Spec a Planetary Axle," and "Why a Powershift Makes Sense." Some of the Burson-Marsteller veterans believe that these articles still hold some records for the number of placements they received. In addition, the articles were inexpensively reprinted from the trade journals and became instant hits at trade shows and as direct mail pieces.

When the 3M Company launched a major marketing effort for its overhead projector system in the business market, Tom Harris helped develop a program called "How to Have More Effective Business Meetings." Articles on this theme were placed in dozens of trade publications serving major business categories. Inquiry cards in the back of many of these trade journals provided hundreds of qualified sales leads, which were converted into installations by the 3M Business Systems sales force.

Trade Shows in B-to-B

In a breakdown of a typical b-to-b marketing budget, without the allocation for the sales staff, the Center for Exhibition Industry Research[5] found that 49 percent of the promotional budget was allocated to trade shows and industry exhibitions. The remaining 51 percent was allocated as follows: 24 percent to Advertising in Trade Journals, 8 percent to Direct Mail, 5 percent to the Internet, 4 percent to Telemarketing, 10 percent to other promotional activities including: PR, brochures, and miscellaneous.

Why such a large allocation of the marcom budget to trade shows? According to a study by Ziff-Davis,[6] in highly technical industries such as computers and software, "Trade shows provide the greatest opportunity for hands-on product comparisons, and they enable participants to explore new technology implementation ideas." A recent ZF survey found that:

- 68 percent of a universe of IT professionals attend events, including trade shows, seminars, and conferences, making these venues an excellent opportunity to reach these opinion leaders.
- Event audiences represent the high end of the market. They tend to:
  —control larger budgets.
  —be more likely to make purchase decisions.
  —come from larger organizations.
  —be better educated.
  —represent higher levels of corporate management.
  —Technical complexity of subject areas seems to drive attendance at trade shows, with the complex areas of networking software and Internet / Intranet Services and software demonstrating over 100 percent increased involvement of attendees over non-attendees.

While the consumer goods industry also has some important exhibitions—most notably the Consumer Electronics Show as well as the many auto, boat, and home and garden shows held annually in cities around the world—the majority of exhibitions are held for the benefit of b-to-b firms. These are major industry events, where most of the key manufacturers, suppliers, and media gather to learn about the latest industry news, meet with customers, show end users the latest technology, and check out the competition.

In its 1996 study, Power of Exhibitions II, CEIR[7] found that companies that integrate such marketing components as advertising, direct marketing, sponsorships, press conferences, and hospitality functions with a trade show activity were more likely to report a "very successful" show. The study also found press conference activities at a show and its surrounding media coverage increased attraction of target audiences to a booth by 77 percent. That study also found that 58 percent of all firms found public relations an important tool in the selling process, and in the healthcare field that number jumped to 67 percent. This suggests that adding public relations to the mix of communications activities surrounding an exhibit would add significant value to the overall exhibition endeavor.

Planning for a Successful Trade Show

The trick to executing a trade show well is to plan it early and include all facets of the marketing department early on. The first important step is insuring that the show has a reasonable expectation that it will attract the key targets of interest to the firm. Show audits and feedback from the sales department play important roles in helping to identify which shows are the most crucial, but those responsible for advertising, direct marketing, and public relations should all be in on the initial plans and all should develop specific and measurable objectives for their role in the show once it is selected.

An after-show post mortem should always be conducted with as much financial analysis as possible. A budget breakdown of all costs incurred and all accomplishments achieved should be prepared. Output measures such as booth attendance and leads generated by customers and prospective customers should always be undertaken using such formulas as attraction efficiency, contact efficiency, and conversion efficiency. Public relations output can be measured by media attendance at the booth and/or special media events, as well as a summary of materials produced and distributed and any other specific objectives that were planned. A qualitative assessment of the event by booth staff should also always be undertaken, with a key question being, "If we could do it over again, what would we do differently?"

Anywhere from three to six months after the event, another assessment should be undertaken for major trade shows to try to establish the outcome measures:

- How many orders can be traced to contacts made at the show?
- How many leads generated at the show were followed up on (and what is their potential value to the firm)?
- How many news articles were generated and what value can you place on them?
- What competitive information was obtained that might be useful?
- Can customers and/or end users recall your presence at the show and remember your message there?

While only a handful of b-to-b firms undertake this level of follow-up and evaluation of their trade show efforts, it is the only way to way to assess the value of the investment and to know if a similar investment should be undertaken next year.

Bosch Converts a Skeptical Trade Press[8]

The following is an excellent example of how both the trade press and a trade show helped meet a specific b-to-b objective. It was undertaken by appliance maker Bosch a year earlier than its consumer campaign, which was discussed in the previous chapter, and it was featured as an award-winning MPR campaign by the public relations trade publication, *Bulldog Reporter*.

When the company decided to relaunch a line of small kitchen appliances in the US after a lackluster and unsuccessful foray into that market 10 years earlier, its MPR team knew it had to follow a two-step marketing approach. The first was aimed at b-to-b audiences to drive distribution, and the second was a b-to-c approach aimed at spreading consumer awareness.

Before consumers could buy the appliances, however, the products first had to reach the stores, and to convince distributors to carry the line, a skeptical trade press had to be convinced that Bosch knew what it was doing this time around. So the first step was aimed directly at the trade media.

For Bosch to attract positive trade media attention, it had to address the skeptics openly and respond with solutions. "Getting to know the trade pubs in the first place and trying to build relationships during holiday time, required very focused media relations," said Erika Price Schulte, PR Director at RiechesBaird, Bosch's integrated marketing firm. "We read back issues to find out which reporters covered which beats and what their opinions were of the competition. This helped us become knowledgeable and articulate in a short time," Schulte said.

Another important factor in Bosch's success was its pursuit of "show dailies" that were distributed at the Housewares Show. Schulte explained:

Show dailies are published during a trade show to coincide with the proceedings. Usually, there's an issue for each day detailing what is happening and who is creating a buzz at the show. We found out who was publishing these and were able to work with the reporters in advance to make sure we were covered prominently. Remember, our challenge was to demonstrate Bosch's commitment to the launch. So dominating the show dailies was a key part of our strategy, and we pitched those reporters the same as the other trades.

In explaining Bosch's focus on the trade publications almost a year in advance of it's consumer media blitz, the *Bulldog Reporter* wrote:

On some campaigns, an all-out media blitz is a fine strategy, but not in this case. To bypass the mistakes of the previous campaign and eliminate unnecessary confusion, Schulte divided her outreach into two stages. In the months before and after the Housewares Show, she concentrated her attention on trade media. Then, as those efforts paid off and the initial swell of coverage subsided, Schulte was in a better position to begin a consumer push. "If we had done the consumer launch first, it would have created frustration that the product was not yet available," she explains.

The resulting positive trade coverage greased the distribution wheels and got Bosch's small appliance launch off to a perfect start. The two-step MPR campaign was awarded a silver medal in the 2003 Bulldog Awards for Excellence in Media Relations & Publicity.

Small Marcom Staffs

Because so much of what is done in PR in the b-to-b environment can either be piggy-backed on to existing marcom activities or can enhance those activities, the same marcom staff can usually be used to accomplish both. This assumes, however, that the firms have staffed themselves with people who are capable of multitasking and are well-versed in each of the key marcom disciplines: advertising, direct marketing, public relations, databases, and special events planning.

MPR Rescues Satellites From Premature Death

In the late 1980s Communications Satellite Corporation (Comsat)[9] used an integrated mix of public relations and other marcom activities to achieve dramatic success. A single set of promotional strategies, initially developed purely for PR purposes, was used to achieve a number of marketing objectives, which not only allows for an efficient use of small marcom budgets, but also small marcom staffs. A number of rumors and misunderstandings were circulating about the technology, but the firm needed to understand them before it could create appropriate messages to combat them, including highly publicized media reports that satellite would become obsolete once the highly publicized undersea fiber optic cable service came on the market within the next year. The firm's public relations agency, Fleishman-Hillard (F-H), was tasked with uncovering key insights about the marketplace's view of satellite technology, F-H conducted extensive qualitative and quantitative research among Comsat's direct customers (large telecommunications companies) and among the end users of the service (large corporate IT departments) to understand each group's knowledge of existing satellite technology and any resistance they had to using it.

Insights from the research led to the creation of Q&A sales literature. Presentation materials were created and used with the marketing staffs of the Comsat's customers, and information materials were provided to them to pass on to their customers to better explain how satellites worked and how their digital capabilities compared with the fiber optic service that would soon be on the market.

Press releases were widely distributed to key media covering the industry along with the Q&As and brochures that were developed for the sales department. The media, always hungry for controversy, reported on it extensively, usually echoing Comsat's position that, like Mark Twain, rumors of the death of satellites were highly exaggerated. *The New York Times* even ran a large cartoon of sharks eating the undersea fiber cable with an accompanying article warning network directors that they should have both systems in place for full backup capabilities.

It was determined that a graphic illustration of how digital satellite technology worked would be a useful tool for the media, so a well-known sci-fi graphic artist was hired to create a dramatic piece of art showcasing the technology's strengths. That artwork became the basis of several print ads that ran in key telecommunications trade publications. It also became the back-drop of the company's trade show booth and was developed into a poster that was used as a trade show give-away, as a premium item that customers and end users could call or write in to request, in exchange for their contact information. Framed copies of the poster, signed by the artist, were also used as gifts to key media and key customers.

Based on existing databases and the new contact names from those who requested the poster, a direct mail campaign was developed to dispel the myths about satellite technology. The materials used in this direct mail campaign included some of the materials already in use by the sales department, but new "how-to" guides and other helpful materials were also created using feedback from the research that identified areas of confusion or concern. These same materials were also used in the trade show booths at various industry events over the next year.

A video was created and a special seminar was developed and conducted at certain trade shows to provide this same information in person to the media, to customers, and to end users. Direct mail was used to invite key people to these events. A live international demonstration was created for the trade show booth, and a special media viewing was arranged. Special media dinners were also organized at several of the trade shows where media could get to know Comsat's executives and technical staff better.

The end result was widespread media coverage of the advantages of digital satellite services and a dramatic increase in orders for the existing technology. Even when the fiber optic systems came on board a year later, orders for digital satellite technology continued to increase, and a second generation of satellites was launched to keep up with demand. The company was named "Telecom Marketing Department of the Year" by *Sales and Marketing Management* Magazine. And it was all done with a PR agency budget of under $100,000 and a marcom staff of five, who were simultaneously working on other products and issues.

Clairol Expands B-to-B Efforts: Procter & Gamble Touts Clairol Professional Products

Direct magazine[10] reported that consumer goods giant Procter & Gamble launched a rare b-to-b integrated marketing effort November 2003 aimed at professional hair stylists. The company used print ads in hair color magazines such as *Professional Modern Salon* and *American Salon*. These were expected to generate more than 4 million impressions.

The architect of the campaign, New York-based Wunderman, tried to appeal to stylists' creativity and reestablish Clairol as a hair color expert. (P&G had only owned the brand two years.) In one ad, a red dahlia burst from the tip of an artist's paintbrush set on a light blue background. The tag line, "A stroke of color genius," ran along the handle of the brush, accompanied by a line at the bottom of the creative that read: "The most colorful things happen when passion is reborn." An 800 number and Web address were used as response mechanisms.

The same theme was used in direct mail and e-mail, and in ad space on the sides of buses. It was also featured in an MPR campaign, which included events at major beauty shows in New York, Chicago and other cities. The overall campaign, which included a heavy focus on education, was viewed as the cornerstone of a major customer relationship management program. P&G also launched a magazine, *The Colorist*, to support the effort. It included tips from experts, information on products and educational classes, and an events calendar.

The first wave of direct mail, which unlike the print ads featured models in its graphics, reached colorists and stylists nationwide in late 2003. That wave of branding messages contained information on educational programs. It was followed by pieces educating stylists on three specific products: Miss Clairol (permanent hair color); Complements (color in a tube); and Kaliedocolors (highlighting). About 300,000 direct mail pieces and e-mail messages had been sent through January 2004.

The eight-page direct mail piece, which read like a book, included a mail-in certificate for a $12 rebate on the purchase of 12 bottles of hair color. It was also translated into Spanish and sent to prospects six months after the initial campaign. The Web site *(www.clairolpro.com)* was also refreshed to be compatible with the campaign, which was expected to run for several years.

Legal B-to-B MPR

In a b-to-b campaign that was more specifically MPR focused, national law firm Foley & Lardner used the confusion in the business world about the latest corporate governance laws, especially the 2001 Sarbanes-Oxley Act, to help promote its new multidisciplinary group of attorneys focused on corporate governance.

The firm, with the help of its PR agency, Weber Shandwick, began the campaign by using the law firm's research unit, KRC Research, to undertake two phases of research. The first was a look at the costs of Sarbanes-Oxley to corporations, and the second was a survey of top executives attitudes toward corporate reform.

PR News, which awarded the campaign "Business-To-Business Campaign of the Year 2004," reported:[11]

> The PR effort that promoted the cost study included a conference call with the media and lawyers on the firm's corporate governance team. For both pieces of research, the results were distributed via a teaser e-mail to media highlighting the issues and attorneys from the team were used as spokespersons. The PR team also sent a PowerPoint deck with full results to key media outlets. The survey results were also posted on the firm's Web site, were also sent to 500 clients and prospective clients.
>
> The campaign resulted in 220 media placements over a three-month period, including coverage in top-tier outlets like The Wall Street Journal, USA Today, CNBC, and numerous industry publications. As a result, Foley & Lardner has received more than 195 requests for the data from research institutions, professional associations, and corporate entities. Also, the Securities and Exchange Commission and the New York Stock Exchange have increased their visits to the law firm's Web site. In August alone, the SEC visited 740 times.
>
> Foley & Lardner attorneys have been asked to speak at a number of conferences, and the firm has been referenced in several important corporate governance discussions, including a *Wall Street Journal* editorial on the rising cost of reform.

Cause-Related Marketing PR

While the term *cause-related marketing* has become synonymous with any marketing tie-in with a good cause and is often used interchangeably with terms such as "social marketing," it originally had a much narrower definition based on a deceptively simple principle: Buy a company's product, and it will make a donation on your behalf to some worthy cause. Sometimes the donation is based on label or coupon redemption. Sometimes the purchase of a specific item or a service transaction results in a contribution.

These sponsorships have not only raised countless millions for good causes over the past thirty years, but they have also been good for business. When consumers become aware of a company's involvement, they are often more inclined to patronize its products and services. Hence, when American Express decided a few years ago to donate two cents to homeless food kitchens for each credit card transaction made by its cardholders, it saw an 8.4 percent increase in its transactions.[1] The campaign was supported by advertising, but it was a public relations activity to be sure. And it is not just the narrow definition of cause-related marketing that can have this level of impact. Firms such as Ben & Jerry's and The Body Shop have created legions of loyal customers by paying attention to environmental issues and supporting worthy causes, regardless of their consumers' transactions. Recent research on corporate reputation might help explain why cause-related activities are such an important part of marketing public relations.

Edelman Public Relations' 2004 Annual Trust Barometer[2] reported that 71 percent of consumers in the US and 66 percent of consumers in Europe believe that "being active in cause-related initiatives" are an important factor in determining a company's reputation and in driving trust in the firm. A 1999 Hill & Knowlton/Yankelovich Partners survey of CEOs[3] on the benefits of a strong corporate reputation found that 77 percent believed that a good reputation helps sell products and services, and 61 percent believe that it makes it easier to attract top employees. Echoing this sentiment, Debra Smith, Vice President of Communications for JP Morgan Chase Company recently said, "People will gravitate to a name and brand they can trust. They want to know they are getting quality service."

Potential Pitfalls for Social Marketing Campaigns

While there is strong evidence that tying marketing endeavors to good causes and good works makes good business sense, effectively pulling it off is much harder than it seems at first glance. Take the following examples. They all have the potential to backfire if not handled well or if treated as pure marketing activities:

- A local convenience store runs a promotion announcing that ten cents from the sale of every hot dog will go to "Jerry's Kids," and sales of hot dogs go up by 20 percent.
- A strip mining company sets aside a thousand acres of land as a nature preserve and gains favor with the local legislature that was about to pass a bill to restrict mining activities.
- A predominantly white-owned hair care products company that has decided to

introduce a new line of products to the African-American community donates several hundred thousand dollars to three of the country's largest black universities for minority scholarships, which results in strong brand recognition among this target group.

Many traditional marketing departments handling these types of causes make the mistake of focusing almost exclusively on influencing the customer. The public relations function, however, will focus on all key stakeholders' interests and concerns, not just the customer. This broader focus is critical to the campaign's success, because there are many stakeholders who could find fault with the company's activities. There could be corporate shareholders who may not want to see corporate profits diminished by what they perceive as inappropriate charitable contributions. There could be media and special interest groups who may interpret the company's actions as self-serving and unethical and may report it in that context. And there could be customers who may not agree with the causes being supported. The public relations professional will (or at least should) consider all of these points of view and will find ways to address them before initiating the cause-related campaign.

The Question of Ethics

Before embarking on a strategy that supports charities or good social causes as those listed above, firms must be able to address the concerns of two groups of potential skeptics of the practice. These two groups have radically different points of view, despite both questioning the ethics of these activities.

The first group not only believes that corporate executives do not have an obligation to take on socially responsible causes, but they believe that it is improper for corporate executives to reduce profits by donating corporate funds to such social causes. Like economist Milton Friedman, they hold that, since these executives do not own their firms and the funds they manage are not their own, they have a fiduciary responsibility to ensure that the funds given to them by investors are used solely for the purposes of maximizing shareholder return. Friedman suggests that if shareholders find value in contributing to social causes, they do so through individual contributions.[4]

Indeed, there have been a growing number of lawsuits by stockholders over this very point. The courts have generally applied the "business judgment rule" that permits small donations to charity when the executives claim they are doing it for the benefit of the company, regardless of whether the company actually benefits from the contributions.[5] But in recent times when corporate profits have been relatively weak, "claiming" benefits is not good enough. Shareholders and judges are beginning to demand "proof" that the charitable tie-in provides value to shareholders in the long run.

To address these concerns, the marketing public relations team should have well-defined objectives for the tie-in with the social cause and a plan to evaluate the benefits achieved through the connection. There does not necessarily need to be an immediate or direct financial payback in terms of sales generated, but some value needs to be assessed for the publicity, goodwill, and relationship-building that will ultimately translate into improved revenues. If there is no tangible evidence that supporting the special cause will result in improved business, then it could be a questionable activity, and the marketing and public relations team should rethink the plan.

The second group of skeptics may be from the very groups being targeted by the cause-related activity or from the media that serve them. The example of the minority scholarships being offered by a firm hoping to break into hair-care products for African-Americans is such a case. If the firm has shown little or no interest in supporting this ethnic group in the past, the motive for the new interest would be suspect, and many in this community might perceive the activity as a shameless bribe.

Supporting this perspective is an article in the *Journal of Mass Media Ethics* by PR Professor David Martinson[6] which suggests that any firm using a cause-related activity with a primary goal of increasing business is acting unethically and is bordering on the dishonest, since their interests lie, not in helping kids with diseases, preserving the environment, or helping minority students complete their education, but in "selling products and manipulating public opinion."

Martinson suggests that companies practicing this form of promotion violate two key premises of ethical behavior—one, that people should be treated as ends, not as means to an end (i.e. corporate profits); and two, that one should do good because it is an inherent duty within every human being. "Individuals should not do good simply because they seek a reward in return for their actions," he says.

Looking for answers to how the news media will cover corporate good works could leave you scratching your head about the right approach to take. Consider the mixed coverage about firms' charitable activities shortly after the September 11, 2001, attacks on the World Trade Center. In some cases, lists were compiled and reported on about how much was being contributed by corporations to victim relief funds. These firms were praised as good corporate citizens. But not all major firms appeared on these lists and some were criticized publicly for being insensitive or poor corporate citizens. In a number of cases, corporate PR people found themselves defending their companies' actions in an endless stream of angry customer calls. This was particularly irksome, because their firms had, indeed, donated generously to the cause, but had either decided to keep their donations quiet to avoid any appearance of self-promotion or had chosen to donate in a way that did not appear on these lists.

Perhaps in response to this level of media scrutiny, some firms began to publicize their charitable efforts. But this was met with even more negative coverage. In a critical article on the practice in the *Wall Street Journal,* author Kris Maher said, "It's not always easy to determine exactly where corporate charity ends and self-promotion begins."[7] The article went on to criticize firms that distributed press releases about their charitable activities. Maher wrote:

> Both Burger King Corp. and McDonald's Corp., for example, have issued releases recently touting aid they have provided. One McDonald's release, titled "Continuing Response to National Tragedy" lists financial support along with a familiar-sounding bullet point: "More Than Half Million Meals to Rescue & Recovery Teams."
>
> In announcing a sponsorship deal with the Harlem Globetrotters, Burger King said the buses the Globetrotters travel in will depict "the American Flag, the Burger King logo and details of the team's contributions to the American Red Cross Liberty Disaster Relief Fund."

In its defense, Rob Doughty, a Burger King spokesman, was quoted in the article saying the company has been careful not to put out too many press releases since the attacks. "But consumers want to know. They want assurances that we are doing something to support the efforts," he said.

The warning here for MPR people is to think carefully about how and when to take credit for their firm's good works, since there is always a chance that someone will call their motives into question.

Addressing Media and Special Interest Skeptics

To overcome skeptics to corporate philanthropy, it is important that the firm begin an early policy of connecting with key causes that are important to their customers and potential targets. If the firm establishes a pattern early on that it respects and supports these causes and the groups that benefit from them, it will be less likely to be accused of trying to buy their favor at the time of a specific promotional campaign. This means that long-term planning and a fair amount of research into what really matters to customers and potential customers are necessary.

In addition, when we look at those firms that have used cause-related marketing effectively—that were able to connect their brands with these worthwhile causes, avoid accusations of self-serving behaviors, and have the media provide strong and supportive coverage of their activities—they have found ways to get involved with the charity beyond just providing financial support. They encourage employees to volunteer, they arrange on-site visits, they lend executives to help in fund-raising or becoming board members, etc. They also tend to emphasize the good works of the charity or social program, and keep a low profile when it comes to publicizing their organization's involvement. They avoid making statements that sound like advertising slogans. They don't say, "We got involved because we are a company with a heart." Instead, they take a more humble approach, along the lines of: "We got involved because we saw a need in a very important community that wasn't being addressed."

In 1988, Robert E. Hope, an executive vice president at Burson-Marsteller, suggested that:

> There is a bridge that must be built between the product and the cause, and that bridge is more than a commercial tie-in. It's a bridge of compatible philosophies, strategies, and mutual benefit. . . . Cause-related marketing is a term that reflects the mission of the originators and was named from the marketer's viewpoint based on the benefits for marketing products . . . a more accurate term might be "cause and product joint marketing" since the benefits must clearly flow both ways.
>
> If cause-related marketing is to grow and help everyone involved in its efforts, nothing can replace the critical need of product marketers and causes in picking only the right things to do and then doing them right. . . . Let's try a new definition. Let's describe cause-related marketing as putting together a cause and a product in a joint, mutually beneficial, marketing effort. . . . When it's all over, all the people in the company that manufactures and sells the product want to feel good about what they have done. In a way, this is the real proof of success . . . proof that there is real 'heart' backing up the credit of being involved.[8]

Cause-Related Campaigns that Worked

Enter American Express

The term *cause-related marketing* was first coined by the Travel Related Services subsidiary of American Express in 1981 and was subsequently trademarked (although we've never seen a challenge to the use of the term by others). Louis V. Gerstner, Jr., then president of American Express, described it as a way to "move from checkbook philanthropy to find new and more creative ways to combine profit objectives with social commitments." He predicted:

> The new stage in this evolution will be an honest, straightforward marriage of corporate interests with worthy social and cultural programs. The net results will be a quantum increase in visibility and support for deserving programs because we will have circumvented the traditional and dismal zero-sum game in which every dollar going to support nonbusiness programs was a grudging subtraction from a corporation's near sacred bottom line.[9]

American Express's cause-related marketing ties philanthropy directly to the marketing of its travel-related services. The company selects causes that need visibility and marketing-and-management help in communities where American Express does business in the United States and throughout the world. Then it donates a small sum to the cause each time a customer uses the American Express card, purchases American Express Travelers Cheques, buys a travel package, or applies for and receives a new American Express card during a typical three-month promotional period. For each cause-related program, American Express creates ads, buys time and space to run them in local media, and generates media coverage that raises public awareness of the projects and their support by American Express, which generates good will for the company. Editorial endorsements occur in news stories and in print and TV editorials commending the company.

McDonald's: Telethon Sponsorships and Ronald McDonald House

Another early believer in the cause-related marketing strategy is McDonald's Corporation. It has practiced the concept of cause-related marketing successfully for more than 30 years. In 1967, at the recommendation of public relations counselor Al Golin, McDonald's became the first corporation to sponsor a national telethon, the Jerry Lewis Labor Day Telethon, which raises funds to fight muscular dystrophy. The company has contributed more than $25 million over the years to help 'Jerry's Kids' by redirecting dimes and quarters from the sale of french fries, Cokes, and other menu items.

Dozens of corporate sponsors have followed McDonald's lead by making contributions based on sales generated by telethon promotions to help muscular dystrophy, Easter Seals, Children's Muscle Network, the United Negro College Fund, and others. Telethons give companies positive exposure in millions of homes.

Another favorite charity of McDonalds is its signature Ronald McDonald House. Since the first Ronald McDonald House opened in 1974, local McDonald's restaurants have raised funds through special promotions to support these facilities where families of seriously ill children can stay for little or no cost while their children are treated at nearby hospitals. Local McDonald's restaurants have served as a catalyst to raise funds for Ronald McDonald Houses. When the first house opened in Philadelphia,

McDonald's restaurants there joined the Philadelphia Eagles in raising the $35,000 needed to purchase the Philadelphia house. In the mid-1980s, Ronald McDonald House Charities (RMHC) was formed, and since 1984, RMHC's global office support to local chapters has totaled more than $84 million. In it 2003 Annual Report, it was noted that 77 percent of its support—more than $15 million—went directly to local chapters and their programs.

There are now 234 Ronald McDonald Houses worldwide offering more than 6,000 bedrooms each night and caring for families in 24 countries. In recent years, McDonald's has attracted national corporate donors to help defray construction and operating costs. Its Web site (*http://www.rmhc.org*) lists the following major corporate donors: American Express, American Farm Bureau, Benjamin Moore & Co., Bissell, Brand Source, Christmas Décor. Coca-Cola, Dillard's, Georgia-Pacific, Kohler, Nestle, NTRA Charities, Select Comfort, Southwest Airlines, Stampin' Up!, United Online, *USA Today*, and Valassis.

Home Depot: Project Homefront[10]

In a cause-related project aimed at showing support for US troops in Iraq, but also wanting to stay close to its area of expertise (home maintenance and improvement), The Home Depot, supported by Ketchum Public Relations, created Project Homefront in 2003. The focus of the project was to provide home repair and maintenance assistance to loved ones whose family members were serving in Iraq. The Home Depot pledged $1 million and 1 million total hours of service through a volunteer corp called Team Depot. In its first year, more than 1,200 houses were repaired and more than 20,000 people participated in the special clinics and kids' workshops that were provided under the program.

The company reported an overwhelming response from consumers and employees alike in scores of e-mails, voice-mails, and letters to the company. The company used corporate advertising to promote the project and solicit more volunteers, using a "thank you note" theme. The ad, which pictured a simple porch with an empty rocking chair and an American flag, had a hand-written note that began, "While they're taking care of our homeland, we're taking care of their homes. Thank you to all the Project Homefront volunteers who continue to help us support the families of those serving our country overseas."

Select Comfort—Catching ZZZs for Charity

Mattress maker and retailer Select Comfort was named "Cause-Related Campaign of the Year 2004" by *PR News* after its successful cause-related marketing strategy that tied its unique positioning of "the sleep number bed" to the Ronald McDonald House Charities.

According to the campaign synopsis:[11]

Sales in 2001 were decreasing, and the company was looking to reposition itself around a unique feature, the Sleep Number—a number between 0 and 100 that represents a combination of comfort, firmness, and support for a particular mattress.

A key component of Select Comfort's rebranding effort was a partnership with Ronald McDonald House Charities (RMHC). Each year, thousands of families stay at Ronald McDonald House while their critically ill children receive treatment at a nearby hospital. In hopes of offering some comfort to these families, the company's ten-year goal was to provide a Sleep Number bed to each of the 4,000 bedrooms in the 150 Ronald McDonald Houses nationwide.

In 2003, Select Comfort looked to its agency of record, Carmichael Lynch Spong (CLS) to leverage its RMHC partnership for greater exposure and help donate 1,000 beds, thus doubling its 2002 efforts. With a budget of $78,000, CLS focused on key markets (and created unique events in several of them).

A Celebrity Bedtime Reading event was held at a Dallas RMHC location, where TV star Angie Harmon read to kids and their families. Select Comfort celebrated its 1000th donation at a newly expanded Ronald McDonald House in Seattle by delivering and assembling 120 beds in one day, the largest single-day, single-house donation. The company celebrated the grand opening of its first stand-alone store in Minneapolis by holding a street-hockey game in the parking lot. The fundraiser included two stars of the NHL's Minnesota Wild. Chicago Bears quarterback Jim Miller also participated in a charity event at a local mall and raised $3,000.

The payoff was huge. More than 52 celebrities actively supported the sponsorship, over 1,100 beds were donated, worth $1.5 million in goods and services, and $75,000 cash were donated to RMHC. Employees volunteered more than 1,200 hours to the cause, while pledging $16,000 in payroll reductions. The Sleep Number brand awareness rose 22 percent in targeted markets, and sales rose 50 percent in October 2003 during the biggest retail promotions. It also was awarded the 2003 Retail Community Service Award from *Executive Technology* magazine and was given a Donor Recognition Award at RMHC's annual international conference.

Campbell's Soup Cause-Related Activities

Campbell Soup Company has been an active follower of the cause-related marketing strategy for many years. Its Labels for Education, introduced nationally in 1973, remains one of the nation's most successful cause-related promotions. In 2005 it still provides the service that allows kids and parents to collect labels from any Campbell's product and redeem them for hundreds of different items that the school could use, including computers, sports/fitness equipment and musical instruments.

Today, the program is Internet driven, and its current Web site (*http://www. labelsforeducation.com*) promotes the program as "an easy, fun way to help schools in your neighborhood get free educational merchandise." Sarah Hughes, 2002 Olympic Gold Medalist, is currently the Labels For Education Ambassador. She encourages children from well equipped schools to collect the labels and donate them to less well off schools.

The Labels for Education Program has resulted in increased use of Campbell products, both nationally and regionally. It also enables retailers who feature Campbell products to enhance their image in the community by earning bonus label certificates to award to local schools.

Lance Armstrong and Cancer Research

Cancer survivor and cycling champion Lance Armstrong became America's hero of the 21st century. *The New York Times* said of him "In his signature color of yellow, the man under the halo is Lance Armstrong, the feel-good bike messenger whose deliverance of inspiration has turned him into America's beloved faith hero."

The Lance Armstrong Foundation (LAF) founded in 1997, provides practical information and tools people with cancer need to live strong. LAF is the favorite philanthropy of many US Corporations. In 2004, as a tribute to the six time Tour de France winner, Nike launched the Wear Yellow Live Strong campaign. Nike donated $1 million to the Foundation and led efforts to raise an additional $5 million through the sale of yellow wristbands engraved with Lance's mantra, "Live Strong." All proceeds from the sale of the wristbands were donated to the foundation's programs that help young cancer patients.

Yellow, the color of Lance's jersey in the Tour de France, was depicted as the color of hope, courage, inspiration, and perseverance. The wristbands, which were offered on his Web site and at Niketown stores, became an overnight sensation with both kids and adults.

Another major corporate supporter of Lance Armstrong's battle against cancer has been Bristol-Myers Squibb. The company describes itself as "a leader in discovering innovative therapies to treat cancer" which" provided the medicines that helped Lance beat his cancer."[12] The company said, "Our medicines are making a difference in the lives of millions of people like Lance across the globe."

The company sponsored the Bristol-Myers Squibb Tour of Hope, a weeklong journey across America by a team of 20 people who have been touched by cancer. The team rode across mountains and over plains, sharing their personal stories in order to motivate communities along the way to learn more about the benefits of cancer research. In the 2004 tour, four teams of five cyclists rode in relay fashion for eight days from Los Angeles to Washington, D.C. The event departed Los Angeles at midnight following a community rally at City of Hope Cancer Center and was joined by Lance Armstrong at points along the way before being welcomed in Washington.

Clean-Up Campaigns

Other programs, like city cleanups, can be more directly related to the specific benefit or use of the product. One of the most popular of these events is The Great American Cleanup™, which has been in existence since 1953. Today, it is the nation's largest annual community improvement program and is held annually between March and May. The program rallies people to make sweeping, dramatic changes from coast-to-coast and provides a number of very high-profile opportunities for companies to get involved. For the second consecutive year, President George W. Bush served as honorary chair of the Great American Cleanup™ in 2004, where more than 2.3 million volunteers worked for more than 7 million hours cleaning, beautifying and improving 15,000 communities during 30,000 different Great American Cleanup™ events. Some of the major corporations that have been involved with the project over the years have been AT&T Wireless, Firestone Tire & Services Centers & Expert Tire & Tire Plus, Georgia-Pacific Corporation, Lysol® Brand Products, Pepsi-Cola Company, Tyco Corporation, and Waste Management, Inc.

Loews Hotels and Career-Building for Women

In 2000, Loews Hotels partnered with The Women's Alliance to host Women on the Path to New Success, a one-day career-building workshop and introduction to the hospitality industry for women on public assistance in 14 cities in the US and Canada. The event gave participants at each hotel an introduction to basic business skills, image consulting, and the chance to learn more about careers in hospitality, one of the world's fastest-growing industries. More than 700 women participated.

Women on the Path to New Success continues the new partnership between Loews Hotels and The Women's Alliance and is the third event in a series of national Loews Hotels Good Neighbor Days held to celebrate the 10th anniversary of the chain's Good Neighbor Policy.

Jonathan Tisch, President and CEO of Loews Hotels, said, "We've spent this year celebrating the tenth anniversary of the Loews Hotels Good Neighbor Policy with a series of national events. And we're thrilled that our final event of the year is an outgrowth of our involvement with the Welfare to Work Partnership and look forward to strengthening our partnership with The Women's Alliance." To date, more than 150 employees throughout the Loews Hotels chain have successfully moved off welfare. We are excited about hosting an event that will give women the skills and encouragement they need to get back into the workforce."[13]

Procter & Gamble Brandsaver Programs

P&G's 2003/2004 Contributions Report outlines the company's mission as it relates to its charitable contributions: "We believe we have a responsibility to use our resources wisely for the long-term benefit of society, as well as the company. We continuously strive to help improve the everyday lives of the world's consumers in all that we do."[14] It goes on to say:

> P&G, its foundation, brands and employees have always been committed to the Company's purpose of improving lives. When the P&G Fund was established in 1952, its chief focus was improving lives in US communities with P&G operations. Now P&G operates in over 80 countries, and we are expanding the scope of our contributions and volunteer activities to touch more of these communities. Our historic focus has grown into a commitment to improve the lives of children in need by preventing disease, providing educational opportunities and teaching life skills. In other words, we want to help children live, learn and thrive. We are particularly interested in helping children get off to a good start because a good start helps ensure a better future. This choice is based on our values and principles, and a belief that we can make a meaningful difference. In this report, you will see how we bring the Company's purpose to life through a variety of programs and partnerships. Its reported contributions are as follows:

> **P&G Global Contributions for Fiscal Year 2003–2004**
> Non-Promotion Related Cash Contributions
> - Education $25,343,961
> - Health / Human Services $13,575,425
> - Civic / Culture / Environment $8,425,606
> - Other $1,144,744
>
> Total Non-Promotion Related Cash Contributions $48,489,736
> - Promotion Related Cash Contributions $25,063,611
> - In-Kind / Product Contributions $30,093,778
>
> **Total P&G Contributions $103,647,125**
> (Amounts do not include employee contributions, volunteer time or administrative expenses.)

Here are some samples of the charitable activities that the firm has most recently supported, as described on the company's Web site:

- USA—Crest Healthy Smiles—Reaching 50 Million Children: Crest Healthy Smiles (CHS) was created in response to the alarming findings from a 2000 Surgeon General report on oral health in the United States. It is designed to improve the state of oral health by providing education, tools and increased access to dental professionals for at least 50 million children and their families by the year 2010. In 2003–2004, CHS 2010 helped improve the oral health of children through a variety of programs.
- USA—Iams—Changing Lives By Empowering Others: In 2004, *Associated Marine Institutes* (AMI) served more than 5,700 troubled youth across the United States in treatment and residential programs. These teens are juvenile offenders who have been referred by the courts.

  AMI students maintain a full schedule of academics and institute chores and responsibilities through group and team activities. One of these team activities is the Dog Assistants Team. Working with a trainer from an assistance dog organization, the students teach dogs not only basic commands such as "sit" and "stay," but also how to open doors, operate light switches, "get the phone" and "go for help." The dogs are being trained to help someone in need—but the students need the dogs just as much as the disabled.
- USA—The Ohio State University—Creating Hope for the Future: The P&G Fund recently made a $1 million pledge to The Ohio State University College of Human Ecology for a breakthrough early childhood development project. The Ohio State University (OSU) is moving its early childhood development center from its on-campus location to one of the poorest neighborhoods in the state. This is a groundbreaking effort—the first time a university has taken their center, including faculty and students, off campus into a neighborhood like this.

Spokespersons

In their book *High Visibility: The Making and Marketing of Professionals into Celebrities*, Rein, Kotler, and Stoller describe the process by which executives, politicians, entertainers, athletes, and other professionals employ to create, market, and achieve successful images. They point out the role of public relations in the process as "the voice of visibility":

> Today PR touches every facet of American life, providing more than 70 percent of all information that is published as "news": As a result, news channels have become highly dependent on PR's output. On Monday, a thirteen-year-old baking wiz—representing the flour manufacturers—makes the rounds on local radio. On Tuesday, a research scientist—funded by a chemical company—describes how a certain mosquito repellent has more resistance power than its competitors. On Wednesday, a well-known actor speaks at the local drugstore chain for Faberge, eats at a local restaurant, attends an art opening, and makes charming, off-the-cuff remarks to senior citizens. Thursday finds the attorney general's office releasing a study on gang crackdowns. As for Friday, Saturday, and Sunday, it is the usual potpourri of football interviews, film reviews, political and social commentary—all arranged by PR.

They list these major functions of public relations professionals in support of their celebrity clients:

- Staging press conferences
- Preparing press kits
- Writing speeches
- Planning and executing publicity tours
- Tracking the movement of the client's image and gathering feedback from media
- Providing or arranging for media skills improvement
- Managing special projects
- Coordinating major events
- Implementing the marketing plan

They point out that, today, public relations professionals have more influence and control over the whole process and are making fundamental strategy decisions. They are exerting greater influence over not only what their corporate clients say, but also over that they do. [1]

Business Celebrities

It is significant that the first celebrity discussed in *High Visibility* was neither an entertainer nor a sports star, but a highly visible business celebrity Lee Iacocca, then chairman of Chrysler Corporation. For Lee Iacocca, high visibility was a strategic tool, and his transformation into a celebrity was "as deliberate as the manufacture of his cars—calculated to use his high visibility to bring buyers into the showroom."

The advent of the modern business celebrity began with Lee Iacocca. He was widely acclaimed in the media as the man behind the Ford Mustang. His boss, Henry Ford II, was the chairman and chief executive of the company founded by his legendary grandfather, and was probably the only business leader who was well known by the public in the 1950s. He clearly resented the acclaim that Iacocca, his president, was receiving from the press. Two weeks after Ford fired him, Iacocca was hired to run Chrysler. He engineered Chrysler's comeback, was given credit for rescuing the company from bankruptcy, and became the biggest star of business. His book, *Iacocca,* became a runaway best-seller, and he was chosen to head the high-profile drive to restore the Statue of Liberty and Ellis Island for the Centennial Celebration on July 4, 1986. The outspoken, headline-making Iacocca was so celebrated that he considered a run for the presidency of the United States.

For Iacocca and latter-day business celebrities, public relations played a vital role in linking the person with their companies and products. Their celebrity rub-off was a marketing plus of immeasurable value. Their appearances at news conferences dramatized the news, brought out the media and assured maximum coverage.

The business celebrity was virtually nonexistent more than forty years ago when Tom Harris wrote his master's thesis at the University of Chicago on "Celebrities as Popular Symbols." At that time, "idols of consumption" from the worlds of entertainment and sports had almost entirely displaced the "idols of production" as subjects of media coverage, and social critics were complaining about the lack of attention to successful business role models who had dominated the media in the first quarter of the century. All of this had changed by the 1990s. Dozens of business leaders had become celebrities and were widely admired by the public.

Donald Trump Superstar

Writing in *Advertising Age,* Jack Bernstein called public relations Donald Trump's "trump card":

> Uncanny luck and a canny sense of public relations weigh heavily in Donald Trump's emergence of success. There's little he can do about luck except take advantage of it, which he does very effectively. But he recognizes the value of good PR and labors to achieve it. Trump says he does not 'enjoy doing press' but understands that media exposure can be very helpful in making deals, so he's willing to talk about them. And does he ever! His appreciation of the value of PR infuses virtually every move he makes, business and personal. Trump is an aggressive advertiser, but his comparison of the worth of advertising versus that of editorial space should insure him a place of privilege in the PR pantheon.
>
> As far back as 1998, Trump was quoted as saying, "If I take a full-page ad in *The New York Times* to publicize a project, it might cost $40,000 and, in any case, people tend to be skeptical about advertising, but if *The Times* writes even a moderately positive one-column story about one of my deals, it doesn't cost me anything, and it's worth a lot more than $40,000."[2]

A decade and a half later, Trump was interviewed by David Segal of *The Washington Post.* Segal reported that "Trump's desk is covered, like every other surface in this room, with Trump-related publicity. Framed on the wall are dozens of magazine covers bearing Trump's face, and on a table is a stack of recent publications waiting for frames. 'This is just a small number of them,' he says, browsing through the pile." [3]

It doesn't hurt that the Trump name appears on Donald's buildings, resorts, and airlines. His first book, *Trump: The Art of the Deal*, became an immediate best-seller with 850,000 hard-cover copies sold, and *Trump, The Game* was one of the most popular board games of the time.

When the nation's news media were having a field day with Trump's marital problems in 1990, *Newsweek* reported that The Donald was clearly enjoying the spotlight, commenting, "What he has missed most in recent months has been the glare of public attention. A friend said 'publicity is his cocaine' and any news was good." Trump told the magazine that the extramarital story had been "great for business, and the blitz of publicity had sent curious people flocking to his various businesses"—the Trump Shuttle airline, the Trump Plaza and Trump Castle casinos in Atlantic City, and New York's Plaza Hotel. *Newsweek* said that, when Trump puts his name on his property, customers seem willing to pay a premium for the name, equating it with "glamour, affluence, and excitement." [4]

Trump opened the Trump Taj Mahal in Atlantic City, at the time the biggest and most expensive casino resort ever built, with what *The New York Times* described as "industrial-strength hoopla." Some 1,800 reporters, photographers, and media types attended the lavish opening to ogle Trump and his 420-million-square-foot, billion-dollar "Eighth Wonder of the World." For the occasion, he brought his companion, Marla Maples, out of hiding for a *Prime Time* interview with Diane Sawyer and personally escorted millions of Americans through the Taj Mahal on network television.

The Donald's second book, *Trump: Surviving at the Top* was "famous before it appeared." Random House planned for "a barrage of media during the first week," including an appearance on *20/20* with Barbara Walters and a two-part interview on NBC's *Today* show, and said it would "maximize free media exposure before committing to buy ad space" to promote the new book. The *Advertising Age* headline: "It's Hype, Hype Hooray for New Book by Trump." The hype worked. [5] *Surviving at the Top* reached the top of *The New York Times* best-seller list the week it was published.

Donald Trump remains the superstar of superstars. His name is plastered on more skyscrapers, casinos, and books about how to get rich than anybody. He has transcended media celebrity to become a media star first on other people's commercials selling everything from credit cards to pizza and then as the star of his own hit reality TV show "The Apprentice." He claimed to be the highest-paid star of prime time television and became universally associated with the phrase "You're fired!" His best-selling books, *Trump: Think Like a Billionaire* and *How to Get Rich: Big Deals from the Star of the Apprentice*, were spin-offs of the TV show. The same year, The Donald launched a bimonthly magazine, *Trump World*, offering real advice on business and real estate and helpful hints on how to spend your earnings. He also lent his name to a fragrance and a line of high-end men's clothing bearing the Trump family crest and suitable for any apprentice of The Donald.

When Trump Hotels and Casino Resorts went into bankruptcy reorganization in 2004, *The New York Times* reported: "Mr. Trump will remain as chairman and," in a nod to the marketing muscle retained by the host of the television show "The Apprentice," "cede to the recapitalized company a perpetual and exclusive worldwide trademark license and royalty fee, to use his name and likeness and all related marks and intellectual property rights."[6] *The Economist* concluded, "The irrepressible Mr. Trump seems to be headed ever upwards, bankruptcy be damned."

The New York Times commented, "However mixed his record as an entrepreneur, Mr. Trump has retained center stage by deftly massaging the news media, distracting attention from his business setbacks and doing just about anything to keep himself in the spotlight. Even in his darkest days, he has rarely attracted much negative publicity, which some observers say is due to his marketing discipline and an unwavering ability to stay 'on message.'"[7]

Business Executive as Celebrity Spokespersons

Al and Laura Ries contend that "products don't create publicity, people do." In their book, *The Fall of Advertising and the Rise of PR*, they state that "the missing ingredient in most marketing programs is the celebrity spokesperson." They are not referring to hired guns like name athletes, movie, TV, or rock stars. They are talking about the chief executive officer of the company who, after all, bears the most responsibility for the success or failure of the brand. They are talking about business stars like Donald Trump, Ted Turner of CNN, Ray Kroc of McDonald's, Dave Thomas of Wendy's, Michael Eisner of Disney, and George Steinbrenner of the New York Yankees.[8]

In his book, *Reputation Marketing*, the prolific marketing author Joe Marconi focuses on Sir Richard Branson, who "may be less well-known in the United States than some other moguls and entrepreneurs, but, in the United Kingdom, his name and reputation are the stuff of legend. His company, Virgin Records, has sold millions of CDs by the Rolling Stones, Janet Jackson, and Tina Turner, among other music industry superstars; Virgin Airlines is regarded as a highly aggressive and competitive carrier; Virgin Megastores in US cities are among the leading retailers of music, videos, books, and electronics equipment; and Virgin Cola is the first serious challenger in a field that Coke and Pepsi had pretty much locked up for years." In the UK, Sir Richard has stamped the Virgin name on nearly two hundred businesses, from health clubs to cosmetics to car dealerships. [9]

As CEO of General Electric for twenty years, Jack Welch earned a reputation as the most admired business leader in the world. He was so well known that, when his book was published in 2001, it was titled simply *Jack: Straight From the Gut*. He received one of the largest advances in book publishing history, and his book became an immediate number one bestseller.

There is a danger when the person and brand become inseparable. Jack lost his luster when reports of an affair with a female journalist appeared in the news media, when he went through a messy divorce, and when his excessive executive retirement perks were revealed. The principal asset of Martha Stewart Living Omnimedia, a publicly owned company, was the reputation of its founder, America's best-known authority on house and home. Martha Stewart was the author of 13 books, plus a library of 32 more books published by *Martha Stewart Living*. Her magazines included *Martha Stewart Living* and *Martha Stewart Weddings*. She produced a one-hour television show also called "Martha Stewart Living." Her name adorned a line of merchandise sold exclusively at Kmart. Her name-brand merchandise was sold on the Internet. Her weekly column was syndicated to 200 newspapers, and her daily radio program was broadcast on 200 radio stations. All of them were put into jeopardy when she was convicted for lying about insider trading.

The Rieses point out that "In the high-tech field, if your CEO is not famous, it's unlikely that your company will be famous and successful too." Their list includes:

- Bill Gates and Microsoft
- Larry Ellison and Oracle
- Lou Gerstner and IBM
- Michael Dell and Dell Computer
- Andy Grove and Intel
- Steve Jobs and Apple Computer[10]

By 2000, tech leaders had become so well known to the public that Jeff Bezos of *Amazon.com* was named *Time* magazine's "Man of the Year." Bill Gates was a cover boy to rival presidents and pop stars. His masterful orchestration of public relations culminated in the smash worldwide campaign to introduce Windows 95.

Consider the story of Steven T. Jobs.

The Steve Jobs Story

Jobs, as everyone knows, was co-founder of Apple Computer, the company that ignited the personal computer revolution in the 1970s with the Apple II and reinvented the personal computer in the 1980s with the Macintosh.

In a political power play, Jobs had been forced out of the company by his hand-picked successor. The company was literally in the dumper by 1997, and Jobs was enjoying great financial rewards from his new company, Pixar Animation Studios, when he responded to a distress call to return to Apple in what was billed as interim chief executive. Pixar was riding high on the great success of *Toy Story*, the first of a series of wildly successful computer films produced with the Disney Company.

When Jobs was beckoned back to Apple, the future of the company was very much in doubt. Apple's market share, customer confidence, employee morale, and share price had plummeted. Things were so bad that the company's CFO said that Apple was in a "death spiral." If Steve Jobs hadn't gone back, there would likely be no Apple today. He took charge, streamlining the company, the product line, and the retail channels. But what made Apple's comeback complete was a series of blockbuster new products.

Then Jobs electrified the industry with iMac. The cool new computer had been a closely guarded secret until, as *The Wall Street Journal* reported, Jobs "blindsided reporters with the new machine."[11] The symbolic setting for the unveiling was the Flint Center in Cupertino, California, the site of the historic launch of the Macintosh 14 years earlier. Jobs kept his sleek new computer under wraps until the dramatic moment when he literally unveiled the translucent teal and white box. Jobs declared, "iMac does for Internet computing what the original Macintosh did for personal computing. Macintosh lets anyone use a computer, and iMac lets anyone get onto the Internet quickly and easily."

Newsweek reported that the crowd, mostly composed of Apple employees and the media, "went bonkers."[12] The massive media coverage that preceded the appearance of iMac in stores rocked the marketplace. Multipage stories in living color appeared in the newsweeklies. *Time* celebrated "Apple's New Crop," and *Newsweek* trumpeted "No More

Beige Boxes." *MacWorld*'s Andrew Gore reported that "it's far too soon to say if the introduction of the iMac on May 6, 1998 will prove to be another of those seminal moments in computing, but it certainly marks a major change for Apple. After years of Apple's panicked rushing to stay apace with an industry that was passing it by, the iMac puts Apple out ahead again. The iMac is innovative, elegant, inexpensive, and everyone's going to want one."[13] The *Fortune* cover story on Steve Jobs reported, "The iMac is the first desktop to get the whole industry excited since the original Macintosh."

Apple worked closely with Macintosh retailers to maximize the impact of the introduction. "Midnight Madness" sales attracted not only hordes of customers but also the media. Quotes from key retailers appearing on Apple's media Web site were picked up in scores of stories, many of them localized with comments from local store managers. CompUSA president and CEO, Jim Halpin, said, "iMac has been the biggest computer launch we've seen in our history. Apple is back, and iMacs are flying off CompUSA store shelves across the US."

Newspaper headlines like these fueled the market:

- "Buyers flock to Apple's iMac" (*USA Today*)
- "Apple Finds it Hard to Meet iMac Demand" (*Wall Street Journal*)

The press coverage even heralded the success of the company's supporting public relations effort. The *Arizona Republic* declared "Debut of Mac Lives Up to Hype." In August, *Macworld* wrote, "After months of carefully crafted publicity and almost unprecedented media attention, Apple's eagerly awaited iMac has arrived." Adding that "although *Macworld* editors have had several opportunities to play with Mac prototypes since its debut last May, today's arrival of the blue-and-white pod marks the first opportunity *Macworld* Lab analysts have had to test an iMac unsupervised. What we found should give Apple and Mac boosters everywhere cause to celebrate."[14]

Apple mounted its largest integrated marketing campaign ever for the iMac. The publicity for iMac was so pervasive and the teal-and-white egg shaped box so well-known that full-page ads on magazine back covers consisted solely of a beauty shot of the iMac on a field of white. The only copy in very discreet typeface is "Think Different" and in even smaller mouse-type "*www.apple.com*." Outdoor boards feature large photos of iMac with cool, catchy headlines like "Chic. Not geek.," "Sorry, no beige," and "Mental floss." The computer had become so familiar that there was no need to identify it by name, even for speeding drivers.

The integrated program included a major product placement push. The fall season found iMacs appearing on all the top-rated TV sitcoms, including "Ally McBeal," "Felicity," "Friends," "Buffy, the Vampire Slayer," "Dawson's Creek," "Melrose Place," "Spin City," "Drew Carey," and even "The X-Files" and ABC's "Home Improvement." Further publicity was assured when Jobs placed five personally signed "golden" tickets in the boxes of five Macs. The lucky winners received free iMacs every year for the next five years.

By the end of its first full month on the market, iMac had become the best-selling computer in the US, a position retained through the introduction of a laptop version and a DVD model that enabled users to direct and edit their own movies. Encouraged by its "boffo intro," Apple introduced iMac in five delicious new "flavors," Jobs-speak for colors—blueberry, grape, lime, strawberry, and tangerine. Steve told *Time*, "We knew we had to name them after things you eat, because you just want to walk up and lick them."[15]

The astonishing success of Apple's iMac marked the convergence of a product that answered a real consumer need: easy access to the Internet, spectacular design, a successful targeting of Mac lovers and first-time computer owners, a marketing partnership with retailers, a memorable print advertising campaign, and an all-inclusive publicity and product placement program, all of which were set in motion by a legendary executive spokesman.

The New iMac

Jobs' mastery of the media was on display again three years later when he introduced a spectacular new iMac. Like its predecessor, nothing like the new iMac had ever been seen. Its distinguishing characteristic was a floating LCD flat screen perched above a six-inch tall dome that contained all its inner works. Its all-in-one hub accommodated music, pictures, movies as well as updates of the traditional computer functions.

Apple's public relations corps and the Edelman PR firm were able to top the phenomenal job they did for the first iMac. There was a *Time* magazine cover story on the man and the machine called "flat-out Cool." Reporter John Quittner could hardly restrain his enthusiasm, describing the new iMacs as "the quintessence of computational coolness —the most fabulous desktop machine that you or anyone else has ever seen." Admitting that "it's hard to remain impassive when you're sitting within the reality-distortion field that surrounds Apple's evangelical CEO when he's obsessing about the dazzling, never-seen-anything-like-it, ultra-top-secret computer.[16]

That's the kind of coverage Apple gets when Steve Jobs gives a chosen magazine an exclusive peek at one of his soon-to-be-revealed marvels. The story was precisely timed to coincide with the big *MacWorld* Show so that free copies of the magazine could be handed out to thousands of attendees. Despite the *Time* exclusive, this was a story that had to be told. Rival newsweekly *Newsweek* reported that "the genius of Steve Jobs is that through vision, inspiration, hard work and, yes, hype, he and his team have come up with a series of triumphs."[17]

The New York Times commented, "There's something cool and hip about Jobs that appeals to journalists."[18] That may be why *Time* has put him on its cover four times compared to six for Bill Gates of Microsoft, the world's leading software company.

Music, Music, Music

By 2001, Jobs had moved beyond computers to become a real force in music and movies. A cover story in *Business Week* showed Steve with his iPod portable music player in hand, addressing the cheering crowd at *MacWorld*. The magazine commented, "Just as the Mac revolutionized computing, Apple is changing the world of on-line music. If Steve Jobs plays his cards right this time, Apple could end up with a big chunk of the digital-entertainment market."

The iPod, introduced in October 2001, could store 10,000 tunes in a package smaller than a deck of cards. *Business Week* proclaimed it "the most radical change in how people listen to music since Sony Corp. introduced the Walkman in 1979."[19] The iPod became the must-have holiday gift of 2001. Apple sold 733,000 iPods during the Christmas season, and even more of them in the normally quiet next quarter. In its first two years on the market, Apple sold two million iPods.

The other huge development was the launch of Apple's iTunes Music Store, which *Time* magazine proclaimed "the Coolest Invention of 2003." It was introduced in 2003, which was a very good year for Steve Jobs.[20] That was the year that his other company, Pixar Animation Studios, released *Finding Nemo,* which became the biggest animated box office hit of all time.

Apple's iTunes Music Store enabled consumers to legally load up on their favorite tunes at 99 cents a tune and rescued the recording industry from Internet pirates like Napster. Its success was the direct result of Jobs' personal salesmanship. He was able to persuade all the major and independent record labels to make their music available legally on one Web site. Heavy media coverage and on-line chat rooms helped iTunes become an immediate hit. One million tunes were sold in the first week and seventy million in the first year. At year-end, Jobs had claimed a 70 percent share of the market for legal music downloads.

With iPod and iTunes, Apple had created another billion-dollar business in a few years. By 2004, Apple had sold more iPods than computers. Jobs had so transformed the company that an interview in *The Wall Street Journal* with Steve Jobs was headlined "The Music Man." The paper called him "the first rock star of the technology business," tracing his evolution from the development of the first successful mass-market personal computer in 1977 to the 1984 reinvention of the personal computer with Macintosh to his major entry into the music business.[21]

The inseparability of the man and his machines was summed up by *Chicago Tribune* columnist James Coates. When Jobs introduced the iTunes Music Store in 2003, Coates wrote: "We probably should be writing about Jobs rather than his potentially earth-shaking scheme. If anybody on the American technology scene still has fire in the belly these days, it's Apple's iconoclastic founder."[22]

He has made an art form out of keeping his new innovations under wraps until he springs them on the press. As *The New York Times* put it, "Surprise is at the heart of all the company's marketing campaigns, and who would expect less from the man who once rented San Francisco's symphony hall to introduce a new computer."[23]

Jobs gave *Newsweek* a first look at the latest version of the iPod in July 2004, resulting in a nine-page cover story titled "iPod, Therefore I Am: Steve Jobs and the Must-Have Music Player Everyone is Talking About." The lead was "How the iPod, a tiny device that's changed the way Americans listen to music—and even live their lives—became a high-tech hit that's now part of the cultural fabric." The magazine proclaimed that iPod had "smacked right into the sweet spot where a consumer product becomes something much, much more: an icon, a pet, a status indicator, and an indispensable part of one's life. To three million-plus owners, iPod not only gives them access to their entire collection of songs and CDs, but membership into an implicit society that's transforming the way music will be consumed in the future."[24]

In 2004, *The Economist* compared Apple's success in the music business with personal computers. "Buying music on-line today is roughly where personal computers were in the mid-1980s: on the verge of spreading from early adopters to the general population. And, as in the 1980s, Apple, then, as now, run by Steve Jobs, is in the lead. Apple's iTunes service has 70 percent of the market for legal downloads of music; the iPod, its near-iconic portable audio player, has about 60 percent of the American market for high capacity, hard-disk-based-players."[25]

Expert Spokespersons

Not all companies are headed by such effective headline-makers as Steve Jobs or Ted Turner. MPR programs often turn to outside authorities or outside celebrities on either the product or a borrowed-interest subject in an effort to bring attention to the product. Company experts are widely utilized in MPR programs. Auto manufacturers make both their division chiefs and their chief engineers available to the car-enthusiast publications at "long lead" press introductions of new models. Pharmaceutical-company research directors and doctors are brought out to lend credibility to new-product introductions and to report on research studies verifying product efficacy. Company home economists frequently are quoted in women's magazines and newspaper food pages and appear on daytime TV talk shows, demonstrating recipes and ways to serve their company's products. Marketing news is covered on cable television and in major daily newspapers like *The New York Times*, *The Chicago Tribune*, *The Los Angeles Times*, and *The Wall Street Journal*. These media frequently quote company marketing executives and market researchers.

Betty Crocker: The Greatest Spokesperson Who Never Lived

In addition to company executives, public relations programs have long been built around a company's advertising spokespersons, real or fictional. This tried-and-true practice predates the ubiquity of television. Although Betty Crocker was never a real person, her name and identity have symbolized General Mills' continuing tradition of service for more than 65 years. Over the years, she has provided a link between the business of food development and the consumer.

In 1921, a promotion for Gold Medal Flour attracted thousands of responses. Betty Crocker was created as a signature for responses to inquiries. In 1924, Betty acquired a voice for daytime radio's first foodservice program. It was an immediate success, and, within months, was expanded to 13 regional stations. Each station had its own Betty Crocker voice, reading scripts written at the Home Service Department in Minneapolis. Subsequently, the *Betty Crocker Cooking School of the Air* became a network program, continuing for 24 years with over one million listeners enrolled. By 1940, surveys showed that Betty Crocker's name was known to 9 out of 10 American homemakers. Special services for schools, under Betty Crocker's name, began in 1956 and included filmstrips and student booklets on baking and meal planning, for classroom use. In 1957, Betty Crocker materials for visually impaired people were developed: "Talking Recipe Records" and a *Cooking with Betty Crocker Mixes* cookbook in large type, with Braille and cassette-tape editions.

Betty Crocker's Picture Cookbook, first published in 1950, became a national best-seller and was followed by a series of cookbooks that today number more than 30. Betty Crocker acquired a new look, her seventh, in 1986. The current Betty Crocker portrait was officially unveiled in connection with the introduction of the sixth edition of *Betty Crocker's Picture Cookbook*.

The new Betty Crocker, according to General Mills, portrayed a professional woman, approachable and friendly, but also competent—in the kitchen as well as in the workplace. A decade later, on the occasion of Betty Crocker's 75th anniversary, she acquired a multicultural look that was a computer-generated composite of 75 women who submitted their photographs and essays on why they embodied the characteristics that best reflected "the spirit of Betty Crocker."

The company recognizes that women of all ages, with or without careers, have active lives outside the home, but they are still concerned about meal preparation and nutrition. Many have grown up expecting advice from Betty Crocker. The goal of General Mills is to provide an image that modern women can relate to, a reassuring reminder of Betty Crocker's promise of thoroughly tested products and up-to-date recipes.

The Toni Twins and Other Living Ads

In 1988, Daniel J. Edelman, chairman of the public relations firm that bears his name, hosted a luncheon to celebrate the 40th anniversary of the first Toni Twins media tour. In 1948 and 1949, two sets of twins traveled throughout Europe and 75 cities in the United States to bring to life the now classic "Which Twin Has the Toni?" advertising campaign, which challenged consumers to identify the twin with the home permanent (rather than the beauty-shop wave).

Twin Toni Twin caravans, trailers painted to look like the Toni Home Permanent Box, carried sets of twins to cities in the East and West. They were greeted by mayors, made guest appearances in department stores, and were interviewed by fashion and beauty editors. They attracted national coverage, like a spread in *Parade* magazine called "The Toni Twins on Parade." When six sets of twins flew to Europe to introduce the home permanent, their arrival was covered by *LIFE* magazine, then the country's best-read weekly magazine.

An *Adweek* story on the anniversary said, "Not only did they make headlines wherever they went, but their odyssey was the forerunner of the media tour, now an integral part of many a marketing strategy." Edelman told the magazine, "You can't just run ads. Whenever you can bring the story to the public on a one-on-one basis, or beyond one-on-one, in local newspapers, local television, or radio, that's going to dramatize your story."[26]

Following the success of the Toni Twins, the Edelman firm created "living ad" MPR programs for Kentucky Fried Chicken founder Colonel Harlan Sanders, 9Lives Cat Food's advertising "spokescat" Morris, and popcorn maker Orville Redenbacher, among others.

Redenbacher was his company's chief public relations spokesperson long before he began to appear in commercials. When he began marketing his gourmet popping corn, major supermarket chains refused to carry it because of its higher price. A skillful MPR program was planned to reach the consumer directly. As a result of massive publicity, mostly featuring interviews with Redenbacher himself, thousands of consumers began demanding it, and the stores responded by stocking it. The brand now holds a three-to-one lead over its closest competitor. Orville Redenbacher himself said that the primary factor in his success is public relations.

Morris, the 9Lives Cat

Effective public relations campaigns can feature real spokespersons or invented ones, like Morris the Cat. The Morris character was created by Leo Burnett Company, the advertising agency for 9Lives Cat Food, and was the focus of the public relations program for the brand, which originated in the early 1970s.

In the early years, the 9Lives PR firm, Edelman, created a national Morris Look-

Alike Contest, an attempt to find a cat with the same looks, charm, and finickiness as Morris. The contest was supported not only by publicity, but also by Morris Look-Alike entry blanks at the point of purchase in supermarkets. The contest was an enormous success; photos of felines claiming a resemblance to Morris poured in from all over the country. A winner selected from each state was sent a year's supply of cat food and a sterling silver, engraved feeding bowl. The winner and its owner were taken to Hollywood for the full star treatment—a suite at the Century Plaza, chauffeured limousine, special dinners, appearances, and press conferences—resulting in widespread national publicity.

Another popular Morris contest was a "Win-A-Date-With-Morris" competition, launched through "purr-sonals" placed in major metropolitan newspapers. All entrants received a valentine, a "paw-tographed" picture, and a coupon for 9Lives Cat Food. The winners from each state won heart-shaped, sterling silver, "My Heart Belongs to Morris" collar tags, and cases of cat food. Morris flew to Indianapolis to personally escort the grand winner to a splashy hometown party.

Since Morris had been found in an animal shelter, he was offered to the American Humane Association as its "spokescat" for an "Adopt-A-Cat Month," to draw attention to the many cats and kittens needing adoption from shelters. Every adopting family received a special kit, including cat-food coupons and an adoption certificate from Morris as a thank you for saving the life of a fellow cat. When Morris appeared at a New York news conference to launch "Adopt-A-Cat Month," the media responded not only with stories, but also with adoption of a dozen cats from the local ASPCA. "Adopt-A-Cat Month" became an annual event; the publicity, promotion, and PSAs led to the adoption of hundreds of thousands of cats and kittens during the month.

"The Morris Award" was another public relations bonanza for the 9Lives brand. In conjunction with the Cat Fanciers Association, a program was created to honor the best non-breed cat of show. The prize, a bronzed statuette of Morris with his 9Lives bowl, was presented to winners of local cat shows throughout the country.

Morris went on to "author" books on cat care, called *The Morris Method, The Morris Approach*, and his own story, *Morris, an Intimate Biography* (complete with nude centerfold), which became a nonfiction best-seller. He also appeared in a television featurette, "The Morris Mystique."

When a 1987 Opinion Research Corporation poll showed that Morris was recognized by 70 percent of the public, more than presidential candidates, he announced his candidacy for the nation's highest office. At a news conference at the National Press Club in Washington, his "campaign manager," Eleanor Mondale, daughter of the former Vice President Walter Mondale, said that Morris would run as an Independent because of his finickiness. She released a "Pawlicy Statement" that included policies on the environment ("Put a litter box on every corner"), voting rights ("One cat: one vote"), politics ("You rub my back and I'll scratch yours"), population control ("Neuter is neater"), education ("It all begins with good paper training"), and Iran-Contra ("Any cat would have smelled a rat").

The launch and campaign fly-around generated 600 million audience impressions in newsweeklies, television, and wire services, with comparable advertising value of $11 million. A national poll following the launch showed consumer awareness of the Morris campaign at nearly 60 percent.

In 2004, Morris became the comeback cat. Off the air for several years, Morris returned in a new 9Lives advertising campaign. The new Morris, the fifth feline to bear the name, was also sent out live on a national publicity and promotional tour. The old Morris can be seen in a retrospective of his finicky commercials on the 9Lives Web site.

23 The Future of Marketing Public Relations

Daniel J. Edelman, chairman of the international public relations firm that bears his name, says that there are three phases in the evolution of public relations. In the first phase from post-World War II to the early 1970s, the founders of the modern practice of public relations created a profession to influence people and effect changes in attitudes and behavior. During the second phase, public relations expanded globally and entered new industries such as technology and healthcare. We are now entering the third phase.

Richard Edelman, who is now CEO of Edelman, says that in the third phase, "We need to expand the footprint of what we do and how we're perceived. Upon receiving the John Hill Award from the New York Chapter of the Public Relations Society of America in 2004, he said that as the power of advertising begins to erode, companies are searching for alternatives. He said:

> Public relations is the answer because the future of business is not about selling, but about sustaining relationships through dialogue, credible sources and relevant experiences. And unlike every other marketing discipline that is precisely what we do.
>
> A company or product builds its reputation through dialogue with the end-user. Companies need an experience that deepens the bond with their customers. To earn trust, companies must provide journalism-quality content and communicate directly to audiences, not simply through the media. Phase three for public relations will be a combination of listening, consulting and classic publicizing. We work at nodes of influence, frame the context and build credibility. We help our clients engage in conversations where understanding is as much a part of the process as messaging.
>
> This is an enormous opportunity for us to become the lead marketing discipline.[1]

Harold Burson, founder of Burson-Marsteller and one of the most influential figures in expanding the boundaries of public relations, has said that there will continue to be a "growing demand for what public relations does even though it may not always be called public relations." He told the Public Relations Society of America's Counselors Academy that:

> Business will continue to face intense competition; business will be pressured to reduce costs; business must continue to develop new markets, to find new niches for its products and services; business will continue to be regulated by governments; business will continue to satisfy the voracious appetites of consumers for information. In other words, business will continue to face problems whose solution is attitude-based and communications-driven. The discipline of public relations is best equipped to deal with problems of that kind. [2]

Public Relations in the Age of Marketing

In order to forecast where marketing public relations is going in the future, it is instructive to look at how public relations has both reflected and supported the marketing milestones of the age of marketing that began in the post-World War II era.

Philip Kotler has identified the most significant marketing concepts to emerge in the past half century. Virtually all of these milestones can be said to have influenced or been influenced by public relations. So closely do the two functions parallel one another that Professor Sidney Levy, former chairman of the marketing department at the prestigious Kellogg School of Management at Northwestern University, has commented that public relations is really a better description of what "we marketers do than marketing." He laments the fact that the public relations people got to the label first.[3]

In the following sections, the milestones of each decade listed by Kotler are described. The concepts have been adapted and enhanced over the years, but they encompass a compendium of contemporary marketing thinking.

Marketing Concepts of the 1950s

- **The Marketing Mix:** The combination of elements used by companies to market their products to consumers. As we have seen, the marketing mix for an increasing number of consumer products now includes marketing public relations along with advertising, promotion, and sales.
- **Product Life Cycle:** The stages from product introduction through growth, maturity, and decline of sales. This concept has undergone many refinements and variations, but whatever the nomenclature, MPR has played an important role in all stages by communicating new news and identifying products with newsworthy associations.
- **Brand Image:** How consumers feel about products and the companies that make them. Introduced in 1955, this idea is, according to Kotler, "especially beloved by advertisers and public relations people."
- **Market Segmentation:** The partitioning of the market into meaningful segments, to focus marketing efforts more precisely. MPR has been especially effective in targeting specific "publics" and developing programs to reach them.
- **The Marketing Concept:** Making what will sell, as defined by the consumer, rather than selling what is made. Public relations supports this concept by communicating messages about how products answer consumer needs and make life easier, happier, and better.
- **The Marketing Audit:** Monitoring marketing strategies, structures, and systems to keep them attuned to changing market conditions. The public relations audit, which arose simultaneously, monitors a company's relationships with its publics. The marketing public relations audit concentrates on analyzing the company's marketing communications to vital audiences, including but not limited to the ultimate consumer, and, importantly, communications to those who influence consumer attitudes and purchasing decisions.

The Soaring 1960s

- **The Four Ps Classification of the Marketing Mix:** Product, price, place, and promotion. Public relations fits in the promotion P. Some public relations practitioners believe that a fifth P may be most important of all. That P is perception, since people's brand preferences and buying behavior are largely the result of how they perceive products and the companies that market them.

- **Marketing Myopia:** Companies fail when they focus on the product and not the consumer. Since editors act as gatekeepers of the news, marketing public relations must focus on disseminating information of value to the consumer, that is, reader, listener, and viewer, in order to gain the implied editorial endorsement of the media.
- **Lifestyles:** The psychographic definition of consumer audiences and appeals. MPR is more and more grounding programs in lifestyle research and shaping product messages and event sponsorships on their appeal to psychographically defined audiences.
- **The Broadened Concept of Marketing:** Advanced by Kotler and Levy, the application of marketing not only to products and services, but also to organizations, persons, places, and ideas. MPR programs are used to market nonprofit organizations, business leaders, and celebrities of all sorts, as well as companies and brands. It has been shown how a corporation's positions on various issues of concern to consumers affect their patronage.

The Turbulent 1970s

- **Social Marketing:** Calling attention to the role that marketing can play in affecting social causes. Public relations is arguably the most effective marketing method for achieving social change. It is used by consumer activists and by proactive companies and trade groups to advance their positions.
- **Positioning:** How brands are ranked against the competition in customers' minds. Introduced by Al Reis and Jack Trout, positioning has been applied to public relations strategies that identify brands with consumer-service programs that set the stage for positive reception of product advertising.
- **Strategic Marketing:** Pursuing marketing strategies, sharply distinguished from marketing tactics, is an offshoot of the corporate strategic planning concept promulgated by the Boston Consulting Group in the early 1970s. Public relations plans of the past focused almost exclusively on tactics. The trick was to come up with a Big Idea that would generate headlines. Today, MPR tactics are more likely to grow out of strategies that work with the other elements of the marketing mix to meet marketing objectives. MPR programs are evaluated on how well ideas/tactics support marketing strategies.
- **Societal Marketing:** Calling upon business to factor into its decisions the long-term interests of consumers and society. Public relations plays a unique role as "the conscience of the company" in counseling marketing management on changes in the social environment to which they must adapt and in identifying opportunities to take actions that will win consumer approval and trust.
- **Macromarketing:** Examining the aggregate effects of business activity on consumer welfare and values. Macromarketing combines the disciplines of marketing public relations (MPR) and the specialized area of corporate public relations (CPR) known as issues management.
- **Service Marketing:** Regarding the marketing of services as having needs that are separate from product marketing. MPR programs have proliferated in recent years in supporting such services as management consulting and financial

services and, more recently, medical services (hospitals and HMOs) and law and accounting firms. These programs build positive awareness of the institution's distinctive competence and tend less to market "product" benefits.

The Uncertain 1980s

- **Marketing Warfare:** Promoting product benefits and positioning brand benefits directly against the marketing strategies of competing brands. Public relations has played a key role and often provided the competitive edge in the cola wars, the beer wars, the burger wars, and the athletic shoe wars, among others.
- **Internal Marketing:** Establishing a marketing culture in a company. Public relations plays a unique role in broadly communicating the company's new marketing orientation to both external and internal audiences in an organized pragmatic way.
- **Global Marketing:** Developing more uniform product and communications plans around the world. Theodore Levitt proposed global marketing in 1983, on the theory that too much adaptation to local markets results in a loss of economies of scale. This theory has been adopted by some multinational advertising agencies and public relations firms through simultaneous worldwide product introductions and sponsorships.
- **Local Marketing:** Marketing efforts tailored to the local market environment. Simultaneous with global marketing, a trend led by the Campbell Soup Company, Nabisco, General Foods, and others, which says that marketing from product variations to benefits to local advertising and promotion starts at the local level. MPR programs have long been adapted to the needs, wants, and lifestyles of consumers, city by city, region by region, or country by country.
- **Direct Marketing:** Reaching the individual consumer with a product or message. Direct marketing has gone beyond door-to-door selling to party selling, telemarketing, TV home shopping, and shopping by personal computer. All of these methods gain credibility when the product or selling company has first earned consumer trust and confidence by gaining endorsement from media and other third-party endorsers reached by MPR.
- **Relationship Marketing:** Building interactions with consumers. The term came into usage in the mid-1980s and holds that relationships, more than transactions, better capture the spirit of marketing. This is, of course, the ultimate public relations-oriented definition of marketing, because building relationships with "publics" is what public relations is all about.
- **Megamarketing:** Harnessing political and public relations skills to overcome marketing barriers. In Kotler's words, megamarketing addresses "the problem of breaking into protected and blocked markets." This book defines the approval of society's gatekeepers as a "pass" strategy that must be considered by today's marketers, in addition to the traditional trade "push" and consumer "pull" strategies.

The One-to-One 1990s

- **Customer Relationship Marketing:** Developing sophisticated database marketing and data mining capabilities that carefully track the wants and needs of individual customers as reflected in the history of their respective relationships with the company. This permitted public relations sources to transmit information directly to customers.

- **Experiential Marketing:** Leveraging a customer's encounter with the brand in an environment that transcends a simple sales transaction. Surrounding the product in an entertaining or dramatic context can enhance the value of the experience the customers attribute to the product or service.
- **Sponsorship Marketing:** Sponsoring events, activities or causes that engage target consumers, enhance their loyalty and reinforce the brand's message. The many ways in which MPR supports sponsorships are discussed in Chapter 17.
- **Marketing Ethics:** Maintaining highly ethical practices that strengthen relationships with customers, many companies are pledged to scrupulously adhere to codes of ethical behavior to operate in the public interest. We consider the impact of company reputation on marketing in Chapter 4.

The Financially Driven 2000s

- **ROI Marketing:** Assessing the impact of marketing tactics requires more precise measurement of value received for dollars spent and the drive to find metrics to evaluate marketing's return on investment. The return on MPR investment can best be measured when it is the only variable factor in the marketplace.
- **Brand Building Marketing:** Building brands has succeeded transactions as the hallmark of marketing. A strong brand evokes associations, performance and expectations. Recent surveys have shown that public relations is most highly valued by brand managers for brand building.
- **Customer Equity Marketing:** Accurately evaluating the value of potential and present customers and implementing systems to acquire and retain best prospects utilizing sophisticated database systems that track each interaction between a company and individual customers to better manage the relationship. MPR is increasingly utilizing one-to-one techniques to deliver information to target customers.
- **Social Responsibility Marketing:** Updating societal marketing, the practice of social responsibility marketing, pioneered by public relations, involved making marketing decisions that positively impact society and are sensitive to social concerns of customers such as discrimination, the environment and product efficacy.[4]

MPR in the Twenty-First Century

Marketing public relations has played an integral role in supporting each step in the evolution of the marketing concept and is certain to continue to do so in the future.

The 1990s saw a period of unprecedented growth driven by emerging hot categories and the acceptance of public relations as essential to marketing success in the technology, healthcare, and financial services fields. The tech field recognized the need to present a nonstop proliferation of products to industry analysts as well as specialized and mainstream media. Hardware and software marketers recognized that public relations was often more important than advertising in influencing both business-to-business customers and consumers. Healthcare marketing public relations exploded with the introduction of breakthrough products and with mature products going over the counter.

Also, MPR was effectively employed by hospitals, HMOs and other organizations in marketing their services to the public.

Financial public relations took on a new look as companies recognized the importance of marketing themselves to current and prospective shareholders. Whereas formerly investor relations was largely confined to annual reports, quarterly earnings releases and security analyst meetings, companies began to market themselves aggressively to investors in the go-go 90s. The excesses of the era were personified by the over-hyping of a parade of IPOs, particularly the proliferation of dot.coms. Big bucks raised by public offerings were spent on advertising and public relations but many of these companies lacked a coherent business plan and were forced to close down.

Beyond these hot categories were extraordinarily successful marketing public relations programs for retailers from Starbucks to Home Depot and Wal-Mart were mounted during the decade. MPR budgets burgeoned in traditional categories like automotives, food, fashion, and travel.

The specific direction of MPR in the future will be shaped by the clarification, if not the resolution, of a number of distinctions and dichotomies.

MPR versus CPR

Some public relations counselors have begun to advocate patterning PR firms like management consultants and law firms. Herbert Corbin, managing partner of KCS&A Public Relations, says the law-firm-type structure engenders continuity of service and holds partners accountable not only to clients but to other partners of the firm. He cites product litigation, handling tender offers, and crisis management as the kind of sophisticated communications problems requiring partner involvement. This kind of organization is most applicable to corporate communications departments and public relations firms that counsel top management on matters involving the company's vital interests with government, the financial community and its shareholders.

On the other hand, marketing public relations serves a parallel purpose to advertising and promotion, and the firm, division or department specializing in MPR is organized similarly to advertising and sales promotion firms. The management level of the MPR firm devises strategies and is responsible for developing creative tactics that support those strategies. The execution of tactics is the responsibility of an account management team, usually headed by a supervisor who keeps the program on course, on schedule, and on budget. The next level on the MPR table of organization are the account executives, who are responsible for the day-to-day implementation of the program.

This functional difference supports the contention of this book that MPR and CPR should be recognized as separate, self-sufficient disciplines and that corporations and PR firms should reorganize to take best advantage of the particular expertise and skills of each. The essential role of MPR should be focused on helping the corporation achieve its marketing objectives, while the role of CPR should be to counsel management on corporate issues, positions and actions as they relate to the achievement of corporate goals. CPR then acts in an advisory staff function, while MPR is a line function whose role is to support the successful marketing of the company's goods and services. The two are closely interrelated when marketing decisions affect or are affected by corporate philosophies and actions. This became especially apparent with the revelations of a series of major corporate scandals that rocked the business world in the late 1990s.

Local versus Global

CPR programs have traditionally included community relations programs in plant and headquarters locations, support of local philanthropies, and events designed for employees and their families, such as open houses and outings. Similarly MPR has long had a local focus. Most "national" programs are, in fact, locally driven and require the development of angles that will attract local media and involve local consumers. A water purifier company recently conducted a media tour that linked the need for its product with a report on the condition of local drinking water compared to other cities. Campbell Soup localized the National Soup Month story by announcing the most popular soups by city.

Peter Gummer, founder of Shandwick Public Relations, contends that "public relations is essentially a local activity." He told *The New York Times*, "It is about changing attitudes and ideas about products and services in a local market. That means getting hold of people who influence opinions—journalists, politician—and changing their attitudes on a local basis."[5]

However Paul Taafe, Worldwide Chairman and CEO of Hill & Knowlton, points out that "while consumer tastes may vary from country to country, the science and technology behind these products stays the same. He says, "The need to communicate to a global audience also extends to the increasingly international group of analysts and regulators who evaluate and make key decisions about pharmaceutical and technology products."[6]

Large international public relations firms like Hill & Knowlton, Burson-Marsteller, Fleishman-Hillard, and Edelman emphasize their ability to provide worldwide "seamless" service to their clients. As early as 1989 *The New York Times* reported that Burson and H&K were "marching across the globe, opening offices in places that once seemed barely worth a business trip." Burson's then-CEO Jim Dowling told the *Times*, "We start our own offices because its cheaper and because we want all of our people steeped in our culture," adding, "you have to be an effective national organization in all of your locations before you become an effective international company."[7]

The move toward worldwide coverage is certain to accelerate in the future, stimulated by the emergence of more multinational client companies, the burgeoning markets in the Asia/Pacific region, the breakdown of European trade barriers, the emergence of free market economies in the countries of Eastern Europe, the growth of Brazil and other Latin American markets, the expansion of markets in Russia and India and the rise of China as a global powerhouse.

Today the top ten PR counseling firms share at least half of the worldwide marketplace. The globalization of public relations can be seen in the ownership of PR firms. A decade ago, all of the world's top five public relations firms were American owned. Today, Burson-Marsteller, Hill & Knowlton and Ogilvy Public Relations are owned by WPP Group, a British conglomerate while MS&L is owned by Paris headquartered Publicis Groupe.

Generalist versus Specialist

Despite the emergence of powerful global PR firms, which are part of publicly-owned communication conglomerates, scores of healthy independent public relations firms have arisen and prospered in recent years. Some are specialists in a particular industry. Many top-flight firms specialize in high tech products or pharmaceuticals. Others specialize in such areas as entertainment, fashion, or food. Automotive companies continue to supplement their large internal staffs with PR firms that have a specialty in marketing cars and trucks. Some firms are expert in marketing in their region. Still others focus on particular target markets, including the Latino market and the African-American market. Firms have been created that specialize in reaching the gay market.

The emergence of public relations mega-agencies is not likely to entirely replace small and midsize public relations firm. There are many clients who prefer to be a larger fish in a small pond. They support small to midsize agencies which may be more accessible, flexible and cost-effective and for whom they represent a significant share of total billings.

Independence versus Advertising Ownership

The ownership of public relations firms by communications conglomerates and advertising agencies has given these firms access to more and better clients and the deep pockets to expand their offices and services. The jury is still out on the workability of the integrated services concept. Many clients value public relations counsel that is independent of advertising control.

Recent experience has shown that when push comes to shove, advertising decisions will and (from a dollars-and-cents point of view) *must* prevail. Martin Sorrell, head of WPP Group, ordered its Hill & Knowlton public relations subsidiary to stop working for the head of Louis Vuitton because of a conflict with the Hennessy Cognac and Chandon Champagne advertising account, which was controlled by a rival of the Moet-Hennessy-Louis Vuitton empire. London's *Sunday Times* reported that when the client reminded Sorrell that H&K's work could jeopardize millions of pounds' worth of cognac and champagne advertising, he intervened and gave 30-days' notice to H&K's client that he was removing the PR firm from the battle.

The split of Golin/Harris from its parent advertising firm, FCB Communications, an otherwise harmonious and productive relationship, was caused because of the threat of a client conflict. When FCB decided to pursue the $200-million Burger King advertising account, a conflict of interest was created with its public relations subsidiary. Golin/Harris had represented industry leader McDonald's Corporation for more than 30 years, and it was the firm's largest and best- known client. Something had to give, and it was the relationship with FCB. The conflict set the wheels in motion for the sale of Golin/Harris to Shandwick.

The acceptance as an article of faith that advertising, especially television advertising, is the universal solution to all marketing problems is breaking down because of the proliferation of channels and the demassification of the market. The top management of the communication conglomerates may be dedicated to helping their clients find the best mix of marketing services to get the job done. But that effort can break down because managers of advertising profit centers are evaluated on how much revenue they produce and not how much business they refer to other units of the parent company.

Integration versus Specialization

While some marketers agree in principle with the notion of one-stop shopping for marketing communications services, there have been problems in execution, organization, fixing of responsibility, and delivery of uniform-quality service across the board.

Ogilvy Group reorganized its operations in an attempt to get more of its clients to use more of its services. Under this organization, a senior executive on an account, known as a "client service director," was made responsible for all client contact and for coordinating the work of all of the agency's services. But questions were raised about the ability of the "client service director" to function as an all-purpose marketing communicator and to understand the various disciplines well enough to orchestrate them. A further complication is the fact that the client "contacts" for advertising, sales promotion, and public relations are often different people in different, unrelated company departments with different reporting structures.

J. Raymond Lewis, senior vice president of marketing at Holiday Inn, Inc., says:

I don't think there is anything inherently beneficial in having all the services under one roof. In my experience, advertising agencies have enough difficulty coordinating all the functions they already have—creative, media, account management—without worrying about bringing public relations into the mix. Furthermore, it doesn't fit our structure. Our advertising agency reports to the vice president of consumer marketing, our PR firm reports to the director of PR. Although both of them report to me, they are autonomous in their own areas. [8]

While some clients may prefer one-stop shopping, an opposite number of clients look to a variety of sources for marketing input and want to be exposed to more options and alternatives rather than a neatly integrated, advertising-centered plan. Susan Henderson, vice president of corporate communications for Willian Wrigley Company, says, "It's not the name on the door that's important, it's the talent in the room."[9]

Some PR clients resist pressure from their ad agencies to use their sister firms. The largest remaining independent PR firms, Edelman and Ruder-Finn, and many small to midsize PR firms have capitalized on their independence from advertising domination to attract clients.

This much is clear: Marketing plans must integrate all elements of the mix. Greater knowledge and understanding of MPR and greater interaction among the communications firms or departments that conceive and execute the plan are called for. The client must inevitably be the coordinator of integrated marketing communications services. It remains to be seen whether the advertising-based conglomerates can become the principal provider of most or all of these services.

Regulation versus Business as Usual

The growth of marketing public relations has benefited not only from the increasing costs and decreasing efficiency of advertising, but from government restrictions and regulations imposed on advertising of certain products and categories. Both the federal government and the states' attorneys general have formed coalitions to prevent marketers from making claims about the health benefits and efficacy of their products. As a result, many marketers have turned to public relations to carry their message to the consumer.

Despite the fact that this product information may pass editorial muster before it is edited and transmitted as news by the media, some critics argue that the public relations message needs to be scrutinized and regulated in the same way as advertising.

The increased use of video news releases (VNRs) by TV stations—a result of the downsizing of news departments, the desire for visually interesting stories, and the interest of viewers in business news—has created particular concern that VNRs are advertising masked as news and thus are subject to regulation. The US Food and Drug Administration is studying whether the use of VNRs, news conferences, and paid "spokesdoctors" and patients by pharmaceutical companies constitutes promotion rather than an exchange of information. The war against smoking resulted in pressure from the US Secretary of Health and Human Services, among others, on cigarette companies to drop their sponsorships of sports events, especially those televised events where cigarette logos are shown on signs, banners, clothing, and vehicles.

Further regulation raises First Amendment questions about the rights of companies to market their products and of consumers to choose to use products that are legally sold. Ironically, the federal government itself uses VNRs extensively. The George W. Bush administration was criticized by the press for producing and distributing a VNR in which an actor portraying a journalist extols the benefits a new Medicare bill.

Blind Faith versus Measurement

The need for improved ways to measure MPR results is greater than ever. The subject is not new. Companies like General Mills and Procter & Gamble, and PR firms like Ketchum, and Porter/Novelli have developed their own systems to evaluate PR programs, but there are no universally accepted and applied research systems that measure outcomes of MPR programs and compare results with industry norms. With more numbers oriented product managers making PR decisions, the need to quantify results has never been greater.

While it is often difficult to separate out the effect on sales of MPR and indeed all of the other components in a well-executed integrated marketing campaign, measurement tools can be applied that evaluate the trust factor that underlies consumer receptivity to many MPR programs. Research is now showing how public relations can drive sales and boost other marketing components. Mark Weiner, CEO of Delahaye Medialink Worldwide Communications Research, says "We now have the tools to trace the impact of public relations in terms of delivering key messages to target media., raising awareness and increasing sales and that in the next decade ROI (return on investment) will be much easier to demonstrate and generate." [10]

Internal versus External

The Thomas L. Harris /Impulse Research Public Relations Clients Surveys have found that client public relations budgets have been divided almost evenly between work done in-house by company public relations departments and work that is assigned to public relations firms. The growth of the PR agency business coincided with the downsizing of internal corporate communications departments that was part of across-the-board corporate cost cutting. The need for companies to step up their use of public relations to support marketing was by that time well established. The result was that corporate departments often assumed the role of managing PR programs executed externally by public relations firms. Outside work was particularly focused on marketing public relations programs for new products and mature brands, designed and conducted entirely by the agency. In recent years there has been a trend for agencies to report directly to company marketing managers rather than corporate communications executives. In fact, fully 24 percent of the public relations clients responding to the 2004 survey identified themselves as marketing officers. The reasons for greater use of PR firms parallel the reasons why, years ago, advertising agencies supplanted fully staffed advertising departments. That is their greater experience in conducting successful campaigns for a wide variety of brands in many fields.

Earned Media versus Paid Placements

One of the strengths of marketing public relations has been the implied endorsement of the media when an editor or news director determines that a product is newsworthy and will be of interest to readers, viewers or listeners. The editorial side of the media has been historically independent of the ad side. There have been always a few exceptions such as coverage of the grand opening of stores that advertise in the newspaper. But with the effectiveness of the traditional 30-second television commercial under fire, advertisers are pressing the media to blend advertising with program content.

The television networks were the first to give in. Product plugs have been around for years in game shows, but the trend accelerated when new technology gave viewers the tools to zap commercials or record shows that delete ads altogether. Paid product placement made significant inroads with the advent of so-called reality shows of the 2000s. Then the networks began to embed advertising in programs such as mini-series and soap operas. Where product placement was once the domain of public relations people and small firms who built their business on relationships with prop masters and set decorators, product placement is now being practiced by advertising agencies, talent agencies and entertainment marketing firms.

Magazines are also under pressure to mix ad messages and content. *The Wall Street Journal* reports that advertisers are leaning on magazines to do this by "running ads next to magazine stories about the same product, getting products mentioned in stories, creating contests linked to magazines and running ads that look like magazine layouts—all of which could blur the traditional lines between editorial and advertising."[11] Mark Whitaker, president of the American Society of Magazine Editors and editor of *Newsweek,* told the *Journal* that the very personal relationship that readers have with magazines "depends in part on magazines having independence and credibility with their readers, as being produced by editors for readers primarily. I think that the problem with product placement is that it runs the risk of undermining that special relationship." He said, "It is absolutely essential for a magazine like *Newsweek* to maintain editorial independence, a sense of journalistic integrity, because it's our stock in trade."[12] It is the stock in trade of MPR to persuade editors that their product stories will be of high interest to readers and be news that readers can use.

MPR versus Marcom

Companies that billed themselves as marcom (marketing communications) agencies began to proliferate in the 2000s. These firms are trying to do on a smaller scale what the large advertising agencies attempted earlier by offering not just advertising but a custom mix of advertising and other marketing services. Their attempt under labels like "The Whole Egg"(Young and Rubicam) and "Orchestration"(Ogilvy and Mather) was undermined by the dominance of advertising profit centers. The large communications conglomerates of today are trying, with some success, to offer their clients a full menu of marketing services including public relations, but they are often too unwieldy to bring the right services together seamlessly.

The new compact marcom firms are more flexible and less advertising dominated. While it is too early to assess their success, public relations firms are scrambling to offer their own menu of marketing services that transcend media relations. *PR Week*, a leading trade publication in the public relations field, initiated a new column "Inside the Mix" in 2004 "to help the industry help clients find ways to reach their target markets that don't necessarily have a slot in any particular disciplinary pigeonhole. Jack O'Dwyer, longtime editor of *O'Dwyer's Newsletter*, even suggests that PR firms that have marketing experience operate under the banner of "marketing communications" because "marcom is adept at finding new markets for products and services and creating events, affiliations, contests and other vehicles to draw attention to the client." He says that "today's executives want marcom activities that produce visible results in a hurry. These activities include all forms of written and electronic communications, He warns that "PR firms must stake a claim to marketing before others do. The PR counseling industry cannot sit still while others encroach on its territory." [13]

This Is Our Time

Just as marketing must expand beyond the leave-it-all to television advertising mindset, Richard Edelman believes that public relations must in the future expand beyond the media relations mindset. He says that "we need a 360-degree communications perspective, because companies must use multiple channels to reach their target audiences and shape perceptions. We can expedite a company's ability to reach all stakeholders with the same story, in a timely, accurate and credible way. We will become the true integrators of communications." [14]

MPR is strategically positioned to assume a role of far greater importance than ever before in marketing of the future. After all, the hallmark of marketing public relations is its unique capability to build bonds, links, and bridges between companies and consumers. Public relations holds that consumers like to do business with companies that they know and trust. MPR programs exist to "relate" companies and their products with consumers and their wants and needs.

Marketing public relations is the made-to-order medium for maintaining brand franchises whether it is by providing information and service to the consumer, identifying the brand with causes that consumers care about, or sponsoring high-visibility events that excite consumers. Credibility is the key, and MPR is uniquely able to add the dimension of credibility to companies and their products.

References

Chapter 1—The MPR Explosion

1. Thomas L. Harris, *Value-Added Public Relations* (Chicago: NTC Business Books, 1998), p. x.
2. "Veronis Suhler Stevenson Forecasts Solid Growth Across All Communications Sectors," Veronis Suhler Stevenson News Release, "August 2, 2004.
3. Alice Gautsch, "Conversation with a Marketer," *Food and Beverage Marketplace* (Spring 1989) p. 12.
4. "WPP's Sorrell Sounds Off on the State of the PR Industry," *PR Week* (January 12, 2002) p. 11.
5. Brad Rodney, "How Brand Managers Use Public Relations," Presentation to PRSA Counselors Academy, April 26, 1999.
6. "The Route to the Consumer," *PR Week* (May 17, 2004) p. 14.
7. James H. Dowling, "No Definition Needed," *PR Week* (November 14, 1988). p. 10.
8. Rene Henry, *Marketing Public Relations: The Hows That Make It Work* (Ames, IA: Iowa State University Press 1995) p. 3.
9. Richard Weiner, *Webster's New World Dictionary of Media and Communications* (New York: McMillan General Reference, 1996), p. 362.
10. Patrick Jackson, "Reconciling the Specific Sphere of Marketing with the Universal Need for Relationships," Position Paper Prepared for the Public Relations Colloquium 1989, San Diego, January 24, 1989.
11. Philip Kotler, "Public Relations versus Marketing: Dividing the Conceptual Domain and Operational Turf," Position Paper Prepared for the Public Relations Colloquium 1989, San Diego, January 24, 1989.
12. Thomas L. Harris/Impulse Research Public Relations Client Survey, September 2004.
13. "WPP's Sorrell Sounds Off on the State of the PR Industry," *PR Week* (January 12, 2002) p. 11.
14. "The Route to the Consumer," *PR Week* (May 17, 2004) p. 14.
15. "The Route to the Consumer," *PR Week*, p. 15.
16. Al Ries and Laura Ries, *The Fall of Advertising and the Rise of PR* (New York: HarperCollins, 2002), p. 8.
17. Arthur Page quote from a 1927 Speech at an AT&T Operations Conference as Captured by Ketchum Productions in an Arthur Page Society video.

Chapter 2—Marketplace Forces Driving MPR

1. "The Vanishing Mass Market," *Business Week* (July 12, 2004), p. 61.
2. Keith Reinhard, 1990 Speech to the Advertising Federation of Australia.
3. Promotional flyer for Northwestern University, Department of Integrated Marketing Communications, Medill School of Journalism, 2005.

4. Patricia Whalen, Srinath Gopalkrishna, and Francis Mulhern, "How Integrated Is Your Exhibit Strategy? Lessons From The Healthcare Field," for *Convene* Magazine (August 2001).
5. "Special Report: The Future of Advertising," *The Economist* (June 26, 2004), p. 69.
6. Sergio Zyman, *The End of Advertising As We Know It* (Hoboken NJ: John Wiley & Sons, 2002), p. 1.
7. Suzanne Vranica, "Ad Agency's Latest Pitch in the Classroom," *The Wall Street Journal* (June 15, 2001).
8. "Paying to Avoid Ads," *The Economist* (August 7, 2004), p. 52.
9. Emily Nelson, "The Top 10 Trends in TV Advertising and Marketing," *WSJ.Com* (March 28, 2004).
10. "The Vanishing Mass Market," *BusinessWeek* (July 12, 2004), p. 61.
11. "Around the Globe With Daniel J. Edelman," *The Strategist* (Winter 2004), p. 24.
12. Michael Morley, *How to Manage Your Global Reputation* (London: Macmillan Press Ltd., 1998) p. 32.
13. Erin White and Jeffrey Trachtenberg, "One Size Doesn't Fit All," *The Wall Street Journal* (October 1, 2003), p. B1.
14. "Around the Globe With Daniel J. Edelman," p. 24.
15. Robert Gray, "Underneath the Arches," *IPRA Frontline* (March 2001), p. 4.
16. Thomas L. Harris, "Spot Remover." *Thomas L. Harris Viewsletter* (March 2003), p. 2.
17. Stuart Elliott, "Product Placement," *New York Times* (Jan. 18, 2003).
18. Joe Cappo, *The Future of Advertising* (New York: McGraw-Hill, 2003), p. 237.
19. White and Trachtenberg, "One Size Doesn't Fit All," *The Wall Street Journal,* p. B2.
20. Al Ries and Laura Ries, *The Fall of Advertising and The Rise of PR* (New York: HarperCollins, 2002).
21. Harold Burson, "The Practice of Public Relations: Where It's Been, Where It's Going," Speech to the Counselors Academy of the Public Relations Society of America, April 5, 1989.
22. "Integrated Approach Helps Consumer Products Achieve High Recall," *The Holmes Report* (February 2, 2004), p. 1.
23. "The Route to the Consumer," *PR Week* (May 17, 2004), pp. 14–21.
24. Sergio Zyman, *The End of Advertising As We Know It* (Hoboken NJ: John Wiley & Sons, 2002), p. 1.
25. Susan Vranica, "Aflac Duck's Paddle to Stardom: Creativity on the Cheap," *The Wall Street Journal* (July 30, 2004), p. B1.
26. Al Ries and Laura Ries, *The Fall of Advertising and The Rise of PR* (New York: HarperCollins, 2002), p. 157.

Chapter 3—Classic MPR

1. Scott M. Cutlip, *The Unseen Power* (Hillside, NJ: Lawrence Erlbaum, 1994), p. 7.
2. Cutlip, *The Unseen Power,* p. 194.
3. Isadore Barmash, *Always Live Better Than Your Clients* (New York: Dodd, Meade & Co., 1983), pp. 80–82.
4. Lee Iacocca with William Novak, *Iacocca: A Biography* (New York: Bantam Books, 1984), pp. 66–67.

5. Iacocca, *Iacocca: A Biography*, pp. 71–73.

Chapter 4—Trust Factor

1. Golin/Harris Trust in *American Business Survey,* May 2003.
2. "A View from the Top: CEOs on Corporate Reputation," *Hill & Knowlton Corporate Reputation Watch* (July 1999).
3. Ellen Ryan Mardiks, "The Next Big Deal," *Reputation Management* (March 2001).
4. Paul Holmes, *The Holmes Report* (Dec. 2003).
5. Al Golin, *Trust or Consequences* (New York: AMACOM, 2004), p. 40.
6. "McDonald's Highlights from Social Responsibility Report," 2002, p. 12.
7. John F. Love, *McDonald's: Behind the Arches* (New York: Bantam Books, 1986), p. 212.
8. Alvin Golin, "Community Relations" in Bill Cantor and Chester, *Experts in Action: Inside Public Relations* (New York: Longman, 1988), p. 73.
9. Golin, "Community Relations," pp. 111–112.
10. Golin, "Community Relations," p. 113.
11. "The Tylenol Comeback," Johnson & Johnson Special Report, undated, p. 8.
12. "The Tylenol Comeback," p. 9
13. Golin, *Trust or Consequences*, p.7.
14. Golin, *Trust or Consequences*, p. 13.

Chapter 5—How MPR Adds Value: Push, Pull, Pass

1. Theodore Levitt, *The Marketing Mode* (New York: McGraw-Hill), 1969, p. 47.
2. Horace Schwerin and Henry Newell, *Persuasion in Marketing* (New York: John Wiley & Sons, 1981), p. 153.
3. Philip Kotler, *Marketing Management*, 6th ed. (Englewood Cliffs, NJ: Prentice-Hall, 1988), p. 612.
4. Alvin Golin, *Trust or Consequences* (New York: AMACOM, 2004), p. 40.
5. Phillip Kotler, "Mega-Marketing," *Harvard Business Review* (Mar. 1, 1986).

Chapter 6—Circumstances for Success: The Harris Grid

1. Daniel J. Edelman, Noel Griffiths Lecture, Sydney, Australia, Feb. 16, 1989.

Chapter 7—The MPR Strategic Planning Process

1. Johnson & Johnson credo from its Web site: *http://www.jnj.com/our_company/our_credo/index.htm*
2. FEDEX mission statement from its corporate Web page: *http://www.fedex.com/us/about/today/mission.html*
3. Celestial Seasonings mission statement from its corporate Web site: *http://www.celestialseasonings.com/whoweare/corporatehistory/mission.php*
4. Diane Witmer, *Spinning the Web: A Handbook for Public Relations on the Internet* (New York: Addison-Wesley Longman, 1999).
5. *Do's and Taboo's Around the World*, Complied by the Parker Pen Company (Elmsford, NY: The Benjamin Company Inc, 1999).
6. Walter K. Lindenmann, "Guidelines and Standards for Measuring the Effectiveness of PR Programs and Activities," The Institute for Public Relations (1997, rev. 2003).

7. Delahaye Medialink promotional flyer: "Integrating Public Relations Measurement into the Marketing Mix Model: How Miller Brewing Tied PR to Barrels of Beer Sold," no date.

Chapter 8—Target Marketing: From Demographics to Lifestyle

1. Al Croft, "PR and the New Consumer," *Relate* (October 30, 1989).
2. Betsy Spethmann, "Loyalty's Royalty," *Promo* Magazine (March 1, 2004). Reprinted with permission from *Promo* magazine.
3. As quoted by Betsy Spethmann, in "Loyalty's Royalty." *Promo* Magazine, March 1, 2004. Reprinted with permission from *Promo* magazine.
4. Gary McWilliams, "Analyzing Customers, Best Buy Decides Not All Are Welcome," *The Wall Street Journal* (November 8, 2004), p. 1.
5. Lisa Fortini-Campbell, *Hitting the Sweet Spot—How Consumer Insights Can Inspire Better Marketing and Advertising* (Chicago, IL: The Copy Workshop, 1992), p. 126.
6. Lasheka Purvis, "The Green Smile," *Reputation Management* (September 2000).
7. Lasheka Purvis, "The Green Smile."
8. Entry Summary for the Public Relations Society of America 2005 Silver Anvil competition: The Clorox Company (Ketchum West) "Clorox Bleach Pen Writes a Bright New Chapter for The Clorox Company."
9. Rick Popely, "Cadillac Gets Younger," *Chicago Tribune* (October 23, 2004), Sec. 2, p. 1.
10. Bill Breen, "Desire: Connecting With What Customers Want." *www.fastcompany .com/on-line/67/desire.html*, February 17, 2003, from *Fast Company*, Issue 67, p. 86.

Chapter 8—Appendix Notes

1. Steve Gillon, *Boomer Nation: The Largest and Richest Generation Ever, and How It Changed America* (New York: Simon and Schuster, 2004).
2. "As an aging population continues to seek the fountain of youth, the medical equipment market promises answers," *Red Herring* (December 6, 2004).
3. David Brooks, *Bobos In Paradise—The New Upper Class and How They Got There* (New York: Simon and Schuster, 2000).
4. Everett M. Rogers, *Diffusion of Innovations* (New York: The Free Press, NY, 1962).
5. *http://users.metro2000.net/~stabbott/genxintro.htm*
6. David Solie, *How to Say It to Seniors: Closing the Communication Gap with Our Elders* (Englewood Cliffs, NJ, Prentice-Hall, 2004).
7. American Marketing Association webinar on YoCos co-sponsored by Iconoculture, October 2004.

Chapter 9—Targeting Multicultural and Global Markets

1. Gina Rudan, "Five Simple Rules for Launching a Multicultural Strategy," *PR Tactics* (August 2004), p. 19.
2. Katie Sweeney, "What Growing Diversity Will Mean for America," *PR Tactics* (August 2004), p. 16.
3. Recounted in J. Walker Smith, Ann Clurman, and Craig Wood, *Coming to Concurrence: Addressable Attitudes and the New Model for Marketing Productivity* (Evanston, IL: Racom Books, 2005), p. 49.
4. Sweeney, "What Growing Diversity Will Mean For America," p. 16.

5. Rudan, "Five Simple Rules for Launching a Multicultural Strategy," p. 19.
6. "Miller Turns Eye Toward Hispanics," *The Wall Street Journal* (October 8, 2004), p. B3.
7. Betsy Spethmann, "Speaking Two Languages," *Promo* Magazine (July 6, 2004), at *http://promomagazine.com*. Reprinted with permission from *Promo* Magazine.
8. Laurel Wentz, "Reverse English," *Advertising Age* (November 19, 2001).
9. Wentz, "Reverse English."
10. Betsy Spethmann, "Speaking Two Languages," at *http://promomagazine.com*.
11. Leon Schiffman and Leslie Kanuk. *Consumer Behavior* (Upper Saddle River, NJ: Pearson/Prentice Hall, 2004), p. 449.
12. "Miller Turns Eye Toward Hispanics," p. B3.
13. Spethmann, "Speaking Two Languages."
14. Schiffman and Kanuk, *Consumer Behavior*, p. 450.
15. Leon Lazaroff, "Time Warner Enters Bidding War for Black Magazine," *Chicago Tribune* (May 1, 2004), Sec. 2, p. 1.
16. Border's Group Web site on community giving: *http://www.bordersgroupinc.com/community/national.htm*
17. "P&G Supplier Diversity Program," at *http://www.pg.com/supplier_diversity/images/pdfs*.
18. Miriam Jordan, "Ethnic Diversity Doesn't Blend in Kids' Lives," *The Wall Street Journal* (June 18, 2004), p. B1.
19. Jordan, "Ethnic Diversity Doesn't Blend in Kids' Lives," p. B1.
20. Shiffman and Kanuk, *Consumer Behavior*, p. 450.
21. Joe Cappo, *The Future of Advertising: New Media, New Clients, New Consumers in the Post-Television Age* (New York: McGraw-Hill, 2003).
22. Jordan, "Ethnic Diversity Doesn't Blend in Kids' Lives."
23. Jordan, "Ethnic Diversity Doesn't Blend in Kids' Lives."
24. Global Best Practices in the Marketing Communications Industry in 2000 sponsored by the IAA, Visa International, and the University of Florida.
25. Nelson D. Schwartz, "Bigger and Bigger—Martin Sorrell Wants WPP to be the World's Largest Marketing Machine," *Fortune* Magazine (November 29, 2004).
26. The Golden Workshop—"Expectations of the Chief Corporate Public Relations Officer In 2001"—Arthur W. Page Society at *http://www.awpagesociety.com/activities/ remarks_speeches/pr2001.asp*
27. Procter and Gamble, Social Responsibility Report, 2004, *http://www.pg.com/company/our_commitment/social_responsibility.jhtml*
28. Mu Jin, "P&G Branch No Plan to Go Public," *The Shanghai Star* (August 15, 2000).
29. The Golden Workshop—Arthur W. Page Society.

Chapter 10—Reaching a Critical Audience: Internal Branding

1. Scott David and Michael Dunn, *Building the Brand-Driven Business*, (Hoboken NJ: Jossey-Bass, 2002).
2. Marc Drizen, "Internalizing Your Brand," *Stakeholder Power*, October 2003. *www.stakeholderpower.com/story.cfm?article_id=374*
3. Juliet Williams in a teleconferenced presentation from London to the Forum for People Performance, November 2003 at Northwestern University, Evanston, IL.

4. R.J. Varey and B.R. Lewis, eds., *Internal Marketing Directions for Management* (New York, Routledge, 2000).

5. Piercy, N. F., "Partnership Between Marketing and Human Resource Management For Implementation Effectiveness in Services Marketing," *Academy of Marketing Conference Proceedings* (Manchester: Metropolitan University, 1997), pp. 865–78.

6. Mohammed Rafiq and Pervaiz K Ahmed, *Internal Marketing: Tools and Concepts for Customer Focused Management* (Woburn, MA: Butterworth-Heinemann, 2002).

7. Rodney Gray, "Finding the Right Direction," *Communication World* (November/December, 2004), pp. 26–32.

8. Patricia T. Whalen, *How Communication Drives Merger Success* (San Francisco: International Association of Business Communicators, 2002).

9. These facts were presented by the Empower Group during a 2003 Internal Branding confererence, Chicago, IL citing the Watson Wyatt "Human Capital Study."

10. Forum for People Performance Conference held November 16, 2004, at Northwestern University, Medill Integrated Marketing Communications and reported at: *http://www.medill.northwestern.edu/medill/inside/imc_feature/summit_stresses_the_importance_of_internal_marketing_in_business_success.html*

11. Don Schultz, "Live the Brand," *Marketing Management* (July/August 2003), p. 8.

12. From the World Famous Pike Street Fish Market Web site: *http://www.pike placefish. com*

13. Procter & Gamble 2004 Contributions Report, at: *http://www.pg.com/company/our_commitment/community.jhtml*

14. Thomas Marlow, "The CEO Refresher," *http://www.refresher.com/!tsmsupply. html*

15. Marlow, "The CEO Refresher."

16. Don Schultz, Live the Brand."

17. David and Michael Dunn, *Building the Brand-Driven Business.*

18. "Creating Brand Ambassadors—How to Help Employees Promote the Brand," Smart Solutions Newsletter, Copyright: JRS Consulting, Inc. 2004.

Chapter 11—MPR Tactics A to Z

1. Monica Davey, "Harley at 100," *The New York Times* (September 1, 2003).

2. Michael J. McCarthy, "New Pop Art Museum Promotes Coke," *The New York Times* (August 2, 1990.).

3. "Ten of the Movies' Most Memorable Role Players," *The New York Times* (October 22, 2003) p. G22.

4. John N. Frank, "Mercedes Tour to Show Off Cars to Consumers, Media," *PR Week* (July 26, 2004), p. 2.

5. John von Rhein, "The CSO in Flux," *The Chicago Tribune* (September 25, 1988).

6. Jeffery Trachtenberg, "Diet Book Found Novel Ways to Get to the Top and Stay," *The Wall Street Journal* (August 2004).

Chapter 12—Getting Coverage in Traditional Media

1. *Advertising Age Fact Pack, Second Annual Guide to Advertising & Marketing,* Supplement to *Advertising Age* (2004).

2. "2004 Facts About Newspapers," Newspaper Association of America: *http://www.naa.org/info/facts04/readership-audience.html*

3. Jeff Bercovici. "Fact: Magazine Readership Is Up—Nix to The Naysayers, 5.3% Increase Since 1998," *Media Life Magazine* (August 28, 2002), *http://www. medialifemagazine.com/news2002/aug02/aug26/3_wed/news1wednesday.html*

4. "Multitasking Dilutes Media Attention" Business View Research Documents, March 23, 2004, Forrester Research, *http://www.forrester.com/findresearch*

5. "TV Still the Favored Media Habit, According to Results of Simultaneous Media Usage Study Released by The Media Center," Press Release Published Thursday, December 2, 2004, *http://www.mediacenter.org/content/5777.cfm*

6. "2004 Communications Industry Forecast," Veronis Suhler Stevenson Partners, New York.

7. Frank Rich, "The Weight of an Anchor," *The New York Times Sunday Magazine* (May 19, 2002), p. 35.

8. Steve Johnson, "The Future of Network News: Follow the Money," *Chicago Tribune* (November 28, 2004), Sec. 7, pp. 1 and 6.

9. "Free Plugs Supply Ad Power," *Advertising Age* (January 29, 1990).

10. Jacques Steinberg, "Rise and Fight: Morning News Wars," *The New York Times* (May 23, 2004), Sec. 3, p. 1.

11. Jacques Steinberg, "Rise and Fight," p. 2.

12. "Get Booked Now: Quick Tips for Helping Your Source Pass TV's Pre-Interview Audition," in *Journalists Speak Out Newsletter* (June 16, 2004), *http://www. bulldogreporter.com.* Copyright: Infocom Group, 2004. Used with permission.

13. RADAR 71 (Fall 2001) and Radio Advertising Bureau.

14. *Advertising Age Fact Pack*, 2004.

15. Michael P. Smith, Managing Director, Media Management Center, Northwestern University. "The Search for New Readers: Growing Audience Requires Newspapers to Adopt an Innovation Mindset," InterAmerican Press Association for Hora de Cierre.

16. *Bulldog Reporter* Promotional E-mail for PR University Conference on Dec 16, 2004: "How To Create Breakthrough E-mail Pitches That Journalists Love to Receive." *http://www.bulldogreporter.com.* Copyright: Infocom Group, 2004. Used with permission.

17. *Bulldog Reporter* e-zine, Journalists Speak Out, 2004 Infocom Group, 5900 Hollis St., Suite L, Emeryville, CA 94608 1-800-959-1059). *http://www.bulldogreporter. com.* Copyright: Infocom Group, 2004. Used with permission.

Chapter 13—Getting Visibility On-Line

1. Weber Shandwick newsletter, *Spotlight!*, 3rd issue. For past issues: *www.weber shandwick.com.*

2. Wikipedia, the free encyclopedia: *http://en.wiki.org/wiki/Main_Page*

3. "E-fluentials®" Copyright 2005, Burson-Marsteller. *http://www.burson-marsteller. com/pages/insights/efluentials*

4. Mark Vangel, "Are You Tracking Blogs? They're Tracking You." *The Gauge*, Volume 17, No. 3 (July 2004). Copyright 2004 Delahaye Medialink Worldwide.

5. Mark Vangel, 2004.

6. Bulldog Reporter's e-zine: "Journalists Speak Out on PR," June 8, 2004. *http:// www. bulldogreporter.com.* Copyright: Infocom Group, 2004. Used with permission.

7. "Blogs: What Are They Good For? Some Savvy Marketers Say Business," *http://www.betuitve.com/Archive/Articles/July_Article01.php*

8. For the full Eyetrack III research report go to: *http://www.poynterextra.org/eyetrack2004/*

9. "Guidelines for the PR Portion of Your Company's Web site," *PR InSite Newsletter*, Volume 1, Issue 1 (March 2003), at *www.prinsite.com*. Reprinted with permission. To order a copy of the Nielsen Norman Group Report, go to: *www.nngroup.com/reports/pr/*

10. Dan Gillmor's letter was reported on in a column entitled "Is PR E-mail Dead?" for the Bulldog Reporter's e-zine, "Journalists Speak Out on PR," (July 6, 2004). Copyright: Infocom Group, 2004. Used with permission.

11. Dan Gillmor, "Is PR E-Mail Dead?"

12. Aparna Kumar, "Concern About New Web Monitors," from *Wired News*, at: *http://www.wired.com/news/print/0,1294,41931,00.html*, Feb. 24, 2001.

Chapter 14—The Bottom Line: Measurement and Evaluation

1. Clark Caywood, presented at the PRSA International Conference in New York, October 25, 2004.

2. Philip Kotler, *Marketing Management*, 11th edition (Englewood Cliffs, NJ: Prentice Hall, 2003).

3. For a complete copy of an article by the IRP on PR measurement, go to *http://www.prfirms.org/docs/pr_measurement2002.pdf*

Chapter 15—Introducing New Products

1. Jack Trout, *The New Positioning* (New York: McGraw-Hill, 1995), p. 147.

2. Al Ries and Laura Ries, *The Fall of Advertising and the Rise of PR* (New York: HarperCollins, 2004).

3. "The Brands That Caught a Wave," *PR Week* (Apr. 26,1999), p. 17.

4. Bob Garfield, "Beetle Would Cruise Even Without Fine Ads," *Advertising Age* (March 16, 1998), p. 43.

5. James Surowiecki, "The Billion Dollar Blade," *The New Yorker* (June 1998), p. 43.

6. The Brands That Caught a Wave," *PR Week* (Apr. 26, 1999), p. 17.

7. "Viagra," *Thomas L. Harris MPR Update* (July 1998), p. 1.

8. Wayne Friedman, "Star Wars: Who Needs Ads," *Advertising Age* (May 10, 1999), p. 4.

9. Scott Donaton, "Galactic Hype-Storm Spawned by Star Wars Prequel," *Advertising Age* (May 31, 1999), p. 44.

10. Mark Starr and Martha Brant, "It Went Down to the Wire," *Newsweek* (July 19. 1999), p. 50.

11. "Marketing Magic Released with a Winning Kick," Associated Press, July 14, 1999.

12. George Lazarus, "World Cup Win Kicks Up Nike Publicity," *The Chicago Tribune* (July 1, 2004).

13. Bernie Miklasz, "US Soccer Players' Challenge: Keep Their Pure Image, Cash In," *St. Louis Post-Dispatch* (July 14, 1999).

14. Karyn Mongret, "Soccer Puts Some Kick into Nike Sports Bras," *Women's Wear Daily* (July 19, 1999), p. 31.

15. Harvey Posert and Paul Franson, *Spinning the Bottle* (St. Helena, CA: HPPR Press, 2002), p. 147.
16. Posert and Franson, *Spinning the Bottle*, pp. 147–48.
17. Rachel Zimmerman, "Botox Gives a Special Lift to These Soirees," *The Wall Street Journal* (April 16, 2002).
18. David Noonan and Jerry Adler, "The Botox Boom," *Newsweek*, pp. 50–58 (Apr. 29, 2002).
19. William Safire, "Farewell, Furrowed Brow," *The New York Times* (May 17, 2002).
20. Paul Gray, "Wild About Harry," *Time* (September 20, 1999), pp. 67–72.
21. Alan Cowell, "All Aboard the Potter Express," *The New York Times* (July 10, 2000), p. B1.
22. Malcolm Jones, "Why Harry's Hot," *Newsweek* (July 17, 2000), cover story.
23. Nancy Gibbs, "The Real Magic of Harry Potter," Time, June, 2003, cover story.
24. "Harry's Order of Millions," *The Wall Street Journal* (May 19, 2003), p. B1.
25. Gibbs, "The Real Magic of Harry Potter."
26. Bruce Horovitz, "Newman, McDonald's Link Up for Salad Days," *USA Today* (March 7, 2003).
27. "McDonald's: Fries with That Salad," *BusinessWeek* (July 5, 2004), p. 82.
28. John Heilemann, "Reinventing the Wheel," *Time* (December 10, 2001), p. 78.
29. Michael Garfield, "Segue to The Segway," *High Tech Texan Newsletter* (9/02) at *http://www.hightechtexan.com/Gadgets/SegwayHT.asp*
30. "Segway Chat with Segway CEO Ron Bills," June 23, 2004, at: *http://www.segwaychat.com/forum*
31. "Segway the Right Way," March 24, 2004, *http://phillips.blogs.com/mwa/2004/ 03/segway_the_righ.html*

Chapter 16—Maintaining Brands and Making Advertising News

1. "Miracle Drug," *BusinessWeek* (August 29, 1988).
2. Gina Kolata, "Aspirin Can Lower Risk of Getting Precancerous Polyps in Colon," *The New York Times* (March 6, 2003), p. A20.
3. "An Aspirin a Day," *Newsweek* (June 7, 2004), p. 79.
4. Randall Rothenberg, "Commercials Become News and the Air Time is Free," *The New York Times* (January 8, 1990).
5. Scott Hume, "Free Association: More Marketers Seek Out Media Exposure to Enhance their Traditional Paid Campaigns," *Advertising Age* (October 23, 1998) p. 9.
6. Hume, "Free Association: More Marketers Seek Out Media Exposure to Enhance their Traditional Paid Campaigns."
7. Mary Wells, *A Big Life in Advertising* (New York: Alfred A. Knopf, 2002), p. 39.
8. Wells, *A Big Life in Advertising*, p. 50.
9. Stuart Elliott, "McDonald's Campaign Aims to Regain the Youth Market," *The New York Times* (September 3, 2003).
10. James Cantalupo, McDonald's Corporation 2003 Annual Report, p. 1.
11. Al Ries and Laura Ries, *The Fall of Advertising and the Rise of PR* (New York: HarperCollins, 2002), Chapter 7.

Chapter 17 Sponsorships and Special Events

1. "The Route to the Consumer," *PR Week* (May 17, 2004) p. 14.
2. International Events Group, "Annual Sponsorship Report," (Jan. 10, 2002).
3. "Sponsownership," *Adweek* (Mar. 17, 2004). p. 11.
4. Steve Lesnik, Kemper Lesnik Communications, promotion piece, no date.
5. Robert Dilenschneider, *Power and Influence* (Englewood Cliffs, NJ: Prentice-Hall, 1989), p. 127.
6. "Sports and Suds: Promotion Meets Ad Profits," *Sports Illustrated* (July 17, 2003).
7. "Sponsorships in NASCAR Breeds Fan Loyalty" NASCAR.com, July 2004.
8. "Sponsorships in NASCAR Breeds Fan Loyalty" NASCAR.com, July 2004.
9. "Sponsorships in NASCAR Breeds Fan Loyalty" NASCAR.com, July 2004.
10. Herb Schmertz with William Novak, *Good-Bye to Low Profile* (Boston: Little Brown & Co., 1986), p. 210–12.
11. Herb Schmertz with William Novak, *Good-Bye to Low Profile* (Boston: Little Brown & Co., 1986), p. 211.
12. Schmertz with Novak, *Good-Bye to Low Profile* (Boston: Little Brown & Co., 1986), p. 212.

Chapter 18—Place Marketing

1. Philip Kotler, Donald Haider, and Irving Rein, *Marketing Places* (New York: The Free Press, 1993), pp. 170–71.
2. Aaron D. Cushman, *A Passion for Winning* (Pittsburgh, PA: Lighthouse Point Press, 2004), pp. 202–3.
3. James Janega, "Harley Festival Gets Fans Motor Running," *The Chicago Tribune* (September 1, 2003) p. 1.
4. Monica Davey, "Harley at 100: Mainstream Meets Mystique," *The New York Times* (September 1, 2003), p. 1.
5. James Strengold, "Low-Key Thrills at Legoland," *The New York Times* (May 9, 1999), p. 10.
6. Ellen Almer, "Shmoozing With the Dolls in Chicago," *The New York Times* (January 18, 2000), p. C2.
7. Nancy Maes, "Show for Girls with Bit of Merchandising," *The Chicago Tribune* (December 3, 1998).
8. "It's The Hottest Place in Town," *The New York Times* (May 16, 2004), p. 1.

Chapter 19—Building Buzz, Placing Product, and Experiential Marketing

1. David Lewis and Darren Bridger, *The Soul of the New Consumer* (London: Nicholas Brealey Publishing, 2001), p. 19.
2. Malcolm Gladwell, "Message in a Bottle," *The Independent on Sunday Magazine,* (June 6, 1997).
3. Faith Popcorn with Lys Marigold, *Clicking* (London: Thorson's, 1996), p. 282.
4. Lewis and Bridger, *The Soul of the New Consumer*, p. 91.
5. *Media Monitoring News On-line* newsletter (December 2004), at *http://www. cyberalert.com/email/newsletter04.html*

6. Rob Walker, "The Hidden (in Plain Sight) Persuaders," *New York Times Magazine* (December 5, 2005).

7. Walker, "The Hidden (in Plain Sight) Persuaders."

8. Walker, "The Hidden (in Plain Sight) Persuaders."

9. Walker, "The Hidden (in Plain Sight) Persuaders."

10. *Media Monitoring News.*

11. P&G Press Release, September 28, 2004.

12. "Next Wave: Too Much Publicity," *Red Herring* (July 28, 2004).

13. "Next Wave," *Red Herring.*

14. "Next Wave," *Red Herring.*

15. B. Jospeph Pine II and James H. Gilmore, "Welcome to the Experience Economy," *Harvard Business Review* (July–August 1998).

16. Case history is excerpted from Bulldog Reporter's "2003 Bulldog Awards for Excellence in Media Relations & Publicity" reported in the e-zine Journalists Speak Out on PR. *http://www.bulldogreporter.com.* Copyright: Infocom Group, 2004. Used with permission.

17. Ellen Byron, "How Neiman Marcus's Tansky Stays Above the Wannabes: Lassoing Manolo Fans Online," *The Wall Street Journal* (December 9, 2004), p. B1.

18. Byron, *The Wall Street Journal.*

19. Byron, *The Wall Street Journal.*

20. "Could Apple Blow Its iPod Lead?" Source: *http://yahoo.businessweek.com/technology/content/dec2004/tc2004127_7607_tc185.htm*

21. "The iPod People Invade Apple's Stores," *Fortune* Magazine (December 13, 2004), p. 79.

22. Lucinda Hahn, "Bentley Makes a Scene," *Chicago Tribune* (August 9, 2004), Sec. 5, p. 3.

23. Pine II and Gilmore, "Welcome to the Experience Economy," p. 101.

Chapter 20—Business to Business MPR

1. Martin P. Block and Tamara S. Block, *Business-to-Business Marketing Research*, 2d ed., (Chicago, IL, Racom Books, 2005).

2. SRDS, *http://www.srds.com/portal/servlet/LoginServlet?action=loginFrame&linkHit=ips*

3. Robert Bly, "What Makes Business-to-Business Marketing Different from Consumer?" in *The Business to Business Marketer*, Vol. 9, No. 5 (July/August 2004), published by the Business Marketing Association.

4. As reported in *Business Brand Leadership*, Volume 4, Issue 1, HSR Business-to-Business, "Building the Hobart Brand," p. 3.

5. Center for Exhibition Industry Research (CEIR), 1999 report on the Packaging Machinery Manufacturers industry.

6. Jeff Stanley, Research Director, of the ZD Comdex-Forums, "IT Trade Shows: A Strategic Marketing Resource. A Survey of the Role of Trade Shows in the IT Universe, Executive Report."

7. CEIR "Power of Exhibitions 2," 1996—*http://www.ceir.org/*

8. Case history is excerpted from *Bulldog Reporter's* "2003 Bulldog Awards for Excellence in Media Relations & Publicity" reported in the e-zine Journalists Speak Out on PR. http://www.bulldogreporter.com. Copyright: Infocom Group, 2004. Used with permission.

9. Comsat was a publicly traded company and the US Signatory to the International Telecommunications Satellite Organization (INTELSAT). It was subsequently acquired by Lockheed Martin Corporation.

10. Patricia O'Dell, "Clairol Expands B-to-B Efforts—Procter & Gamble Touts Clairol Professional," *Direct* Magazine (March 1, 2003). Copyright 2003 Primedia Business Magazines & Media Inc.

11. Reported in *PR Week*, "PR Awards 2004," (Dec. 17, 2004) p. 17.

Chapter 21—Cause-Related MPR

1. Tom Duncan, *IMC: Using Advertising & Promotion to Build Brands* (New York: McGraw-Hill Irwin, 2002).

2. "Edelman's Annual Trust Barometer," January 20, 2004, *http://www.edelman.com/events/Trust/startwm.html*

3. Hill Knowlton/Yankelovich's Survey on "The Value of Corporate Reputation: The ROI of Public Affairs," 2002.

4. Thomas Carson, "Friedman's Theory of Corporate Social Responsibility," *Business and Professional Ethics Journal*, Vol. 12, No. 1 (Spring, 1993), pp. 3–32.

5. Thomas Carson. "Friedman's Theory of Corporate Social Responsibility," citing Smith vs. Barlow, 1950, p. 23.

6. David Martinson, "Enlightened Self-Interest Fails as an Ethical Baseline in Public Relations," in *Journal of Mass Media Ethics*, Vol. 9, No. 2 (1994), pp. 100–9.

7. Kris Maher, "Thin Line Between Philanthropy, Corporate Branding Begins to Blur." *The Wall Street Journal* (October 4, 2001),

8. Robert E. Hope, "Cause-Related Marketing." Speech to the Public Affairs Council, Philadelphia, May 24, 1988.

9. Louis V. Gerstner, Jr., "Value in Cause Related Marketing," *Financier* (May 1985).

10. Home Depot Web site: *www.homedepot.com.*

11. "Community Relations Campaign of the Year 2004," in *PR News*, "PR Awards 2004," p. 21.

12. Bristol Meyers Corporate Report, 1998.

13. Loews Corporate Report, 2002.

14. From P&G 2004 Contributions Report—*http://www.pg.com/content/pdf/01_about_pg/01_about_pg_homepage/about_pg_toolbar/download_report/contributions_report.pdf*

Chapter 22—Spokespersons

1. Philip Kotler, Irving Rein, and Martin Stoller, *High Visibility* (Lincolnwood, IL: NTC Business Books, 1997), p. 278.

2. Jack Bernstein, "Donald's Trump Card," *Advertising Age* (March 7, 1988).

3. "David Segal, "Donald Trump: The Size of His Ego is No Act," *The Chicago Tribune* (September 16, 2004) p. 10.

4. "Divorce Isn't His Only Worry," *Newsweek* (March 5, 1990), pp. 32–33.

5. Jennifer Lawrence, "It's Hype, Hype Hooray for New Book by Trump," *Advertising Age* (August 6, 1990).

6. Timothy L. O'Brien, "Trump Hotels Plans to Seek Bankruptcy," *The New York Times* (August 10, 2004).

7. Timothy L. O'Brien and Eric Dash, "The Midas Touch With Spin on It," *The New York Times* (September 8, 2004), p. C1.

8. Al Ries and Laura Ries, *The Fall of Advertising and the Rise of PR* (New York: HarperCollins), p. 163.

9. Joe Marconi, *Reputation Marketing* (New York: McGraw-Hill, 2002), p. 198.

10. Ries and Ries, *The Fall of Advertising and the Rise of PR*, p. 164.

11. Jim Carlton, "From Apple, a New Marketing Blitz," *The Wall Street Journal* (August 14, 1998) p. B1.

12. Steven Lacy, "Hello Again," *Newsweek* (May 18, 1998) p. 46.

13. Andrew Gore, "The Vision Thing: Defying Gravity Again," *MacWorld Online* (September 28, 1998).

14. Gore, "The Vision Thing."

15. Michael Krantz, "What Flavor is Your Mac?" *Time* (January 18,1999), p. 92.

16. Josh Quittner, "Apple's New Core," *Time* (January 14, 2002), p. 46.

17. Steven Levey, "With a Little Bit of Luxo," *Newsweek* (January 21, 2002), p. 48.

18. Felecity Barringer, "A Cover for Steve Jobs," *The New York Times* (January 14, 2002), p. C2.

19. Peter Burroughs, "Show Time!" *BusinessWeek* (February 2, 2004), p. 57.

20. Chris Taylor, "Steve Jobs' New Music Store," *Time* (November 17, 2003).

21. Walter S. Mossberg, "The Music Man," *The Wall Street Journal* (June 14, 2004), p. B1.

22. James Coates, "Jobs' Performance Keeps Apple Shining," *The Chicago Tribune* (May 4, 2003).

23. John Markoff, "Oh, Yeah, He Also Sells Computers," *The New York Times* (April 25, 2004), Sunday Business, p. 8.

24. Steven Levey, "iPod Nation," *Newsweek* (July 26, 2004), p. 44.

25. "A Big Week for Apple," *The Economist* (July 31, 2004), p. 53.

26. "Around the Globe With Daniel J. Edelman," *The Strategist* (Winter 2004), p. 24.

Chaper 23—The Future of Marketing Public Relations

1. Richard Edelman, "This is Our Time," *The Strategist* (Summer 2004), p. 60.

2. Harold Burson, "The Practice of Public Relations: Where It's Been, Where It's Going," Speech to the Counselors Academy of the Public Relations Society of America, April 5, 1989.

3. Edelman, "This is Our Time."

4. Philip Kotler, *Marketing Management,* 11th ed. (Englewood Cliffs, NJ: Prentice Hall, 2003).

5. Randall Rothenberg, "Shandwick Promotes Smallness," *The New York Times* (May 31, 1989).

6. Paul Taafe, "The Future of Global Public Relations: An Agency Perspective," *The Strategist* (Winter 2004), p. 22.

7. James H. Dowling, "No Definition Needed," *PR Week* (November 14, 1988), p. 10.

8. Paul Taafe, "The Future of Global Public Relations: An Agency Perspective," p. 22.

9. Paul Taafe, "The Future of Global Public Relations: An Agency Perspective," p. 22.

10. Mark Weiner, "The External Factors Shaping Public Relations in 2014," *PR Tactics* (July 2004), p. 29.

11. "A Marriage of Inconvenience, Part 2" *Relate* (June 26, 1989), p. 24.

12. Mark Weiner, "The External Factors Shaping Public Relations in 2014," p. 29.

13. Jack O'Dwyer, *O'Dwyer's Newsletter* (August 18, 2004), p. 8.

14. Richard Edelman, "This Is Our Time."

Bibliography

Ellen Almer, "Shmoozing With the Dolls in Chicago," *The New York Times*, January 18,2000, p. C2.

Isadore Barmash, *Always Live Better Than Your Clients*. New York: Dodd, Meade & Co., 1983.

Jeff Bercovici. "*Fact: Magazine Readership Is Up*—Nix To The Naysayers, 5.3% Increase Since 1998," *Media Life Magazine*, August 28, 2002, *http://www.medialifemagazine .com/news2002/aug02/aug26/3_wed/news1wednesday.html*

Martin P. Block and Tamara S. Block, *Business-to-Business Marketing Research*. Chicago: Racom Books, 2005.

Robert Bly, "What Makes Business-to-Business Marketing Different From Consumer?" in *The Business To Business Marketer*, July/August 2004, Vol. 9, No. 5. Published by the Business Marketing Association.

Bill Breen, "Desire: Connecting With What Customers Want." www.fastcompany.com/online/67/desire.html, February 17, 2003, from *Fast Company* Issue 67, p. 86.

David Brooks, *Bobos In Paradise—The New Upper Class and How They Got There*. NY: Simon and Schuster, 2000.

Bulldog Reporter Promotional Email for PR University Conference on Dec 16, 2004: "How To Create Breakthrough Email Pitches That Journalists Love to Receive."

Burson-Marsteller, *http://www.blogger.com/*

Ellen Byron, "How Neiman Marcus's Tansky Stays Above the Wannabes; Lassoing Manolo Fans Online," *The Wall Street Journal*, December 9, 2004, Page B1.

Joe Cappo, *The Future of Advertising: New Media, New Clients, New Consumers in the Post-Television Age*. New York: McGraw-Hill, 2003.

Thomas Carson, "Friedman's Theory of Corporate Social Responsibility," *Business and Professional Ethics Journal*, Vol. 12, No. 1 (Spring, 1993), 3–32.

Clarke Caywood, *The Handbook of Strategic Public Relations and Integrated Communications*. New York: McGraw-Hill, 1997.

———, Presented at the PRSA International Conference in New York, NY, October 25, 2004.

Al Croft, "PR and the New Consumer," *Relate*, October 30, 1989.

Aaron D. Cushman, *A Passion for Winning*. Pittsburgh, PA: Lighthouse Point Press, 2004.

Scott M. Cutlip, *The Unseen Power*. Hillsdale, NJ: Lawrence Erlbaum, 1994.

Scott M. Cutlip, Allen H. Center, and Glen M. Broom *Effective Public Relations*, 6th ed. Englewood Cliffs, NJ: Prentice-Hall, 1985.

Monica Davey, "Harley at 100," *The New York Times* (September 1, 2003).

———, "Harley at 100:Mainstream Meets Mystique," *The New York Times*, September 1, 2003, p.1.

Scott David and Michael Dunn, *Building the Brand Driven Business*. Hoboken, NJ: Jossey-Bass, 2002.

Delahaye Medialink promotional flyer: "Integrating Public Relations Measurement into the Marketing Mix Model: How Miller Brewing Tied PR to Barrels of Beer Sold."

James H. Dowling, "No Definition Needed," *PR Week* (November 14, 1988).

Marc Drizen, "Internalizing Your Brand," *Stakeholder Power.* October 2003. *www.stakeholderpower.com/story.cfm?article_id=374*

Tom Duncan, *IMC: Using Advertising & Promotion to Build Brands.* New York: McGraw-Hill Irwin, 2002.

Stuart Elliott, "Product Placement," *New York Times* (Jan. 18, 2003.

Lisa Fortini-Campbell, *Hitting the Sweet Spot—How Consumer Insights Can Inspire Better Marketing and Advertising.* Chicago, IL: The Copy Workshop, 1992, p. 126.

John N. Frank, "Mercedes Tour to Show Off Cars to Consumers, Media," *PR Week* (July 26, 2004) p. 2.

Louis V. Gerstner, Jr., "Value in Cause Related Marketing," *Financier* (May 1985).

Steve Gillon, *Boomer Nation: The Largest and Richest Generation Ever, and How It Changed America.* New York: Simon and Schuster, 2004.

Malcolm Gladwell, "Message in a Bottle," *The Independent on Sunday Magazine,* 1997: 6.

Alvin Golin, *Trust or Consequences.* New York: Amacom, 2003.

_____, "Community Relations" in Bill Cantor, *Experts in Action:Inside Public Relations.* New York: Longman, Inc., 1984.

Howard Gossage, *The Book of Gossage.* Chicago: The Copy Workshop, 1998.

Robert Gray, "Underneath the Arches," *IPRA Frontline* (March 2001), p. 4.

Rodney Gray, "Finding the Right Direction," *Communication World* (November/ December 2004), p. 26–32.

Lucinda Hahn, "Bentley Makes a Scene," *Chicago Tribune,* August 9, 2004, Sec. 5, p. 3.

Thomas L. Harris, *Value-Added Public Relations.* Chicago: NTC Business Books, 1998.

Rene Henry, *Marketing Public Relations: The Hows That Make It Work.* Ames, IA: Iowa State University Press 1995.

Hill Knowlton/Yankelovich's survey on "The Value of Corporate Reputation," "The ROI of Public Affairs," 2002.

Robert E. Hope, "Cause Related Marketing." Speech to the Public Affairs Council, Philadelphia, May 24, 1988.

Lee Iacocca with William Novak, *Iacocca: A Biography.* New York: Bantam Books, 1984.

Patrick Jackson, "Reconciling the Specific Sphere of Marketing with the Universal Need for Relationships," Position Paper Prepared for the Public Relations Colloquium 1989, San Diego, January 24, 1989.

James Janega, "Harley Festival Gets Fans Motor Running," *The Chicago Tribune* (September 1, 2003).

Mu Jin, "P&G Branch No Plan to Go Public," *The Shanghai Star* (August 15, 2000).

Steve Johnson, "The Future of Network News: Follow the Money," *Chicago Tribune* (November 28, 2004), Sec. 7, pp. 1 & 6.

Miriam Jordan, "Ethnic Diversity Doesn't Blend in Kids' Lives," *The Wall Street Journal* (June 18, 2004), p. B1.

Philip J. Kitchen and Don E. Schultz, *Raising the Corporate Umbrella.* New York: Palgrave, 2001.

Philip Kotler, *Marketing Management,* 6th ed. Englewood Cliffs, NJ: Prentice-Hall, 1988.

_____, *Marketing Management.* 11th ed. Englewood Cliffs, NJ: Prentice Hall, 2003.

_____, *Kotler on Marketing.* New York: The Free Press, 1999.

Philip Kotler, "Public Relations versus Marketing: Dividing the Conceptual Domain and Operational Turf," Position Paper Prepared for the Public Relations Colloquium 1989, San Diego, January 24, 1989.

Phillip Kotler, "Mega-Marketing," *Harvard Business Review* (Mar. 1, 1986).

Kotler, Philip, Donald H. Haider and Irving Rein. *Marketing Places.* New York: The Free Press 1993.

Philip Kotler and William Mindak, "Marketing and Public Relations," *Journal of Marketing* (October 1978).

Philip Kotler, Irviing Rein, Martin Stoller, *High Visibiity: The Making and Marketing of Celebrities.* (Lincolnwood, IL: NTC Business Books, 1997).

Aparna Kumar, "Concern About New Web Monitors, " from *Wired News,* at: *http://www.wired.com/news/print/0,1294,41931,00.html,* Feb. 24, 2001.

Leon Lazaroff, "Time Warner Enters Bidding War for Black Magazine," *Chicago Tribune* (May 1, 2004), Sec. 2, p. 1.

Theodore Levitt, *The Marketing Mode.* New York: McGraw-Hill, 1969.

David Lewis and Darren Bridger, *The Soul of the New Consumer.* London: Nicholas Brealey Publishing, 2001.

Walter K. Lindenmann, "Guidelines and Standards for Measuring the Effectiveness of PR Programs and Activities," The Institute for Public Relations (1997, rev. 2003).

John F. Love, *McDonald's: Behind the Arches.* New York: Bantam Books, 1986.

Michael J. McCarthy, "New Pop Art Museum Promotes Coke," *The New York Times* (August 2, 1990).

Gary McWilliams, "Analyzing Customers, Best Buy Decides Not All are Welcome," *The Wall Street Journal* (November 8, 2004).

Nancy Maes, "Show for Girls with Bit of Merchandising," *The Chicago Tribune* (December 3, 1998).

Joe Marconi, Joe *Reputation Marketing.* New York: McGraw-Hill, 2002.

_____, *Public Relations: The Complete Guide.* Mason, Ohio: Thomson Learning/Racom Books, 2004.

Ellen Ryan Mardiks, "The Next Big Deal" *Reputation Management* (March 2001).

David Martinson, "Enlightened Self-Interest Fails as an Ethical Baseline in Public Relations," in *Journal of Mass Media Ethics* (1994) Vol. 9, No. 2, 100–109.

Kris Maher, "Thin Line Between Philanthropy, Corporate Branding Begins to Blur." *The Wall Street Journal* (October 4, 2001).

Morley, Michael. *How To Manage Your Global Reputation.* London: Macmillan Press, 1998.

Emily Nelson, "The Top 10 Trends in TV Advertising and Marketing, *WSJ.Com* (March 28, 2004).

Patricia O'Dell, "Clairol Expands B-to-B Efforts—Procter & Gamble touts Clairol Professional," in *Direct* Magazine (March 1, 2003).

Parker Pen Company, *Do's and Taboo's Around the World.* Elmsford, NY: the Benjamin Company Inc., 1985.

N. F. Piercy, "Partnership Between Marketing and Human Resource Management For Implementation Effectiveness in Services Marketing" in *Academy of Marketing Conference Proceedings*, Manchester Metropolitan University (1997).

B. Joseph Pine II and James H. Gilmore, "Welcome to the Experience Economy," *Harvard Business Review* (July-August 1998).

Faith Popcorn with Lys Marigold, *Clicking*. London: Thorson's, 1996.

Rick Popely, "Cadillac Gets Younger" *Chicago Tribune* (October 23, 2004), Sec. 2.

Harvey Posert and Paul Franson, *Spinning The Bottle*. St. Helena, CA: HPPR Press, 2004.

Lasheka Purvis, "The Green Smile," *Reputation Management* (September 2000).

Mohammed Rafiq and Pervaiz K Ahmed, *Internal Marketing: Tools and Concepts for Customer Focused Management*. (Woburn, MA: Butterworth-Heinemann, 2002).

Frank Rich, "The Weight of an Anchor," *The New York Times Sunday Magazine* (May 19, 2002) , p. 35.

Al Ries and Laura Ries, *The 22 Immutable Laws of Branding*. New York: HarperCollins, 1998.

_____, *The Fall of Advertising & The Rise of PR*. New York: HarperCollins, 2003.

Everett M. Rogers, *Diffusion of Innovations*. New York: The Free Press, 1962.

Gina Rudan, "Five Simple Rules for Launching a Multicultural Strategy," *PR Tactics* (August 2004).

Leon Schiffman and Leslie Kanuk, *Consumer Behavior*. Upper Saddle River, NJ: Pearson/Prentice Hall, 2004.

Don E. Schultz, "Live the Brand," *Marketing Management* (July/August 2003).

Don E. Schultz and Philip J. Kitchen. *Communicating Globally: An Integrated Approach*. Lincolnwood, IL: NTC Business Books, 2000.

Nelson D. Schwartz, "Bigger and Bigger—Martin Sorrell Wants WPP to be the World's Largest Marketing Machine" *Fortune* Magazine (November 29, 2004).

Horace Schwerin and Henry Newell, *Persuasion in Marketing*. New York: John Wiley & Sons, 1981.

J.Walker Smith, Ann Clurman, and Craig Wood, *Coming to Concurrence: Addressable Attitudes and the New Model for Marketing Productivity* (Evanston/Chicago, IL: Racom Books, 2005).

David Solie, *How to Say It to Seniors: Closing the Communication Gap with Our Elders*. Englewood Cliffs, NJ, Prentice-Hall, 2004.

Betsy Spethmann, "Loyalty's Royalty," *Promo* Magazine (March 1, 2004).

_____, "Speaking Two Languages," *Promo* Magazine (July 6, 2004), at *http://promomagazine.com*

Jacques Steinberg, "Rise and Fight: Morning News Wars," *The New York Times* (May 23, 2004), Sec. 3, p. 1.

James Strengold, "Low-Key Thrills at Legoland," *The New York Times* (May 9, 1999).

Katie Sweeney, "What Growing Diversity Will Mean For America," *PR Tactics* (August 2004).

Jeffery Trachtenberg, "Diet Book Found Novel Ways to Get to the Top and Stay," *The Wall Street Journal* (August 2004).

Jack Trout with Steve Rivkin, *The New Positioning*. New York: McGraw-Hill, 1996.

Larry Tye, *The Father of Spin*. New York: Crown, 1998.

Mark Vangel, "Are You Tracking Blogs? They're Tracking You," *The Gauge* (July 2004), Volume 17, No. 3. Delahaye Medialink Worldwide.

"The Vanishing Mass Market," *BusinessWeek* (July 12, 2004).

R. J. Varey and B. R. Lewis (eds.), *Internal Marketing Directions for Management*. New York, Routledge, 2000.

John von Rhein, "The CSO in Flux," *The Chicago Tribune* (September 25, 1988).

Susan Vranica, "Ad Agency's Latest Pitch in the Classroom," *The Wall Street Journal* (June 15, 2001).

_____, "Aflac Duck's Paddle to Stardom: Creativity on the Cheap," *The Wall Street Journal* (July 30, 2004) p. B1.

Rob Walker, "The Hidden (in Plain Sight) Persuaders," *New York Times Magazine* (December 5, 2005).

Richard Weiner, *Webster's New World Dictionary of Media and Communications*. New York: Macmillan, 1996.

Wells, Mary. *A Big Life in Advertising*. New York: Alfred A. Knopf, 2002.

"WPP's Sorrell Sounds Off on the State of the PR Industry," *PR Week* (January 12, 2002).

Laurel Wentz, "Reverse English," *Advertising Age* (November 19, 2001).

Patricia T. Whalen, *How Communication Drives Merger Success*. San Francisco: International Association of Business Communicators, 2002.

Patricia Whalen, Srinath Gopalkrishna, and Francis Mulhern, "How Integrated Is Your Exhibit Strategy? Lessons From The Healthcare Field," *Convene* Magazine (August 2001).

Weber Shandwick newsletter: Spotlight!, 3rd issue. For past issues: *www.webershandwick.com*

Diane Witmer, *Spinning the Web: A Handbook for Public Relations on the Internet*. New York: Addison-Wesley Longman, 1999.

Erin White and Jeffrey Trachtenberg, "One Size Doesn't Fit All," *The Wall Street Journal* (October 1, 2003), p.B1.

Steve Yastrow, *Brand Harmony*. New York: Select Books, 2003.

Sergio Zyman, *The End of Marketing as We Know It*. New York: HarperCollins, 1999.

_____, *The End of Advertising As We Know It*. Hoboken, N.J.: John Wiley & Sons, 2002.

Index

About TEXERE

Texere, a progressive and authoritative voice in business publishing, brings to the global business community the expertise and insights of leading thinkers. Our books educate, enlighten, and entertain, and provide an intersection where our authors and our readers share cutting-edge ideas, practices, and innovative solutions. Texere seeks to cultivate, enhance, and disseminate information that illuminates the global business landscape.

www.thomson.com/learning/texere

About the Typeface

This book was set in 10 point Minion. The Minion font family, created in 1992 by Robert Slimbach, is based on classical old-style types from the late Renaissance period. This clear, balanced typeface adapts well to today's digital technology, presenting the richness of the late baroque forms within modern text formats.

Library of Congress Cataloging-in-Publication Data

Harris, Thomas L., 1931–
    The marketer's guide to public relations in the 21st century / Thomas L. Harris, Patricia T. Whalen ; foreword by Philip Kotler.
        p. cm.
    Rev. ed. of: The marketer's guide to public relations : how today's top companies are using the new PR to gain a competitive edge. 1991.
    Includes bibliographical references and index.
    1. Corporations—Public relations. 2. Marketing—Management. 3. Public relations. I. Whalen, Patricia T. II. Harris, Thomas L., 1931– Marketer's guide to public relations. III. Title.
    HD59.H276 2006
    659.2—dc22
                    2006003288